A select collection of English plays. From the best authors ... Volume 1 of 3

812
Sel

ECCO
PRINT EDITIONS

A select collection of English plays. From the best authors ... Volume 1 of 3
Multiple Contributors, See Notes
ESTCID: N021664
Reproduction from British Library
The titlepages are engraved; each volume has an individual printed titlepage dated 1759 and reading: 'A select collection of English plays. In three volumes.'. Each volume contains five plays, each with separate titlepage and pagination, all with imprint: Edinburgh, printed for A. Donaldson, 1759. Vol.1 contains: 'Mahomet the impostor', 'The orphan of China', 'The siege of Damascus', 'The Christian hero', and 'Don Sebastian'; vol.2 contains: 'The Indian emperor', 'All for love', 'Theodosius', 'King Henvy V', and 'Oroonoko'; vol.3 contains: 'The miser', 'The provok'd wife', 'The recruiting officer', 'The constant couple', and 'Sir Harry Wildair'.
Edinburgh : sold by A. Donaldson, 1760.
3v. ; 8°

Gale ECCO Print Editions

Relive history with *Eighteenth Century Collections Online*, now available in print for the independent historian and collector. This series includes the most significant English-language and foreign-language works printed in Great Britain during the eighteenth century, and is organized in seven different subject areas including literature and language; medicine, science, and technology; and religion and philosophy. The collection also includes thousands of important works from the Americas.

The eighteenth century has been called "The Age of Enlightenment." It was a period of rapid advance in print culture and publishing, in world exploration, and in the rapid growth of science and technology – all of which had a profound impact on the political and cultural landscape. At the end of the century the American Revolution, French Revolution and Industrial Revolution, perhaps three of the most significant events in modern history, set in motion developments that eventually dominated world political, economic, and social life.

In a groundbreaking effort, Gale initiated a revolution of its own: digitization of epic proportions to preserve these invaluable works in the largest online archive of its kind. Contributions from major world libraries constitute over 175,000 original printed works. Scanned images of the actual pages, rather than transcriptions, recreate the works *as they first appeared.*

Now for the first time, these high-quality digital scans of original works are available via print-on-demand, making them readily accessible to libraries, students, independent scholars, and readers of all ages.

For our initial release we have created seven robust collections to form one the world's most comprehensive catalogs of 18th century works.

Initial Gale ECCO Print Editions collections include:

History and Geography
Rich in titles on English life and social history, this collection spans the world as it was known to eighteenth-century historians and explorers. Titles include a wealth of travel accounts and diaries, histories of nations from throughout the world, and maps and charts of a world that was still being discovered. Students of the War of American Independence will find fascinating accounts from the British side of conflict.

Social Science

Delve into what it was like to live during the eighteenth century by reading the first-hand accounts of everyday people, including city dwellers and farmers, businessmen and bankers, artisans and merchants, artists and their patrons, politicians and their constituents. Original texts make the American, French, and Industrial revolutions vividly contemporary.

Medicine, Science and Technology

Medical theory and practice of the 1700s developed rapidly, as is evidenced by the extensive collection, which includes descriptions of diseases, their conditions, and treatments. Books on science and technology, agriculture, military technology, natural philosophy, even cookbooks, are all contained here.

Literature and Language

Western literary study flows out of eighteenth-century works by Alexander Pope, Daniel Defoe, Henry Fielding, Frances Burney, Denis Diderot, Johann Gottfried Herder, Johann Wolfgang von Goethe, and others. Experience the birth of the modern novel, or compare the development of language using dictionaries and grammar discourses.

Religion and Philosophy

The Age of Enlightenment profoundly enriched religious and philosophical understanding and continues to influence present-day thinking. Works collected here include masterpieces by David Hume, Immanuel Kant, and Jean-Jacques Rousseau, as well as religious sermons and moral debates on the issues of the day, such as the slave trade. The Age of Reason saw conflict between Protestantism and Catholicism transformed into one between faith and logic -- a debate that continues in the twenty-first century.

Law and Reference

This collection reveals the history of English common law and Empire law in a vastly changing world of British expansion. Dominating the legal field is the *Commentaries of the Law of England* by Sir William Blackstone, which first appeared in 1765. Reference works such as almanacs and catalogues continue to educate us by revealing the day-to-day workings of society.

Fine Arts

The eighteenth-century fascination with Greek and Roman antiquity followed the systematic excavation of the ruins at Pompeii and Herculaneum in southern Italy; and after 1750 a neoclassical style dominated all artistic fields. The titles here trace developments in mostly English-language works on painting, sculpture, architecture, music, theater, and other disciplines. Instructional works on musical instruments, catalogs of art objects, comic operas, and more are also included.

The BiblioLife Network

This project was made possible in part by the BiblioLife Network (BLN), a project aimed at addressing some of the huge challenges facing book preservationists around the world. The BLN includes libraries, library networks, archives, subject matter experts, online communities and library service providers. We believe every book ever published should be available as a high-quality print reproduction; printed on-demand anywhere in the world. This insures the ongoing accessibility of the content and helps generate sustainable revenue for the libraries and organizations that work to preserve these important materials.

The following book is in the "public domain" and represents an authentic reproduction of the text as printed by the original publisher. While we have attempted to accurately maintain the integrity of the original work, there are sometimes problems with the original work or the micro-film from which the books were digitized. This can result in minor errors in reproduction. Possible imperfections include missing and blurred pages, poor pictures, markings and other reproduction issues beyond our control. Because this work is culturally important, we have made it available as part of our commitment to protecting, preserving, and promoting the world's literature.

GUIDE TO FOLD-OUTS MAPS and OVERSIZED IMAGES

The book you are reading was digitized from microfilm captured over the past thirty to forty years. Years after the creation of the original microfilm, the book was converted to digital files and made available in an online database.

In an online database, page images do not need to conform to the size restrictions found in a printed book. When converting these images back into a printed bound book, the page sizes are standardized in ways that maintain the detail of the original. For large images, such as fold-out maps, the original page image is split into two or more pages

Guidelines used to determine how to split the page image follows:

• Some images are split vertically; large images require vertical and horizontal splits.
• For horizontal splits, the content is split left to right.
• For vertical splits, the content is split from top to bottom.
• For both vertical and horizontal splits, the image is processed from top left to bottom right.

Select Collection

of

ENGLISH PLAYS.

from

THE beſt AUTHORS

VOL. I.

☞ *See the Contents on the other ſide.*

EDINBURGH, ſold by A. DONALDSON
at Pope's Head *oppoſite the* Exchange.
MDCCLX

A

SELECT COLLECTION

OF

ENGLISH PLAYS.

IN THREE VOLUMES.

VOLUME I.

CONTAINING,

MAHOMET THE IMPOSTOR.
THE ORPHAN OF CHINA.
THE SIEGE OF DAMASCUS.
THE CHRISTIAN HERO.
DON SEBASTIAN.

EDINBURGH:

Printed for A. DONALDSON, at *Pope's* Head,
opposite to the Exchange.

MDCCLIX,

MAHOMET

THE

IMPOSTOR.

A

TRAGEDY.

By Monf. VOLTAIRE.

EDINBURGH:

Printed for A. DONALDSON, at *Pope's* Head opposite the Exchange.

M,DCC,LIX.

PROLOGUE.

Spoken by Mr. HAVARD.

TO point what Lengths *credulity* has run,
　　What concils fhaken, and what ftates undone;
What hellifh fury wings th' *Euthufiaft's* rage,
And makes the troubled earth one tragic ftage;
What blafphemies *Impofture* dares advance,
And build what terrors on weak ignorance,
How fraud alone rage to *religion* binds,
And makes a *pandæmonium* of our minds:
Our *Gallic Bard*, fir'd with thefe glorious views,
Fuft to this *crufade* led the tragic Mufe,
Her power through FRANCE his charming numbers bore,
But FRANCE was deaf —for all her priefts were fwore.

ON Englifh ground fhe makes a firmer ftand,
And hopes to fuffer by no hoftile hand.
No clergy here ufurp the free-born mind,
Ordain'd to teach and not enflave mankind;
Religion here bids *perfecution* ceafe,
Without, all order, and *within*, all peace;
Truth guards her happy pale with watchful care,
And *frauds*, tho' *pious*, find no entrance there.

Religion, to be facred, muft be *free*,
Men will fufpect ———— where *bigots* keep the key.
Hooded and train'd like hawks, th' *Enthufiafts* fly,
And the prieft's victims in their pounces die.
Like who is born blind, by mother-church they're bred,
Nor wake to *fight*, to know themfelves mifled.

Murder's the game —————— and to the sport unpriest,
Proud of the *sin*, and in the *duty* blest,
The *Layman*'s but the *blood hound* of the priest.
Whoe'er thou art, that dar'st such themes advance,
To priest rid SPAIN repair, or slay in FRANCE,
For JUDAS' hire there do the Devil's task,
And trick up *slavery* in *religion*'s mask.
ENGLAND still free, no surer means requires
To sink their sottish souls, and damp their martial fires.

    BRITONS, those numbers to yourselves you owe;
VOLTAIRE hath strength to shoot in SHAKESPEAR's
      bow.
Fame led him at his *Hippocrene* to drink,
And taught to write with *nature* as to think:
With ENGLISH freedom, ENGLISH wit he knew,
And from th' inexhausted stream profusely drew.
Cherish the noble Bud yourselves have made,
Nor let the frauds of FRANCE steal all our trade.
Now of each *prize* the winner has the wearing,
E'en send our ENGLISH stage a-privateering:
With your *commission*, we'll our sails unfold,
And from their loads of *dross* import some *gold*.

                           D R A

DRAMATIS PERSONÆ.

MAHOMET.	Mr. DELANE.
MIRVAN, *his General.*	Mr. BRIDGES.
ALI,	
HERCIDES, } *Officers of* MAHOMET. }	Mr. GREEN.
AMMON,	
ZAPHNA, } *Captives brought up*	Mr. GARRICK.
PALMIRA, } *under* MAHOMET.	Mis GIFFARD.
ALCANOR, *Chief of the Senate of* Mecca,	Mr GIFFARD.
PHARON, *his Friend.*	Mr. WINSTONE.

SCENE, MECCA.

MAHOMET

THE

IMPOSTOR.

ACT I. SCENE I.

Scene, an apartment in the Temple of MECCA.

Enter ALCANOR *and* PHARON.

ALCANOR.

——P HARON, no more——Shall I
    Fall proftrate to an arrogant Impoftor,
Homage in MECCA one I banifh'd thence,
And incenfe the delufions of a rebel!
No——blaft ALCANOR, righteous Heav'n! if e'er
This hand, yet free and uncontaminate,
Shall league with fraud, or adulate a tyrant.
    PHA. Auguft and facred chief of ISHMAEL's fenate,
This zeal of thine, paternal as it is,
Is fatal now——our impotent refiftance
Controuls not MAHOMET's unbounded progrefs,
But, without weak'ning, irritates the tyrant.
When once a citizen, you well condemn'd him
As an obfcure, feditious innovator:
But now he is a conqu'ror, prince and pontiff,
Whilft nations numberlefs embrace his laws,
And pay him adoration——Ev'n in MECCA
He boafts his profelytes

ALC,

ALC Such profelytes
Are worthy of him——low, untutor'd reptiles
In whom fenfe only lives——moft cred'lous ftill
Of what is moft incredible!
    PHA Be fuch
Difdain'd, my Lord ; but mayn't the peft fpread up-
          wards,
And feize the head——Say, is the fenate found ?
I fear fome members of that rev'rend clafs
Are mark'd with the contagion, who, from views
Of higher pow'r and rank, or canker'd with
The gangrenous defilement of a bribe,
Worfhip this rifing fun, and give a fanction
To his invafions
    ALC If, ye powers divine!
Ye mark the movements of this nether world,
And bring them to account, crufh, crufh thofe vipers,
Who, fingled out by a community
To guard their rights, fhall for a grafp of ore,
Or paltry office, fell 'em to the foe
    PHA. Each honeft citizen, I grant, is thine,
And, grateful for thy boundlefs bleffings on them,
Would ferve thee with their lives, but the approach
Of this ufurper to their very walls
Strikes 'em with fuch a dread, that ev'n thefe
Implore thee to accept his proffer'd peace.
    ALC. O people, loft to wifdom, as to glory!
Go, bring in pomp, and ferve upon your knees
This idol, that will crufh you with its weight ;
Mark, I abjure him   by his favage hand
My wife and children perifh'd, whilft in vengeance
I carry'd carnage to his very tent,
Tranffix'd to earth his only fon, and wore
His trappings, as a trophy of my conqueft.
This torch of enmity thus lighted 'twixt us,
The hands of time itfelf can ne'er extinguifh.
    PHA. Extinguifh not, but fmother for a while
Its fatal flame, and greatly facrifice
Thy private fuff'rings to the public welfare.
O fay, ALCANOR, wert thou to behold
(As foon thou may'ft) this fam'd metropolis
With foes begirt , behold its pining tenants

                             Prey

Prey on each other for the means of life,
Whilst lakes of blood, and mountains of the slain,
(As erst in July) putrify the air,
And sweep off thousands with their pois'nous steams,
Would thy slain children be aveng'd by this?

   Alc. No, Pharon, no; I live not for myself.
My wife and children lost, my country's now
My family

   Pha. Then let not that be lost.

   Alc. 'Tis lost by cowardice.

   Pha. By rashness, often.

   Alc. Pharon, desist.

   Pha. My noble Lord, I cannot,
Must not desist, will not, since you're possess'd
Of means to bring this insolent invader
To any terms you'll claim.

   Alc. What means!

   Pha. Palmira.
That blooming fair, the flow'r of all his camp,
By thee born off in our last skirmish with him,
Seems the divine ambassadress of peace,
Sent to procure our safety. Mahomet
His, by his heralds, thrice propos'd her ransom,
And bid us fix the price.

   Alc. I know it, Pharon.
And would'st thou then restore this noble treasure
To that Barbarian? Would'st thou, for the frauds,
The deaths, the devastations he brings on us,
Enrich his ruffian hands with such a gem,
And render beauty the reward of rapine?——
Smile not, my friend, nor think that at these years
Well travell'd in the winter of my days,
I entertain a thought tow'rds this young beauty,
But what's as pure as is the western gale,
That breathes upon the uncropt violet——

   Pha. My Lord——

   Alc.——This heart, by age and grief congeal'd,
Is no more sensible to love's endearments,
Than are our barren rocks to morn's sweet dew,
That balmy trickles down their ruggid cheeks.

   Pha. My noble chief, each master-piece of nature
Commands involuntary homage from us.

Alc.

ALC. I own a tenderness, unfelt before,
A sympathetic grief, with ardent wishes
To make her happy, fill'd my widow'd bosom.
I dread her being in that monster's power,
And burn to have her hate him, like myself.
'Twas on this hour I, at her modest suit,
Promis'd her audience in my own pavilion.
PHARON, go thou mean while, and see the senate
Assembled strait——I'll sound 'em as I ought.
                              [*Exeunt severally.*

SCENE *changes to a room of state.*

Enter PALMIRA

PAL. What means this boding terror that usurps,
In spite of me, dominion o'er my heart,
Converting the sweet flow'r of new blown hope
To deadly *Night shade;* pois'ning to my soul
The fountain of its bliss——O holy Prophet!
Shall I ne'er more attend thy sacred lessons?
O ZAPHNA! much lov'd youth! I feel for thee
As for myself——But hold, my final audit
Is now at hand——I tremble for th' event!
Here comes my judge—Now liberty, or bondage!

Enter ALCANOR.

ALC. PALMIRA, whence those tears? trust me, fair
                              maid,
Thou art not fall'n into *Barbarians* hands.
What *Mecca* can afford of pomp or pleasure,
To call attention from misfortune's lap,
Demand and share it.
    PAL. No, my generous victor,
My suit's for nothing *Mecca* can afford;
Pris'ner these two long months beneath your roof,
I've tasted such benignity and candor,
Whilst your own hands so labour'd to beguile
The anxious moments of captivity,
That oft I've call'd my tears ingratitude.
    ALC. If ought remains, that's in my pow'r, to smooth
The rigour of your fate, to crown your wishes,
And make you say, *I'm happy,* why, 'twould fill

                                        The

The furrows in my cheeks, and make old age
Put on its summer's garb.

    PAL. Thus low I bless thee. [*Kneeling*]
It is on you, on you alone, ALCANOR,
My whole of future happiness depends.
Restore me then, restore me to my country,
Restore me to my father, prince, and Prophet;
Restore me to my——Oh!————

    ALC. To what, PALMIRA? [*Raising her*]
Those meaning blushes, that articulate pause,
Render my question vain. This subtile robber
Has trespass'd on thy heart ——Art thou not promis'd
To be inroll'd his wife, to swell the number
Of his licentious *Haram*?

    PAL. No, my Lord.
Train'd up from infancy at MAH'MET's feet,
Watch'd by his eye, and by his precepts form'd,
I rev'rence him, nay, view him as inspir'd
By that tremenduous Pow'r whose sword he bears;
But never did this humble breast conceive
A hope so big with vanity as that.

    ALC. With vanity! Now, by my sword, PALMIRA,
'Twere vanity in him to aim so high.
That gen'rous soul, superior to misfortune,
That breast where every virtue finds a mansion,
And that fair form where beauty sits enthron'd
Amidst the smiles and graces, speak yon sprung
From such a race, as would disdain to match
With this fierce *Arab*.

    PAL. No, the pride of birth
I am a stranger to, a captive infant,
Nurs'd in the camp, I ne'er could yet discover
Who was my father. But our holy Prophet
Has well supply'd that loss. Have pity then?
Pity, ALCANOR, one who's torn from all
That's dear or venerable to her soul;
And O restore her to her faith and country.

    ALC. Is slav'ry dear then? Is fraud venerable?
What country! a tumultuous wand'ring camp!

    PAL. My country, Sir, is not a single spot
Of such a mold, or fix'd to such a clime,
No, 'tis the social circle of my friends,

                              The

The lov'd community in which I'm link'd,
And in whose welfare all my wishes center.

ALC. Excellent maid! then *Mecca* be thy country.
Robb'd of my children, would PALMIRA deign
To let me call her child, the toil I took
To make her destiny propitious to her,
Would lighten the rough burden of my own.
But no, you scorn my country and my laws.

PAL. Can I be yours when not my own? Your bounties
Demand and share my gratitude ——But MAHOMET
Claims right o'er me of parent, prince, and prophet.

ALC. Of parent, prince, and prophet! Heav'ns! that robber
Who, a 'scap'd felon, emulates a throne,
And, scoffer at all faiths, proclaims a new one!

PAL. O cease, my Lord, this blasphemous abuse
On one, whom millions with myself adore,
Does violence to my ear, such black profaneness
'Gainst Heav'n's interpreter, blots out remembrance
Of favours past, and nought succeeds but horror.

ALC. O superstition! thy pernicious rigours,
Inflexible to reason, truth and nature,
Banish humanity the gentlest breasts,
PALMIRA, I lament to see thee plung'd
So deep in error.——

PAL. Do you then reject
My just petition? Can ALCANOR's goodness
Be deaf to suff'ring virtue? Can his justice
Be blind to injur'd right? Name but the ransom,
And MAHOMET will treble what you ask

ALC. There is no ransom MAHOMET can offer
Proportion'd to the prize. Trust me, PALMIRA,
I cannot yield thee up: What! to a tyrant,
Who wrongs thy youth, and mocks thy tender heart
With vile illusions, and fanatic terrors!——

Enter PHARON.

What would'st thou, PHARON?

PHA. From yon western gate,
Which opens on *Moradia*'s fertile plains,
MAHOMET's gen'ral, MIRVAN. hastes to greet thee.

ALC

ALC MIRVAN, that vile apoftate!

PHA. In one hand
He holds a fcimitar, the other bears
An olive-branch, which to our chiefs he waves,
An emblem of his fuit——a martial youth,
ZAPHNA by name, attends him for our hoftage.

PAI. [*Apart.*] ZAPHNA! myfterious Heav'n!

PHA. MIRVAN advances
This way, my Lord, to render you his charge.

ALC. MIRVAN advance! How dare the traitor fee
   me?
PALMIRA, thou retire——PHARON, be prefent.
                                    [*Exit* PALMIRA.

Enter M I R V A N

After fix years of infamous rebellion
Againft thy native country, doft thou, MIRVAN,
Again profane, with thy detefted prefence,
Thefe facred walls which once thy hands defended,
But thy bad heart has vilely fince betray'd?
Thou poor deferter of thy country's Gods,
Thou bafe invader of thy country's rights,
What would'ft thou have with me?

MIR. I'd pardon thee——
Out of compaffion to thy age and fuff'rings,
And high regard for thy experienc'd valour,
Heav'n's great apoftle offers thee in friendfhip
A hand could crufh thee, and I come commiffion'd
To name the terms of peace he deigns to tender.

ALC He deigns to tender! Infolent impoftor!
Muft MAHOMET then, ye pow'rs! give peace to *Mecca*,
Or plunder it?——Doft thou not, MIRVAN, blufh
To ferve this wretch——this bafe of foul, as birth?

MIR MAHOMET's grandeur's in himfelf, he fhines
With borrow'd luftre, raifes not his ftature   [not
By perching on his father's monument:
Born of himfelf, himfelf's the only fountain
Of all the flowing honours that adorn him.
Such is the mafter I have chofen, fuch
Is Heav'n's elect to rule the world in truth.

ALC. MIRVAN, I know thee, this infidious blazon

                    B   Dazzles

Dazzles not me. Banish, for once, imposture,
And view with reason's eye this homag'd prophet;
Then villain, or enthusiast, thou must grant him.——
A pilf'ring camel-driver, one so vile
His own vile crew renounc'd him——Out-cast thus
Of out-casts, straight, he arrogates the prophet,
Stiles himself Heav'n's apostle, and, by means
Of a forg'd dream, draws o'er to his imposture
The refuse of all nations ——Banish'd *Mecca*,
From cave to cave with he FATIMA fled,
Whilst scatter'd, persecuted and proscrib'd,
Through wastes and deserts his disciples stray'd.

PHA Stray'd, till *Medina*, poison'd with their errors,
Gave them a home, and prop'd the impious sect

ALC. 'Twas then that thou, that thou thyself, more
brave,
More just and gen'rous, didst attack this tyrant,
Whose voluntary slave thou'rt now become.
If a true prophet, durst thou wound him then?
If an impostor, dar'st thou now obey him?

MIR Plung'd in the night of prejudice, and bound
In fetters of hereditary faith,
My judgement slept, but when I found him born
To mold anew the prostrate universe,
I started from my dream, join'd his career,
And shar'd his arduous, and immortal labours.
Once, I must own, I was as blind as thou,
Then wake to glory, and be chang'd like me

PHA. O what a fall from virtue was that change!

ALC. What death to honour, wak'ning to such glory!

MIR. Embrace our faith then, reign with MAHOMET,
And, cloath'd in terrors, make the vulgar tremble.

ALC. 'Tis MAHOMET, and tyrants like to MAHO-
MET,
'Tis MIRVAN, and apostates like to MIRVAN,
I only would make tremble ——Is it, say'st thou,
Religion that's the parent of this rapine,
This violence and rage?——No, true religion
Is always mild, propitious and humane;
Plays not the tyrant, plants no faith in blood,
Nor bears destruction on her chariot wheels,
But stoops to polish, succour and redress,

                                          And

And builds her grandeur on the public good.

MIR. Thou art turn'd Chriſtian, ſure ' ſome ſtrag-
  gling monk
Has taught thee theſe tame leſſons——

AIC. If the Chriſtians
Hold principles like theſe,- which reaſon dictates,
Which all our notions of the pow'ıs divine
Declare the ſocial laws they meant for man,
And all the beauties and delights of nature
Bear witneſs to, the Chriſtians may be right :
Thy ſect cannot, who, nurs'd in blood and ſlaughter,
Woıſhip a cruel and ıevengeful being,
And dıaw him always with his thundeı round him,
As ıipe for the deſtıuction of mankınd.

MIR. If clemency delights thee, learn ıt here.
Though banıſh'd by thy voice his native city,
Though by thy hand robb'd of his only ſoн,
MAHOMET pardons thee ; nay further, begs
The hatred burnıng 'twixt you be extınguıſh'd
With reconcıliatıon's gen'rous tear.

ALC I know thy maſter's arts ; his gen'rous tears,
Like the refreſhing drops that pıevious fall
To the wıld outrage of o'erwhelmıng earthquakes,
Only forerun deſtruction ; his beſt friendſhip
Is but a guileful clue, whereby to ſeize
Your heart's each fort, and turn ıts garrıſon
Agaınſt ıtſelf. Courage he has, not bıav'ıy,
Foı blood and havock are the ſuıe attendants
Oп his victorıous car.

PHA. Leagues he will make too——

ALC. Lıke other gıaſpıng tyıants, tıll he eyes
A lucky junctuıe to enlarge hıs bounds ,
Then he'll deııde 'em, leap o'er ev'ry tie
Of ſacred guarantee, or ſwoın protection,
And, when th' oppreſſed ally imploıes aſſiſtance,
Beneath that maſk, invade the wıſh'd for ıealms,
And fıom puıe friendſhip take them to himſelf.

MIR MAHOMET fights Heav'n's battles, bends the
  bow
To ſpread Heav'n's laws, and to ſubject to faith
The ıron neck of crror.

AIC. MIRVAN, Yes,

His new religion, molded in his aims,
Holds out a heav'nly kingdom to his followers,
Whilst humble he courts but an earthly one.
Lust and ambition, MIRVAN, are the springs
Of all his actions, whilst, without one virtue,
Dissimulation, like a flatt'ring painter,
Bedecks him with the colouring of them all.
This is thy master's portrait——But no more.——
My soul's inexorable, and my hate
Immortal as the cause from whence it sprang.

MIR　What cause——

ALC.　The diff'rence between good and evil.

MIR.　Thou talk'st to me, ALCANOR, with an air
Of a stern judge, that from his dread tribunal
Intimidates the criminal beneath him.
Resume thy temper, act the minister,
And treat with me as with th' ambassador
Of Heav'n's apostle, and *Arabia*'s king.

ALC.　*Arabia*'s king! What king? Who crown'd
him?——

MIR.　Conquest——
Whilst to the stile of conqu'ror and of monarch,
Patron of peace he'd add——Name then the price
Of peace and of PALMIRA——Boundless treasures,
The spoils of vanquish'd monarchs, and the stores
Of riffl'd provinces are thrown before thee.
Our troops, with unwont ardour, hasten hither
To lay in ruin this rebellious city,
Stem then the rushing torrent: MAHOMET
In person comes to claim a conference with thee
For this good purpose.

ALC.　Who! MAHOMET!

MIR.　Yes, he conjures thou'lt grant it.

ALC　Traitor, were I sole ruler here in *Mecca*,
I'd answer thee with chastisement——

MIR　Hot man!
I pity thy false virtue——But farewel——
And since the senate share thy power in *Mecca*,
To their serener wisdoms I'll appeal.

Exit MIRVAN.

ALC. I'll meet thee there, and see whose voice is victor.
Come, PHARON, aid me to repulse this traitor;

To

To bear him, with impunity, amongft us,
Is treafon 'gainft ourfelves——Ye facred powers,
My country's gods, that for three thoufand years
Have reign'd protectors of the tribe of *Ifhmael*!
And thou, O fun, refplendent torch of day,
The Image of thofe Gods, who in thy march
Beam'ft their light on us, O fupport my fpirit
In that firm purpofe it has always held,
To combat violence, fraud and ufurpation ;
To pluck the fpoil from the oppreffor's jaws,
And keep my country, as I found it, free!

[*Exeunt.*

A C T II. Scene I.

Scene, Palmira's *Apartment.*

Palmira *Difcovered*

Palmira.

CEASE, ceafe ye ftreaming inftruments of woe
From your ignoble toil——take warmth, my
     heart ;
Collect thy fcatter'd powers, and brave misfortune.
In vain the ftorm-toft manner repines,
Were he within to raife as great a tempeft
As beats him from without, it would not fmooth
One boift'rous furge· impatience only throws
Difcredit on mifchance, and adds a fhame
To our affliction.

Enter Z A P H N A.

Hah! All gracious Heav'n !
Thou, Zaphna ! is it thou? What pitying Angel
Guided thy fteps to thefe abodes of bondage? [powers;
    Zaph. Thou fov'reign of my foul, and all its
Object of ev'ry fear and ev'ry wifh ;
Friend, Sifter, Love, Companion, all that's dear!
Do I once more behold thee, my Palmira?

B 3   O,

O, I will set it down the whitest hour
That ZAPHNA e'er was blest with————

   PAL. Say, my hero————
Are my ills ended then ? they are, they are :
Now ZAPHNA's here I am no more a captive,
Except to him , O blest captivity !

   ZAPH. Those smiles are dearer to my raptur'd breast,
Sweeter those accents to my list'ning heart,
Than all *Arabia*'s spices to the sense.

   PAL. No wonder that my soul was so elate,
No wonder that the cloud of grief gave way,
When thou, my sun of comfort, wert so nigh.

   ZAPH. Since that dire hour, when on *Sabaria*'s strand,
The barb'rous foe depriv'd me of PALMIRA,
In what a gulph of horror and despair
Have thy imagin'd perils plung'd my soul !
Stretch'd on expiring coarses, for a while
To the deaf stream I pour'd out my complaint,
And begg'd I might be number'd with the dead,
That strow'd its banks————Then starting from despair,
With rage I flew to MAHOMET for vengeance.
He, for some high mysterious purpose, known
To Heav'n and him alone, at length dispatch'd
The valiant MIRVAN to demand a truce.
Instant on wings of light'ning I pursu'd him,
No order had————no leave obtain'd————pursu'd him,
And enter'd as his hostage————fix'd, PALMIRA,
Or to redeem, or die a captive with thee.

   PAL. Heroic youth !

   ZAPH. But how have these *Barbarians*
Treated my fair ?

   PAL. With high humanity
I, in my victor, found a friend ————ALCANOR
Has made me feel captivity in nothing,
But absence from my ZAPHNA and my friends————

   ZAPH. I grieve a soul so generous is our foe.
But now presented as an hostage to him,
His noble bearing and humanity
Made captive of my heart, I felt, methought,
A new affection lighted in my breast,
And wonder'd whence the infant ardor sprang.

   PAL. Yet, gen'rous as he is, not all my pray'rs,

                                      Not

Not all the tears I laviſh at his feet,
Can move him to reſtore me———
   Zaph But he ſhall———
Let the *Barbarian* know he ſhall, Palmira.
The God of Mahomet, our divine protector,
Whoſe ſtill triumphant ſtandard I have born
O'er piles of vanquiſh'd infidels.———That power,
Which brought unnumber'd battlements to earth,
Will humble *Mecca* too.

Enter MIRVAN.

Well, noble Mirvan,
Do my Palmira's chains ſit looſe upon her ?
Say, is it freedom ? This preſumptuous ſenate———
   Mir. Has granted all we aſk'd, all we could wiſh.——
The truce obtain'd, the gates to Mahomet
Flew open———
   Zaph Mahomet in *Mecca!* ſay'ſt thou ?
Once more in *Mecca !*
   Pal. Tranſport, bid him welcome ! .
   Zaph. Thy ſuff'rings then are o'er, the ebb is paſt,
And a full tide of hope flows in upon us.
   Mir. The ſpirit of our prophet, that inſpir'd me,
Breath'd ſuch divine perſuaſion from my lips,
As ſhook the reverend fathers,———Sirs, cried I,
This fav'rite of high Heav'n, who rules in battle,
Before whoſe footſtool tributary kings
Bow the anointed head, born here in *Mecca,*
Aſks but to be inroll'd a Senator,
And you refuſe his pray'r ! deluded ſages !
Although your conqueror, he requeſts no more
Than one day's truce, pure pity to yourſelves !
To ſave you, if he can, and you———O ſhame !——
At this a gen'ral murmur ſpread around,
Which ſeem'd propitious to us.———
   Zaph. Greatly carried !
Go on———
   Mir Then ſtraight th'inflexible Alcanor
Flew through the ſtreets, aſſembling all the people,
To bar our prophet. Thither too I fled,
Urg'd the ſame arguments, exhorted, threat'ned,
'Till they unhing'd the gates, and gave free paſſage

                   To

To MAHOMET and his chiefs——In vain ALCANOR,
And his dishearten'd party, strove t'oppose him ;
Serene and dauntless through the gazing croud,
With more than human majesty he mov'd,
Bearing the peaceful olive, whilst the truce
Was instantly proclaim'd——

    PAL. But where's the prophet ?

    MIR. Reclin'd in yonder grott that joins the temple,
Attended by his chiefs.

    ZAPH, There let us haste
With duteous step, and bow ourselves before him.

                      Exeunt.

SCENE *changes to a spacious Grotto.*

MAHOMET *with the* ALCORAN *before him.*

HERCIDES, AMMON, ALI, *&c attending at a distance*

    MAH Glorious hypocrisy ! What fools are they,
Who, fraught with lustful or ambitious views,
Wear not thy specious mask——Thou, ALCANOR !
Hast won more battles, ta'en more cities for me
Than thrice my feeble numbers had atchiev'd,
Without the succour of thy sacred impulse.

                      [*Coming forward.*
Invincible supporters of our grandeur !
My faithful chiefs, HERCIDES, AMMON, ALI !
Go and instruct this people in my name ;
That faith may dawn, and, like a morning-star,
Be herald to my rising.
Lead them to know, and to adore my God ,
But above all to fear him——Lo PALMIRA !

                   Exeunt HERCIDES, *&c.*
Her angel-face, with unfeign'd blushes spread,
Proclaims the purity that dwells within.

Enter MIRVAN, ZAPHNA *and* PALMIRA.
[*To* PALMIRA) The hand of war was ne'er before so
      barbarous,
Never bore from me half so rich a spoil

                        As

As thee, my fair !

PAL Joy to my heav'nly guardian !
Joy to the world that MAHOMET's in *Mecca* !

MAH. My child, let me embrace thee ———— how's
        this, ZAPHNA !
Thou here ! ————

ZAPH. [*Kneeling*] My father, chief, and holy pontiff!
The God that thou'rt infpir'd by, march'd before me.
Ready, for thee, to wade through feas of danger,
Or cope with death itfelf, I hither haften'd
To yield myfelf an hoftage, and with zeal
Prevent thy order.

MAH. 'Twas not well, rafh boy :
He that does more than I command him, errs
As much as he who faulters in his duty,
And is not for my purpofe ———— I obey
My God————implicitly obey thou me.

PAL. Pardon, my gracious Lord, his well-meant ardor.
Brought up from tender infancy beneath
The fhelter of thy facred patronage,
ZAPHNA and I've been animated ftill
By the fame fentiments. alas' great Prophet,
I've had enough of wretchednefs, ———— to languifh
A prifoner here, far both from him and you :
Grudge me not then the ray of confolation
His prefence be im d, nor cloud my dawning hope
Of rifing freedom and felicity.

MAH. PALMIRA, 'tis enough I read thy heart————
Be not alarm'd ; tho' burden'd with the cares
Of thrones and altars, ftill my guardian eye
Will watch o'er thee, as o'er the univerfe.
Follow my generals, ZAPHNA : fair PALMIRA,
Retire, and pay your powerful vows to Heav'n,
And dread no wrongs but from ALCANOR.
        [ZAPHNA *and* PALMIRA *go out feparately.*

MIRVAN ————
Attend thou here ———— 'tis time, my trufty foldier,
My long try'd friend, to lay unfolded to thee
The clofe refolves and councils of my heart.
The tedious length of a precarious fiege
May damp the prefent ardor of my troops,
And check me in the height of my career.

                            Let

Let us not give deluded mortals leisure,
By reason, to dispeise the mystic gloom
We've cast about us ——— Prepossession, friend,
Reigns monarch of the million ———*Mecca*'s croud
Gaze at my rapid victories, and think
Some awful power directs my arm to conquest.
But whilst our friends once more renew their efforts,
To win the wav'ring people to our interest,
What think'st thou, say, of ZAPHNA and PALMIRA?
    MIR. As of thy most resign'd and faithful vassals
    MAH. O! MIRVAN, they're the deadliest of my foes.
    MIR. How!
    MAH. Yes, they love each other ———
    MIR. Well ——— what crime ———
    MAH. What crime, dost say? ——— Learn all my
         frailty, then ———————
My life's a combat, keen austerity
Subjects my nature to abstemious bearings.
I've banish'd from my lips that trait'rous liquor,
That either works to practices of outrage,
Or melts the manly breast to woman weakness,
Or on the burning sands, or desart rocks,
With thee I bear th' inclemency of climates,
Freeze at the Pole, or scorch beneath the Line.
For all these toils love only can retaliate,
The only consolation or reward!
Fruit of my labours, idol of my incense,
And sole divinity that I adore!
Know then, that I prefer this young PALMIRA
To all the ripen'd beauties that attend me,
Dwell on her accents, doat upon her smiles,
And am not mine but her's: now judge, my friend,
How vast the jealous transports of thy master,
When at his feet he daily hears this charmer
Avow a foreign love, and, insolent!
Give MAHOMET a rival?
    MIR. How! and MAHOMET
Not instantly revenge! ———————
    MAH. Ay, should he not?
But better to detest him, know him better:
Learn then, that both my rival, and my love,
Sprang from the loins of this audacious tyrant.

                                        MIR.

MIR. ALCANOR! ——————

MAH. Is their father: old HERCIDES,
To whose sage institution I commit
My captive infants, late reveal'd it to me ——
Perdition! I myself light up their flame,
And fed it till I set myself on fire.
Well, means must be employed; but see, the father:
He comes this way, and launches from his eye
Malignant sparks of enmity and rage.
MIRVAN, see all ta'en care of, let HERCIDES,
With his escorte, beset yon gate, bid ALI
Make proper disposition round the temple,
This done, return, and render me account
Of what success we meet with 'mongst the people:
Then, MIRVAN, we'll determine or to loose,
Or bridle in our vengeance, as it suits.

[*Exit* MIRVAN.

Enter ALCANOR.

MAH. Why dost thou start, ALCANOR? whence that
          horror?
Is then my sight so baneful to thee?
    ALC. Heav'ns!
Must I then bear this? Must I meet in *Mecca*,
On terms of peace, this spoiler of the earth?
    MAH. Approach, old man, without a blush, since
          Heav'n
For some high end, decrees our future union.
    ALC I blush not for myself, but thee, thou tyrant,
For thee, bad man! who com'st with serpent-guile
To sow dissension in the realms of peace,
Thy very name sets families at variance,
'Twixt son and father bursts the bonds of nature,
And scares endearment from the nuptial pillow,
Ev'n truce with thee is a new stratagem
For leave to plunge the dagger in our hearts.
And is it, insolent dissembler! thus
Thou com'st to give the sons of *Mecca* peace,
And me an unknown God? ——————
    MAH Were I to answer any but ALCANOR,
That unknown God should speak in thunder for me:
But here with thee I'd parley as a man.

                                        ALC

ALC. What can'ft thou fay? what urge in thy defence?
That, like a hunger-ftung and rav'nous wolf
Prowling for prey, thou traverfeft the world,
Seizing on all that comes within thy grafp.

MAH. Each nation of the peopl'd globe by turns
Have foar'd to triumph, and immortal fame;
At length *Arabia's* happy hour is come.
Her gen'rous fons too long, alas! unknown,
Have fuffer'd all their glory to lie buried:
New days, by vict'ry mark'd, at length proceed,
And *Mecca's* now the deftin'd feat of power.

ALC. Power is a curfe when in a tyrant's hands,
But in a Bigot tyrant's —— treble curfe.

MAH. Behold-from North to South the ravag'd globe
Lies defolate, a wafte of crumbled empires.
Perfia ftill bleeding, and her throne revers'd,
India yok'd to flav'ry, *Egypt* fpoil'd,
And CONSTANTINE's late grandeur now no more.
Behold the well-built *Roman* empire mould'ring
On ev'ry fide; whilft, ruining beneath
Its own enormous weight, its fcatter'd members,
Like branches from the parent-tree lopt off,
Lie dead and wither'd —— On this wreck of nations
Let lov'd *Arabia* rife: a new religion,
New laws, new ties, and a new God are wanting,
To roufe the flumbering world to deeds of glory

ALC. To deeds of rapine, bloodfhed, and impofture!

MAH. *Minos* in *Crete*; in *Afia*, *Zoroafter*,
At *Egypt* fam'd *Ofiris*, and in *Latium*
The pious *Numa*, gave thofe barb'rous people
Their ineffective laws; I'm therefore come,
After a thoufand annual funs, to banifh
Their crude impoftures, and unite all nations
Under one faith and fovereign. ——

ALC. At thy nod, then,
The face of the creation muft be chang'd
By menaces and carnage, modeft thou!
Would'ft force all mortals to believe alike •
What right haft thou receiv'd to plant new faiths,
Or lay a claim to royalty and priefthood?

MAH. The right that a refolv'd and tow'ring fpirit
Has o'er the grov'ling inftinct of the vulgar ——

ALC.

ALC. Patience good Heav'ns! Have I not known thee,
    MAHOMET,
When void of wealth, inheritance, or fame,
Rank'd with the lowest of the low at *Mecca*?
    MAH. Dost thou not know, superb, yet feeble man!
That the low insect lurking in the grass,
And the Imperial eagle which aloft
Ploughs the etherial plain, are both alike
In the eternal eye————Mortals are equal.
It is not birth, magnificence, or pow'r,
But virtue only makes the diff'rence 'twixt them.
    ALC. [*Apart*] What sacred truth, from what pol-
    luted lips!
    MAH. By virtue's ardent pinions bore on high,
Heav'n met my zeal, gave me in solemn charge
I's sacred laws, then bade me on and publish.
    ALC And did Heav'n bid thee on and plunder too?
    MAH. My law is active, and inflames the soul
With thirst of glory what can thy dumb gods?
What laurels spring beneath their footy altars?
Thy slothful sect disgrace the human-kind,
Enervate lifeless images of men!
Mine bear th' intrepid soul, my faith makes heroes
    ALC. Go preach these doctrines at *Medina*, where
By prostrate wretches thou art rais'd to homage
    MAH. Hear me, thy *Mecca* trembles at my name:
If therefore thou would'st save thyself or city,
Embrace my proffer'd friendship————What, to-day,
I thus solicit, I'll command to morrow
    AIC Contract with thee a friendship! frontless man!
Know'st thou a God can work that miracle?
    MAH I do————Necessity. Thy interest.
    ALC. Interest is thy God, Equity is mine.
Propose the tie of this unnatural union,
Say, is't the loss of thy ill-fated son,
Who in the field fell victim to my rage,
Or the dear blood of my poor captive children,
Shed by thy butchering hands,
    MAH Ay, 'tis thy children.
Mark me then well, and learn th' important secret
Which I'm sole master of————Thy children live.
    ALC Live!

C   MAH.

MAH. Yes————both live————

ALC. What fay'ft thou? both!

MAH Ay, both.

ALC And doft thou not beguile me?

MAH No, old man.

ALC Propitious Heav'ns! fay, MAHOMET, for now
Me thinksI could hold endlefs converfe with thee,
Say, what's their portion! Liberty, or bondage?————

MAH. Bred in my camp, and tutor'd in my law,
They wait upon my will

ALC. And haft thou ne'er
Let loofe thy vengeance on them? Never wrung 'em
With fhackles, rack, or fcourge? Ne'er thought of me,
And then————

MAH. No, I difdain'd to punifh them
For injuries done by thee————Hear then, ALCANOR,
I hold the balance of their deftinies,
And now 'tis on the turn————their lives, or deaths————
'Tis thine to fay which fhall preponderate.

ALC. Mine! Can I fave them? Name the mighty
          ranfom————
If I muft bear their chains, double the weight,
And I will kifs the hand that puts them on
Or if my ftreaming blood muft be the purchafe,
Drain ev'ry fluice and channel of my body,
My fwelling veins will burft to give it paffage.

MAH I'll tell thee then—Renounce thy Pagan faith,
Abolifh thy vain Gods, and————

ALC. Hah!

MAH. Nay, more,
Surrender *Mecca* to me, quit this temple,
Affift me to impofe upon the world,
Thunder my *Koran* to the gazing croud,
Proclaim me for their prophet, and their king,
And be a glorious pattern of credulity
To *Korah*'s ftubborn tribe. Thefe terms perform'd,
Thy fon fhall be reftor'd, and MAH'MET's felf
Will deign to wed thy daughter.

ALC Hear me, MAHOMET,
I am a father, and this bofom boafts
A heart as tender as e'er parent bore.
After a fifteen years of anguifh for them,

                                        Once

Once more to view my children, clasp 'em to me,
And die in their embraces! melting thought!
But were I doom'd, or to enslave my country,
And help to spread black error o'er the earth;
Or to behold those blood-embrued hands
Deprive me of 'em both——Know me then, MAHO-
  MET,
I'd not admit a doubt to cloud my choice——
   [*Looking earnestly at* MAHOMET *for some*
    time before he speaks.
Farewel.

        [*Exit* ALCANOR!

 MAH. Why, fare thee well then——Churlish dotard!
Inexorable fool! Now, by my arms,
I will have great revenge, I'll meet thy scorn
With treble retribution.

     Enter MIRVAN.
Well, my MIRVAN,
What say'st thou to it now?
 MIR. Why, that ALCANOR,
Or we must fall.
 MAH. Fall then th' obdurate rebel!
 MIR. The truce expires to morrow, when ALCANOR
Again is *Mecca*'s master, and has vow'd
Destruction on thy head; the senate too
Have pass'd thy doom.
 MAH. Those heart chill'd, paltry bablers,
Plac'd on the bench of sloth, with ease can nod,
And vote a man to death, why don't the cowards
Stand me in yonder plain?——With half their numbers
I drove 'em headlong to their walls for shelter,
And he was deem'd the wisest senator,
That enter'd first the gate, but now they think
They've got me in the toil, their spirits mount,
And they could prove most valorous assassins——
Well, this I like——I always ow'd my greatness
To opposition, had I not met struggle
I'd been obscure——enough——perish ALCANOR!
He marbl'd up, the pliant populace,
Those dupes of novelty, will bend before us
Like osiers to a hurricane.——

MIR No time
Is to be loft,
　MAH But for a proper arm?
For, howoever irkfome, we muft fave
Appearances, and mafk it with the vulgar.
　MIR. True, my fage chief——What think'ft thou
　　　then of ZAPHNA?
　MAH. Of ZAPHNA, fay'ft thou!
　MIR Yes, ALCANOR's hoftage——
He can in private do thee vengeance on him.
Thy other tav'rites of maturer age,
And more difcreetly zealous, would not rifk it:
Youth is the ftock, whence grafted fuperftition
Shoots with unbounded vigour. He's a flave
To thy defpotick faith, and urg'd by thee,
However mild his nature may appear,
Howe'er humane and noble is his fpirit,
Or ftrong in reafon, where allow'd to reafon,
He would, for Heav'n's fake, martyr half mankind.
　MAH. The brother of PALMIRA!
　MIR. Yes, that brother,
The only fon of thy outragious foe,
And the inceftuous rival of thy love.
　MAH. I hate the ftripling, loath his very name:
The *Manes* of my fon too cries for vengeance
On the curft fire, but then, thou know'ft my love,
Know'ft from whofe blood fhe fprang; this ftaggers,
　　　MIRVAN.
And yet I'm here furrounded with a gulph
Ready to fwallow me; come too, in queft
Of altars and a throne—What muft be done?——
My warring paffions, like contending clouds,
When fraught with thunder's fatal fuel, burft
Upon themfelves, and rend me with a fhock.
And fhall enervating, contagious love,
Hag my afpiring fpirit, fink me down
To woman's fhackles, make a lap-thing of me?
Glory: that muft not be! ambition ftill,
And great revenge, impetuous urge their claims,
And muft be notic'd. MIRVAN, found this youth:
Touch not at once upon the ftartling purpofe,
But make due preparation.
　　　　　　　　　　MIR.

MIR. I'll attack him
With all the forces of enthusiasm:
There lies our strength.
 MAH. First then, a solemn vow
To act whatever Heav'n by me enjoins him.
Next, omens, dreams, and visions may be pleaded:
Hints too of black designs by this ALCANOR
Upon PALMIRA's virtue, and his life ————
But to the proof————Be now propitious, Fortune,·
Then love, ambition, vengeance, jointly triumph.

ACT III. SCENE I.

ZAPHNA *and* PALMIRA.

ZAPHNA.

ALCANOR claim a private conference with us!
 What has he to unfold?
 PAL I tremble, ZAPHNA.
 ZAPH. Time press'd too, did he say?
 PAL. He did, then cast
A look so piercing on me, it o'erwhelm'd
My face with deep confusion; this he mark'd,
Then, starting, left me.
 ZAPH [*Aside*] Hah! this gives me fear
That MERVAN's jealousies are too well grounded,
But I must not distract her tender bosom
With visionary terrors. [*To PAL.*] Both in private?
 PAL. In private both.
 ZAPH. Her virtue, and my life! [*Apart*]
It cannot be; so reverend a form
Could ne'er be pander to such black devices.
 PAL But let us shun it, ZAPHNA; much I fear
ALCANOR has deceiv'd us, dread the treach'ry
Of this blood-thirsty senate. Trust me, ZAPHNA,
They've sworn the extirpation of our faith,
Nor care by what vile means————
ZAPH.

ZAPH. My foul's beft treafure,
For whole fecurity my ev'ry thought
Is up in arms, regardlefs of my own,
Shun thou ALCANOR's prefence. I would meet him
Intrepid inftantly, but duty calls
To more important deeds. This hour, PALMIRA,
MIRVAN, by order of our royal Pontiff,
Prepares to folemnize fome act of worfhip
Of a more hallow'd and myfterious kind,
Than will admit of vulgar eye. Myfelf
Alone am honour'd to affift.

   PAL. Alone!
   ZAPH. Yes, to devote myfelf by folemn vow
For fome great act, of which my fair's the prize.
   PAD. What act?
   ZAPH No matter, fince my lov'd PALMIRA
Shall be the glorious recompence————
   PAL. Oh ZAPHNA!
Methinks I do not like this fecret vow!
Why muft not I be prefent? Were I with thee
I fhould not be fo anxious, I'd then guard thee
'Gainft ought that offer'd in the fhape of danger.
For, truft me, ZAPHNA, my affection for thee
Is of that pure, difinterefted nature,
So free from paffion's taint, I've no one wifh
To have thee more than thus, have thee my friend,
Share thy lov'd converfe, wait upon thy welfare,
And view thee with a fifter's fpotlefs eye.
   ZAPH. Angelic excellence!
   PAL. And, let me tell thee,
This MIRVAN, this fierce MIRVAN gives me terrors,
So far from tend'ring confolation to me,
His theme is blood and flaughter; as I met him
His eyes flam'd fury, whilft in dubious phrafe
He thus befpoke me————" The deftroying angel
" Muft be let loofe————PALMIRA, Heav'n ordains
" Some glorious deed for thee, yet hid in darknefs,
" Learn an implicit rev'rence for it- will.
" And, above all, I warn thee, fear for ZAPHNA."
   ZAPH What can he mean? Can I believe, ALCANOR,
Thy fair deportment but a treacherous mafk?
Perhaps in thofe blefs'd moments, when once more

I

I felt the sunshine of PALMIRA's smiles,
My soul, wrapt up in its own transport, full,
Too full to let in any stranger-thought,
Forgetting all its griefs, and all its fears,
O'erlook'd the artful windings of his heart,
For, since, I've held me happy in his friendship,
And bondage wore the livery of choice.
But this was wrong, and henceforth I will hate him
With double zeal for thus seducing me.
Yet, spite of all the rage that ought to fire me
Against this rebel to our faith and prophet,
'Tis hard to hate, where one's inclin'd to love

    PAL. How has Heav'n fraught our love-link'd hearts,
       my ZAPHNA,
With the same thoughts, aversions, and desires!
But for thy safety, and our dread religion
That thunders hatred to all infidels,
With great remorse I should accuse ALCANOR.

    ZAPH. Let us shake off this vain remorse, PALMIRA,
Resign ourselves to Heav'n, and act its pleasure.
The hour is come that I must pledge my vow.
Doubt not but the Supreme, who claims this service,
Will prove propitious to our chaste endearments.
Farewel, my Love, I fly to gain the summit
Of earth's felicity————to gain PALMIRA.   [*Exit.*

    PAL. Where'er I turn me here, 'tis all suspicion!
What means this vow? MIRVAN, I like thee not.
ALCANOR too distracts my timorous breast!
Ev'n MAH'MET's self I dread whilst I invoke him!
Like one benighted 'midst a place of tombs,
I gaze around me, start at ev'ry motion,
And seem hem'd in by visionary spectres.
All-righteous Power, whom trembling I adore,
And blindly follow! O deliver me
From these heart-rending terrors ——Ha! who's here?

Enter M A H O M E T.

'Tis he! 'tis MAHOMET himself, kind Heav'n
Has sent him to my aid————My gracious Lord,
Protect the dear, dear idol of my soul,
Save ZAPHNA, guard him from————

                       MAH.

MAH. From what ?———Why ZAPHNA ?
Whence this vain terror ? Is he not with us ?

PAL. O Sir, you double now my apprehenfions.
Thofe broken accents, and that eager look,
Shew you have anguifh fmothering at the heart,
And prove, for once, that MAHOMET's a mortal.

MAH. [*Apart*] Hah ! I fhall turn a traitor to myfelf—
O woman ! woman !——Hear me, ought I not
To be enrag'd at thy profane attachment ?
How could thy breaft, without the keeneft fting,
Harbour one thought not dictated by me ?
Is that young mind, I took fuch toil to form,
Turn'd an ingrate and infidel at once ?
Away, rebellious maid——

PAL. What doft thou fay,
My Royal Lord ? Thus proftrate at your feet,
Let me implore forgivenefs, if in ought
I have offended ; talk not to me thus ;
A frown from thee, my father and my king,
Is death to poor PALMIRA. Say then, MAHOMET,
Didft thou not deign to juftify his choice ?
Didft thou not in this very place permit him
To tender me his vows ?

MAH. [*Apart*] His vows ! perdition !
How the foft trait'refs racks me !—Rife, PALMIRA——
[*Apart.*] Down, rebel love ! I muft be calm.——Come
        hither ,
Beware, rafh maid, of fuch imprudent fteps,
They lead to guilt. What wild, pernicious errors
Mayn't the heart yield to, if not greatly watch'd !

PAL. In loving ZAPHNA, fure it cannot err ;
There's nothing wild, nothing pernicious——

MAH. How !
This theme delights you——

PAL. I muft own it does.
Yes, my great mafter ; for I ftill have thought
That Heav'n itfelf approv'd of my affection,
And gave a fanction to our mutual ardours
From Heav'n, you oft have told us, ev'ry bent
And proper tendency of nature fprings.
Heav'n knows not change , how can it then to-day
Condemn a paffion yefter's fun approv'd ?

                                        Can

Can what was virtue once be now a crime?
Can I be guilty————————
    MAH. Yes————towards me you are————
You! nurs'd from infancy beneath my eye,
Child of my care, and pupil of my faith!
You, whom my partial fondness still distinguish'd
From all the captive youth that grac'd my triumphs;
And you, who now, without my leave, permit
A slave to bear thee from my sight for ever.
    PAL. No, we both live, nay more, would die for thee;
And, O my Lord, if all that earth can offer
Of grandeur, opulence, or pleasure, e'er
Shall make me deaf to gratitude's demands,
May ZAPHNA's self be evidence against me,
And plead for double vengeance on my treach'ry.
    MAH [*Apart.*] ZAPHNA again! Furies, I shall relapse!
And make her witness of my weakness.
    PAL. Sir!
What sudden start of passion arms that eye?
    MAH. O, nothing, pray retire a while, take courage,
I'm not at all displeas'd; 'twas but to sound
The depth of thy young heart. I praise thy choice.
Trust then thy dearest int'rest to my bosom:
But know, your fate depends on your obedience.
If I have been a guardian to your youth,
If all my lavish bounties past weigh aught,
Deserve the future blessings which await you.
Howe'er the voice of Heav'n dispose of ZAPHNA,
Confirm him in the path where duty leads,
That he may keep his vow, and merit thee.
    PAL. Distrust him not, my Sov'reign, noble ZAPHNA
Disdains to lag in love or glory's course.
    MAH. Enough of words————————
    PAL. As, boldly, I've avow'd
The love I bear that hero at your feet,
I'll now to him, and fire his gen'rous breast,
To prove the duty he has sworn to thee. [*Exit Palmira.*

MAHOMET *alone.*

Confusion! must I, spite o' me, be made
The confident of her incestuous passion!
What could I say? Such sweet simplicity

Lur'd

Lur'd down my rage, and innocently wing'd
The arrow through my heart.   And shall I bear this?
Be made the sport of curst ALCANOR's house;
Check'd in my rapid progress by the sire,
Supplanted in my love by his rash boy,
And made a gentle pander to the daughter!
Perdition on the whole detested race!

Enter MIRVAN

* MIRV. Now, MAHOMET's the time to seize on *Mecca*,
Crush this ALCANOR, and enjoy PALMIRA;
This night the old enthusiast offers incense
To his vain Gods in sacred *Caaba.*
ZAPHNA, who flames with zeal for Heav'n and thee,
May be won o'er to seize that lucky moment.

   MAH   He shall, it must be so, he's born to act
The glorious crime, and let him be, at once,
The instrument and victim of the murder.
My law, my love, my vengeance, my own safety,
Have doom'd it so.——But, MIRVAN, dost thou think
His youthful courage, nurs'd in superstition,
Can e'er be work'd——

   MIR. I tell thee, MAHOMET,
He's tutor'd to accomplish thy design,
PALMIRA too, who thinks thy will is Heav'n's,
Will nerve his arm to execute thy pleasure.
Love and enthusiasm blind her youth
They're still most zealous who're most ignorant.

   MAH. Didst thou engage him by a solemn vow?

   MIR   I did, with all th' enthusiastic pomp
Thy law enjoins; then gave him, as from thee,
A consecrated sword to act thy will.
O, he is burning with religious fury!
But hold, he comes——

Enter ZAPHNA.

   MAH. Child of that awful and tremenduous Pow'r,
Whose laws I publish, whose behests proclaim,
Listen, whilst I untold his sacred will.
'Tis thine to vindicate his ways to man,
'Tis thine his injur'd worship to avenge.

ZAPH.

ZAPH. Thou Lord of nations, delegate of Heav'n,
Sent to shed day o'er the benighted world,
O say, in what can ZAPHNA prove his duty?
Instruct me how a frail earth-prison'd mortal
Can or avenge or vindicate a God.

MAH By thy weak arm he deigns to prove his cause:
And launch his vengeance on blaspheming rebels.

ZAPH. What glorious action, what illustrious danger
Does that Supreme, whose image thou, demand?
Place me, O place me in the front of battle,
'Gainst odds innumerable, try me there,
Or, if a single combat claim my might,
The stoutest *Arab* may step forth, and see
If ZAPHNA fail to greet him as he ought

MAH. O greatly said, my son, 'tis inspiration!
But heed me, 'tis not by a glaring act
Of human valour, Heav'n has will'd to prove thee,
This infidels themselves may boast, when led
By ostentation, rage, or brute-like rashness.
To do whate'er Heav'n gives in sacred charge,
Nor dare to found its fathomless decrees,
This, and this only's meritorious zeal.
Attend, adore, obey, thou shalt be arm'd
By death's remorseless angel, which awaits me.

ZAPH Speak out, pronounce What victim must I
offer?
What tyrant sacrifice? Whose blood requir'st thou?

MAH The blood of a detested infidel,
A murderer, a foe to Heav'n and me;
A wretch who slew my child, blasphemes my God,
And like a huge *Colossus* bears a world
Of impious opposition to my faith,
The blood of curst ALCANOR

ZAPH. I!———ALCANOR!

MAH What! dost thou hesitate? rash youth, beware,
He that deliberates is sacrilegious
Far, far from me be those audacious mortals,
Who for themselves would impiously judge,
Or see with their own eyes, who dares to think,
Was never born a proselyte for me.
Know who I am Know, on this very foot,
I've charg'd thee with the just decree of Heav'n.

And

And when that *Heav'n* requires of thee no more
Than the bare off'ring of its deadliest foe,
Nay, thy foe too, and mine, why dost thou balance,
As thy own father were the victim claim'd!
Go, vile idolater, false *Muffulman*,
Go seek another master, a new faith.

    ZAPH. O *Mahomet*——

    MAH. Just when the prize is ready,
When fair PALMIRA's destin'd to thy arms——
But what's PALMIRA? or what's Heav'n to thee,
Thou poor, weak rebel to thy faith and love?
Go, serve and cringe to our detested foe

    ZAPH O pardon, MAHOMET; methinks I hear
The oracle of Heav'n———It shall be done.

    MAH Obey then, strike, and for his impious blood,
PALMIRA's charms and paradise be thine.
[*Apart to* Mirvan.] MIRVAN, attend him close, and let
        thy eyes
Be fix'd on ev'ry movement of his soul.   [*Exeunt.*

ZAPHNA *alone*

Soft, let me think———this duty wears the face
Of something more than monstrous———pardon Heav'n!
To sacrifice an innocent old man,
Weigh'd down with age, unsuccour'd, and unarm'd!
When I am hostage for his safety too———
No matter, Heav'n has chose me for the duty,
My vow is pass'd, and must be straight fulfill'd.
Ye stern, relentless ministers of wrath,
Spirits of vengeance, by whose ruthless hands
The haughty tyrants of the earth have bled,
Come to my succour, to my flaming zeal,
Join your determin'd courage; from this breast
Banish the stripling pity And thou, angel
Of MAHOMET, exterminating angel,
That mow'st down nations to prepare his passage,
Give me the scorpion's rage, the basilisk's eye,
That I may look, and look till I can murder.
Hah! who comes here!

                       Enter

Enter ALCANOR.

ALC. Whence, ZAPHNA, that deep gloom,
That, like a blasting mildew on the ear
Of promis'd harvest, blackens o'er thy visage?
Grieve not that here, thro' form, thou art confin'd:
I hold thee not as hostage, but as friend,
And make thy safety partner with my own.

ZAPH. [*Apart*] And make my safety partner with
thy own!

ALC. The bloody carnage, by this truce suspended
For a few moments, like a torrent check'd
In its full flow, will with redoubled strength
Bear all before it ————I must say no more,
But, ZAPHNA, trust me this, my heart is touch'd
To think that thou'rt in *Mecca*, 'midst thy foes,
Sworn-foes to MAHOMET, and all his friends.
For when confusion reigns, and insurrection
With indiscriminating fury stalks
Through ev'ry street, what mercy can be hop'd?
In this impending scene of public horror,
Be then, dear youth, these mansions thy asylum.
I'll be thy hostage now, and with my life
Will answer that no mischief shall befal thee.
I know not why, but thou art precious to me.

ZAPH. Heav'n, duty, gratitude, humanity! [*Apart*.
What didst thou say, ALCANOR? Didst thou say,
That thy own roof should shield me from the tempest?
That thy own life stood hostage for my safety?

ALC. Why thus amaz'd at my compassion for thee?
I am a man myself, and that's enough
To make me feel the woes of other men,
And labour to redress 'em.——Sacred Powers
Root from the fair creation those dire fiends,
Who place their joy in plunder and oppression.

ZAPH. [*Apart*] What melody these accents make!
My soul
Turns its each faculty into attention;
And whilst my own religion spurs to murder,
His precepts of humanity prevail.
[*To* Alc.] Can then a foe to MAH'MET's sacred law,
Be virtue's friend?

ALC Thou know'ſt but little, ZAPHNA,
If thou doſt think true virtue is confin'd
To climes or ſyſtems , no, it flows ſpontaneous,
Like life's warm ſtream throughout the whole creation,
And beats the pulſe of ev'ry healthful heart.
Thy tender ſpirit, by this tyrant form'd,
Holds all but *Muſſulmen* for criminals.
Thou look'ſt on me with horror, 'ere thou know'ſt me ;
Whilſt barb'ious prejudice with yoke of iron
Weighs down thy reaſon, warps thy honeſt ſoul,
And turns thy actions counter to thy will.
How canſt thou, ZAPHNA, worſhip for thy God
A being claiming cruelty and murders
From his adorers ? Such is thy maſter's God————

ZAPH. [*Apart*] O my relenting ſoul! thou'rt al-
        moſt thaw'd
From thy reſolve.————I pray you, ſir, no more ;
Talk me not into treaſon againſt Heav'n,
And MAHOMET at once. [*Apart*] Peace, reaſon, peace!
Oft has our Prophet ſaid, thy earth-ſprung dictates,
Like the bewild'ring meteor of the night,
Delude the wretch who truſts their flatt'ring ſhine.

ALC. [*Apart*] The more I view him, talk with him,
        obſerve
His underſtanding tow'ring 'bove his age :
His candour, which ev'en bigotry can't ſmother ;
And all the radiant undiſſembled virtues
Which emanate from his accompliſh'd ſoul ;
The more my breaſt takes int'reſt in his welfare.
[*To Zaphna.*] ZAPHNA, come near—I oft have thought
        to aſk thee,
To whom thou ow'ſt thy birth ; whoſe gen'rous blood
Swells thy young veins, and mantles at thy heart

ZAPH. That dwells in darkneſs ; no one friendly beam
E'er gave me glimpſe from whom I am deſcended.
The camp of godlike MAHOMET has been
My cradle, and my country ; whilſt of all
His captive infants no one more has ſhar'd
The ſunſhine of his clemency and care.

ALC I do not blame thy gratitude, young man:
But why was MAHOMET thy benefactor ?
Why was not I ? I envy him that glory.

                                        Heav'ns !

Heav'ns! it reflects such lustre on himself,
As half atones for his atrocious crimes.
Why then, this impious man has been a father
Alike to thee, and to the fair PALMIRA,

 ZAPH. Oh!

 ALC. What's the cause, my ZAPHNA, of that sigh,
And all that language of a smother'd anguish?
Why didst thou snatch away thy cordial eye,
That shone on me before?

 ZAPH. [*Apart.*] O my torn heart!
PALMIRA's name revives the racking thought
Of my near blunted purpose:

 ALC. Come, my friend:
The flood-gates of destruction soon thrown ope
Will pour in ruin on that curse of nations.
If I can save but thee, and fair PALMIRA,
From this o'erflowing tide, let all the rest
Of his abandon'd minions be the victims
For your deliverance——————I must save your blood.

 ZAPH. [*Apart*] Just Heav'n! and is't not I must shed
   his blood?

 ALC. Nay, tremble, if thou dar'st to hesitate——————
Follow me straight.

Enter PHARON.

 PHA. ALCANOR, read that letter,
Put in my hands this moment by an *Arab*
With utmost stealth, and air bespeaking somewhat
Of high importance.

 ALC [*Reads.*] Whence is this?——————HERCIDES!
Cautious my eyes! be sure you're not mistaken
In what you here insinuate. Gracious Heav'n!
Will then thy Providence at length o'er-rule
My wayward fate, and by one matchless blessing,
Sweeten the suff'rings of a threescore years!

  [*After looking, for some time, earnestly at* Zaphna.
Follow me.

 ZAPH. Thee?——————But MAHOMET——————

 ALC. Thy life
And all its future bliss dwells on this moment.
Follow, I say.   *Exeunt* Alcanor *and* Pharon.

D 2   *Enter*

Enter M I R V A N *and his attendants haftily on the
other fide of the ftage.*

MIR. [*To* Zaph.] Traitor, tuin back; what means
This conference with the foe? To MAHOMET
Away, this inftant, he commands thy prefence.
    ZAPH. [*Apart.*] Where am I! Heav'ns! How fhall I
        now refolve!
How act! A precipice on every fide
Awaits me, and the fiift leaft ftep's perdition.
    MIR. Young-man, our Prophet brooks not fuch delay;
Go, ftop the bolt that's ready to be launch'd
On thy rebellious head.
    ZAPH. Yes,' and renounce
This horrid vow, that's poifon to my foul.
                        Exit with Mirvan, *&c.*

Re-enter A L C A N O R *and* P H A R O N.
    ALC. Where is this ZAPHNA?——But he flies me ftill:
In vain I call in all the foft'ning arts
Of pity, love, and friendfhip to engage him:
His breaft is fear'd by that Impofter's precepts
'Gainft all who bid defiance to his laws.
But, PHARON, didft thou mark the baneful gloom,
The fomewhat like reluctance, rage, and pity,
That blended fat upon his penfive brow?
    PHA. I did, there's fomething at his heart——
    ALC. There is——
Would I could fathom it! this letter, PHARON,
His afpect, age; the tranfport that I tafte
When he is near me; the anxiety
His abfence gives, do too much violence
To my diftracted fenfe. HERCIDES here
Defires to fee me; t'was his barb'rous hands
That robb'd me of my children: They are living,
He tells me, undei MAHOMET's protection;
And he has fomething to unfold, on which
Then deftiny and mine depends. This ZAPHNA
And young PALMIRA, vaffals of that tyrant,
Are ignorant fiom whom they are defcended.
                                    Imagination's

Imagination's pregnant with the thought.
My wifhes mock me. Sinking with my grief,
I blindly catch at ev'ry flatt'ring error,
And fupplicate deception's felf for fuccour.

PHA. Hope, but yet fear, ALCANOR; think, my chief,
How many infants from their parents torn,
E're confcious whofe they are; attend that tyrant,
Drink in his dictates, place their being in him,
And deem him an infallible difpenfer
Of Heav'ns decifions————-

ALC. Well, no matter, PHARON;
At noon of night conduct HERCIDES hither:
Thy mafter, in th' adjoining fane, once more
Will importune the Gods with pray'rs and incenfe,
That he may fave his friends, and fee his children.

PHA. Thou fhalt not find thy PHARON flack in ought,
That tends to thy deliverance from this anguifh.

[*Exit* Pharon.

ALC. Juft Heav'n, if by erroneous thought or act,
I have drawn down your fierce difpleafure on me,
Point me to right; I'll onward to its goal
With double energy; will expiate all,
That in the days of ignorance might offend.
Only reftore my children to my care,
Give to my craving arms my haplefs children,
That I may form them; turn 'em back from wrong,
Weed their young minds of thofe pernicious errors
The arch-impoftor has implanted in 'em ;
Train 'em in virtue's fchool, and lead them on
To deeds of glorious and immortal honour.

[*Exit.*

ACT IV. SCENE I.

MAHOMET's *Apartment.*

MAHOMET *alone.*

AMBITION knows not confcience——Well, this
    ZAPHNA
Is fix'd at length———I leffon'd him fo home,
Dealt to his young enthufiaftic foul
Such promifes and threats————————

Enter MIRVAN

MIRVAN, What news?
   MIR O, MAHOMET, I fear the nice-wov'n web
Of our defign's unravell'd   E're thy fpirit
Had re inflam'd young ZAPHNA with the thirft
Of old ALCANOR's blood, he had reveal'd
The dreadful pu pofe to HERCIDES ————————
   MAH. Hah!
   MIR. HERCIDES loves the youth, and ZAPHNA ftill
Has held him as a father.
   MAH. That I like not.
What does HERCIDES fay? thinks he with us?
   MIR. O no, he trembles at the very thought
Of this dread fcene, compaffionates ALCANOR,
And————
   MAH He's but half a friend then, and half friend
Is not a fpan from traitor. MIRVAN, MIRVAN,
A dangerous witnefs muft be fome way dealt with ;
Am I obey'd?
   MIR. 'Tis done.
   MAH. Then for the reft————————
Or e'er the harbinger of 'morrow's dawn
Gleam in the eaft, ALCANOR thou muft fet,
Or MAHOMET and all his hopes muft perifh.
That's the firft ftep, then——ZAPHNA, next for thee.
Soon as thy hands have dealt the midnight mifchief,
In thy own blood the fecret muft be drown'd.
Thus quit of fon and father (thofe curft rivals

Who elbow me at once in love and grandeur,)
Both *Mecca* and PALMIRA, shall be mine.
O tow'ring prospect! how it fills the eye
Of my aspiring, and enamour'd soul!
Night put on double sable, that no star
May be a spy on those dark deeds —— Well, MIRVAN,
Shall we accomplish this?

MIR. We shall, my chief.

MAH What tho' I seize his life from whom she sprung?
He's not her father as she knows it not.
Trust me, those partial ties of blood, and kindred,
Are but th' illusive taints of education:
What we call nature is mere habit, MIRVAN;
That habit's on our side; for the whole study
Of this young creature's life has been obedience;
To think, believe, and act, as pleasur'd me.
But hold, the hour, on which our fortune hangs,
Is now at hand. While ZAPHNA seeks the temple,
Let us look round us, see that not a wheel
Lag in the vast machine we have at work.
It is success that consecrates our actions.
The vanquish'd rebel, as a rebel, dies;
The victor-rebel plumes him on a throne.   [*Exeunt.*

SCENE *changes to the Temple.*

Enter ZAPHNA, *with a drawn sword in his hand.*

ZAPH. Well then, it must be so, I must discharge
This cruel duty —— MAHOMET enjoins it,
And Heav'n thro' him demands it of my hands.
Horrid, tho' sacred act! —— my soul shrinks back,
And won't admit conviction —— ay, but Heav'n!
Heav'n's call I must obey —— O dire obedience,
What dost thou cost me? my humanity!
Why, duty, art thou thus at war with nature?

Enter PALMIRA.

Thou here, PALMIRA! O! what fatal transport
Leads thee to this sad place, these dark abodes,
Sacred to death? thou hast no business here.

PAL. O ZAPHNA, fear, and love, have been my guides.
What

What horrid facrifice is this enjoin'd thee?
What victim does the God of MAHOMET
Claim from thy tender hand?

ZAPH. My guardian angel,
On whofe determination ever turns.
The hinge of my elections; fpeak, refolve me;
How can affaffination be a virtue?
How can the gracious Parent of mankind
Delight in mankind's fuff'rings? Mayn't this Prophet,
This great announcer of his heav'nly will,
Miftake it once?

PAL. O tremble to examine.
He fees our hearts ———— to doubt, is to blafpheme.

ZAPH. Be fteady then my foul, firm to thy purpofe,
And let religion fteel thee againft pity.
Come forth, thou foe to MAHOMET and Heav'n,
And meet the doom thy rebel faith deferves;
Come forth, ALCANOR.

PAL. Who? ALCANOR!

ZAPH. Yes.

PAL. The good ALCANOR!

ZAPH. Why d'ye call him good?
Can impious have fellowfhip with good?
Curfe on his pagan virtues! he muft die;
So MAHOMET commands. And yet, methinks,
Some other Deity arrefts my arm,
And whifpers to my heart ——— ZAPHNA, forbear.

PAL. Diftracting ftate!

ZAPH. Alas, my dear PALMIRA,
I'm weak, and fhudder at this bloody bus'nefs:
Yet the beheft of Heav'n, howe'er it feem
To crofs on nature, or take captive reafon,
Is facred to the will, and claims obedience.
Help me, O help, PALMIRA, I am torn,
Diftracted with this conflict in my breaft.
I'd not be barbarous, nor facrilegious;
I find, I wear not an affaffin's heart,
Yet Heav'n here bids me wear affaffin's hands.
Zeal, horror, love, and pity feize my breaft,
And drag it diff'rent ways. Alas, PALMIRA,
You fee me toffing on a fea of paffions,
An ebb and flow of contrarieties,

Which

Which now feem kindly wafting me to fhore,
And the next moment plunge me back me again
Into the bofom of th' outragious deep.
'Tis thine, my angel, to appeafe this tempeft,
Fix my diftracted will, and teach me ——

PAL. —————— What ?
What can I teach thee in this ftrife of paffions ?
O ZAPHNA ! I revere our holy Prophet,
Think all his laws are regifter'd in Heav'n,
And every mandate minted in the fkies ,

ZAPH. But then to break through hofpitality,
And murder him by whom we are protected!
O ! it makes reafon ftagger, will rebell,
And the whole tribe of the exalted paffions
Rife up in arms, and combat with the duty.

PAL. O poor ALCANOR ! gen'rous, good ALCANOR!
My heart bleeds for thee.

ZAPH. Does it bleed for him ?
Were ZAPHNA's fate as piteous as his
'Twould bleed for ZAPHNA too.

PAL. Canft thou doubt that ?

ZAPH. Know then, unlefs I act this horrid fcene;
Unlefs I plunge this dagger in the breaft
Of that old man, I muft be more undone,
A more forlorn, abandon'd, fhipwreck'd wretch,
Than earth e'er bore. I muft ——

PAL. What —————

ZAPH. Muft, PALMIRA —————
(O agonizing thought !) lofe thee for ever.
This tyrant Prophet (Heav'n forgive my rafhnefs !),
Our royal pontiff, makes this facrifice
The price, by which I muft obtain PALMIRA.

PAL. Am I the price of good ALCANOR's blood!

ZAPH. So MAHOMET ordains.

PAL. Can cruelty
And love join hands ?

ZAPH. Alas, they muft PALMIRA,
If ours are ever join'd. Heav'n's fubftitute
Will give thee only to a murderer.

PAL. Horrible dow'ry !

ZAPH. But if Heav'n enjoins it,
If by this dreadful action I can ferve

Love

Love and religion ⸺⸺⸺⸺

   PAL. Is that poffible?   [nounc'd

   ZAPH Thou know'ft the curfe our Prophet has de-
Of endlefs tortures on the difobedient:
Thou know'ft with what an oath I've bound myfelf,.
To vindicate his laws, extirpate all
That dare oppofe his progrefs. Say then, fair one,
Thou tutorefs divine, inftruct me how,
How to obey my chief, perform my oath,
Yet lift' to mercy's call.

   PAL. This rends my heart.

   ZAPH. How to avoid being banifh'd thee for ever.

   PAL. O fave me from that thought ! muft that e'er be?

   ZAPH. It muft not: thou haft now pronounc'd his
      doom.

   PAL. What doom? ⸺⸺ Have I!

   ZAPH. Yes thou haft feal'd his death.

   PAL. What did I fay? I feal his death ! did I?

   ZAPH. 'Twas Heav'n fpoke by thee, thou'rt its oracle,
And I'll fulfil its laws. This is the hour
In which he pays at the adjoining altar
Black rites to his imaginary Gods.
Follow me not, PALMIRA.

   PAL. I muft follow,
I will not, dare not leave thee.

   ZAPH. Gentle maid,
I beg thee fly thefe walls, thou can'ft not bear
This horrid fcene ⸺⸺O thefe are dreadful moments!
Be gone ⸺⸺ quick ⸺⸺ this way ⸺⸺

   PAL No, I'll follow thee,
Re-tread thy ev'ry footftep, tho' they lead
To the dark gulph of death. There is no horror
So chilling to the blood, not any anguifh
So bitter to the foul but I could fuffer
With tranfport, rather than the fingle thought
That ZAPHNA felt one pang I did not fhare.

   ZAPH. Thou matchlefs maid ! ⸺⸺ To the due
      trial then.

                      [*Exeunt.*

                       SCENE

SCENE *draws, and difcovers the inner part of the temple, with a Pagan altar and images.* ALCANOR *addreffing himfelf to the idols.*

ALCANOR

Eternal Powers, that deign to blefs thefe manfions,
Protectors of the fons of *Ifhmael*,
Attend the vows I offer for my country !
Let *Mecca* ftand fecure amongft the nations,
And ftem the rage of rapine and impofture.
Blaft, blaft this blafphemous invader's force,
And turn him back with fhame   If pow'r be yours,
O fhield your injur'd votaries, and lay
Oppreffion bleeding at your altar's foot.

Enter ZAPHNA *and* PALMIRA.

PAL. [*Entering.*] Act not this bloody deed , O fave
     him, fave him
   ZAPH Save him, and lofe both Paradife and thee !
   PAL Hah! yon he ftands —O ZAPHNA, all my blood
Is frozen at the fight.
     ALC 'Tis in your own behalf that I implore
The terrors of your might , 'tis the laft hour
You'll e'er be worfhip'd in this facred dome,
This hallow'd *Caaba*, unlefs you fwift
Pour vengeance on this vile apoftate's head,
Who dares profanely wreft your thunder from you,
And lodge it with an unknown, fancy'd God
     ZAPH Hear how the wretch blafphemes ! fo, now—
   PAL Hold, ZAPHNA.
   ZAPH. Let me go ———
     PAL. I cannot—— cannot
     ALC But if, for reafons, which dim-fighted mortals
Can't look into, you'll crown this daring rebel
With royalty and priefthod, take my life
And if, ye gracious Pow'rs, you've ought of blifs
In ftore for me, at my laft hour permit me
To fee my children, pour my bleffing on them,
Expire in their dear arms, and let them clofe
Thefe eyes, which then would wifh no after-fight.
     PAL. His children, did he fay ?

                                        ZAPH

ZAPH. I think he did ————

ALC. For this I'll at your altar pay my vows,
And make it smoke with incense,
                    [*Retires behind the altar.*

ZAPH. Now's the time.   [*Drawing his sword.*
Insulting Heav'n, he flies to stones for refuge:
Now let me strike.

PAL Stay but one moment, ZAPHNA.

ZAPH. It must not be ———— unhand me.

PAL What to do?

ZAPH. To serve my God and king, and merit thee.
        [*Breaking from* PALMIRA, *and going towards
        the altar, he starts, and stops short.*
Ha! what are ye, ye terrifying shades?
What means this lake of blood that lies before me?

PAL. O ZAPHNA, let us fly these horrid roofs

ZAPH. No, no ———— go on, ye ministers of death;
Lead me the way. I'll follow ye.

PAL. Stay, ZAPHNA.
Heap no more horrors on me, I'm expiring
Beneath the load.

ZAPH. Be hush'd ———— the altar trembles!
What means that omen? does it spur to murder,
Or would it rein me back? No, 'tis the voice
Of Heav'n itself, that chides my lingering hand.
Now send up thither all thy vows, PALMIRA,
Whilst I obey its will and give the stroke.
        [*Goes out behind the altar after* ALCANOR.

PAL. What vows! will Heav'n receive a murderer's
                    vows?
For sure I'm such, whilst I prevent not murder.
Why beats my heart thus? what soft voice is this
That's waken'd in my soul, and preaches mercy?
If Heav'n demands his life, dare I oppose?
Is it my place to judge? ———— Hah! that dire groan
Proclaims the bloody bus'ness is about.
ZAPHNA! O ZAPHNA!

Re-enter ZAPHNA.

ZAPH. Hah! where am I?
Who calls me? where's PALMIRA? She's not here:
What friend has snatch'd her from me?

                                        PAL.

PAL. Heav'ns! he raves!
Doft thou not know me, ZAPHNA? her who lives
For thee alone? —— why doft thou gaze thus on me?
   ZAPH. Where are we?
   PAL. Haft thou then difcharg'd
The horrid duty?
   ZAPH What doft fay?
   PAL ALCANOR——
   ZAPH. ALCANOR! what, ALCANOR?
   PAL Gracious Heav'n,
Look down upon him!
Let's be gone, my ZAPHNA,
Let's fly this place.
   ZAPH O whither fly! to whom?
D'ye fee thefe hands? who will receive thefe hands?
   PAL. O come, and let me wafh them with my tears.
   ZAPH. Who art thou? let me lean on thee——I find
My pow'rs returning. Is it thou, PALMIRA?
Where have I been? what have I done?
   PAL I know not.
Think on't no more.
   ZAPH. But I muft think, and talk on't too, PALMIRA.
I feiz'd the victim by his hoary locks ——
(Thou, Heav'n, did'ft will it—can'ft thou will a crime!)
Then, fhuddering with horror, buried ftrait
The poinard in his breaft. I had redoubl'd
The bloody plunge —— (what cannot zeal perfuade?)
But that the venerable fire pour'd forth
So piteous a groan; look'd fo, PALMIRA,——
And with a feeble voice cry'd, is it ZAPHNA?
I could no more. O had'ft thou feen, my love,
The fell, fell dagger in his bofom, view'd
His dying face, where fat fuch dignity,
Cloath'd with compaffion tow'rds his bafe affaffin,
'Twould have converted thee to breathlefs marble,
And made thee, to futurity, at once,
A monument of cruelty and pity
              [*Throwing himfelf on the ground.*
The dire remembrance weighs me to the earth ——
Here let me die ——
   PAL. Rife, my lov'd ZAPHNA, rife,
And let us fly to MAH'MET for protection.

            E   If

If we are found in these abodes of slaughter,
Tortures and death attend us ; let us fly.

    ZAPH. [*Starting up.*] I did fly at that blasting sight,
      PALMIRA.
When, drawing out the fatal steel, he cast
Such tender looks! I fled —— The fatal steel,
The voice, the tender looks, the bleeding victim
Blessing his murderer —— I cou'd not fly.
No, they clung to me, riv'd my throbbing heart,
And set my brain on fire   What have we done?

    PAL   Huk! what's that noise? I tremble for thy life.
O, in the name of love, by all the ties,
Those sacred ties that bind thee mine for ever,
I do conjure thee, follow me.

    ZAPH   Be gone ——
Leave me.   Say, was't not the destroyer, love,
That urg'd me on to this detested deed?
Had it not been for thee, consulting thee,
But for thy irresistible decision,
I had been deaf to Heav'n, and spurn'd its order.

    PAL.   Why dost thou load me with this dire reproach?
O ZAPHNA, this is cruelty indeed !
Was not my soul abhorrent of the action,
As much as thine? did not I call thee back ?
Didst not thou shake me off by violence,
When I hung on thee, would have forc'd thy stay?

    [ALCANOR *comes from behind the altar, leaning*
      against it, with the bloody sword in his hand.

    ZAPH. Hah! look, PALMIRA, see; what object's that
Which bears upon my tortur'd sight? is't he?
Or is't his bloody *Manes* come to haunt us?   [death,

    PAL.   'Tis he himself, poor wretch ! struggling with
And feebly crawling tow'rds us.   Let me fly,
And yield what help I can   Let me support thee,
Thou much lamented, injur'd, good old man.

    ZAPH.   Why don't I move? my feet are rooted here,
And all my frame is struck, and wither'd up,
As with the lightning's blast.

    ALC.   My gentle maid,
Wilt thou support me?
Weep not, my PALMIRA.   [thee.

    PAL. I could weep tears of blood, if that would serve
                    ALC

ALC. [*Sitting down*] ZAPHNA, come hither, thou
    haſt ta'en my life,
For what offence, or what one thought tow'rds thee
That anger or malevolence gave birth,
Heav'n knows I am unconſcious. Do not look ſo;
I ſee thou doſt relent.

Enter PHARON *haſtily*

PHA [*Starting back.*] Hah! 'tis too late then.
ALC Would I could ſee HERCIDES ! PHARON, lo,
Thy martyr'd friend, by his diſtemper'd hand,
Is now expiring
PHA. Dire, unnatural crime !
O wretched parricide ! —— behold thy father.
                [*Pointing to* ALCANOR.
ZAPH My father !
PAL Father ! hah !
ALC. Myſterious Heav'n!
PHA. HERCIDES, dying by the hand of MIRVAN,
Who ſlew him, leſt he ſhould betray the ſecret,
Saw me approach, and, in the pangs of death,
Cry'd, fly, and ſave ALCANOR; wreſt the ſword
From ZAPHNA's hand, if 'tis not yet too late,
That's deſtin'd for his death, then let him know
That ZAPHNA and PALMIRA are his children.
PAL. That ZAPHNA and PALMIRA are his children !
Doſt hear that ZAPHNA !
ZAPH. 'Tis enough, my fate !
Canſt thou ought more ?
ALC O nature ! O my children !
By what vile inſtigations wert thou driven,
Unhappy ZAPHNA, to this bloody action ?
ZAPH. [*Falling at his father's feet*] Love of my
    duty, nation and religion,
Inſpir'd me with the raſh, accurſed zeal,
To perpetrate an act more black, more horrid,
Than e'er the Sun caſt eye on, than e'er tears
Can cleanſe from its foul ſtain, than e'er ſweet mercy
Can intercede for, or than hell can puniſh.
Reſtore me, Sir, reſtore me that damned weapon,
That I for once may make it, as I ought,
An inſtrument of juſtice.
          E 2   PAL.

PAL. [*Kneeling.*] O my father,
Strike here, the crime was mine, 'twas I alone
That work'd his will to this unnatural deed.
Upon these terms alone he cou'd be mine,
And inceſt was the price of parricide.

ZAPH Strike your aſſaſſins ————

ALC. I embrace my children,
And joy to see them, tho' my life's the forfeit.
Kind Heav'n thus mingles in my bitter cup
So ſweet a conſolation, that I bleſs
My deſtiny, and think the draught divine.
Riſe, children, riſe and live, live to revenge
Your father's death ———— But, in the name of nature,
By the remains of this paternal blood
That's oozing from my wound, raiſe not your hands
'Gainſt your own being ZAPHNA, wou'dſt thou do me
A ſecond deadlier miſchief thro' thyſelf?
Then thou wou'dſt ſtab me to the heart indeed:
Self ſlaughter can't atone for parricide.

ZAPH Go on, Sir, pray go on then I will live,
Live to ſome purpoſe, this is glorious ſuffering.
Ten thouſand ſwords had been a needle's point,
To this moſt exquiſitely tort'ring goodneſs:
Bleſſing, where curſing's due, is cruelty.

ALC. Thy undetermin'd arm haſn't quite fulfill'd
Its bigot-purpoſe, morn's at hand, the truce
Is broke; I hope to live to animate
Our friends 'gainſt this impoſtor, lead 'em, ZAPHNA,
To root out a rapacious baneful crew,
Whoſe zeal is phrenzy, whoſe religion murder.

ZAPH Swift, ſwift, ye hours! celeſtial charioteer,
Laſh on thy courſers! light me to revenge!
Why linger for the day? flaming revenge
Is torch ſufficient. Inſtantly I'll fly
Through ev'ry ſtreet, rend with my bitter cries
The cypreſs veil of ſleep; ſound ſuch a trump
As might burſt ope death's palace, and awake
His breathleſs guards Then, then, infernal weapon,
                          (*Snatches the bloody ſword.*
I'll waſh off thy foul ſtain with the heart's blood

Of that malignant fanctify'd affaffin.

(*As* ZAPHNA *is going off,* MIRVAN *and his followers enter and ftop him.*

MIR. Seize ZAPHNA,
And load the traiterous murderer with chains.
Help you the good ALCANOR. —— Haplefs man!
Our Prophet, in a vifion, learnt to-night
The mournful tale of thy untimely end,
And fent me ftraight to feize the vile affaffin,
That he might wreck fevereft juftice on him.
MAHOMET comes to vindicate the laws,
Not fuffer, with impunity, their breach.

ALC. Heav'ns! what accumulated crimes are here!

ZAPH. Where is the monfter? bear me inftant to him,
That I may blaft him with my eye, may curfe him
With my laft hefitating voice.

PAL. Thou tyrant,
Did not thy own death-doing tongue enjoin
This horrid deed?

MIR. Not mine, by Heav'n!

ZAPH. Not thine!

MIR. No, by our Prophet, and his holy faith,
Of all the thoughts e'er harbour'd in this breaft,
It ne'er had fuch a monfter for its tenant.

ZAPH. Doft hear him, Heav'n? O moft accomplifh'd
villain!
MIRVAN, look at me——dar'ft thou——

MIR. Off with him,   [*To the foldiers.*
And fee him well fecur'd, till MAHOMET
Demands him of you.

PAL. Villain, hold!
              [*Laying hold of* ZAPHNA.

MIR. Away.

ZAPH. Juft, juft reward of my credulity!

PAL. Let me go with him, I will fhare thy fate,
Unhappy ZAPHNA, for I fhare thy guilt.
But then——   [*Looking back at* ALCANOR.

MIR. No more——you muft to MAHOMET.
Obey without reluctance; our great Prophet
In pity to your tender frame and years,
Will take you under his divine protection.

      E 3   PAL.

PAL. [*Apart*] O death, deliver me from such pro-
　　tection.

MIR. If you would ought to save the destin'd
　　ZAPHNA,
Follow me to the Prophet, you may move him
To mitigate his doom ——Away
　　　　　　　　[*To the soldiers who hold* ZAPHNA.
You this way.　　　　　　　　[*To* PALMIRA.

ZAPH. Pardon !

PAL. O pardon !
　　　[*They are led off by degrees, looking alternately*
　　　　at their father and each other.

ALC. What a wretch now am I!
Both from me torn, then when I wanted most
Their consolation.

PHA. Did you hear that shout ?
The citizens are rous'd, and all in arms
Rush on to your defence.

ALC. PHARON, support me
Some moments longer.———Help, conduct me
　　　　tow'rds 'em,
Bare this wound to 'em ; let that speak the cause,
The treach'rous cause, for words begin to fail me :
Then, if in death I can but serve my country,
Save my poor children from this tyger's gripe,
And give a second life to that lov'd pair,
By whose misguided zeal I lose my own ,
What patriot, or parent, but wou'd wish
In so divine a cause to fall a martyr !

　　　　　　　　　　　　　　　[*Exeunt.*

✤✤✤✤✤✤✤✤✤✤✤✤✤✤✤✤✤✤✤✤✤✤✤✤✤✤✤

ACT V. SCENE I.

MAHOMET *and* MIRVAN.

MAHOMET.

WRONG will be ever nurs'd and fed with
　　　　blood———
So ! this boy-bigot held his pious purpose ?

　　　　　　　　　　　　　　　　MIR.

Mir. Devoutly.

Mah What a reafonlefs machine
Can fuperftition make the reas'ner man !
Alcanor lies then on his bed of earth ?

Mir This moment he expir'd, and *Mecca's* youth
In vain lament their chief.   To the mad croud
That gather'd round, good Ali, and myfelf,
(Full of thy dauntlefs heav'nly-feeming fpirit)
Difclaim'd the deed, and pointed out the arm
Of righteous Heav'n, that ftrikes for Mahomet ——
" Think ye," we cried, (with eyes and hands uprear'd),
" Think ye our holy Prophet would confent
" To fuch a crime, whofe foulnefs cafts a blot
" On right of nations, nature, and our faith ?
" O rather think he will avenge his death,
" And root his murd'rer from the burden'd earth,"
Then ftruck our breafts, and wept the good old man ;
And only wifh'd, " He'd dy'd among the faithful,
" And flept with Ibrahim."

Mah. Excellent Mirvan !

Mir. We then both at large
Defcanted on thy clemency and bounty.
On that, the filent and defponding croud
Broke out in murmurs, plaints, and laft in fhouts,
And each mechanic grew a *Muffulman.*

Mah. O worthy to deceive, and awe the world,
Second to Mahomet ! Let me embrace thee.——
But fay, is not our army at their gates,
To back our clemency ?

Mir. Omar commands
Their nightly march thro' unfufpected paths,
And with the morn appears,

Mah. At fight of them,
The weak remaining billows of this ftorm
Will lafh themfelves to peace —But where is Zaphna ?

Mir. Safe in a dungeon, where he dies apace,
Unconfcious of his fate ; for well thou know'ft,
Whilft at the altar's foot he flew his fire,
In his own veins he bore his guilt's reward.

Mah. I would be kind, and let him die deceiv'd,
Nor know that parent-blood defiles his foul.

Mir. He cannot know it : if the grave be filent,

I'm

I'm sure HERCIDES is————

MAH. Unhappy ZAPHNA!
Something like pity checks me for thy death.
But why————I must not think that way————shall
    MAHOMET
Give a new paradile to all mankind,
And let remoise and confcience be the hell
Of his own breaft! My fafety claim'd his life,
And all the Heav'n of fair PALMIRA's charms
Shall be my great reward
    MIR My noble Lord,
PALMIRA is at hand, and waits your pleafure.
    MAH At hand! How, MIRVAN, could'ft thou let
      me talk
On themes of guilt when that pure angel's near?
    MIR The weeping fair, led on by flatt'ring hope
Of ZAPHNA's life, attends your facred will.
A filent, pale dejection fhrouds her cheeks,
And, like the lily in a morning fhow'r,
She droops her head, and locks up all her fweets.
    MAH. But now, MIRVAN,
Affemble all our chiefs, and on this platform
Let them attend me ftraight.
                  [*Exit* MIRVAN.

Enter PALMIRA, *with Attendants.*
    PAL. [*Apart.*] Where have they led me?
Methinks each ftep I take, the mangled corpfe
Of my dear father, (by poor ZAPHNA mangled,)
Lies in my way, and all I fee is blood———   [*Starting.*
'Tis the impoftor's felt———Burft, heart, in filence.
    MAH. Maid, lay afide this dread. PALMIRA's fate,
And that of *Mecca*, by my will is fixt.
This great event that fills thy foul with horror,
Is myftery to all but Heav'n and MAHOMET.
    PAL. [*Apart.*] O ever-righteous Heav'n, canft thou
      fuffer
This facrilegious hypocrite, this fpoiler,
To fteal thy terrors, and blafpheme thy name,
Nor doom him inftant dead?
    MAH. Child of my care,
At length from galling chains I've fet thee free,
                     And

And made thee triumph in a juft revenge:
Think then thou'rt dear to me, and MAHOMET
Regards thee with a more than father's eye:
Then know, (if thou'lt deferve the mighty boon),
An higher name, a nobler fate awaits thee.

PAL. What wou'd the Tyrant? ———————

MAH. Raife thy thoughts to glory,
And fweep this ZAPHNA from thy memory,
With all that's paft———Let that mean flame expire,
Before the blaze of empire's radiant fun
Thy grateful heart muft anfwer to my bounties,
Follow my laws, and fhare in all my conquefts.

PAL. What laws! what bounties! and what con-
          quefts, Tyrant!
Fraud is thy law, the tomb thy only bounty;
Thy conquefts fatal as infected air,
Difpeopling half the globe ———See here, good Heav'n,
The venerable Prophet I rever'd
The King I ferv'd, the God that I ador'd.

MAH. [*Approaching her.*] Whence this unwonted lan-
          guage, this wild phrenzy?

PAL. Where is the fpirit of my martyr'd father?
Where all the odour of my ZAPHNA's fame?
Where poor PALMIRA's infant innocence?
Blafted by thee, by thee, infernal monfter———
Thou found'ft us angels, and haft made us fiends:
Give, give us back our lives, our fame, our virtue,
Thou can'ft not, Tyrant;———Yet thou feek'ft my love:
Seek'ft with ALCANOR's blood his daughter's love:

MAH. [*Apart*] Horror, and death! The fatal fecret's
          known!

Enter MIRVAN.

MIR. O MAHOMET, all's loft! thy glory tarnifh'd,
And the infatiate tomb ripe to devour us
HERCIDES' parting breath divulg'd the fecret;
The prifon's forc'd, the city all in arms.
See where they bear aloft their murder'd chief,
Fell ZAPHNA in their front, death in his looks,
Rage all his ftrength. Spite of the deadly draught
He holds in life but to make fure of vengeance.

                                        MAH.

MAH. What doft thou here then ? Inftant with our
      guards,
Attempt to ftem their progrefs, 'till th' arrival
Of OMAR with the troops
    MIR. I hafte, my Lord   [*Exit* Mirvan.
    PAL. Now, now thy hour's at hand.
Hear'ft thou thofe fhouts that rend the ambient air,
See'ft thou thofe glancing fires that add new horrors
To the night's gloom ? frefh from thy murd'ring poi-
    nard,
(For thine it was, tho' ZAPHNA gave the blow,)
My father's fpirit leads the vengeful fhades,
Of all the wretches whom thy fword has butcher'd,
I fee them raife their unfubftantial arms
To fnatch me from thy rage, or worfe thy love.
Shadows fhall conquer in PALMIRA's caufe.
    MAH. [*Apart*] What terror's this that hangs upon
      her accents ?
I feel her virtue, tho' I know her weaknefs.
    PAL. Thou afk'ft my love ! go feek it in the grave
Of good ALCANOR,——Talk'ft of grateful minds !
Bid ZAPHNA plead for thee, and I may hear thee.
Till then thou art my fcorn ——May'ft thou, like me,
Behold thy deareft blood fpilt at thy feet.
Mecca, Medina, all our *Afian* world,
Join, join to drive th' Impoftor from the earth;
Blufh at his chains, and fhake 'em off in vengeance !
Thefe are th' endearments, thefe the cordial vows
PALMIRA's grateful heart returns to MAHOMET.
    MAH. [*Apart*] Be ftill, my foul, nor let a woman's
      rage
Ruffle thy wonted calm——Spite of thy hate
Thou'rt lovely ftill, and charming ev'n in madnefs.
    (*A fhout and noife of fighting*)
    PAL [*Apart*] Roll, roll your thunders, Heav'n, and
      aid the ftorm !
Now hurl your light'nings on the guilty head,
And plead the caufe of injur'd innocence !
    MAH. My fair, retire, nor let thy gentle foul
Shake with alarms ; thou'rt my peculiar care.
I go to quell this trait'rous infurrection,
And will attend thee ftraight.
                      PAL.

PAL. No, Tyrant, no.
I'll join my brother, help to head our friends,
And urge 'em on——————— [*Exit* Palmira.

Enter A L I.

MAH. Whence, ALI, that furprize!

ALI My Royal Chief,
The foe prevails———Thy troops led on by MIRVAN,
Are all cut off, and valiant MIRVAN's felf,
By ZAPHNA flain, lies welt'ring in his blood.
The guard that to our arms fhould ope the gates,
Struck with the common phrenzy, vow thy ruin,
And death and vengeance is the general cry.

MAH. Can ALI fear? Then MAHOMET be thy felf

ALI See thy few friends whom wild defpair hath arm'd,
(But arm'd in vain,) are come to die befide thee

MAH. Ye heartlefs traitors! MAHOMET alone
Shall be his own defender, and your guard,
Againft the crouds of *Mecca* ———————Follow me.

Enter ZAPHNA, PALMIRA, *and* PHARON, *with
citizens, and the body of* Alcanor *on a bier.*

MAH. Hah!

ZAPH See, my friends, where the Impoftor ftands,
With head erect, as if he knew not guilt,
As if no tongue fpake from ALCANOR's wound,
Nor call'd for vengeance on him.

MAH Impious man!
Is't not enough to've fpilt thy parent blood?
But with atrocious and blafpheming lips,
Dar'ft thou arraign the fubftitute of Heav'n!

ZAPH. The fubftitute of Heav'n! fo is the fword,
The peftilence, the famine, fuch art thou.
Such are the bleffings Heav'n has fent to man,
By thee its delegate · nay more, to me.
O he took pains, PALMIRA, upon us,
Religion'd us into fuch monftrous crimes
As nature ficken'd at conception of.————
How could'ft thou damn us thus?

MAH. Babler, avaunt!

ZAPH. Well thou upbraid'ft me; for to parley with
thee

Half

Half brands me coward⌐ O revenge me, friends,
Revenge ALCANOR's maſſacre · Revenge
PALMIRA's wrongs, and cruſh the ranc'rous monſter.

MAH. Hear me, ye ſlaves born to obey my will.

PAL. Ah! hear him not, fraud dwells upon his
    tongue.

ZAPH. Have at thee, fiend.——Hah! Heav'n.

[ZAPHNA *advancing, reels, and reclines on his ſword.*
What cloud is this
That thwarts upon my ſight, my head grows dizzy,
My joints unlooſe, ſure 'tis the ſtroke of fate

MAH. [*Aſide*] The poiſon works ——Then triumph
    MAHOMET!

ZAPH. Off, off baſe lethargy.

PAL. Brother, diſmay'd!
Haſt thou no power, but in a guilty cauſe,
And only ſtrength to be a parricide?

ZAPH. Spare that reproach ——Come on——It will
    not be.

[*Hangs down his ſword, and reclines on* PHARON,
Some cruel pow'r unnerves my willing arm,
Blaſts my reſolves, and weighs me down to earth.

MAH. Such be the fate of all who brave our law.
Nature and death have heard my voice, and now
Let Heav'n be judge 'twixt ZAPHNA and myſelf,
And inſtant blaſt the guilty of the two.

PHA. ZAPHNA revive——What means this gen'ral
    terror?
They ſtand aghaſt, and tremble at his voice!   o

PAL. Brother! O ZAPHNA!

ZAPH. ZAPHNA now no more.

[*Sinking down by* ALCANOR's *body, and leaning on
    the bier,* PHARON *kneeling down with him, and
    ſupporting him*
Down, down, good PHARON——Thou poor injur'd
    corſe,
May I embrace thee? Won't thy pallid wound
Purple anew at the unnatural touch,
And ooze freſh calls for vengeance?

PAL. O my brother!

ZAPH. In vain's the guiltleſs meaning of my heart:
High Heav'n deteſts th' involuntary crime,

                                        And

And dooms for parricide—Then tremble, tyrant.
If the supreme can punish error thus,
What new invented tortures must await
Thy soul, grown leprous with such foul offences,
As might make dim the very eye of day?
But soft—Now fate and nature are at strife.—
Sister, farewel; with transport should I quit
This toilsome, perilous, delusive stage,
But that I leave thee on't; leave thee, PALMIRA,
Expos'd to what is worse than fear can image,
That bad man's mercy. But I know thee brave,
Know that thou'lt act a part—look on her Heav'n,
Guide her, and————Oh!   [*Dies.*

    PAL. Think not, ye men of *Mecca*,
This death inflicted by the hand of Heav'n,
'Tis he————That viper ——

    MAH. Know, ye faithless wretches,
'Tis mine to deal the bolts of angry Heav'n
Behold them there, and let the wretch who doubts,
Tremble at ZAPHNA's fate, and know that MAHOMET
Can read his thoughts, and doom him with a look.
Go then, and thank your pontiff, and your prince,
For each day's sun he grants you to behold.
Hence, to your temples, and appease my rage.
       [*The people go off.*

    PAL. Ah! stay, my brother's murder'd by this ty-
       rant,
By poison, not by piety, he kills.

    MAH. 'Tis done————Thus ever be our law receiv'd!
       [*Apart.*

Now fair PALMIRA————

    PAL. Monster, is it thus
Thou mak'st thyself a God by added crimes,
And murders justify'd by sacrilege?

    MAH. Think, exquisite PALMIRA, for thy sake——

    PAL. Thou'st been the murderer of all my race.
See where ALCANOR, see where ZAPHNA lies:
Do they not call for me too at thy hands?
O that they did!————But I can read thy thoughts;
PALMIRA's sav'd for something worse than death,
That modesty denies her tongue to utter.
       F   This

This to prevent———— ZAPHNA, I follow thee.
                    [*Stabs herself with* ZAPHNA's *sword.*
  MAH. Slaves, feize her defp'rate hand.
  PAL. Thou ftriv'ft in vain,
    Reclining on her attendants, and then laying herfelf
      againft the fide of the bier, oppofite to ZAPHNA.
To hold a foul refolv'd.————O ZAPHNA, biother,
We burnt not with fo criminal a flame
As does that tyrant.————When the heart is pure,
Small is the difference, eafy is the change,
A lover's paffion for a fifter's fondnefs.
  MAH. What haft thou done?
  PAL. A deed of glory, tyrant!
Thou'ft left no object worth PALMIRA's eye;
And when I fhut out light, I fhut out thee————
                                        [*Dies.*

  MAH. Farewel, dear victim of my boundlefs paffion!
The price of treachery, the reward of murder,
Crown of my hopes, and fruit of all my crimes,
Sink with thee to the earth————O juftice! juftice!
In vain are glory, worfhip and dominion!
All conqueror as I am, I am a flave,
And, by the world ador'd, dwell with the damn'd.
My crimes have planted fcorpions in my breaft————
There is remorfe! Is confcience then! O furies!
Here, here I feel ye. 'Tis in vain to brave
The hoft of terrors that invade my foul,
I might deceive the world, myfelf I cannot.
  ALI. Be calm a while, my Lord, think what you are.
  MAH. Hah! What I am!   [*Turning to the bodies.*
    Ye breathlefs family!
Let your loud-crying wounds fay what I am.
O fnatch me from that fight, quick, quick tranfport me
To nature's lonelieft manfion, where the fun
Ne'er enter'd, where the found of human tread
Was never heard————But wherefore? Still I there,
There ftill fhall find myfelf————Ay, that's the hell!
I'll none on't ————————   [*Drawing his fword.*
  ALI. Heav'ns! help, hold him!
                    [ALI, &c. *difarm him.*
  MAH. Paltry daftards!
You fled the foe, but can difarm your mafter.

                   Angel

Angel of death, whofe pow'r I've long proclaim'd,
Now aid me, if thou canft, now, if thou can'ft,
Draw the kind curtain of eternal night,
And fhroud me from the horrors that befet me.
O what a curfe is life, when felf conviction
Flings our offences hourly in our face,
And turns exiftence torturer to itfelf,

FINIS.

EPILOGUE,

By a FRIEND.

Spoken by Mr. GARRICK.

LONG has the shameful licence of the age,
With senseless ribaldry, disgrac'd the stage,
So much indecencies have been in vogue,
They pleaded custom in an Epilogue;
As if the force of reason was a yoke
So heavy——they must ease it with a joke;
Disarm the moral of its virtuous sway,
Or else the audience go displeas'd away.

How have I blush'd to see a tragic Queen,
With ill-tim'd mirth disgrace the well-wrote scene;
From all the sad solemnity of woe,
Trip nimbly forth————to ridicule a beau;
Then, as the loosest airs she had been gleaning,
Cocquette the fan, and leer a double meaning.

Shame on these arts that prostitute the bays!
Shame on the bard, who this way hopes for praise!

The bold, but honest author of To-night,
Disdains to please you, if he please not right.
If in his well-meant scene you chance to find
Aught to ennoble or enlarge the mind;
If he has found the means, with honest art,
To fix the noblest wishes in the heart;
In softer accents to inform the *Fair*,
How bright they look, when virtue drops the tear,
Enjoy with friendly welcome the repast,
And keep the heart-felt relish to the last.

B ⚜ L

THE

ORPHAN of CHINA.

A

TRAGEDY.

Translated from the FRENCH of

M. DE VOLTAIRE.

First Acted at PARIS, on the 20th of *August*,
1 7 5 5.

E D I N B U R G H:

Printed for A. DONALDSON, at *Pope's Head*
oppofite the Exchange.

M,DCC,LIX.

DAVID GARRICK, Efq;

S I R,

THE ftory of *Voltaire's* ORPHAN *of* CHINA is fo very affecting, and fome of the characters fo ftrongly marked, that I cannot help taking this method of recommending it to your notice. A play built on the fame fable, could not fail of being well received on our ftage. The following tranflation, lame as it may appear, would bid fair for as many admirers as moft of our modern tragedies, if ZAMTI was reprefented by Mr *Garrick,* and IDAME by Mrs. *Cibber,* or Mrs. *Pritchard*; for either of thofe performers would appear to advantage in that character. You will fmile perhaps at this laft infinuation; but I can affure you, I am the moft difinterefted of any who have offered their plays to you, fince I fhall not pretend to lay any claim to the benefit of third nights.

BUT if you ferioufly intended to bring on a tragedy founded on this ftory, fome few alterations in the plan might be made, which, I think, would render it ftill more excellent. The two alarming fcenes in the firft and laft act could, indeed, admit of no improvement; and are convincing proofs of the fenfe our author muft entertain of *Shakefpear's* excellencies, and how much he has profited by a judicious imitation of his manner, notwithftanding the difrefpect with which he has more than once mentioned that great mafter of the drama. It appears to me, that the plot would be more artfully conducted, if the audience were not fo foon apprized, that IDAME is the perfon for whom GENGIS formerly entertained an unfuccefsful paffion.

A 2
THIS.

THIS, I think, will be evident to every one, who will read over the scene between GENGIS and OCTAR, in the second act, and for a moment suppose to himself, that he has not already been let into the secret: after which let him consider whether the natural amazement of GENGIS, on seeing IDAME, at the opening of the third act, would not have been doubly interesting, if the discovery had by that means been first made to the spectator. Besides this alteration, I cannot help thinking, that the account given by OSMAN, at the latter part of the second act, of the behaviour of ZAMTI and IDAME, might be very successfully thrown into action, and would more affectingly engage the attention of the audience, than a long narration, which would appear the more tedious, as it would probably be put into the mouth of an inferior player. The character of GENGIS might also be heightened with some pathetic touches, which would not only be more natural, but would also make him less resemble one of those angry strutting kings, so frequent in our plays, and which have so long made majesty appear ridiculous on the *English* stage.

THESE, and some few other alterations, might perhaps be found expedient, if you should think proper to naturalize this *French* performance. I hope you will on no account deprive the public of so exquisite an entertainment, since *Voltaire*'s original must fall into very bad hands indeed, if they contrive to make it half so insipid as any new tragedies lately exhibited, *Barbarossa* excepted. I am,

SIR.

Your Admirer,

and Humble Servant,

The TRANSLATOR.

✠✠✠✠✠✠✠✠✠✠✠✠✠✠✠✠✠✠✠✠✠✠✠✠✠✠✠✠✠✠✠✠✠✠✠✠✠

TO THE

LORD MARSHAL,

DUKE of *RICHELIEU*,

PEER of *FRANCE*,

First Gentleman of the KING's Chamber, Commandant in LANGUEDOC, one of the Forty of the Academy.

MY LORD,

I WOULD fain present you with beautiful marble like the *Genoese*, and I have only *Chinese* figures to offer you. This little work does not seem made for you. There is no hero in this piece, who has reconciled all opinions by the charms of his genius, or who has supported a falling republic, or who has attempted to overthrow an *English* column with four cannons*. I am

A 3   more

* At the battle of *Fontenoy*, the *English* army was drawn up in a column, divided into three parts, which had made its way against all opposition, and remained masters of the field. Marshal SAXE himself had given orders to prepare for a retreat, when by the advice of the Duke of RICHELIEU, four cannons were advanced against the Body of the *English* Forces, which were the chief means of their being routed, and the victory falling on the side of the *French*. To which circumstance the Dedicator here alludes.

more aware than any body of the trifle that I offer you: but all muſt be forgiven to an attachment of forty years. It will be ſaid, perhaps, that the foot of the *Alps,* and in the midſt of eternal ſnows, whither I am retired, and where I ought to be merely a philoſopher, I have yielded to the vanity of publiſhing to the world, that the moſt eminent perſon on the banks of the *Seine* has never forgot me. yet I have only conſulted my own heart; that alone directs me; that has always inſpired my words and actions: it deceives itſelf ſome times, you know, but not after proofs of ſo long ſtanding. Let it then be known, if this weak Tragedy can laſt any time after me, that its author was not indifferent to you; let it be known, that if your Uncle founded the polite arts in *France,* you have ſupported them in their decline.

THE idea of this Tragedy was firſt conceived ſometime ago on reading *The Orphan of Tchao,* a *Chineſe* Tragedy, tranſlated by Father *Brémare,* which may be found in the collection publiſhed by Father *Du Halde.* This *Chineſe* piece was compoſed in the fourteenth century, within the very Dynaſty of GENGIS-KAN. It is a new proof that the victorious *Tartars* did not change the manners of the nation vanquiſhed, they protected all the Arts eſtabliſhed in *China,* they adopted all its Laws.

THIS is a ſtriking inſtance of the natural ſuperiority of reaſon and genius over blind and barbarous force and the *Tartars* have twice afforded this example. For when they had again made a conqueſt of this great Empire, at the beginning of the laſt century, they ſubmitted a ſecond time to the wiſdom of the nation they had ſubdued, and the two people have formed but one nation,

tion, governed by the moſt antient laws in the world : a ſtriking event, which has been the main ſcope of my work.

THE *Chineſe* Tragedy called *The Orphan*, is taken from a large collection of Dramatic pieces of that nation. They cultivated above three thouſand years ago that art, found out a little time after by the *Grecians*, of drawing living portraits of the actions of men, and of eſtabliſhing thoſe ſchools of morality, where virtue is inculcated by action and dialogue. Dramatic Poetry was for a long time in repute, only in the vaſt country of *China*, ſeparated from, and unknown to the reſt of the world, and in the one town of *Athens*. *Rome* did not cultivate it till at the end of four hundred years after. If you look for it among the *Perſians*, among the *Indians*, who paſs for people of invention, you will not find it ; it never came to them. *Aſia* contented itſelf with the Fables of *Pilpay* and *Lokman*, which include the whole of morality, and which inſtruct by allegory all nations and all ages

ONE would imagine, that after having made animals talk, there remained but one ſtep to make men converſe, to bring them on the ſtage, and to form the Dramatic Art · yet theſe ingenious people never once thought of it. One may infer from hence, that the *Chineſe*, the *Greeks*, and the *Romans* are the only ancient people, who had a true notion of ſociety. Nothing, in effect, makes men more ſociable, more ſoftens their manners, brings their reaſon to greater perfection, than aſſembling them to taſte together the pure pleaſures of the ſoul. Thus we ſee that ſcarce had *Peter the Great* poliſhed *Ruſſia*, and built *Petersburg*, than Theatres were eſtabliſhed. *Germany*, the more it has

improved,

improved, the more it has adopted public spectacles. The few countries, where they have not been received within the last century, have not been placed in the rank of civilized nations.

THE *Orphan of Tchao* is a precious monument, which serves better to shew us the genius of *China* than all the relations ever made, or that ever can be made, of that vast Empire. It is true, that that piece is quite barbarous, in comparison of the correct works of our time; but at the same time it is an absolute master-piece, if we compare it to those of ours written in the fourteenth century Certainly our * *Troubdours*, our *Bazoche*, our *Societé des enfans sans souci*, and our *Mére sotte*, are infinitely below the *Chinese* Author. It must also be observed, that that piece is written in the language of the *Mandarines*, which is not at all changed, and that we scarce understand the language spoken in the times of *Lewis* XII. and *Charles* VIII.

THE *Orphan of Tchao* can only be compared to the *English* and *Spanish* Tragedies of the seventeenth century, which please even now beyond the *Pyrenees*, and beyond the sea. The action of the *Chinese* Piece lasts twenty-five years, as in the monstrous Dramas of *Shakespear* and *Lopez de Vega*, which they have named Tragedies: it is a heap of incredible events. The enemy of the house of *Tchao* first attempts to destroy the chief of it, by letting loose on him a hudge mastiff, which is supposed to be endowed with the instinct of discovering criminals, as *Jacques Aimar* among us discovered robbers by his wand. Then he supposes an order of the Emperor, and sends to his enemy *Tchao* a rope, a bowl of poison, and a poignard. *Tchao* sings,
according

* Names of *French* Plays, and *French* Authors.

according to the cuſtom, and cuts his own throat, in virtue of that obedience due, of right divine, from all mankind to the Emperor of *China*. The perſecutor deſtroys three hundred perſons of the houſe of *Tchao*. The Princeſs Dowager then lyes in of the *Orphan*. They convey away the infant from the fury of him who has extirpated his whole family, and who would yet murder in his cradle the only one remaining. This deſtroyer iſſues orders to murder all the infants in the villages round about, that the *Orphan* may be enveloped in the general deſtruction.

ONE ſeems reading *the thouſand and one nights*, in action and ſcenes : but notwithſtanding the incredibilty, it is ſtill intereſting ; and in ſpite of the heap of incidents, the whole is remarkably perſpicuous. Theſe have been the two grand excellencies in all ages and all nations ; and theſe excellencies are wanting in many of our modern pieces It is true, the *Chineſe* piece has no other beauties : unity of time and action, opening of ſentiments, painting of manners, eloquence, argument, paſſion, are all wanting ; and yet, as I have already ſaid, the work is ſuperior to any of our own, of the ſame date.

YET the *Chineſe*, who in the fourteenth century, and ſo long before, compoſed better dramatic poems than all the *Europeans*, have always remained in the mere infancy of the art, while, by time and diligence, our nation has produced about a dozen pieces, which, if they are not perfect, are yet infinitely beyond any thing that all the reſt of the world has produced in that kind The *Chineſe*, like the other *Aſiaticks*, have ſtopt at the firſt elements of poetry, eloquence, phyſicks, aſtronomy, painting, known by them ſo long before

tore

fore us. They began all things so much sooner than other people, never afterwards to make any progress in them They have resembled the ancient *Ægyptians*, who having first instructed the *Grecians*, were afterwards incapable of being their disciples.

THESE *Chinese*, to whom we have made voyages among so many dangers, these people of whom we have with so much difficulty obtained leave to carry them, the money of *Europe*, and to come and instruct them, are yet ignorant that we are their superiors : they are not enough advanced, to dare only to try to imitate us. We have gone into their history for subjects of tragedy, and they are ignorant that we have an history.

THE famous Abbé *Metastasio* has taken, for the subject of one of his Dramatic poems, nearly the same subject with myself: that is to say, an *Orphan* escaped from the slaughter of his family , and he has carried that adventure back to a dynasty which reigned nine hundred years before our æra.

THE *Chinese* tragedy of the *Orphan of Tchao*, is quite another subject. I again have chose a subject quite different from the two others, and which only resembles them in name. I have fix'd at the grand epocha of *Gengis-Kan*, and have endeavoured to paint the manners of the *Tartars* and of the *Chinese*. Adventures the most interesting are nothing, unless they paint the manners; and that painting, which is one of the great secrets of the art, is also a mere frivolous amusement, unless it inspires virtue.

I MAY venture to say, that from the *Henriade* down to *Zara*, and quite down to this *Chinese* piece, good or bad, such has always been the principle that has in-

spired

fpired me, and that in the hiſtory of the age of *Lewis* XIV. I have celebrated my king, and my country, without flattering either the one or the other It is in ſuch a labour that I have conſumed more than forty years. But obſerve the words of a *Chineſe* author, tranſlated into *Spaniſh* by the celebrated *Navaretto*.

" If you compoſe any work, ſhew it only to your " friends; dread the public and your fellows; for " they will falſify and empoiſon that which you have " done, and impute to you that which you have not " done. Calumny, who has a hundred trumpets, ſhall " ſound them all to deſtroy you, while Truth, who is " mute, ſhall reſt with you. The famous *Ming* was " was accuſed of having thought irreverertly of *Tien* " and *Li*, and of the Emperor *Vang*. They found the " old man dying, who had juſt finiſhed the panegyric " of *Vang*, and a hymn to *Tien* and *Li*," &c.

DRA-

DRAMATIS PERSONÆ.

GENGIS-KAN, Emperor of the *Tartars*.

OCTAR,
OSMAN, } Officers of the *Tartars*.

ZAMTI, *Mandarine* and Prieſt.

IDAME, Wife to *Zamti*.

ASSELI, Friend to *Idame*.

ETAN, Friend to *Zamti*.

The SCENE *is in a Palace of the* Mandarines, *joining to the Imperial Palace, in the City of* Cambalu, *now* Pekin.

THE

ORPHAN of CHINA.

A

TRAGEDY.

ACT I. SCENE I.

IDAME, ASSELI.

IDAME.

CAN there, in this fad day of defolation,
In this dire hour of carnage and deftruction,
When ev'n this palace, open to the *Tartars*,
Falls with the world beneath barbarian hands,
Can there, amid this heap of public horrors,
Remain for me frefh caufe of private woe ?

ASSELI. Ah! who, alas! among the common lofs,
Feel not the preffure of their own misfo·tunes ?
Who fends not up to heav'n her feeble cries
To fave a fon, a father, or a hufband ?
Within this pale, ftill ftranger to the foe,
Whither the King withdrew from public view
The weak defencelefs minifters of peace ;
Th' interpreters of law, the holy priefts,
Decrepit age, and cradled infancy,
And we the trembling band of fearful women,
Whom cruel flaughter yet has left untouch'd,
Know not, alas! to what enormous lengths
The haughty victor may extend his rage
We hear the thunder roll, and tempefts roar :
The ftorm hangs o'er us, and we dread its fall.

B   IDAME.

IDAME. O fortune! O thou more than earthly pow'r!—
Know'st thou, my ASSELI, beneath what hand
Once pow'rful *Cathay*'s bleeding empire groans,
The hand, that thus oppresses all the world?

ASSELI. They call the cruel tyrant King of Kings:
Fierce GENGIS KAN, whose dread exploits in war
Have made proud *Asia* one vast sepulchre.
OCTAR his officer, to murder train'd,
With sword and fire already seeks the palace,
And conquer'd *Cathay* to new masters yields
This city, sometime sovereign of the world,
Lies drown'd in blood, and all its hundred streets,
Floating in gore, proclaim the dismal tale.

IDAME. Know'st thou, this tyrant of the subject earth,
This fell destroyer of our helpless state,
This dread of Kings, imbrued in royal blood,
Is a rough *Scythian*, bred to war and arms,
A warrior, wandring in those savage desarts,
Where angry heaven lours with endless storms.
'Tis he, who, mad for pow'r above his fellows,
Was hither driv'n by persecution's rage,
And whom thou lately saw'st in this great city,
Begging protection at the palace gates;
This King of Kings, this victor's TEMUGIN.

ASSELI How! TEMUGIN! who paid his vows to
     thee!
That fugitive! whose homage and whose love
Appear'd an insult to your angry parents!
Is't he draws after him this train of kings,
He, whose bare name strikes terror to mankind!

IDAME. The same, my ASSELI, his haughty courage,
His future greatness shone upon his visage
All, I confess, seem'd poor and mean to him;
And even, while he begg'd our court's assistance,
Unknown, a fugitive, he seem'd commanding.
He lov'd me, and perhaps my foolish heart
Approv'd his love: perhaps it was my pride
To tame this lion shackled in my chains,
To our soft forms to bend his savage grandeur,
To polish with our virtues his rough soul,
And make him one day worthy to be rank'd
Among the number of our citizens.

He

He would have ferv'd the ftate he has deftroy'd,
And he we fcorn'd has brought on all our woes.
Thou know'ft, the fierceneſs of our jealous people,
The antient honours of our arts and laws,
Our holy faith, thrice fanctified and pure,
And the long glories of a hundred ages,
All, all forbad, with one united voice,
A bafe alliance with the barb'rous nations.
A holier Hymen has engaged my vows,
And virtuous ZAMTI merits all my love.
Who would have thought, in thofe bleft hours of peace,
That a ſcorn'd *Scythian* thus fhould lord it o'er us ?
This, this alarms me, I refufed his hand,
And am the wife and partner of another.
He comes in blood, the world at his command
To give him means of vengeance.—O ſtrange fate !
O heaven ! can it be, that this great people
Should, like bafe flocks of cattle fent to flaughter,
Fall, without fight, beneath a *Scythian* fword !

ASSELI. The *Coreans*, it is faid, have troops affembled:
But we know nothing but by vague report,
And are abandon'd to the victor's rage.

IDAME. O how uncertainty increaſes grief !
I know not where our miferies extend,
Whether amid the palace of his fathers
The Emperor has refuge found, or help ;
Whether the Queen by th' enemy is feiz'd ;
Or, if of one or both the hour is come :
Too fad reward, alas! of wedded love.
The hapleſs infant to our care confign'd
Again excites my fear and my compaſſion.
My ZAMTI too with raſh ſtep treads the palace ;
Haply, refpect of his moft holy office
May touch thefe favages   'Tis faid, the ruffians,
Bred to the trade of death, have yet preferv'd
Some notion of a GOD   fo much ev'n nature,
In barb'rous climes, untaught and unimprov'd,
Proclaims to all, RELIGION and a GOD.
Yet, ah! I fondly dream of their refpect,
I talk of hope, but am a flave to fear.
O mifery !

SCENE II.

IDAME, ZAMTI, ASSELI.

IDAME. O fay, unhappy Zamti,
Is then our flavery, our woe determin'd ?
Ah! what haft thou beheld ?
                        Zamti. The height of horrors.
Our fortune's fixt, and *China* is no more.
Beneath the ftranger fword all falls.   Ah! what avail'd
A life of virtue ? Fair peace fmil'd in vain ;
In vain our laws gave pattern to the world ;
Grey wifdom dies by brutal violence.
I faw the favage troop of northern ruffians
Making their way in blood ; o'er flaughter'd heaps,
Carrying the fword and fire.   In crowds they fought
The facred manfion of our haplefs Monarch.
He with majeftic brow expected death,
And held within his arms his fainting Queen.
Thofe of their children, whofe increafing valour
Began to grow with years, whofe little arms
Could wield a fword, were all already fall'n.
Round them clung thofe, whofe tender infancy
Had nought but cries and tears for their defence.
While they prefs'd round him, and embrac'd his knees,
I by a fecret path approach'd the place,
And view'd with horror the unhappy father.
I faw thofe fiends, thofe monfters of the defart,
Lifting the murd'rous fteel againft our King,
And thro' the palace drag with bloody hands
The father, children, and their dying mother.
While all was fury, havock, death, and plunder,
The wretched monarch turn'd on me his eyes,
And thus addrefs'd me in the facred tongue,
Unknown to th' conqu'ring *Tartar* and the people,
O fave at leaft from death my youngeft fon !
Think, if I did not fwear I would preferve him,
O think, how loudly duty call'd upon me.
I felt my fainting fpirits new revived,
Hither I flew.   The bloody ravifhers
Stopt not my paffage : whether hideous joy,
Intent on plunder, turn'd their eyes afide ;

Whether

Whether this badge of my moſt rev'rend office,
This ſymbol of the GOD that I adore,
Struck their fierce ſouls with awe, or Heav'n itſelf
Determin'd to preſerve this Royal Infant,
Athwart their watch'ul eyes dim miſts ſuffus'd,
Dazzled their ſight, and mollified their rage.

IDAME. Yes, we will ſave him. Be this royal charge,
With our dear child away convey'd, and bred.
Deſpair not, but with haſte prepare our flight:
Let ETAN have the care of our depart,
And fly tow'rds *Corea*, to the ocean ſide,
Where the ſea girds this mournful univerſe.
The earth has deſarts and wild ſavages
Away then with theſe infants, while the foe
Invades not yet this ſanctified aſylum.
Come, time is precious, and complaint in vain.

ZAMTI. Alas! has then the race of kings no refuge!——
The troops from *Corea* linger in their march.
Mean while deſtruction rages in our walls:
Seize we, if poſſible, th' auſpicious moment
To place in ſurety this our precious charge.

SCENE III.

ZAMTI, IDAME, ASSELI, ETAN.

ZAMTI. Why thus, my ETAN, frighted and amazed?
IDAME. Fly, fly this place abandon'd to the *Scythian*.
ETAN. You are obſerv'd, and flight impoſſible.
The pale's encircled by a cruel guard,
Forming around the frighted multitude
A dreadful fence thick-ſet with pikes and darts.
The conqu'ror ſpoke, and ſlavery heard his voice:
The people, motionleſs with fear and horror,
Sink in deſpair; now murder's reeking ſword
With impious rage has drank our Emp'ror's blood.
ZAMTI. Is he then dead?
IDAME. O heav'nly powers, the Emperor!
ETAN. Words cannot paint the horrors of the ſcene.
His bleeding wife, their children torn and mangled—
O GODS! ador'd on earth! how ſhall I ſpeak it?

Their

Their fufferings only mov'd the victor's fcorn,
While their poor fubjects, fearful to complain,
Hung down thofe eyes that fpoke their grief too plainly.
The fhamelefs foldiers on their coward knees
Refign'd their arms ; when now the conquerors
Tir'd with the toil of murder, drunk with blood,
Inftead of death pronounc'd our flavery.
Yet ftill new woes remain.   This GENGIS KAN,
That leads this fwarm from forth the Northern hive,
This tyrant, born to be the bane of *China*,
Here formerly abode, unknown and fcorn'd.
Now all incens'd, implacable he comes,
To glut his anger, and revenge his wrongs.
His favage nations form'd by other laws
Than our foft people: Fields, and tents, and cars
Their wonted dwelling, ev'n the wide extent
Of this vaft city would appear confinement.
No fenfe have they of our fair arts and laws,
But mean with barb'rous rage to overturn
Thefe walls, fo long the wonder of the world.

   IDAME.   Too fure the victor comes refolv'd on ven-
       geance
In my obfcurity I plac'd fome hopes ;
But heav'n, alas! determin'd to deftroy us,
Has fcatter'd the kind cloud that late conceal'd us.

   ZAMTI.   Perhaps ev'n yet the Gods will fave *the
       Orphan:*
Be his fecurity our only care————
What means this *Tartar* here ?
             IDAME.   O fhield me, Heav'n!

SCENE IV.

ZAMTI, IDAME, ASSELI, OCTAR *and* Guards.

   OCTAR   Hear, and obey, ye flaves, there yet remains
The laft and youngeft fon of all your kings.
'Tis ye protect him, and your rafh compaffion
Preferves an enemy we would deftroy
I here command you, in the mighty name
Of the great conqueror of all mankind,
Give up this infant , fee it quickly brought me.

If you delay, again within thefe walls
Shall havock ftalk in blōod, and you the firft
Shall fall a facrifice. Day flies, night comes ;
Think, and beware, befoie the clofe of eve,
If life is precious, fee that ye obey.

SCENE V.

ZAMTI, IDAME.

IDAMF. Where will our forrows end, when ev'ry
    moment
Teems wrth new horrors, and produces evils,
Which, till this day of death, th' affrighted foul
Could ne'er conceive Alas! you anfwer not,
But figh in vain to Heaven, that opprefies us——
And muft thou, offspring of fo many kings!
Be facrific'd to pleafe a ruffian foldier ?
    ZAMTI. I've promis'd, I have fworn to fave his life.
    IDAME. Ah! what can your weak help avail him now?
Your oaths, your fond endearments, or your promife ?
We have not ev'n hope left
            ZAMTI. O Heav'n! my IDAME,
And could'ft thou then behold this child of kings
Butchei'd by *Scythians* ?
            IDAME. No; the very thought
Makes my fad eyes run o'er and it, alas!
Our own dear child demanded not my care,
I would fay, Death! my ZAMTI, fince our kings
Fall by the *Scythian*, let not us furvive them !
    ZAMTI. Who, plung'd in mifery, views death with
        dread ?
The guilty fear, the wretched wifh for death,
The brave defy, and triumph in the face on't ;
The wife, who know that death at laft muft come,
Without a fhock receive it.
            IDAME. Why is this ?
What mean thefe dreadful words? upon the ground
You fix your eyes, your hair ftands all on end,
Your cheek grows pale, tears are in your eyes.
My bofom anfwers yours, feels all its griefs;
But what refolve you?

                            ZAMTI,

ZAMTI. To obſerve my oath.
Go, wait my coming near the Royal infant.

IDAME. O, that my cries and prayers could protect
[him!

SCENE VI.

ZAMTI, ETAN.

ETAN. Alas! my Lord, your pity can't preſerve him.
His death alone can ſave the ſtate from ruin,
The people's ſafety aſk it

ZAMTI. Yes——I ſee,
A ſacrifice moſt dreadful muſt be made——
Attend me, ETAN!——Is your country dear?
Say, do you own that GOD of Heav'n and Earth
Worſhip'd by all our fathers, but unknown
To the rude *Bonze*, and by theſe *Scythians* ſcorn'd?

ETAN. Own him? he is my boſom's ſole ſupport:
I mourn my country's woes, nor hope redreſs
But from his power.

ZAMTI. By his ſacred name,
By all his power, ſwear thou'lt ne'er reveal
The ſecret purpoſe, which to thy performance
I now commend · ſwear that thou wilt accompliſh
That which the laws, the int'reſts of thy country,
My duty, and my GOD by me command thee.

ETAN. I ſwear it; and may all our common woes
Be heap'd on me alone, if e'er betraying
Your ſacred charge, or faultering in my zeal,
My tongue or hand ſhall ever prove unfaithful!

ZAMTI. I muſt delay no longer.

ETAN. How! in tears!
Alas! amid ſo many miſeries,
Whence this new cauſe of grief?

ZAMTI. His fate is fix'd.
The cruel order's given.

ETAN. Time grows ſhort;
Yet ſure this child, which is to you a ſtranger——

ZAMTI. Stranger! this ſtranger child! my King a
ſtranger!

ETAN. His father was indeed our King. Alas!

I

I know it, and I freeze with horror: ſpeak,
What muſt I do?

   ZAMTI. My very looks are watch'd,
And all my ſteps obſerv'd; but thou'rt unnotic'd.
Thou know'ſt th'aſylum of our ſacred charge;
Avail thyſelf of thine obſcurity,
And for a time within the monuments,
Built by our ſires, conceal this Royal Infant.
Thence ſhall be ſoon convey'd to *Corea*'s chief
This tender ſhoot of *China*'s Royalty.
Save we at leaſt from theſe fell murderers
This hapleſs child, the object of their fears.
Save we our King, and leave the reſt to me.

  ETAN. Without this mournful pledge what threatens
    you?
Say, can you anſwer all the victor's rage?

  ZAMTI. Yes, I can ſatisfy it.

     ETAN. You, my Lord!

  ZAMTI. O nature! O tyrannic duty!

     ETAN How!

  ZAMTI. Go, from his cradle take my only ſon.

  ETAN. Your ſon!

   ZAMTI. Think of the King you ought to ſave.
Take my ſon——let his blood——I can no more.

  ETAN. Ah! what do you command me?

     ZAMTI. Spare a father,
His miſeries, and moſt of all his weakneſs.
Oppoſe not my deſign, but quick fulfil
The ſolemn vow thou'ſt made

    ETAN. Alas! you wrung
That raſh vow from me. To what dreadful duty
Does the performance bind me! your great ſoul,
And generous purpoſe I admire with horror.
But if my friendſhip——

    ZAMTI No, it muſt be ſo.
I am a father, and a father's grief
Hath told me more, much more than thou canſt ſay.
I've ſilenc'd blood, do thou bid friendſhip peace.
Away.

  ETAN. I muſt obey.

   ZAMTI. For pity leave me.

      SCENE

SCENE VII.

ZAMTI *solus.*

I've filenc'd blood!——Ah, moſt unhappy father!
That voice, alas! too loudly calls upon me.
My wife and ınfant rend my foul with angȗıſh:
O charm to ſilence, Heav'n, the voice of grief,
Nor let me know the weakneſs of my foul.
Man is too weak, alas! to conquer nature:
Support him, Heaven! and when his cares are vain,
His drooping virtue with thy grace ſuſtain!

ACT II. SCENE I.

ZAMTI *solus.*

ETAN too long delays his ſad return.
I long, yet fear, to know the deed's diſpatch'd;
I wiſh, yet dread, his coming. Oh! my ſon,
My dear, dear infant! art thou then deſtroy'd?
Have they made up this horrid ſacrifice?
I could not to the *Scythian's* butcher hand
Myſelf deliver you. Heav'n give me ſtrength
To hear the ſad ſucceſs of my attempt,
And hide the anguiſh of my tortur'd foul!

SCENE II.

ZAMTI, ETAN.

ZAMTI My friend!——I underſtand—— your tears ex-
    plain it.
ETAN. Your helpleſs ſon——
                    ZAMTI Ah! ſpeak of him no more;
Speak of our Monarch's ſon, the hope o' th' Empire.
Say, is he ſafe?
                    ETAN The holy monuments
Of his great anceſtors from hoſtile eyes

His life and woes conceal. To you he owes
A life, whofe dawn in heavinefs comes on :
Too fatal gift perhaps.
    Zamti. He lives enough.
O you, my Royal Mafters, to whofe fhades
My only child I facrifice, forgive
A father's tears !
    Etan. Within thefe conquer'd walls
Your forrows fpeak too loudly.
    Zamti. Oh ! my friend,
In what fad manfion fhall my grief have vent ?
And how fhall I fuftain the firft approach,
Bitter upbraidings, yellings, wild defpair,
And imprecations of a furious mother ?
Let us at firft, if poffible, deceive her !
 Etan. The ruffians, in her abfence, took your fon,
And to the cruel victors ftrait convey'd him.
I flew immediately to fave, if poffible,
Th' endanger'd *Orphan*.
    Zamti Tell her, my good Etan,
That we have fav'd the Heir of *China*, tell her,
Our boy is fafe, and thus with kind delufion
Win her, if poffible, to fond belief.
Alas ! that truth fo often fhould be cruel !
Mankind adore it, and it makes them wretched
Come then, my Etan !—Heav'n ! my wife approaches,
And death and madnefs ftare within her eyes.

S c e n e III.

ZAMTI, IDAME

 Idame What have I feen ? Barbarian ! is it poffible ?
Did you command this horrid facrifice ?
Ah ! no, I can't believe it, angry heav'n
Ne'er fill'd your bofom with fuch cruelty,
You cannot be more hard and barbarous
Than the rough Tut : Canft thou weep then, Zamti ?
 Zamti Ah ! weep with me, my Idame, but try
To fave your King
    Idame How ! facrifice my fon ?
        Zamti.

ZAMTI. Such is our haplefs lot : but think, dear
    wife,
That CITIZEN's a holier tie than MOTHER.

IDAME. Rules nature then fo feebly in your breaft?

ZAMTI. Alas! too ftrong; but weaker than my duty.
I would preferve our child, but more, much more,
To my unhappy mafter's blood I owe.

IDAME. No, I difclaim this favage ftrength of foul.
I've feen thefe walls in afhes, this high throne
O'erturn'd, and wept our monarch's haplefs fate :
But by what madnefs, ftill more horrible,
Will you bring on a poor wife's death, and fhed
The blood of your own child, they not demand ?
Our kings interr'd, and vanifh'd into duft,
Are they your Gods, and do you dread their thunder?
And have you fworn to thefe weak Gods intomb'd
To facrifice your fon? Alas! my ZAMTI,
The great and fmall, the fubject and the monarch,
Diftinguifh'd for a time by idle marks,
Equal by nature, equal by misfortune,
Each bears enough, that bears his own diftrefs.
It is our part, amid this gen'ral wreck
To gather up our fad remains.—Good heav'n!
Where had I been, if my credulity
Had fall'n into the net was fpread before me!
If by the ORPHAN's fide I had remained,
My infant-victim would to butcher hands
Have been deliver'd; I no more a mother
Had fall'n beneath the knife that kill'd my child.
Thanks to my love, that troubled and unquiet
Call'd me, like inftinct, to the fatal cradle!
I found them carrying off my lovely babe,
And with a mother's fury tore him from them.
Barbarian! ev'n the cruel ravifhers
Wanted thy favage firmnefs. To a flave,
Whofe breaft with nurfing care has long fuftain'd
His little life, the precious charge I gave.
Thus have I fav'd from death the child and mother,
Nay more, my ZAMTI, fav'd th' unhappy fire.

ZAMTI. How! is my fon then living?

        IDAME. Yes, thank heaven!
Kind, in thine own defpight, to blefs thee ftill.

Repent

Repent you of your rafhnefs.

     Z A M T I. God of heaven !
Forgive this joy that will not be reprefs'd,
And for a moment mixes with my grief.
O my dear IDAME, his days are few :
In vain you would prolong his life, in vain
Conceal this fatal off'ring. On demand,
If we not render up his forfeit life,
The jealous tyrants foon will be reveng'd ,
And all the citizens with us deftroy'd,
Too fadly fhall repay thy cruel care.
Inclos'd by foldiers, there's no refuge left ;
And my poor boy, thou fondly ftriv'ft to fave,
Cannot be refcu'd from the hand of flaughter.
He muft die.

  IDAME. Stay ! dear ZAMTI, ftay, I charge thee !
 ZAMTI. Ah !—he muft die

     IDAME. Muft die ! hold, on thy life !
Fear my defpair and fury, fear a mother.

  ZAMTI I know no fear but to betray my duty.
Abandon yours; me and my life abandon
To the detefted conqu'ror's impious rage.
Go, afk my death of GENGIS ; go, he'll grant it.
Bathe in a hufband's blood your hands, and fill
With monftrous deaths this day of parricide :
Horror on horror's head ftill heap, at once
Betray your GOD, your COUNTRY, and your KING.

  IDAME. My king ! what claim have monarchs in the
   grave ?
Owe I my blood a tribute to their afhes ?
Or does a fubject's duty bind thee more,
Than the ftrong ties of father and of hufband ?
Nature and marriage are the firft of laws,
The duties, and chief bonds of all mankind ·
Thefe laws defcend from heav'n, the reft are human.
O make me not abhor the blood of kings !—
Yes, fave the ORPHAN from the victor's fword,
But fave him not by parricide. O let
His days be bought at any *other* price :
Far from abandoning, I fly to aid him.
I pity him. O pity thou thyfelf,
Pity thy guiltlefs infant, and O pity
      C   His

His poor diftracted mother, who doats on thee!
No more I threaten ; at thy knees I fall.——
O haplefs father, dear though cruel hufband,
For whom I fcorn'd, which hap'ly you remember,
The man whom fortune now has made our mafter ;
Grant me the offspring of our pureft love ;
Nor O! oppofe the ftrong and tender cries
Of love, that even now fhake all your frame!

ZAMTI. Ah! do not thus abufe thy power o'er me,
Nor join with nature to oppofe my duty.
O thou too weak of foul! if you but knew !——

IDAME. Yes I am weak , a mother fhould be fo.
Yet thou fhould'ft not upbraid my foul of weaknefs,
Were I to follow thee to death or torture :
And if, to glut the bloody victor's rage,
The mother's murder may redeem the child,
I'm ready : Idame fhall ne'er complain ;
And her heart beats as nobly as thy own.

ZAMTI. Alas! I know thy virtues.

S C E N E   IV.

ZAMTI, IDAME, OCTAR, with Guards.

OCTAR. Dare ye, flaves,
Refume the pledge that I commanded from you ?
Follow them, foldiers, and the child conceal'd
See they refign. Away, your Emp'ror comes ·
Here bring the victim to your mafter's feet.
Soldiers, obferve them.

ZAMTI. We'll obey your orders :
We will refign the infant.

IDAME. Never, never.
No, I'll not yield him up, but with my life.

OCTAR. Away with that bold woman. Lo, the Em-
          peror !·
Let not thefe captive flaves approach his prefence.

SCENE V.

GENGIS, OCTAR, OSMAN, Soldiers.

GENGIS. Too far they pufh my right of victory.
Sheath'd be the fword, and flaughter check its courfe!
And henceforth let the vanquifh'd breathe fecure!
Terror I fent before me, but bring peace.
The child of kings deftroy'd fhall glut my rage:
In his blood will I choak the fatal feeds
Of dark confpiracy and bold rebellion,
Which fuch weak phantoms of a prince infpire.
His fathers are all fallen: he muft follow.
Let the kings die, the fubjects all fhall live.

Ceafe to deftroy thofe noble monuments;
Refpect thofe facred prodigies of art,
And let them ftand as the rewards of valour.
Ceafe to commit to flames and defolation
Thofe Archives of the Laws, vaft fcrolls of writing,
And all thofe works of genius you defpife.
From error if they fprung, that error's ufeful;
It makes the people docile and obedient.

OCTAR, I deftine you to bear my banners
Where the fun rifes from his watry bed.

[To one of his followers.

In conquer'd *India*, humble in its ruin,
Of my decrees be thou th' interpreter;
While in the Weft my victor fons fhall fly
From *Samarcand's* proud walls to *Tanais'* banks.
Away: OCTAR remain.

SCENE VI.

GENGIS, OCTAR.

GENGIS. Could'ft thou believe
That fate would lift me to this height of glory?
I trample on this throne, and here I reign,
Where late I fcarcely durft uplift my eyes:
Here in this palace, this proud city, where
Mix'd with the vulgar crowd, and feeking refuge,

I underwent the scorn, which in distress
The stranger takes of th' haughty citizen.
A *Scythian* they disdain'd, with shame and outrage
Receiv'd my ill form'd wishes   Nay, my OCTAR,
A peevish woman here refus'd that hand
Beneath whose pow'r now trembles all mankind.

OCTAR. Why, now exalted to this height of glory,
When the whole world lies prostrate at your feet,
Comes o'er your memory this idle thought?

GENGIS. My soul, I do confess, was always hurt
With the affronts my humble fortune suffer'd
I never knew but this one thought of anguish,
And here believ'd my soul would find repose:
But 'tis not in the splendor of my fortune,
The pleasure fame, or love, they say, bestows.
I feel an indignation that's below me;
And yet methinks, I'd have her know her king,
Make her look up from baseness, to his glory,
Whose tenderness her folly turn'd to rage;
That when she sees the lot she might have shar'd,
Her fury and despair may give me vengeance.

OCTAR. My ear, my Lord, has ever been accustom'd
To cries of fame and victory; of walls
O'erturn'd and smoaking at your feet: Of love
And all these tender tales I nothing know.

GENGIS. No, since the hour my soul was here subdued.
Since all my fierceness was so poorly conquer'd,
I guarded my firm heart from the return
Of that mean softness, which they here call Love.
Thou, IDAME, I own, within this breast
Mad'st an impression I ne'er knew till then.
In our rough females of the frozen North
There is no beauty that enchains the soul.
Those savage consorts of our hardy labours
Are barb'rous, rude, robust, and masculine.
But here a new infection seiz'd my soul,
Darting from th' eyes of IDAME: Her words,
Her looks breath'd tenderness. Her scorn,
I thank it, nourish'd this my noble fury,
And her disdain releas'd me from her bonds.
This tyrant charm, this sov'reign of the heart
Would have destroy'd my honour. My whole soul

Is due to glory. I've fubdu'd the world,
Inftead of wafting in mean love my days.
No, this difgraceful wound, I once endur'd,
Shall ne'er re-enter this offended breaft.
I banifh the low thought: a woman rule me!
No, I'll forget her, will not fee her, OCTAR.
Let her at leifure mourn her foolifh fcorn;
Enquire not of her, I forbid thy fearch.

 OCTAR. Here more important cares call out upon us.
 GENGIS. Yes, I reflect too deeply on thefe errors.

SCENE VII.

GENGIS, OCTAR, OSMAN.

 OSMAN. The facrifice, my Liege, was juft prepar'd,
And the guards rang'd in order all around,
But an event, which I expected not,
Demands new orders, and fufpends his fate:
A woman all diftract', and bath'd in tears,
Came raving to the guard with outftretch'd arms;
And pierc'd our ears with her alarming cries.
Stop, 'tis my fon you would affaffinate:
'Tis my fon, they deceive you in the victim.
The black defpair that fpoke within her eyes,
Her face, her voice, her cries and exclamations,
Her rage, intrepid in the midft of grief,
Were the plain marks of nature and a mother.
But then, at our command, appear'd her hufband,
Not lefs diftrefs'd and wretched than herfelf,
But dark, and all-collected in his grief:
You have, he cried, the laft of all our kings;
Strike, that's the child whofe blood was your demand.
His eyes, while thus he fpoke, ran o'er with tears:
The woman, ftruck with horror at his words,
Long time remain'd without fpeech, life, or motion;
But fhe no fooner felt returning life,
Than, O my fon! reftore my fon! fhe cry'd.
Griefs fo fincere were never counterfeit,
Such bitter tears delufion never fhed.
Doubt and confufion overwhelm'd us all,
And here I came to know your dread commands.

GENGIS

GENGIS   I fhall difcover this weak artifice,
And who deceives me furely feels my vengeance :
What, wou'd this race of flaves delude their Lord ?
And muft their blood begin to ftream again ?

OCTAR. This woman cannot baffle your high prudence.
The Emp'ror's infant offspring was her care ;
Fond of her mafter's children, love and grief,
And fond enthufiafm equals nature.
Her grief fo unaffected aids th' impofture :
But foon difcovering her hidden purpofe,
This cloud of darknefs fhall clear up before you.

GENGIS. What is this woman ?

OCTAR. Wife, they fay, my Lord,
To a grave chief, one of thofe letter'd fages
All *Afia* treats with rev'rence and refpect ;
Who proud of th' honours of their facred laws,
Upon their vain tribunal dar'd to brave
A hundred kings.   Their croud's innumerable ;
But now they're all in chains, and own the force
Of laws more fovereign.   This haughty flave
Is ZAMTI call'd, who o'er the infant watch'd
Due to the facrifice.

GENGIS. Examine them
And make this guilty pair confefs the truth.
Moreover let our guards, their poft preferv'd,
Watch, where our prudent caution lately plac'd them.
Let none efcape. they talk of a furprife,
And fome attempt from *Corea*.   Soldiers too
Upon the river banks have late been feen.
See, if thefe wretches will provoke their fate,
And rouze the fleeping lion from his den.
See, if, while earth owns GENGIS for its Lord,
The rebel world muft groan beneath his fword.

ACT

ACT III. SCENE I.

GENGIS, OSMAN, Guards.

GENGIS.

HAVE they clear'd up th'impofture of thefe flaves?
Their crimes detected, and reveng'd my wrongs
Say, is this phantom of a prince, their care,
Reftor'd at laft to OCTAR?

OSMAN. All's confufion.
This fteady *Mandarine*, at fight of torture
Still undifmay'd, perfifted in his anfwer,
And feem'd upon his brow to carry truth.
His trembling wife by tears alone replied,
And ftill appear'd more beautiful in grief.
Spite of our manly fpirit, our rough fouls
Were foften'd into pity. never ought
So beauteous ftruck our fight. This haplefs fair
Demands to throw her at your Highnefs' feet.
" Let the great Conqueror of Kings but hear me!
" Let him protect an infant's innocence!
" Even in his anger I will hope for mercy;
" Since he's all-powerful he will needs be noble.
" Can he refufe the cries of the unhappy?"
'Tis thus fhe fpoke; and I would fain have promis'd
That you'd admit her to your royal prefence.

GENGIS. Yes, I will know what means this myftery.
[*To his Train.*

Let her come; go, and ftrait conduct her hither.
Let her not think by whinings and complainings,
By deep fetch'd fighs, and fome few idle drops,
To blind the eyes of caution or revenge.
The women of this place can ne'er abufe me ·
Too well, alas! I know their faithlefs tears,
And my firm heart hath long been fteel'd againft them.
She feeks a boon on which her fate depends.
And if fhe tries to practife on my faith,
She meets with certain death.

OSMAN. My Lord, fhe comes.
GENGIS.

GENGIS. What do I see! is't poffible? O Heaven!
Do I not dream · and is't not all delufion?
'Tis IDAME, 'tis fhe, and my rapt foul———

SCENE II.

GENGIS, IDAME, OCTAR, OSMAN, Guards.

IDAME. Kill, kill, my Lord, a moft unhappy woman!
Revenge is all your own, and I expect it,
But, O preferve from death a guiltlefs child!
 GENGIS. Take comfort, Madam; lay thofe fears
   afide———
I am amaz'd, I own, as well as you———
Fortune, that governs all, deceiv'd us both,
And much the times are chang'd. But tho' high Heaven,
Of a rough *Scythian,* whom you lately fcorn'd,
Has made the conqueror of fubject *Afia,*
Be not difmay'd. Your Emperor forgets
Th'affronts which here were thrown on TEMUGIN.
This laft remainder of a hoftile race,
To vict'ry and my throne I facrifice.
The quiet of the ftate demands his life,
And this pledge muft be render'd up. The death
Of your own child you need not fear: Myfelf
From danger will protect him.
    IDAME. O misfortune!
 GENGIS. But of the truth I muft be fatisfied:
With what delufion they would blind my rage,
And how yourfelf and hufband would deceive me.
 IDAME. O pity the diftreffes of the wretched!
 GENGIS You know I ought to hate this rafh offender.
 IDAME. Hate him! my Lord.
   GENGIS. I've faid too much.
     IDAME. Reftore,
O quick reftore the infant to my arms!
You've promis'd me, and have pronounc'd his fafety.
 GENGIS. His fafety's in your hands? my glory's
   fcorn'd,
My orders all contemn'd, and pow'r difgrac'd:
You know the full extent of all my wrongs.
To take away the victim to my rage,

           To

To difobey my fovereign command,
Is poor offence to all my former wrongs.
'Tis not the infult of to-day alone
That juftifies my rage. Your hufband——hufband!'
Hell! hell! that name alone demands my vengeance.
What is this hufband, that beneath his fway
Could bend your captive heart? what is this flave
That thinks to brave my fury? Let him come.

IDAME. My virtuous hufband, now the wretched caufe
Of all my grief, has ferv'd his God and King
With honeft love, and I was happy in him.

GENGIS. In him?—when did you form this curft alliance?

IDAME. While, far from our bleft walls, your profp'rous
fate
Remoteft nations to your arms fubdu'd.

GENGIS. Ay, in that day that GENGIS was difpis'd;
That day, that calls for vengeance on you both,
And bids me *China* with my hate purfue.

S C E N E III.

GENGIS, OCTAR, OSMAN, on one fide.
IDAME, ZAMTI, on the other, Guards,

GENGIS. Speak? are my fovereign commands obey'd?
Haft thou refign'd the Son o' th' Emperor?

ZAMTI. I have fulfill'd my duty: it is done.

GENGIS. You know that I can punifh fraud and in-
folence;
You know that nothing can efcape my rage,
That if the Royal infant you've conceal'd,
Spite of your artifice he'll foon be found,
And death alone fhall anfwer for your crime.
                                        [*To his guards.*
But I'll believe you: Go, and feize the child
This flave has render'd up a facrifice.
Kill him.

ZAMTI. Unhappy father!

IDAME. Stay, Barbarians!
Ah! my good Lord, is this then your compaffion,
And is it thus a conqu'ror keeps his word?

GENGIS. Is't thus I am abufed, and fool'd by flaves?
Lt

It is too much: hear now my laſt reſolve.
Tell me this moment who, this infant is,
Inform me the whole truth, or elſe he dies.

　　IDAME. My ſon prevails, and if this ſad confeſſion,
Which nature tears from my afflicted ſoul,
Appears a new offence; and if for blood
Your ſoul ſtill thirſts, ſtrike here: for worſe than death
Already racks my breaſt. Strike here, but ſave,
O ſave the generous, the noble ZAMTI!
It is too true that our moſt Royal Maſter,
Who, but for GENGIS, might have ſtill ſurviv'd,
Committed to our care that ſacred charge,
Honour'd by all but thee. Too many horrors
Follow'd your victory; too much, alas!
Has ſavage cruelty eclips'd your fame.
So many innocents all plung'd in blood,
The Emperor and his Queen, and five ſons ſlain,
This mighty Empire by the ſword laid waſte,——
Could not ſo much of carnage glut your rage?
A ſtern barbarian came to aſk the child,
That deareſt pledge committed to our care,
Son of ſo many kings, our only hope.
My huſband, at this cruel order, ſtill retain'd
His faith inviolate, nor ſwerv'd from duty.
He gave up his own ſon. His tortur'd ſoul
The agonies of nature ſhook in vain;
In vain affection pleaded for a ſon.
You never ſhould have known this fatal ſecret;
I ſhould have more admir'd his noble firmneſs,
I ſhould have copied it· But I'm a mother.
My ſoul could not ſuſtain the cruel conflict,
And for a ſacrifice reſign my ſon.
Alas! my grief and violent deſpair
Too plainly ſpoke the weakneſs of a mother
There ſtands the hapleſs father of the child,
Whoſe virtues were his only crimes. O ſpare
The babe, whoſe innocence could ne'er offend,
And ſpare the father, whoſe offence was virtue.
Me, puniſh me, who have at once betray'd
My huſband and my king. O noble ZAMTI,
Thrice worthy all my love and admiration,
Forgive the weakneſs of maternal love.

I

If you die, fo will I. At leaft forgive
That I from flaughter have preferv'd your fon.

ZAMTI. I forgive all: no more will I complain:
For my king's fon I have no more to fear.
He's plac'd in fafety.

GENGIS. Traitor, flave, he is not.
Or bring him, villain, or your abject life
Shall anfwer for your crime.

ZAMTI. My crime? it were
Indeed a crime, if I obey'd thefe orders
The fov'reign voice of my right noble Mafters
Speaks from the grave more loud than thy command.
You are my conqueror, but not my king.
If I ow'd you a fubject's faith, to you
I would be faithful. Take my life, but ftill
Refpect my zeal. I gave you up my fon;
I could refign my deareft child a victim:
Can you then think I tremble for my life?

GENGIS. Away with him

IDAME. O, hear me?——

GENGIS Drag him hence.

IDAME. On me, on me vent all your rage O Heaven!
Could I have thought that by your cruel hand
I e'er fhould lofe a king, a fon, and hufband?
What! will foft pity never touch your foul?

GENGIS. Go, follow him to whom your fate has
bound you:
Follow your hufband. Tears fhall never move me,
Nor keen reproaches melt me to compaffion.

IDAME. This I forefaw: now all my hopes are flown.

GENGIS Go, IDAME: if in my own defpight
Pity again fhould enter my weak heart,
You know the wrongs which muft be fatisfied.

S C E N E IV.

GENGIS, OCTAR

GENGIS. Whence come thefe fighs? thefe doubtings
whence? what God
Spoke in her, and maintain'd her finking caufe?
Is there a pow'r in virtue or in beauty

Above

Above my high authority? Ah! OCTAR,
Stay! for I fear, I tremble for myself:
I want a friend; my weak soul needs support.

OCTAR. Since I must speak, receive my honest counsel
If you wou'd sacrifice this hostile race,
If the last branches from the wither'd trunk
You would lop off, delay not your revenge.
The cruel rigour of those bloody deeds,
Which must support a throne by conquest gain'd,
Should fall immediate, rapid, sure, and quick.
The bloody stream in torrents should descend.
Time restores peace and order, reconciles
The people to their fate, and wipes away
The bloody traces of their former woes.
They soon forgive, and e'en forget their wrongs.
But when the blood's drawn from them drop by drop,
When the wound slowly clos'd, is soon again
Torn open by the hand of violence,
When slaughter seems to shape his course anew,
Then fierce despair stirs up to deeds of rage
Then coward souls, and makes a feeble race
A race of stubborn potent adversaries,
More dangerous, the more they are subdu'd.

GENGIS. But then this IDAME! this haughty
        woman!
Wife to a slave that braves me in my anger!

OCTAR You owe her no compassion, but revenge
Your love for her, you own, was idle passion,
Of a light transient flame the hasty sparks:
Her foolish scorn, her anger, and the time,
Have in your breast its weak remains extinguish'd.
She's in your eyes a guilty wretch, the wife
Of a low criminal.

GENGIS He shall be punish'd:
I should, I will have vengeance. Pity him!
What! spare a slave I hate! that braves me too!
My rival!

OCTAR. Why is not his death pronounc'd?
You have him in your pow'r, and yet he lives.

GENGIS Just heav'n! is't come to this? and does
        my heart,
Subdu'd by beauty, and disarm'd by tears,

Forego

Forego its rage, heave shameful sighs, and feel?
Th' alarms of love? I rival to a slave!
A happy slave! and yet permit him live;
Yet know she doats upon him! Ah! I feel
Respect for IDAME ev'n in her husband:
I fear to plunge the dagger in his breast,
Lest the dire stroke should wound her bosom too.
Is it then true I love? is't I that sigh?
What then is love that has such sov'reign pow'r?

OCTAR. I've only learnt to fight and to obey.
My cars, my steeds, my arrows and my quiver,
These are my only passions, only science,
To this capriciousness of soul a stranger.
I only know of victory and plunder;
That captives always to the victors yield.
This melting softness, to our race unknown,
Belies your fortune and your character.
What is't to you that one more slave attends
In bitterness of soul your dread decree?

GENGIS. I am aware how far my pow'r extends:
I may, too well I know, use violence.
But O! what cruel, what imbitter'd joy,
To force a heart that renders not itself!
To see those eyes that should be lighted up
With transport, sunk beneath a cloud of tears!
And to possess a slave, who views your love
With horror, and the agonies of grief!
The monsters of the forests we inhabit,
See happier days, and know less barb'rous loves.
Spite of myself, my anger, and revenge,
The lovely IDAME subdued my soul.
I tremble that my heart should recollect it.
I was enrag'd; and yet her soul o'er mine,
Over my character, and sov'reign will,
Rul'd with a pow'r more absolute and sure,
Than I received from war, and victory
Over a hundred kings dethron'd, enslav'd.
'Tis this enflam'd my rage and indignation:
But I'll for ever chase her from my heart;
I will forget her, my sole aim be glory——
Alas! she comes, she triumphs, and I love.

D   SCENE

S C E N E   V.

GENGIS, OCTAR, OSMAN.

GENGIS. The news? what fays fhe? what does fhe
    refolve?
OSMAN. Sooner to perifh at her hufband's fide,
Than to difcover where the child's conceal'd.
They fwear to me unmov'd the worft of deaths.
Her hufband holds her trembling in his arms,
Supports her conftancy, and fteels her foul.
Thus let us die together, cry they, while around
The people weep, and feem to fhake with horror.
    GENGIS. Does IDAME demand her death of me?
Ah! bid her be of comfort, let her know
Each minute of her life is precious to me.
Enough, go, fly!

S C E N E   VI.

GENGIS, OCTAR

OCTAR. What orders do you give
Touching this Infant they conceal from vengeance?
    GENGIS. Any.
    OCTAR   You fhould command your faithful guards
To force the Infant e'en from IDAME.
    GENGIS. O hurt not IDAME: but hafte, good
        OCTAR,
To make her haughty hufband know my pow'r.
This Infant's blood were poor and low revenge,
My rage demands a nobler facrifice.
                        OCTAR. ZAMTI?
GENGIS. Ay, ZAMTI.
        OCTAR. Oh! beware, my Lord,
Nor let a thought fo mean debafe your foul.
Would you new firmnefs add to his defpair?
    GENGIS. I would preferve my IDAME: the reft
I leave to thee. Away!
                    OCTAR. What would you do?
What is your hope?
                            GENGIS.

GENGIS. To talk with her again,
To fee her, love her, and of her be lov'd,
Or elfe to be reveng'd, and give her death——
Alas! you fee the weaknefs of my heart
Spite of my haughty foul, weak paffion's flave
I threaten, love, defpair, and madly rave.

A C T IV. SCENE I.

GENGIS, and Guards.

GENGIS.

AND is it thus that happinefs and peace,
The aim of all my labours, fly my fearch?
Ah! now I feel the heavy cares of power.
To the fad bufinefs of my tortur'd heart
I cannot give an hour. O IDAME!
For thee I wifh; yet round me nought behold
But furly warriors, and an irkfome train.

[*To his train.*

Go, take your ftation near the city walls,
Left haughty *Corea*'s troops attempt furprife
They have proclaim'd this Infant, Emperor,
And with his forfeit head I'll march againft them.
For the laft time tell ZAMTI to obey;
I have too long delay'd this child's deftruction

[*He remains alone.*

Away. Their diligence is tedious now,
When other cares take up my foul. Alas!
To awe the vanquifh'd and the victors rule,
To forefee dangers, half-form'd plots to crufh,
And all the cruel bufinefs of a king,
Falls heavy on my heart, with foreign woes
And other cares perplext ——O happier far
My humble fortune, abject, and unknown!

D 2   SCENE

SCENE II.

GENGIS, OCTAR

GENGIS. Well, haſt thou ſeen this ſtubborn *Mandarine?*

OCTAR No fear or danger moves him fro n his purpoſe.
My Lord, I bluſh'd to parley in your name
With a vile ſlave, whom you ſhould ſacrifice.
He view d the torture with indifference,
And talk'd of duty to his king, and juſtice:
He braves his vanquiſhers, as if his voice
Preſcrib'd them laws Him and his rebel wife
At once deſtroy, noi languiſh for a ſlave.
Puniſh the hated pair, whoſe inſolence
Affronts that power which all the world obeys.

GENGIS. Amazement! what a people have I conquer'd!
Whence are they? whence theſe elevated thoughts,
This native grandeur of the noble ſoul,
Which we in our rough climes ne'er felt or knew!
To a King dead, each ſacrificing nature,
One without murmur ſees his ſon deſtroy'd,
The other for a huſband aſks to die:
Nothing can ſhake them, nothing move their fear.
Whence, whence is this? with ſteady reaſon's eye,
When fall'n, enſlav'd, this people I ſurvey,
Though conqueror, my captives I revere,
And praiſe their virtues, while I give them chains.
I ſee their labours have adorn'd the world;
I ſee them an induſtrious, noble people;
Their kings on wiſdom's baſis built their power,
To all the neighbour nations giving laws,
And reigning without conqueſt or the ſword.
Heav'n has aloted us rude force alone;
Battles our arts, and all our labours death.
Ah! what avails ſo much ſucceſs in war?
Or what the glories of a world enſlav'd?
We made the car of conqueſt red with blood:
Yet there's a greater fame, a nobler glory.

I'm

I'm jealous of their virtue, blush to see
The conquer'd soar above the conqueror.

OCTAR. Can GENGIS such a feeble race admire?
What boot their puny arts, that cannot save
The practisers from slavery or death?
The weak should serve the strong. All earth must yield
To toil and valour. Why then stain your power
By insults unreveng'd, and suffer slaves
To brave their conqu'ror? why, when lord of all,
Submit to bonds, to our brave race unknown?
And draw upon yourself reproach from those
Whose arms have made you monarch of the world?
Shall then the brave companions of your labours
See all those victories effac'd by love?
They blush at the mean thought, their souls disdain it;
And by my voice their clamours reach your ears.
In theirs, as the state's name, I call upon you.
Pardon a *Tartar*, pardon a rough soldier,
Grown grey in armour worn in your defence,
Who cannot see you a mean slave to love,
But presents glory to your dazzled eyes.

GENGIS. Let them seek IDAME.

OCTAR. You would——

GENGIS Obey.
Seek her. Your zeal grows troublesome and bold.
My subjects ev'n my frailties shall revere.

S C E N E III.

GENGIS *solus.*

Fate will not be oppos'd, and doubtless Heav'n
Destines her for me ——What avails my greatness?
I have made wretches, and myself am wretched.
Of all the savages that fill my train,
Greedy of combat, prodigal of blood,
Has ever one spoke words of comfort to me,
Or sooth'd the anguish of my aching soul?
Have all these states enslav'd e'er given my breast
One hour of peace? Ah! no: my wearied soul
Still sought some pleasing error, to dispense
The gloomy night of care, and to afford

Some

Some confolation on the throne of Empire.
OCTAR has fhock'd me with his horrid counfel.
I am environ'd with a bloody train
Of fell affaffins, difciplin'd to death,
And form'd for ravage ; born alone for war,
And fhocking to a foul refin'd by love.
Let them fight for me, follow me to death,
But never dare my actions to arraign.
Where is my IDAME ?——'Tis fhe ; fhe comes.

SCENE IV.

GENGIS, IDAME.

IDAME. Are then my griefs your fport ? and am I call'd
To be receiv'd with fcorn ?   O fpare a woman,
Nor add new anguifh to a mother's woes !
GENGIS. Be not difmay'd.   Your hufband may atone
His paft offence, and ftill receive our pardon.
I have already bid my vengeance fleep,
And you alone could move my heart to mercy.
Perhaps 'tis not without high heav'ns decree,
That fortune has conducted me to you.
For furely IDAME was form'd by fate,
To make a conqu'ror ftoop, enflave a mafter,
And melt in me that ftubbornnefs of foul,
The rough diftinction of my native clime
Then be advis'd, and mark me well . I reign
Within thefe walls, yet you may re-affume
Dominion o'er me, though perhaps your fcorn
Might rather warrant fury and revenge.
Our law permits divorce ; fubmit to that,
And make the conqu'ror of the world your flave.
If he is odious, yet a throne has charms,
And royal wreaths may wipe away your tears.
The int'reft of the ftate and of the city
Forbid you to refufe my proffer'd love.
Of love to parley now, may move your wonder :
The man, who overturn'd your Monarch's throne,
And all your Kings has mingled with the duft,
Was fcarce expected, while his furious arm

Was

Was dealing death, again to fall before you.
But you was robb'd of your too eafy heart,
And a bafe rival has ufurp'd my place.
You owe it to the conqu'ror of mankind,
Who now with twenty fceptres is return'd,
To claim that love, once due to TEMUGIN.
You fix your eyes on earth, nor can I guefs
What you refolve.   Forget my pow'r, forget
My fiercenefs, well reflect, and freely fpeak.

   IDAME. Still to new changes every hour condemn'd,
Yet I confefs that you have mov'd my wonder
But if I can recal my fcatter'd fpirits,
My anfwer fhall amaze you more   That time
You may remember, and that humble life,
In which Heav'n once obfcur'd your future fame,
You was not then the terror of the world,
But lowly TEMUGIN: whole nations then
Bow'd not beneath your fovereign command.
Then, when your hand was pure, 'twas proffer'd to me;
And know, that then I would not have refus'd it

   GENGIS. What do I hear? O Heav'n! and did you
       love me?
Did you————

   IDAME. I own, againft your fighs and vows
My fubject foul would never have rebell'd,
Had not the virtuous pair that gave me life,
Refign'd its duty to another Lord.
The power of parents over us, you know:
They are the image of the God we ferve,
And we for ever owe obedience to them.
This fallen Empire, on parental right
Was founded, on the folemn marriage faith,
On honour, juftice, and refpect of oaths:
On thefe 'twas built; and though beneath your arms
It fink for ever, yet the noble fpirit
Which taught us thefe, fhall never, never die.
Your fortunes are much chang'd, but mine remain
Unalter'd and the fame,

     GENGIS. And did you love me?
  IDAME What though I did? that very love were now
A threefold bar againft our union,
Another reafon I fhould now refufe you.

                    My

My marriage-bonds by Heav'n itſelf were form'd ;
My huſband ſacred , to ſay more, I love him.
Before yourſelf, your throne, and all its greatneſs
I would prefer him.   O forgive this warmth
That flows from honeſt love , nor think I boaſt
My conqueſt o'er your heart, or mean to brave
Your anger, or take pride in theſe denials,
Which riſe alone from juſtice and my duty.
I ſigh not for a throne , ſome other fair
Make happy with your ſceptre and your love,
Withdrawn from me, who knew not how to prize them :
And O let me beſeech with earneſt pray'r,
That ZAMTI know not of your proffer'd love.
He'll be leſs proud o' th' triumph, than enrag'd
At this new outrage offer'd to my faith.

   GENGIS   Concerning him, my firm reſolve you know,
And he'll obey, if life is precious to him.

   IDAME   He will not do't, he never can obey .
And if the cruel agonies of torture
Could ſhake his ſoul from its integrity,
My faith and duty ſhould ſuſtain his weakneſs.
I would ſupport his fainting heart, and plead
Thoſe ſacred bonds his baſeneſs would diſhonour.

   GENGIS. What do I hear ? can I believe it ? Gods !
Can you thus love him after what has paſs'd
When the barbarian huſband would have giv'n
Your child to certain death ?

          IDAME. Barbarian huſband !
'Twas virtue in him , I admire him for it ;
Though I felt all the weakneſs of a mother.
And was I ſo unjuſt, to hate him for it,
My pride would not permit me to deſert him.

   GENGIS   Still all you ſay amazes, and diſtracts me ,
Thoſe virtues I adore, I wiſh to hate.
I love you more, the more you ſcorn my love,
At once you make my heart a ſlave, and rebel.
Fear me , for know, that ſpite of all my love,
My fury may outſtrip my tenderneſs.

   IDAME. I know your pow'r, and that you may exact
Death, or obedience to your dread command :
Yet the laws live, and are above you ſtill.

                GENGIS.

GENGIS..The laws! what laws dare contradict my will?
Here are no laws, but such as I impose:
I, a rough *Scythian*, your king, your conqueror.
The laws you follow have been fatal to me.
Yes, when e'er while our fortunes here were equal,
Our thoughts, our hearts were mutually inclin'd,
(For spite of all your scorn I now believe it)
When all united us, those laws I hate
Ordain'd my shame, and your accursed marriage.
I make them void, I speak, and they're annull'd,
Thou, with the subject universe, obey.
Those manners, usages, and laws you boast,
Are criminal, if they oppose my will.
I've order'd it? your husband must resign
Into my hands your Emperor and You.
Their lives shall be the pledge of your obedience.
Think on't, you know how far I may revenge:
Think at what price you may appease a King,
Who loves you, and yet blushes at his passion.

SCENE V.

IDAME, ASSELI.

IDAME. Or death or infamy——no other choice——
O Royal Infant! O my dearest husband!
When in my hands I hold your destiny,
My voice without one doubt pronounces Death.
    ASSELI Ah! rather re-assume that pow'r, which Heav'n
Has given to virtuous beauty: re-assume
That pow'r, which makes this *Scythian* bend before you,
And own your influence. Sometimes a word
Can soften anger, and disarm fierce rage.
Try: they can ev'ry thing, who know to please.
    IDAME. That I have pleas'd is now my greatest grief.
    ASSELI. Yet that alone can give the vanquish'd rest.
In our calamities the bounteous Heavens
Have ordain'd you to check the tyrant's rage.
You saw how soon his irritated soul
Lost all its fierceness, and was hush'd to peace;
Else long ago in ZAMTI he had destroy'd

A

A hated rival : ZAMTI brav'd his rage,
And yet he lives, he lives too unremov'd
From you his wife, they tender you in him.
This conqu'ior, though he has laid wafte the world,
Still honours you; you may remember too
That he firft wrought upon your virgin heart :
His paffion formerly was pure and lawful.

IDAME. Peace; fay no more; 'tis bafenefs but to
think on't.

SCENE VI.

ZAMTI, IDAME, ASSELI.

IDAME. Am I then ftill, 'mid all our woes, your wife?
And are we ftill permitted thus to meet?

ZAMTI. Permitted? 'tis the tyrant's fov'reign order,
And to his rage I owe this happy moment.

IDAME. Have they inform'd you at what horrid price
The tyrant would grant your's and th' *Orphau*'s life?

ZAMTI. O mention not, confider not my life:
A fingle citizen's a trivial lofs.
Forget it then : But O remember, IDAME,
That 'tis our duty to preferve our King.
To him our lives and fervices we owe,
And ev'n the blood of children born to ferve him;
But owe him not the forfeit of our honour.
Yet certain death awaits the haplefs *Orphan*,
Whom I've fecreted in that dark afylum,
Where all our ancient monarchs are intomb'd;
And where, unlefs we can afford him aid,
He'll with his fathers fhare the fleep of death.
In vain the generous Prince of *Corea*
Waits the dear charge, my zeal has promis'd him.
ETAN, the faithful guardian of his life,
Loaded with chains, my cruel lot partakes.
You are the *Orphan's* only refuge left
'Tis you alone that muft his threaten'd life,
Your fon, your glory, and my honour fave.
We will obey our tyrant's dread commands:
I'll give them up my fon: I'll give up more

Freed

Freed by my death, go, foothe the ruffian *Tartar* :
Pafs o'er my grave to this barbarian's arms.
Yet now I firft behold grim death with horror,
Since it abandons you to this ufurper.
But my King afks it, and I expiate
By my juft death this impious facrifice.
Wed, with thefe horrid aufpices, the tyrant,
And with a mother's care ftill guard your King.
Reign, that your King may live, and hufband die.
Reign at this price.   It fhall be fo——

IDAME. O hold !
Do you then know me ? think you, I would buy
A throne with fhame, my ZAMTI, and thy death ?
Or do you think I'm lefs a wife than mother ?
Alas ! you dream, and your too rigid virtue
Twice in one day hath finn'd againft itfelf,
Scorning the cries of nature and of love.
Ah ! cruel to your fon, to me more cruel,
Do you forget that I'm your wife, and love you ?
All-righteous Heav'n has better taught my foul ;
I'll fave my King, yet not difhonour you.
The tyrant, be it love, or be it fcorn,
Conftrains me not, nor watches my defigns.
Within thefe walls, with bloody gore o'erflow'd,
I ftill am free, nor are my fteps obferv'd.
The Prince of *Corea* by the fecret path
May reach the tombs, wherein this precious charge
From the deftroyer's eye now lyes conceal'd.
I know each winding paffage of the place ,
I fly to give him timely nourifhment,
To render him to *China*'s faithful friends,
Within my arms among their warlike ranks
To carry him, a gift from Heav'n, their aid.
I know that you muft die ; but full of glory,
Our memory fhall ever be rever'd.
When equal to the nobleft we fhall rife,
O judge, if IDAME has ftain'd your fame !
    ZAMTI. Heav'n ! that infpireft, with thy arm fuftain her !
O IDAME ! thy virtues o'ertop mine.
Haply for thee from ruin Heav'n may fave
Thy country, and thy Monarch from the grave.

ACT

ACT V. SCENE I.

IDAME, ASSELI.

ASSELI.

HOW? is all loft? are all our hopes then fled?
And are you ftill a captive and a flave?
Alas! 'twere better not to have incens'd
This conqueror. What could a feeble woman,
A helplefs child, againft fuch force and pow'r
In vain oppofing weaknefs?

IDAME. Now all's o'er.
I've done my duty, ftrove with vain attempt
To wreftle with my fate: It will not be.
I am again a flave, and doom'd to wear
The tyrant's chains.

ASSELI. Again the haplefs *Orphan*
Becomes his prey, and dies as foon as born;
And ZAMTI muft partake the Infant's fate

IDAME. The hour of both approaches: if then death
Is yet delay'd, 'tis only to prepare
More grievous torments for them. My dear fon
Perhaps muft follow them. The haughty victor
Call'd me before him, to increafe my woes.
His very looks fhot terror and difmay:
Full oft he rais'd his arm, all red with blood,
Againft the *Orphan*, and my haplefs fon.
I all in tears fell proftrate at his feet,
And lay 'tween him and th' objects of his rage:
But he with roughnefs threw me from before him,
And with dire threats and angry looks departed,
Then foon again return'd ftill more enrag'd.
Now cried for vengeance, now delay'd his purpofe,
While round him ftood a train of favage warriors,
Who feem'd to afk his orders for my death.

ASSELI. GENGIS would never give fuch horrid orders.
Your hufband, whom he hates, ftill lives; the *Orphan*
To th' hand of flaughter is not yet refign'd.
But afk for pardon, all will be forgiven.

IDAME.

IDAME. No, all his furious love is turn'd to rage.
Oh! had you seen him double my diſtreſs,
Swear his fixt hate, and mock me in my tears!——

ASSELI. This rage, a word, a tear from you abates.
This conquer'd lion, that roars thus in his chain,
Did he not love, would never threaten hate.

IDAME. Or love or hate, 'tis time to end that life
Which without horror I cannot preſerve.

ASSELI. Ah! what do you reſolve?
IDAME. When angry Heav'n
Has fill'd the meaſure of our miſeries,
It oft ſupports us in the blackeſt grief,
And gives us courage equal to our woes.
Amid the horrors of the preſent hour
I feel my ſoul dilate with unknown ſtrength;
I fear no more this conqu'ror of mankind;
But on myſelf alone my fate depends.

ASSELI. But then this ſon, this object of your fears,
Will you abandon him?
IDAME. Ah! there you touch
My tend'reſt part, you pierce me to the ſoul.
O horrid ſacrifice! does ought remain
That can be done to ſave him from deſtruction?
Perhaps the tyrant, proud in his ſucceſs,
By Kings encircl'd humbled to the duſt,
Amid the crowd of wretches in his train,
Will not reflect on my unhappy child:
Or ſee perhaps with aſpect leſs ſevere
The guiltleſs child, whoſe mother once he lov'd.
In that one hope I reſt; the ſoothing thought
Flatters my ſoul in death. If me he lov'd,
He will not hate my aſhes, when I'm dead,
He'll not purſue my ſon.

SCENE II.

ZAMTI, ASSELI, OCTAR.

OCTAR. Stay, IDAME;
Here wait the Emperor. [*To his train.*] Guards, watch
thoſe infants:
See, that none enter here, none hence depart.
Do you retire. [*To* ASSELI
IDAME.

E

IDAME. Will the Emperor
See me again ? I muſt obey ; yet wiſh
That with my huſband I might firſt confer.
Perhaps the conqueror, his rage appeas'd,
Will render juſtice to a hapleſs pair.
Alas ! I ſee that my requeſt is vain,
And conqueſt is with you inexorable.
Is then compaſſion in your climes unknown !
And may I not your friendly voice implore ?

　　OCTAR. When th' Emperor has ſpoke, t' implore's a
　　　　criine.
You are not now beneath your ancient kings,
Who could abate the rigour of their laws :
The ſword reigns now ; nor pray'rs, nor tears we know.
He ſpeaks, and all earth trembles and obeys.
Stay, and attend the order of the Emperor.

SCENE III.

IDAME, *ſola.*

GOD of the wretched ! who behold'ſt my woes,
Amid theſe horrors, O ſupport my ſoul !
O give, me firmneſs ! pour into my boſom
The virtues of the huſband you have giv'n me !

SCENE IV.

GENGIS, IDAME.

　　GENGIS. No, I have not enough diſplay'd my rage,
Enough made humble your raſh haughtineſs,
Enough reproach'd the baſeneſs of that heart,
Which anſwers mercy with ingratitude.
You do not ſee the height of your offending,
Nor think on what a dreadful point you ſtand,
Nor know the horror that inſpires my breaſt :
You, whom I've madly lov'd, but ought to hate ;
You, who've betray'd me, and I ought to puniſh ?

IDAME

IDAME. Punifh me: but, O punifh me alone!
T e only boon I afk of my deftroyer,
Whofe flinty heart, nor pray'rs, nor tears can melt.
Ah, quench your rage and fiercenefs in my blood!
Deftroy a woman faithful to her duty;
And let her torments end:

GENGIS. Ah! 'no, I cannot.
Too cruel IDAME! O could I end
The tortures more fevere that rack my foul!
I came to punifh; and can pardon all;
Pardon!——I pardon you!——no, fear my vengeance.
Your Monarch's Son, and you'rs are in my power.
I mention not that abject flave your hufband;
Your love is caufe-enough that he fhould die.
He has betray'd me, brav'd me, been a rebel,
And merited ten thoufand deaths. Your pray'rs
Have ftay'd that arm, that fhould fall heavy on him.
Ev'n to this hour the traitor lives. But now
No more will I implore my flave, my captive.
Forget him, or he dies. Your ftubborn heart
Has now no mean pretext to fcreen its purpofe:
He is no more your hufband, now condemn'd.
He'll die for you; for ever break the chain
That binds him to you, by a fhameful death.
'Tis you conftrain me you, that faithful wife,
With idle fcruples feal your hufband's death.
I know, I might, all-cover'd with his blood,
Force you fubmit, and grant my utmoft wifh.
But know this Savage, *Scythian*, this Deftroyer,
Has fentiments as noble as your own.
Fate, IDAME, defigns us for each other,
And my foul longs for gentle fway o'er thine.
Abjure your marriage; and that very hour
Your fon fhall rank as mine. On your decree
The deftiny of more than one depends:
Of your King's Son, now doom'd full foon to die,
And of your hufband, whom your voice may fave.
His fon's fate, your's, nay mine itfelf, on you
Depends; for GENGIS loves you, doats upon you.
And yet beware that you oppofe me not,
Infult not the fond weaknefs of my foul,
For even now rage chides my tendernefs,

E 2   And

And threatens danger, while I talk of love.
Tremble at my love, my very kindness fear.
My soul is too familiar with revenge,
And I shall punish you, because I've lov'd.
Fo give me, for I rave, and then, alas!
I threaten most, when most I would implore.
O, sooth to peace this conflict of my soul!
One word from you this Empire's fate decrees,
But this important word you must pronounce.
O, quick pronounce it! and inform my heart,
If it must burn with love, or hatred tow'rds you.

IDAME. Nor love nor hatred should infl me it now.
Your love's unworthy both of you and me:
You owe me justice if you are a king,
I will demand it, ev'n against yourself.
I do not mean to brave your sov'reign power,
But rather grace and dignify your greatness,
And you in secret must applaud me for it.

GENGIS. 'Tis well: you chuse my hate then: and
  shall have it.
My bosom pants already for revenge.
I know you not; and my just indignation
Awakes the cruelty that slept within me.
Your Prince, your husband, and your infant son,
Shall answer with their blood your rebel scorn,
GENGIS condemns, but IDAME's the cause.

IDAME. Barbarian!

GENGIS. 'Tis resolv'd; they are no more.
Your sometime lover's now an angry master.
A bloody, merciless, fierce enemy,
Whose hatred rises equal to your scorn.

IDAME. I fall then at this angry master's feet,
Whom Heav'n has made my king, and on my knees
Implore him to comply with one request.

GENGIS. Cruel! rise IDAME: I'm all attention.
O! could I tell my soul you would relent!
What would you? speak.

IDANE. That GENGIS would permit
My husband to confer with me in secret.

GENGIS. Your husband to confer——

IDAME. Deny me not.
This conference shall be our last, that o'er

Yo"

You better shall interpret my resistance.

GENGIS. No, 'twere not meet you should consult with
    him :
Yet I'll permit this interview. Perhaps
His haughty soul hath better learnt its duty,
And taught him to forego the fatal honour
Of rivaling the conqu'ror of mankind.
He hid his Prince, when I in fury sought him ;
He has possess'd my IDAME! What crimes !
And yet he lives, is pardon'd, if you ask it.
You fix his fate ; his death, or his divorce.
Yes, he shall see you. OCTAR, watch this gate.
Alas ! what doubts perplex my tortur'd soul !
O ! shall I yet be happy in her love ?

IDAME *sola*. I feel new spirit glow within my breast,
That constancy I doubted of till now.

SCENE V.

ZAMTI, IDAME.

IDAME. O thou, whom next to Heaven I revere,
Mortal more great and noble in my eyes,
Than all the Conqu'rors men have rais'd to Gods ;
The horror of our fate too well you know :
Our doom is fixt, and our last hour is come.

ZAMTI. I know it.

IDAME. Twice you've try'd with vain attempt
To save the offspring of our hapless Kings.

ZAMTI. Ah ! think of it no more ; all hope is lost.
Fail not in the performance of your duty,
I die in peace.

IDAME. What fate attends my son ?
Forgive this thought, that flows from my despair
Forgive my sighs, and think but of my courage.

ZAMTI. Our kings are dead, our country is enslav'd.
To die is happiness : lament not me,
But, O bewail the wretches doom'd to live.

IDAME. They mean you, ZAMTI, a most shameful death.

ZAMTI. Well, let it come. I wait their savage orders.
They dally with my miseries too long.

                                                               IDAME

IDAME. Attend me, ZAMTI. Cannot we then die
Without a tyrant's order?   At the altar.
The ox is facrific'd : the criminal,
Like a vile flave, is dragg'd to punifhment ;
But the great, ZAMTI, their own fate determine,
Nor from a haughty mafter wait their death.
Why, why attend the hour of death from him ?
Man was not born for fuch a bafe dependance.
No, copy rather the brave conftancy
Of our intrepid neighbours.   They fupport
The rights of nature ; live while free, but die
Rather than fuffer flav'ry or difhonour,
To live difgrac'd is bitter to their fouls,
Nor dread they ought fo much as infamy.
The noble *Japanefe* ne'er meanly waits
A haughty ruler's voice to fpeak his death.
We have inftructed thofe brave Iflanders,
Nor let us blufh to learn their virtues too ;
To learn like them to die.

                ZAMTI. O matchlefs woman !
I praife thy conftancy, and fure fuch woes
May warrant this tranfgreffion of our laws.
I had already form'd this noble purpofe ;
But without arms, flaves, victims, and alone,
There are no means of death but from our Tyrants.
    IDAME, [*drawing a dagger.*] Slaves! victims!—There—
           take this—with me be free ;
Strike and deliver us.
                ZAMTI. O Heaven ! with thee ?
    IDAME. Yes, tear this breaft, this heart they would
           difhonour.
My feeble arm ftill traitor to its purpofe,
Could not with fteady aim direct the blow :
Do thou with nobler firmnefs guide its point,
And bravely facrifice a faithful wife ;
Then, cover'd with her blood, befide her fall.
In my laft moments I'll embrace my hufband,
And GENGIS fhall with jealoufy behold us.
    ZAMTI Yes, IDAME, thy virtues ftand the trial,
And thou difplay'ft the warmeft marks of love.
Thrice worthy wife, this laft farewel receive——.
The dagger now,——and turn thine eyes afide.
                            IDAME

IDAME, [*giving him the dagger*] There—now ftrike
here : nay, paufe not, nor delay.

ZAMTI. I cannot do't.

IDAME. You muft.

ZAMTI. O horror !

IDAME. Strike :
Stiike here, then turn the poniard on yourfelf.

ZAMTI. Then copy me.

IDAME, [*feizing his arm.*] Here, ZAMTI, here——

SCENE VI.

GENGIS, OCTAR, IDAME, ZAMTI, Guards.

GENGIS.
[*Accompanied by his Guards, and difarming* ZAMTI.]
Hold, hold !
Stay your rafh hand ! O Heav'n ! what would you do ?

IDAME. Deliver ourfelves from thee, and end our woes.

ZAMTI. Will you not let us even die in peace ?

GENGIS. O hold !——All gracious Heav'n, King of
Kings !
To whom my foul now lifts itfelf in pray'r,
Witnefs of all my wrongs, and all my weaknefs,
By whom fuch States and Monaichs I've fubdued,
Shall I at length grow worthy of my glory ?——
You move my anger, ZAMTI, thus to reign
Over a heart that once felt love foi me,
A heart that I adore. Your faithful wife
Had rather fall a facrifice to duty,
Fall by thy hand, than fhare a throne with me.
But you fhall both endure, and own my pow'r;
Perhaps do moie.

IDAME. What more can vengeance do ?

ZAMTI. What new device to add to oui afflictions ?

IDAME. Why are we not already doom'd to die ?

GENGIS. Your doom is fix'd, and you fhall know your
fate
You have done juftice, I'll do juftice too
What I have now beheld I fcarce believe
Your fiimnefs I admire, and am your convert.

Upon

Upon the throne to which my arms have rais'd me,
I blush to see how much I fall below you.
In vain by my exploits in war distinguish'd,
I am degraded , and would equal you,
I knew not the best conquest man could make
Was to subdue himself: to you I owe it.
Rejoice with me, that you could change my soul,
I come to re-unite, and to protect you.
Watch, happy husband, o'er the guiltless life
Of your King's Son · to your care I resign him.
By right of conquest I might have destroy'd him,
But I lay down that right I late abus'd.
With all a father's care I'll henceforth guard
The ORPHAN and your Son.   Fear not my faith.
I was but conqu'ror, you have made me King.
                                        [*To* ZAMTI.

Of the laws here, be thou th' Interpreter ;
With ministry right worthy of thyself.
Teach reason, justice, and morality.
The victors let the vanquish'd rule ! let wisdom
Preside o'er courage ! triumph o'er rude force,
That owes you homage ! I will give th' example.
Your Sov'reign, all invincible in arms,
Shall own himself obedient to your laws.

  IDAME. What do I hear ? O Heav'n ! can this be true?
  ZAMTI. Now, you indeed are worthy of your glory :
Nor shall your captives groan beneath your yoke.
    IDAME. What could inspire so noble a design?
    GENGIS. YOUR VIRTUES. These to friendship turn'd
            my hate,
And taught me, TO BE GOOD, IS TO BE GREAT.

The E N D.

THE

SIEGE of DAMASCUS.

A

TRAGEDY.

By JOHN HUGHES, Esq;

EDINBURGH:

Printed for A. DONALDSON, at Pope's Head
opposite the Exchange.

M,DCC,LIX.

B🔷L

To The Right Honourable

EARL *COWPER.*

My Lord,

MY Obligations to Your Lordſhip are ſo great and ſingular, ſo much exceeding all acknowledgment, and yet ſo highly demanding all that I can ever make, that nothing has been a greater uneaſineſs to me than to think that I have not publicly owned them ſooner. The honour of having been admitted to your Lordſhip's acquaintance and converſation, and the pleaſure I have ſometimes had of ſharing in your private hours and retirement from the town, were a happineſs ſufficient of itſelf to require from me the utmoſt returns of gratitude. But your Lordſhip was ſoon pleaſed to add to this, Your generous care of providing for

A 2   One

One who had given you no follicita-
tion; and before I could afk, or even
expected it, to honour me with an
employment, which, tho' valuable on
other accounts, became moft fo to me,
by the fingle circumftance of its plac-
ing me near your Lordfhip. But I
am not to bound my acknowledgments
here: When your Lordfhip withdrew
from public bufinefs, your care of me
did not ceafe till you had recommend-
ed me to your fucceffor, the prefent
Lord Chancellor. So that my having
fince had the felicity to be continued
in the fame employment, under a patron to whom I have many obligations, and who has particularly fhewn
a pleafure in encouraging the lovers of
learning and arts, is an additional obligation for which I am originally in-
debted to your Lordfhip.

AND yet I have faid nothing as I
ought of your Lordfhip's favours, unlefs I could defcribe a thoufand agree-
able

able circumſtances which attend and heighten them. To give is an act of power common to the great, but to double any gift by the manner of beſtowing it, is an art known only to the moſt elegant minds, and a pleaſure taſted by none but perſons of the moſt refin'd humanity.

As for the Tragedy I now humbly dedicate to your Lordſhip, part of it was written in the neighbourhood of your Lordſhip's pleaſant ſeat in the country ; where it had the good fortune to grow up under your early approbation and encouragement ; and I perſuade myſelf it will now be received by your Lordſhip with that indulgence, the exerciſe of which is natural to you, and is not the leaſt of thoſe diſtinguiſhing virtues by which you have gain'd an unſought popularity, and without either ſtudy or deſign have made yourſelf one of the moſt belov'd perſons of the age in which you live.

A 3 Here

Here, my Lord, I have a large subject before me, if I were capable of pursuing it, and if I were not acquainted with your Lordship's particular delicacy, by which you are not more careful to deserve the greatest praises than you are nice in receiving even the least. I shall therefore only presume to add, that I am, with the greatest zeal,

My LORD,

Your Lordship's most Obliged,

Most Dutiful, and

Devoted Humble Servant,

Feb. 6. 17½⅖.

JOHN HUGHES.

INTRODUCTION.

THE time of the following action is about two years after *Mahomet*'s death, under the next succeeding Caliph, *Abubeker*. The Saracen Caliphs were supreme both in spiritual and temporal affairs ; and *Abubeker*, following the steps of *Mahomet*, had made a considerable progress in propagating his new superstition by the sword. He had sent a numerous army into *Syria*, under the command of *Caled*, a bold and bloody Arabian, who had conquered several towns. The spirit of enthusiasm, newly poured forth among them, acted in its utmost vigour; and the persuasion, that they who turned their backs in fight were accursed of God, and that they who fell in battle passed immediately into paradise, made them an over-match for all the forces which the Grecian Emperor, *Heraclius*, could send against them. It was a very important period of time, and the eyes of the whole world were

fixed

fixed with terror on these successful savages, who committed all their barbarities under the name of religion; and soon after, by extending their conquests over the Grecian empire, and thro' *Persia* and *Egypt*, laid the foundation of that mighty empire of the Saracens, which lasted for several centuries; to which the Turks of later years succeeded.

The Saracens were now sat down before *Damascus*, the capital city of *Syria*, when the action of this Tragedy begins. This was about the Year of our Lord 634. All who have written of those times represent the state of Christianity in great confusion, very much corrupted, and divided with controversies and disputes, which, together with an universal depravity of manners, and the decay of good policy and antient discipline in the Empire, gave a mighty advantage to *Mahomet* and his followers, and prepared the way for their amazing success.

To

To the Memory *of Mr.* HUGHES.

O Loft too early! and too lately known !
My love's intended marks receive in one ;
Where new to eafe, and recent from thy pains,
With ampler joy thou tread'ft the blifsful plains :
If there, regardful of the ways of men,
Thou feeft with pity, what thou once haft been,
O gentle fhade ! accept this humble verfe,
Amidft the meaner honours of thy herfe.

How does thy PHOCYAS warm BRITANNIA's youth,
In arms to glory, and in love to truth !
O ! if the Mufe of future ought prefige,
Thefe feeds fhall ripen in the coming age ;
Then youths, renown'd for many a field well fought,
Shall own the glorious leffons thou haft taught ;
Honour's ftrict laws fhall reign in every mind;
And every PHOCYAS his EUDOCIA find.
O ! yet be this the loweft of thy fame ;
To form the hero, and inftruct the dame ;
I fee the Chriftian, Friend, Relation, Son,
Burn for the glorious courfe that thou haft run.

IF aught we owe thy pencil, or thy lyre,
Of manly ftrokes, or of fuperior fire,
How muft thy Mufe be ever own'd divine,
And in the facred lift unrival'd fhine !
Nor joyous health was thine, nor downy eafe,
To thee forbidden was the foft recels,
Worn with difeafe, and never-ceafing pain,
How firmly did thy foul her feat maintain !
Early thy fide the mortal fhaft receiv'd ·
All, but the wounded Hero, faw and griev'd :

No fenfe of fmart, no anguifh cou'd controul,
Or turn the generous purpofe of his foul.
Witnefs the nobler arts, by heav'n defign'd
To charm the fenfes, and improve the mind ;
How thro' your mazes, with inceffant toil,
He urg'd his way to reap th' immortal fpoil !
So fabled ORPHEUS tun'd his potent fong,
Death's cireling fhades, and STYGIAN glooms among.

OF thy great labours this the luft, and chief,
At once demands our wonder, and our grief;
Thy foul in clouded majefty 'till now,
Its finifh'd beauties did but partly fhow ;
Wond'ring we faw difclos'd the ample Store,
Griev'd in that inftant, to expect no more.

So, in the evening of fome doubtful day,
And clouds divided with a mingl'd ray,
Haply the golden Sun unveils his light,
And his whole glories fpread at once to fight ;
Th' enliven'd world look up with gladfome cheer,
Blefs the gay fcene, nor heed the night too near ;
Sudden the lucent orb drops fwiftly down
Thro' weftern fkies to fhine in worlds unknown.

MARCH 28. 1720.   WILLIAM COWPER.

On

On Mr. HUGHES' TRAGEDY *of the* SIEGE *of* DAMASCUS.

INFERIOR bards enervate ftrains indite,
  And void of vigour and of meaning write;
Their languid lines one even tenour keep,
And with the fame unvary'd cadence creep:
But *here* the fenfe is ftrong, the diction bold,
And truths fublime in manly verfe are told.
So tow'ring SOPHOCLES and SHAKESPEAR wrote,
Drew to the life, and painted human thought!

  No *modern* phrafes in thefe fcenes appear,
Antiquity's more noble drefs they wear;
This mafter hand with nicest judgement draws
Th' *Arabian* notions, manners, rites and laws;
Difplays degen'rate Chriftians growing crimes,
And the vain pomp of thofe corrupted times.

  On every fide what lovely landfkips rife!
The gay defcriptions cheat our ravifh'd eyes!
Here, fig-trees, vines, and olives bloom below;
And there, proud LEBANON's afpiring brow,
With ftately groves of palms and cedars crown'd,
Does the grand profpect beautifully bound!
What eye but fees the *moon's fair rifing light*
Drive back the hov'ring fhades, and chear the night!

  WHILE in the luftre of *thefe* glowing lines,
Th' impoftor's paradife fo gaily fhines,
With winy rivers nect'rine fruits fupply'd,
And beauties fparkling in immortal pride.
No more we wonder, fuch outrageous fire
Did the bold *Arab's* zealous breafts infpire.

  SILENCE is pleas'd, and wrapt *attention* waits,
While PHOCYAS with himfelf of death debates;
But when he rifes, wildly from the ground,
And *paffion* mocks him with imagin'd found,

Terror

Terror and grief at once poſſeſs the ſoul,
And ev'ry ſenſe and faculty controul.
Back to its ſource the vital current flies,
When, SAVE HER! SAVE HER! ravingly he cries.

THESE ſcenes improve, as well as warm the heart,
And nobleſt morals to the mind impart.
How juſt the draught! How elegantly true,
Which lets that ſoothing nymph, fair *Fame*, to view!
What ſolemn truths theſe awful lines contain:
Death's no where to be found. Thou fly'ſt in vain
From life; with what thou fly'ſt, to meet again!
Pride drops her plums, and *envy* dies away,
As the ſtars fade before the dawning day,
When chang'd EUMENES, in his ruin'd ſtate,
By ſage *affliction* diſciplin'd too late,
Does juſtly of *proſperity* complain,
That *ſelf-deſtroying monſter*, *Virtue's bane!*
A large diffuſive love of humankind,
Shines forth in brave ABUDAH, unconfin'd,
How amiable the virtuous chief appears,
When mildly he diſtreſsful PHOCYAS chears,
Supports his drooping head, condoles his grief,
And gives his noble foe a friend's relief!

O! that my muſe, in ſoft melodious verſe,
Could bright EDUOCIA's matchleſs charms rehearſe!
Her flowing words, like honey-dews, diſtil,
And ev'ry breaſt with riſing rapture fill:
Honour and *love*, like harneſs'd doves, unite,
And round her ſpread a ſweetly-vary'd light:
True to herſelf, and to her ſpotleſs fame,
Thro' ev'ry ſcene ſhe ſhines, illuſtriouſly the ſame!

WM. DUNCOMBE.

April, 1720.

PRO.

PROLOGUE

Spoken by Mr. M I L L S.

OFT has the Muse here try'd her magic arts,
    To raise your fancies, and engage your hearts.
When o'er this little spot she shakes her wand,
Towns, cities, nations, rise at her command:
And armies march obedient to her call,
New states are form'd, and ancient Empires fall.
To vary your instruction and delight,
Past ages roll renew'd before your sight.
His awful form the *Greek* and *Roman* wears,
Wak'd from his slumber of two thousand years:
And man's whole race, restor'd to joy and pain,
Act all their little greatness o'er again.

No common woes to-night we set to view;
Important is the time, the story new.
Our opening scenes shall to your sight disclose,
How spiritual dragooning first arose;
Claims drawn from Heav'n by a *Barbarian* Lord,
And faith first propagated by the sword.
In rocky *Araby* this pest began,
And swiftly o'er the neighbour-country ran:
By faction weaken'd, and disunion broke,
Degenerate provinces admit the yoke.
Nor stopp'd their progress, till, resistless grown,
Th' Enthusiasts made all *Asia's* world their own.

BRITONS,

B

BRITONS, be warn'd; let e'en your pleasures here
Convey some moral to th' attentive ear.
Beware, left bleffings long possess displease;
Nor grow supine with liberty and ease.
Your country's glory be your constant aim,
Her safety all is yours, think yours her fame.
Unite at home———forego inteſtine jars;
Then scorn the Rumours of religious wars;
Speak loud in thunder from your guarded shores,
And tell the continent, the sea is yours.
Speak on,———and say, by war you'll peace maintain,
Till brighteſt years, referv'd for GEORGE's reign,
Advance, and shine in their appointed round;
Arts then shall flourish, plenteous joys abound,
And, chear'd by him, each loyal Muse shall sing,
The happieſt iſland, and the greateſt KING.

PROLOGUE,

Spoken by Mr. MILWARD, on the Re-
vival in *March* 1734-5.

HERE force and fancy, with united charms,
 Mingle the fweets of love with war's alarms.
Our Author fhows, in Eaftern pomp array'd,
The conqu'ring Hero and the conftant Maid.
None better knew fuch noble heights to foar,
Tho' PHÆDRA, and tho' CATO charm'd before.

WHILE in the luftre of his glowing lines
Th' ARABIAN Paradife fo gaily fhines,
With winy rivers, racy fruits fupply'd,
And beauties fparkling in immortal pride;
Gallants, you'll own that a refiftlefs fire
Did juftly their enamour'd breafts infpire.

AT firft, a numerous audience crown'd this play,
And kind applaufes mark'd its happy way,
While he, like his own PHOCYAS, fnatch'd from view,
To fairer realms with ripen'd glory flew.
Humane, tho' witty; humble, tho' admir'd;
Wept by the great, the virtuous fage expir'd!

STILL may the Bard, beneath kind planets born,
Whom every Grace, and every Mufe adorn,
Whofe fpreading fame has reach'd to foreign lands,
Receive fome tribute too from BRITISH hands.

Dramatis

DRAMATIS PERSONÆ.

CHRISTIANS.

EUMENES, Governor of *Damascus*. Mr. WILKS.

EUDOCIA, his Daughter. Mrs. PORTER.

HERBIS, his Friend, one of the Chiefs } Mr WILLIAMS.
of the City.

PHOCYAS, A Noble and Valiant }
Syrian, privately in Love with } Mr. BOOTH.
EUDOCIA. }

ARTAMON, an Officer of the Guards. Mr. W. MILLS.

SERGIUS, an Express from the Emperor HERACLIUS.

Officers, Soldiers, Citizens, and Attendants.

SARACENS.

CALED, General of the *Saracen* Army. Mr. MILLS.

ABUDAH, the next in Command un- } Mr. THURMOND.
der CALED. }

DARAN, a wild *Arabian*, professing }
Mahometanism for the sake of the } Mr. WALKER.
Spoil. }

SERJABIL, }
RAPHAN, &c. } *Saracen Captains.*

Officers, Soldiers, Attendants.

SCENE, *the City of* DAMASCUS *in* Syria, *and the* Saracen *Camp before it. And in last Act a Valley adjacent.*

THE

THE

SIEGE of DAMASCUS.

A

TRAGEDY.

ACT I.   SCENE I.

SCENE, *The City.*

Enter EUMENES, *followed by a croud of people.*

EUMENES.

I'LL hear no more.   Be gone '
Or stop your clamorous mouths, that still are open
To bawl sedition, and consume our corn.
If you will follow me, send home your women,
And follow to the walls ;   there earn your safety,
As brave men shou'd— Pity your wives and children!
Yes, I do pity them , Heav'n knows I do,
E'n more than you ; nor will I yield 'em up,
Tho' at your own request, a prey to Ruffians—
HERBIS, what news '

Enter HERBIS.

HERB. News '——We're betray'd, deserted ;
The works are but half mann'd ;   the *Saracens*
Perceive it, and pour on such crouds, they blunt
Our weapons, and have drain'd our stores of death.
What will you next ?
EUM. I've sent a fresh recruit ,
The valiant PHOCYAS leads 'em on——whose deeds
In early youth assert his noble race,

A

A more than common ardour feems to warm
His breaft, as if he lov'd and courted danger.

HERB. I fear 'twill be too late.

EUM. [*Afide.*] I fear it too :
And tho' I brav'd it to the trembling croud,
I've caught th' infection, and I dread th' event.
Wou'd I had treated '——but 'tis now too late ——
Come, HERBIS.   *Exeunt.*

[*A noife is heard without, of officers giving orders.*

1 OFF. Help there ! more help ! All to the Eaftern gate !

2 OFF. Look where they cling aloft like clufter'd bees !
Here, Archers, ply your bows.

1 OFF Down with the ladders ;
What, will you let them mount ?

2 OFF. Aloft there ! give the fignal, you that wait
In *St. Mark's* Tower.

1 OFF. Is the town afleep ?
Ring out th' alarum bell !

[*Bell rings, and the citizens run to and fro in confufion. A great fhout. Enter* HERBIS.

HERB So—the tide turns, PHOCYAS has driv'n it back.
The gate once more is ours.

Enter EUMENES, PHOCYAS, ARTAMON, *&c*

EUM. Brave PHOCYAS, thanks ! mine and the people's
        thanks ! [*People fhout and cry, A* Phocyas ! *&c.*
Yet, that we may not lofe this breathing fpace,
Hang out the flag of truce You *Artamon*,
Hafte with a trumpet to th' *Arabian* chiefs,
And let them know, that, hoftages exchang'd,
I'd meet them now upon the Eaftern plain.   } *Exit* AR-
                                                  } TAMON.
PHO. What means EUMENES ?

EUM PHOCYAS, I wou'd try
By friendly treaty, if on terms of peace
They'll yet withdraw their powers.

PHO On terms of peace !
What peace can you expect from bands of robbers ?
What terms from flaves, but flavery ?——You know
Thefe wretches fight not at the call of honour ;
For injur'd rights, or birth, or jealous greatnefs,
That fets the princes of the world in arms.
Bafe born, and ftarv'd amidft their ftony defarts,

                                                  Long

Long have they view'd from far, with wishing eyes,
Our fruitful Vales, our fig-trees; olives, vines,
Our cedars, palms, and all the verdant wealth
That crowns fair *Lebanon's* aspiring brows.
Here have the locusts pitch'd, nor will they leave
These tasted sweets, these blooming fields of plenty,
For barren lands, and native poverty,
Till driv'n away by force.

    Eum What can we do?
Our people in despair, our soldiers harrass'd,
With daily toil, and constant nightly watch;
Our hope of succours from the Emperor
Uncertain, Eutyches not yet return'd
That went to ask them; one brave army beaten;
Th' *Arabians* numerous, cruel, flush'd with conquest.

    Herb. Besides, you know what frenzy fires their minds
Of their new faith, and drives them on to danger

    Eum. True;——they pretend the gates of paradise
Stand ever open to receive the souls
Of all that die in fighting for their cause.

    Pho. Then would I send their souls to paradise,
And give their bodies to our *Syrian* eagles.
Our ebb of fortune is not yet so low
To leave us desperate. Aids may soon arrive;
Mean time, in spite of their late bold attack,
The city still is ours; their force repell'd,
And therefore weaker; proud of this success,
Our soldiers too have gain'd redoubl'd courage,
And long to meet them on the open plain.
What hinders then but we repay this outrage,
And sally on their camp?

    Eum. No——let us first
Believe th' occasion fair, by this advantage,
To purchase their retreat on easy terms.
That failing, we the better stand acquitted
To our own citizens   Howe'er, brave Phocias,
Cherish this ardour in the soldiery,
And in our absence form what force thou canst.
Then, if these hungry blood hounds of the war
Shou'd still be deaf to peace, at our return
Our widen'd gates shall pour a sudden flood
Of vengeance on them, and chastise their scorn. [*Exeunt.*
                            S C E N E

SCENE *changes to a plain before the city.*
A prospect of tents at a distance.

CALED, ABUDAH, DARAN.

DAR. To treat, my chiefs?———What! are we mer-
    chants then.
That only come to traffic with these *Syrians*,
And poorly cheapen conquest on conditions?
No, we were sent to fight the Caliph's battles,
Till ev'ry iron neck bend to obedience.
Another storm makes this proud city ours;
What need to treat?———I am for war and plunder.

CAL. Why, so am I———and but to save the lives
Of Mussulmans, not Christians, wou'd not treat.
I hate these Christian dogs, and 'tis our task,
As thou observ'st, to fight, our law enjoins it;
Heav'n too is promis'd only to the valiant.
Oft' has our Prophet said, the happy plains
Above, lie stretch'd beneath the blaze of swords.

ABU. Yet DARAN's loth to trust that Heav'n for pay;
This earth, it seems, has gifts that please him more.

CAL. Check not his zeal, ABUDAH.

ABU. No, I praise it,
Yet I could wish that zeal had better motives.
Has victory no fruits but blood and plunder?
That we were sent to fight, 'tis true; but wherefore?
For conquest, not destruction. That obtain'd,
The more we spare, the Caliph has more subjects,
And Heav'n is better served.———But see they come.

Enter EUMENES, HERBIS, ARTAMON

CAL. Well, Christians, we are met—and war a while,
At your request, has still'd its angry voice,
To hear what you'll propose.

EUM. We come to know,
After so many troops you've lost in vain,
If you'll draw off in peace, and save the rest.

HERB. Or rather to know first—for yet we know not—
Why on your heads you call our pointed arrows,
In our own just defence? What means this visit?
And why we see so many thousand tents

Rise

Rife in the air, and whiten all our fields?

CAL. Is that a queftion now?—you had our fummons,
When firft we march'd againft you, to furrender.
Two moons have wafted fince, and now the third
Is in its wane. 'Tis true, drawn off a while,
At *Aiznadin* we met, and fought the powers
Sent by your Emperor to raife our fiege.
Vainly you thought us gone; we gain'd a conqueft.
You fee we are return'd; our hearts, our caufe,
Our fwords the fame.

HERB But why thofe fwords were drawn,
And what's that caufe, inform us.

EUM. Speak your wrongs,
If wrongs you have receiv'd, and by what means
They may be now repair'd

ABU. Then, Chriftians, hear,
And Heav'n infpire you to embrace its truth!
Not wrongs t'avenge, but to eftablifh right
Our fwords were drawn: For fuch is Heav'n's command
Immutable. By us great MAHOMET,
And his fucceffor holy ABUBEKER,
Invite you to the faith,

ART. [*Afide*] So———then it feems
There's no harm meant; we're only to be beaten
Into a new religion.——If that's all,
I find I am already half a convert.

EUM. Now, in the name of Heav'n, what faith is this
That ftalks gigantic forth thus arm'd with terrors,
As if it meant to ruin, not to fave?
That leads embattell'd legions to the field,
And marks its progrefs out with blood and flaughter?

HERB. Bold frontlefs men! that impudently dare
To blend religion with the worft of crimes!
And facrilegioufly ufurp that name,
To cover frauds, and juftify oppreffion!

EUM. Where are your priefts? What doctors of your
law
Have you e'er fent, t'inftruct us in its precepts?
To folve our doubts, and fatisfy our reafon,
And kindly lead us thro' the wilds of error
To thefe new tracts of truth?——This wou'd be friendfhip,
And well might claim our thanks.

CAL.

CAL. Friendship like this
With scorn had been receiv'd; your numerous vices,
Your clashing sects, your mutual rage and strife
Have driv'n religion, and her angel guards,
Like out-casts from among you.   In her stead,
Usurping superstition bears the sway,
And reigns in mimic state, 'midst idol shews,
And pageantry of pow'r.   Who does not mark
Your lives? rebellious to your own great Prophet
Who mildly taught you —— therefore MAHOMET
Has brought the sword to govern you by force,
Nor will accept obedience so precarious.

    EUM. O solemn truths! tho' from an impious
            tongue!   [*Aside.*
That we're unworthy of our holy faith,
To heav'n with grief and conscious shame we own.
But what are you, that thus arraign our vices,
And consecrate your own? vile hypocrites!
Are you not sons of rapine, foes to peace,
Base robbers, murderers——

    CAL. Christian, No——
    EUM. Then say,
Why have you ravag'd all our peaceful borders?
Plunder'd our towns? and by what claim e'en now
Tread you this ground?

    HERB. What claim, but that of hunger?
The claim of ravenous wolves, that leave their dens
To prowl at midnight round some sleeping village,
Or watch the shepherd's folded flock for prey?   [ours.

    CAL. Blasphemers, know, your fields and towns are
Our Prophet has bestow'd 'em on the faithful,
And heav'n itself has ratify'd the grant.

    EUM. Oh! now indeed you boast a noble title!
What cou'd your Prophet grant? a hireling slave!
Not e'en the mules and camels which he drove
Were his to give; and yet the bold impostor
Has canton'd out the kingdoms of the earth,
In frantic fits of visionary power,
To sooth his pride, and bribe his fellow-madmen!

    CAL. Was it for this you sent to ask a parley,
T'affront our faith, and to traduce our Prophet?
Well might we answer you with quick revenge

                                        For

For such indignities. —— Yet hear once more,
Hear this our last demand; and this accepted
We yet withdraw our war. Be Christians still;
But swear to live with us in firm alliance,
To yeild us aids, and pay us annual tribute.

 Eum. No; —— Should we grant you aid, we must
    be rebels;
And tribute is the slavish badge of conquest.
Yet since, on just and honourable terms,
We ask but for our own ——Ten silken vests,
Weighty with pearls and gems, we'll send your Caliph;
Two, Caled, shall be thine; two thine, Abudah.
To each inferior captain we decree
A turbant, spun from our Damascus flax
White as the snows of heav'n; to every soldier,
A scimitar. This, and of solid gold
Ten ingots, be the price to buy your absence.

 Cal. This, and much more, e'en all your shining
    Wealth,
Will soon be ours; look round your *Syrian* frontiers!
See, in how many towns our hoisted flags
Are waving in the wind; *Sachna*, and *Hauran*,
Proud *Tadmor*, *Aracah*, and stubborn *Bosia*
Have bow'd beneath the yoke,——Behold our march
O'er half your land, like flames thro' fields of harvest.
And last view *Aiznadin*, that vale of blood!
There seek the souls of forty thousand *Greeks*
That, fresh from life, yet hover o'er their bodies.
Then think, and then resolve.

 Herb Presumptuous men!
What tho' you yet can boast successful guilt,
Is conquest only yours? Or dare you hope
That you shall still pour on the swelling tide,
Like some proud river that has left its banks,
Nor ever know repulse?

 Eum. Have you forgot?
Not twice seven years are past since e'en your Prophet,
Bold as he was, and boasting aid divine,
Was by the tribe of *Coresh* forc'd to fly,
Poorly to fly, to save his wretched life,
From *Mecca* to *Medina*?

          Abu.

ABU. No';——forgot?
We well remember how *Medina* screen'd
That holy head, preserv'd for better days,
And rip'ning years of glory!

DAR. Why, my chiefs,
Will you waste time ; in offering terms despis'd
To these idolaters.———Words are but air,
Blows wou'd plead better.

CAL. DARAN, thou say'st true.
Christians, here end our truce. Behold once more
The sword of Heav'n is drawn! nor shall be sheath'd
But in the bowels of DAMASCUS.

EUM. That,
Or speedy vengeance, and destruction due
To the proud menacers, as Heav'n sees fit!

[*Exeunt severally.*

SCENE *changes to a garden.*

EUDOCIA.

All's hush'd around!——No more the shouts of soldiers,
And clash of arms tumultuous fill the air.
Methinks this interval of terror seems
Like that when the loud thunder just has roll'd
O'er our affrighted heads, and in the Heav'ns
A momentary silence but prepares
A second and a louder clap to follow.

Enter PHOCYAS

O no——my hero comes, with better omens,
And every gloomy thought is now no more.

PHO. Where is the treasure of my soul!——EUDOCIA,
Behold me here impatient, like the miser
That often steals in secret to his gold,
And counts with trembling joy, and jealous transport,
The shining heaps which he still fears to lose.

EUD. Welcome, thou brave, thou best deserving lover!
How do I doubly share the common safety,
Since 'tis a debt to thee!——But tell me, PHOCYAS,
Dost thou bring peace?——thou dost, and I am happy!

PHN. Not yet, EUDOCIA, 'tis decree'd by Heav'n
I must do more to merit thy esteem.

Peace,

Peace, like a frighted dove, has wing'd her flight
To diftant hills, beyond thefe hoftile tents;
And thro' 'em we muft thither force our way,
If we would call the lovely wanderer back
To her forfaken home.

   EUD. Falfe flattering hope!
Vanifh'd fo foon!——alas, my faithful fears
Return, and tell me, We muft ftill be wretched!

   PHO Not fo, my fair; if thou but gently fmile,
Infpiring valour, and prefaging conqueft,
Thefe barbarous foes to peace and love fhall foon
Be chec'd, like fiends before the morning light,
And all be calm again.

   EUD. Is the truce ended?
Muft war, alas, renew its bloody rage?
And PHOCYAS ever be expos'd to danger;

   PHO Think for whofe fake danger itfelf has charms?
Difmifs thy fears, the lucky hour comes on,
Full fraught with joys, when my big foul no more
Shall labour with this fecret of my paffion,
To hide it from thy jealous father's eyes
Juft now, by fignals from the plain, I've learn'd
That the proud foe refufe us terms of honour;
A fally is refolv'd, the citizens -
And foldiers, kindled into fudden fury,
Prefs all in crouds, and beg I'll lead 'em on.
O my EUDOCIA! if I now fucceed————
Did I fay If————I muft, I will, the caufe
Is love, 'tis liberty, it is EUDOCIA!————
What then fhall hinder fince our mutual faith
Is pledg'd, and thou confenting to my blifs.
But I may boldly afk thee of EUMENES,
Nor fear a rival's more prevailing claim?

   EUD. May Bleffings ftill attend thy arms!—Methinks
I've caught the flame of thy heroic ardor!
And now I fee thee crown'd with palm and olive;
The foldiers bring thee back with fongs of triumph,
And loud applauding fhouts, thy refcu'd country
Refounds thy praife; our Emperor *Heraclius*
Decrees the honours for a city fav'd,
And pillars rais'd of monumental brafs
Infcrib'd————*To* PHOCYAS *the* DELIVERER.

     C

                          PHO:

PHO. The honours and rewards which thou haſt nam'd
Are bribes too little for my vaſt ambition.
My ſoul is full of thee!——Thou art my all
Of fame, of triumph, and of future fortune.
'Twas love of thee firſt ſent me forth in arms ;
My ſervice is all thine, to thee devoted,
And thou alone canſt make e'en conqueſt pleaſing.

EUD. O do not wrong thy merit, nor reſtrain it
To narrow bounds ; but know, I beſt am pleas'd
To ſhare thee with thy country. O my PHOCYAS!
With conſcious bluſhes oft' I've heard thy vows,
And ſtrove to hide, yet more reveal'd my heart ;
But 'tis thy virtue juſtifies my choice,
And what at firſt was weakneſs, now is glory.

PHO. Forgive me, thou fair pattern of all goodneſs
If in the tranſport of unbounded paſſion,
I ſtill am loſt to ev'ry thought but thee.
Yet ſure to love thee thus is ev'ry virtue ;
Nor need I more perfection.————Hark ! I'm call'd.

[*Trumpet ſounds.*

EUD. Then go——and Heav'n with all its angels
guard thee

PHO. Farewel!——for thee once more I draw the ſword.
Now to the field to gain the glorious prize ;
'Tis victory—the word ; EUDOCIA's eyes ! [*Exeunt.*

ACT II. SCENE I.

SCENE, *The Governor's palace.*

EUMENES, HERBIS.

HERBIS   [NES.
STILL I muſt ſay 'twas wrong, 'twas wrong, EUME-
And mark th' event !
EUM. What cou'd I leſs? You ſaw
'Twas vain t' oppoſe it, whilſt his eager valour,
Impatient of reſtraint————

HERB.

HERB. His eager valour ?

His rashness, his hot youth, his valour's fever !

Must we, whose bufiness is to keep our walls,

And manage warily our little ftrength,

Muft we at once lavish away our blood,

Becaufe his pulfe beats high, and his mad courage

Wants to be breath'd in fome new enterprife ?——

You fhou'd not have confented.

 EUM You forgot,

'Twas not my voice alone ; you faw, the people

(And fure fuch fudden inftincts are from Heav'n ')

Rofe all at once to follow him, as if

One foul infpir'd 'em, and that foul were PHOCYAS.

 HERB. I had indeed forgot , and afk your pardon.

I took you for EUMENES, and I thought

That in DAMASCUS you had chief command.

 EUM. What doft thou mean ?

 HERB. Nay, who's forgetful now ?

You fay, the people———Yes, that very people,

That coward tribe that prefs'd you to furrender !

Well may they fpurn at loft authority ;

Whom they like better, better they'll obey.

 EUM. O I cou'd curfe the giddy changeful flaves.

But that the thought of this hour's great event

Poffeffes all my foul.——If we are beaten !——

 HERB. The poifon works, 'tis well——I'll give

  him more.   [*Afide.*

True, if we're beaten, who fhall anfwer that ?

Shall you, or I ?——— Are you the Governor ?———

Or fay we conquer, whofe is then the praife ?

 EUM. I know thy friendly fears ; that thou and I

Muft ftoop beneath a beardlefs rifing hero ,

And in HERACLIUS' court it fhall be faid,

DAMASCUS, nay perhaps the empire too,

Ow'd its deliverance to a boy ———Why, be it,

So that he now return with victory ;

'Tis honour greatly won, and let him wear it ;

Yet I could wifh I needed lefs his fervice.

Were EUTYCHES return'd———

 HERB. [*Afide.*] That, that's my torture.

I fent my fon to th' Emperor's court, in hopes

His merit at this time might raife his fortunes ;

But PHOCYAS——Curse upon his forward virtues!——
Is reaping all this field of fame alone,
Or leaves him scarce the gleanings of a harvest.

   EUM. See, ARTAMON with hasty strides returning:
He comes alone!—O friend, thy fears were just,
What are we now, and what is lost DAMASCUS?

Enter ARTAMON.

   ART. Joy to EUMENES!
   EUM Joy!————is't possible?
Dost thou bring news of victory?
   ART. The sun
Is set in blood, and from the Western skies
His seen three thousand slaughter'd *Arabs* fall.
   HERB. Is PHOCYAS safe?
   ART. He is, and crown'd with triumph.
   HERB [*Aside.*] My fears indeed were just.
          [*Shout,* A PHOCYAS, A PHOCYAS.
   EUM. What noise is that?
   HERB The people worshipping their new divinity,
Shortly they'll build him temples.
   EUM. Tell us, soldier,
Since thou hast shar'd the glory of this action,
Tell us how it began.
   ART At first the foe
Seem'd much surpris'd; but taking soon th' alarm
Gather'd some hasty troops, and march'd to meet us.
The Captain of these bands look'd wild and fierce,
His head unarm'd as if in scorn of danger,
And naked to the waste, as he drew near
He rais'd his arm, and shook a pond'rous lance;
When all at once, as at a signal giv'n,
We herd the TECBIR, so these *Arabs* call
Their shouts of onset, when with loud appeal
They challenge Heav'n, as if demanding conquest.
The battle join'd, and thro' the barbarous host
Fight, Fight, and *Paradise* was all the cry.
At last our leaders met, and gallant PHOCYAS——
But what are words to tell the mighty wonders
We saw him then perform?————their chief unhors'd,
The *Saracens* soon broke their ranks and fled;
And had not a thick evening fog arose
                     (Which

(Which fure the Devil rais'd up to fave his friends!)
The flaughter had been double——But, behold!
The Hero comes.

Enter P H O C Y A S. E U M E N E S *meeting him.*

Eum. Joy to the brave Phocyas!
Eumenes gives him back the joy he fent.
The welcome news has reach'd this place before thee.
How fhall thy country pay the debt fhe owes thee?

Pho. By taking this as earneft of a debt
Which I owe her, and fain wou'd better pay.

Herb. In fpite of envy, I muft praife him too. [*Afide.*
Phocyas, thou haft done bravely, and 'tis fit
Succefsful virtue take a time to reft.
Fortune is fickle, and may change; befides,
What fhall we gain, if from a mighty ocean
By fluices we draw off fome little ftreams?
If thoufands fall, ten thoufands more remain.
Nor ought we hazard-worth fo great as thine
Againft fuch odds; fuffice what's done already:
And let us now, in hope of better days,
Keep wary watch, and wait th' expected fuccours.

Pho. What!——to be coop'd whole months within
    our walls?
To ruft at home, and ficken with inaction?
The courage of our men will droop and die,
If not kept up by daily exercife.
Again the beaten foe may force our gates;
And victory, if flighted thus, take wing,
And fly where fhe may find a better welcome.

Art. [*Afide.*] It muft be fo——he hates him! on
    my foul,
This Herbis is a foul old envious knave.
Methinks Eumenes too might better thank him.

Eum. [to Herbis *afide.*] Urge him no more;——
I'll think of thy late warning.
And thou fhalt fee I'll yet be governor.
            A letter brought in.
Phocyas [*looking on it.*] 'Tis to Eumenes.

Eum. Ha! from *Eutyches.*

[*Reads.*] 'The Emperor, awakened with the danger
' That threatens his dominions, and the lofs
            C 3   'At

' At *Aiznadin,* has drain'd his garrisons
' To raise a second army.   In a few hours
' We will begin our march.   SERGIUS brings this,
' And will inform you further————

HERB. [*Aside.*] Heav'n, I thank thee!
'Tis e'en beyond my hopes.

EUM. But where is SERGIUS?

Mess. The letter, fasten'd to an arrow's head,
Was shot into the town.

EUM. I fear he's taken.————
O PHOCYAS, HERBIS, ARTAMON! my friends!
You all are sharers in this news, the storm
Is blowing o'er, that hung like night upon us,
And threaten'd deadly ruin ————Haste, proclaim
The welcome tidings loud thro' all the city.
Let sparkling lights be seen from every turret
To tell our joy, and spread their blaze to heav'n!
Prepare for feasts, danger shall wait at distance,
And fear be now no more.   The jolly Soldier
And Citizen shall meet o'er their full bowls,
Forget their toils, and laugh their cares away,
And mirth and triumphs close this happy day.
                    [*Exeunt* HERB *and* ART.

    PHO.   And may succeeding days prove yet more
                happy!
Well dost thou bid the voice of triumph sound
Thro' all our streets, our city calls thee father;
And say, EUMENES, dost thou not perceive
A father's transport rise within thy breast,
Whilst in this act thou art the hand of heav'n
To deal forth blessings, and distribute joy?

    EUM. The blessings heav'n bestows are freely sent,
And shou'd be freely shar'd.

    PHO. True, ———— Generous minds
Redoub'd feel the pleasures they impart,
For me, If I've deserv'd by arms or counsels,
By hazard's greatly sought and greatly prosper'd,
Whate'er I've added to the public stock,
With joy I see it in EUMENES' hands,
And wish but to receive my share from thee.

    EUM. I cannot, if I wou'd, withhold thy share.
                                        What

What thou haſt done is thine ; the fame thy own ;
And virtuous actions will reward themſelves.

   PHO. Fame ?——What is that, if courted for herſelf ?
Leſs than a viſion , a mere ſound, an echo,
That calls with mimic voice thro' woods and labyrinths
Her cheated lovers ; loſt and heard by fits,
But never fix'd , a ſeeming nymph, yet nothing.
Virtue indeed is a ſubſtantial good,
A real beauty ; yet with weary ſteps
Thro' rugged ways, by long laborious ſervice,
When we have trac'd, and woo'd, and won the dame,
May we not then expect the dower ſhe brings ?

   EUM. Well—aſk that dower, ſay, can DAMASCUS
                  pay it ?
Her riches ſhall be tax'd, name but the ſum,
Her merchants with ſome coſtly gems ſhall grace thee,
Nor can HERACLIUS fail to grant thee honours,
Proportion'd to thy birth and thy deſert.

   PHO. And can EUMENES think I wou'd be bribed
By traſh, by ſordid gold, to venal virtue ?
What ! ſerve my country for the ſame mean hire,
That can corrupt each villain to betray her ?
Why is ſhe ſav'd from theſe Arabian ſpoilers,
If to be ſtripp'd by her own ſons ?——forgive me
If the thought glows upon my cheeks ; I know
'Twas mention'd, but to prove how much I ſcorn it.
As for HERACLIUS, if he own my conduct,
I ſhall indulge an honeſt pride in honours
Which I've ſtrove to merit. Yes EUMENES,
I have ambition——yet the vaſt reward
That ſwells my hopes, and equals all my wiſhes
Is in thy gift alone——— it is EUDOCIA.

  EUM. EUDOCIA ! PHOCYAS, I am yet thy friend,
And therefore will not hold thee long in doubt.
Thou muſt not think of her——

   PHO. Not think of her ?
Impoſſible !——— ſhe's ever preſent to me,
My life, my ſoul ; ſhe animates my being,
And kindles up my thoughts to worthy actions.
And why, EUMENES, why not think of her ?
Is not my rank———

   EUM. Forbear———what need a herald

                               To

To tell me who thou art ?———Yet once again—
Since thou wilt force to a repetition,
I fay, thou muft not think of her.

 PHO. Yet hear me ;
Why wilt thou judge, e'er I can plead my caufe ?

 EUM. Why wilt thou plead in vain ? haft thou not
   heard
My choice has deftin'd her to EUTYCHES ?

 PHO. And has fhe then confented to that choice ?

 EUM. Has fhe confented ?—What is her confent ?
Is fhe not mine ?

 PHO. She is————and in that title
E'en kings with envy may behold thy wealth,
And think their kingdoms poor !—and yet EUMENES,
Shall fhe, by being thine, be barr'd a privilege
Which e'en the meaneft of her fex may claim ?
Thou wilt not force her ?

 EUM. Who has told thee fo ?
I'd force her to be happy.

 PHO. That thou canft not.
What happinefs fubfifts in lofs of freedom ?
The gueft conftrain'd but murmurs at the banquet ;
Nor thanks his hoft, but ftarves amidft abundance.

 EUM. 'Tis well, young man — why then I'll learn
   from thee
To be a very tame obedient father.
Thou haft already taught my child her duty.
I find the fource of all her difobedience,
Her hate of me, her fcorn of EUTYCHES ;
Ha ! is't not fo ?———come tell me , I'll forgive thee.
Haft thou not found her a moft ready fcholar ?
I know thou haft———why, what a dull old dotard
Was I, to think I ever had a daughter !

 PHO I'm forry that EUMENES thinks————

 EUM. No ———— forry !
Sorry for what ? then thou doft own thou'ft wrong'd
  me !
That's fomewhat yet———curfe on my ftupid blindnefs !
For had I eyes I might have feen it fooner.
Was this the fpring of thy romantic bravery,
Thy boaftful merit, thy officious fervice ?

 PHO. It was—with pride I own it—'twas EUDOCIA!

I

I have ferv'd thee in ferving her, thou know'ft it,
And thought I might have found a better treatment.
Why wilt thou force me thus to be a-braggard,
And tell thee that which thou fhou'dft tell thyfelf;
It grates my foul—I am not wont to talk thus.
But I recall my words—I have done nothing,
And wou'd difclaim all merit but my love.

Eum. O no—fay on, that thou haft fav'd DAMASCUS,
Is it not fo?——Look o'er her battlements,
See, if the flying foe have left their camp!
Why are our gates yet clos'd if thou haft fieed us?
'Tis true, thou fought'ft a fkirmifh—what of that?
Had EUTYCHES been prefent——

Pho. EUTYCHES!
Why wilt thou urge my temper with that trifler?
O let him come! that in yon fpacious plain
We may together charge the thickeft ranks,
Rufh on to battle, wounds, and glorious death,
And prove who 'twas that beft deferved EUDOCIA.

Eum. That will be feen ere long—but fince I find
Thou arrogantly wou'dft ufurp dominion,
Believ'ft thyfelf the guardian genius here,
And that our fortunes hang upon thy fword;
Be that firft try'd—for know, that from this moment
Thou here haft no command—Farewel!—So ftay,
Or hence and join the foe—thou haft thy choice.

[*Exit* EUMENES.

Pho. Spurn'd and degraded!—proud ungrateful man!
Am I a bubble then, blown up by thee,
And to's'd into the air to make thee fport?
Hence to the foe? 'tis well——EUDOCIA,
O I will fee thee, thou wrong'd excellence!
But now to fpeak thy wrongs, or my difgrace?
Impoffible—O rather let me walk
Like a dumb ghoft, and burft my heart in filence.

S C E N E, *The Garden.*

Enter E U D O C I A

Eud. Why muft we meet by ftealth, like guilty
lovers!
But 'twill not long be fo——What joy it will be

To

To own my Hero in his ripen'd honours,
And here applauding crouds pronounce me bleſt !——
Sure he'll be here——See ! the fair riſing moon,
Ere day's remaining twilight ſcarce is ſpent,
Hangs up her ready lamp, and with mild luſtre
Drives back the hov'ring ſhades! Come, PHOCYAS, come;
This gentle ſeaſon is a friend to love,
And now methinks I cou'd, with equal paſſion,
Meet thine, and tll thee all my ſecret ſoul.

Enter P H O C Y A S,

He hears me — O my PHOCYAS ! — What ? — not
　　anſwer ?——
Art thou not he ? or art ſome ſhadow ?——ſpeak
　　PHO. I am indeed a ſhadow——I am nothing——
　　EUD. What do'ſt thou mean ? —— for now I know
　　　　thee, PHOCYAS.
　　PHO. And never can be thine.
It will have vent—O barbarous curſt—but hold——
I had forgot,——it was EUDOCIA's father !——
O cou'd I too forget how he has us'd me !
　　EUD. I fear to aſk thee——
　　PHO. Doſt thou fear !——Alas !
Then wilt thou pity me—O generous maid !
Thou haſt charm'd down the rage that ſwell'd my
　　　　heart,
And chock'd my voice—now I can ſpeak to thee.
And yet 'tis worſe than death what I have ſuffer'd ;
It is the death of honour !—Yet that's little ;
'Tis more, EUDOCIA, 'tis the loſs of thee !
　　EUD. Haſt thou not conquer'd ?—What are all theſe
　　　　ſhouts,
This voice of general joy, heard far around ?
What are theſe fires, that caſt their glimmering light
Againſt the ſky ? Are not all theſe thy triumph ?
　　PHO. O name not triumph ! talk no more of conqueſt !
It is indeed a night of general joy,
But not to me, EUDOCIA, I am come
To take a laſt farewel of thee for ever
　　EUD. A laſt farewel !
　　PHO. Yes ;——How wilt thou hereafter
Look on a wretch deſpis'd, revil'd, caſhier'd,

　　　　　　　　　　　　　　　　　　Stripp'd

Stripp'd of command, like a bafe beaten coward?
Thy cruel father—I have told too much,—
I fhou'd not but for this have felt the wounds
I got in fight for him—now, now they bleed.
But I have done—and now thou haft my ftory,
Is there a creature fo accurft as PHOCYAS?

EUD. And can it be? Is this then thy reward?
O PHOCYAS? never wou'dft thou tell me yet
That thou hadft wounds; Now I muft feel them too
For it is not for me thou haft borne this?
What elfe could be thy crime?—wer't thou a traitor,
Hadft thou betray'd us, fold us to the foe————

PHO. Woul'd I be yet a traitor, I have leave,
Nay, I am dar'd to it with mocking fcorn.
My crime indeed was afking thee, That only
Has cancell'd all, if I had any merit,
The city now is fafe, my fervice flighted,
And I difcarded like an ufelefs thing,
Nay, bid be gone—and, if I like that better,
Seek out new friends, and join yon barb'rous hoft.

EUD. Hold—let me think a while— [*Walks afide*
—Tho' my heart bleed,
I wou'd not have him fee thefe dropping tears—
And wilt thou go then, PHOCYAS?

PHO. To my grave,
Where can I bury elfe this foul difgrace?
Alas! that queftion fhews how poor I am,
How very much a wretch, for if I go,
It is from thee, thou only joy of life:
And death will then be welcome.

EUD. Art thou fure
Thou haft been us'd thus?—Art thou quite undone?

PHO. Yes, very fure—What doft thou mean?

EUD. That then, it is a time for me—O heav'n!
    that I
Alone am grateful to this wond'rous man!—
To own thee PHOCYAS, thus— [*giving her hand.* nay,
    glory in thee,
And fhew without a blufh, how much I love.
We muft not part————

PHO. Then am I rich again! [*Embracing her.*
O no—we will not part!—confirm it heav'n!

                          Now

Now thou shalt see how I will bend my spirit,
With what soft patience I will bear my wrongs,
Till I have wearied out thy father's scorn.
Yet I have worse to tell thee——EUTYCHES——

EUD. Why wilt thou name him?

PHO Now, e'en now he's coming!
Just hov'ring o'er thee, like a bird of prey.
Thy father vows——for I must tell thee all——
'Twas this that wrung my heart, and rack'd my brain,
E'en to distraction!——vows thee to his bed;
Nay threaten'd force, if thou refuse obedience.

EUD. Force?—threaten'd force!—my father—where
      is nature?
Is that too banish'd from his heart?——O then
I have no father——How have I deserv'd this?——
                                      [*Weeping.*
No home, but am henceforth an outcast orphan,
For I will wander to earth's utmost bound,
E'er give my hand to that detested contract.
O save me, PHOCYAS! thou hast sav'd my father——
Must I yet call him so, this cruel father.——
How wilt thou now deliver poor EUDOCIA?

PHO. See! how we're join'd in exile, how our fate
Conspires to warn us both to leave this city!
Thou know'st the Emperor is now at *Antioch*;
I have an uncle there, who, when the *Persian*,
As now the *Saracen*, had nigh o'er-run
The ravag'd empire, did him signal service,
And nobly was rewarded. There, EUDOCIA,
Thou might'st be safe, and I may meet with justice.

EUD. There—any where, so we may fly this place
See, PHOCYAS, what thy wrongs and mine have wrought
In a weak woman's frame! for I have courage
To share thy exile now thro' every danger.
Danger is only here, and dwells with guilt,
With base ingratitude, and hard oppression

PHO. Then let us lose no time, but hence this night.
The gates I can command, and will provide
The means of our escape. Some five hours hence
('Twill then be turn'd of midnight) we may meet
In the piazza of *Honoria*'s convent.

EUD. I know it well; the place is most secure,

                                      And

And near adjoining to this garden wall.
There thou fhalt find me—O protect us, Heav'n!
PHO. Fear not,—thy innocence will be our guard.
I've thought already how to fhape our-courfe.
Some pitying angel will attend thy fteps,
Guide thee unfeen, and charm the fleeping foe,
Till thou art fafe!——O I have fuffer'd nothing,
Thus gaining thee, and this great generous proof;
How bleft I am in my EUDOCIA's love!
My only joy, farewel!——
  EUD. Farewel, my PHOCYAS!
I've now no friend but thee—yet thee I'll call
Friend, father, lover, guardian!——Thou art all
                                    [*Exeunt.*

A C T III. SCENE I.

SCENE, Caled's *Tent.*

CALED *attended.* SERGIUS *brought in, bound with cords.*

CALED

MERCY! What's that?——Look yonder on the field
Of our late fight!——Go, talk of mercy there.
Will the dead hear thy voice?
  SERG. O fpare me yet!
  CAL. Thou wretch!——Spare thee? to what? to
    live in torture?
Are not thy limbs all bruis'd, thy bones disjointed,
To force thee to confefs? And would'ft thou drag,
Like a crufh'd ferpent, a vile mangled being?
My eyes abhor a coward——Hence, and die!
  SERG. O, I have told thee all?—When firft purfu'd,
I fix'd my letters on an arrow's point,
And fhot them o'er the walls——
  CAL. Haft thou told all?
Well then thou fhalt have mercy to requite thee;
Behold, I'll fend thee forward on thy errand.
                    D   Strike

Strike off his head, then caft it o'er the gate,
There let thy tongue tell o'er its tale again.
   SERG. O bloody *Saracen !*————————
       [*Exit* SERGIUS, *dragg'd away by guards.*

Enter A B U D A H.

   CAL. ABUDAH, welcome !
   ABU. O CALED ! what an evening was the laft !
   CAL. Name it no more, remembrance fickens with it,
And therefore fleep is banifh'd from this night ;
Nor fhall to-morrow's fun open his eye
Upon our fhame, e're doubly we've redeem'd it.
Have all the captains notice ?
   ABU. I have walk'd
The rounds to-night, e're the laft hour of pray'r,
From tent to tent, and warn'd them to be ready.
What muft be done ?
   CAL. Thou know'ft th' important news,
Which we have intercepted by this flave,
Of a new army's march.   The time now calls,
While thefe foft *Syrians* are diffolv'd in riot,
Fool'd with fuccefs, and not fufpecting danger,
Neglectful of their watch, or elfe faft bound
In chains of fleep, companion of debauches,
To form a new attack e're break of day ;
So, like the wounded leopard, fhall we rufh
From out our covert on thefe drowfy hunters,
And feize 'em unprepar'd to 'fcape our vengeance.
   ABU Great Captain of the armies of the Faithful !
I know thy mighty and unconquer'd fpirit,
Yet hear me, CALED ; hear and weigh my doubts.
Our angry Prophet frowns upon our vices,
And vifits us in blood.   Why elfe did terrors
Unknown before feize all our ftouteft bands ?
The angel of deftruction was abroad ;
The archers of the tribe of *Thoal* fled,
So long renown'd, or fpent their fhafts in vain ;
The feather'd flights err'd thro' the boundlefs air,
Or the death turn'd on him that drew the bow !
What can this bode ?————Let me fpeak plainer yet ;
Is it to propagate th' unfpotted law
We fight ? 'tis well ; it is a noble caufe !
                      But

But much I fear infection is amongst us;
A boundless lust of rapine guides our troops.
We learn the Christian vices we chastise,
And, tempted with the pleasures of the soil,
More than with distant hopes of paradise,
I fear, may soon——but Oh! avert it Heav'n!
Fall e'en a prey to our own spoils and conquests.

CAL. No——thou mistak'st, thy pious zeal deceives
Our Prophet only chides our sluggard valour. [thee.
Thou saw'st how in the vale of *Honan* once
The troops, as now defeated, fled confus'd
E'en to the gates of *Mecca's* holy city,
'Till MAHOMET himself there stopt their entrance,
A javelin in his hand, and turn'd them back
Upon the foe, they fought again, and conquer'd.
Behold how we may best appease his wrath!
His own example points us out the way.

ABU. Well—be it then resolv'd. Th' indulgent hour
Of better fortune is, I hope, at hand:
And yet since PHOCYAS has appear'd its champion,
How has this city rais'd its drooping head!
As if some charm prevail'd where-e'er he fought;
Our strength seems wither'd, and our feeble weapons
Forgot their wonted triumph——were he absent——

CAL. I would have sought him out in the last action
To single fight, and put that charm to proof,
Had not a foul and sudden mist arose
E're I arriv'd to have restor'd the combat.
But let it be——'tis past. We yet may meet,
And 'twill be known whose arm is then the stronger.

Enter DARAN

DAR. Health to the race of *Ismael!* and days
More prosp'rous than the last—a Christian captive
Is fall'n within my watch, and waits his doom.

CAL. Bring forth the slave!——O thou keen vulture
    death!
Do we then feed thee only thus by morsels?
Whole armies never can suffice thy hunger.

DARAN *goes out, and re-enters with* PHOCYAS.

Cal. Whence, and what art thou!—Of *Damascus*?—
    Daran,
Where didst thou find this dumb and sullen thing,
That seems to lour defiance on our anger? [me,

Dar. Marching in circuit with the horse thou gav'st
T' observe the city gates, I saw from far
Two persons issue forth, the one advanc'd,
And e're he could retreat, my horsemen seiz'd him.
The other was a woman, and had fled,
Upon a signal giv'n at our approach,
And got within the gate.   Wou'dst thou know more,
Himself, if he will speak, can best inform thee.

Cal. Have I not seen thy face?

Abu. [*To* Caled.] He hears thee not;
His eyes are fix'd on earth; some deep distress
Is at his heart.   This is no common captive.

Cal. A lion in the toils! We soon shall tame him.
Still art thou dumb!——Nay, 'tis in vain to cast
Thy gloomy looks so oft around this place,
Or frown upon thy bonds——thou can'st not 'scape.

Pho. Then be it so——the worst is past already,
And life is now not worth a moment's pause,
Do you not know me yet?——think of the man
You have most cause to curse, and I am he.

Cal. Ha! Phocyas?

Abu. Phocyas?——Mahomet, we thank thee!
Now thou dost smile again.

Dar. [*Aside*] O Devil, Devil!
And I not know him?——'twas but yesterday
He kill'd my horse, and drove me from the field.
Now I'm reveng'd! No; hold you there, not yet,
Not while he lives.

Cal. [*Aside*] This is indeed a prize!——
Is it because thou know'st what slaughter'd heaps
There yet unbury'd lie without the camp,
Whose ghosts have all this night, passing the *Zorat*,
Call'd from that bridge of death on thee to follow,
That now thou'rt here to answer to their cry?
Howe'er it be, thou know'st thy welcome——

                                            Pho.

PHO. Yes,
Thou proud, blood-thirſty ARAB !——Well I know
What to expect from thee ; I know ye all.
How ſhould the authors of diſtreſs and ruin
Be mov'd to pity ? that's a human paſſion ;
No————in your hungry eyes, that look revenge,
I read my doom. Where are your racks, your tortures ?
I'm ready————lead me to 'em ; I can bear
The woiſt of ills from you. You're not my friends,
My countrymen.————Yet were ye men, I cou'd
Unfold a ſtory————but no more——EUMENES,
Thou haſt thy wiſh, and I am now————a worm !
    ABU. [*to* CALED *aſide.*] Leader of armies, hear him!
        for my mind
Preſages good accruing to our cauſe
By this event.
    CAL. I tell thee then, thou wrong'ſt us,
To think our hearts thus ſteel'd, or our ears deaf
To all that thou may'ſt utter. Speak, diſcloſe
The ſecret woe that throbs within thy breaſt.
Now, by the ſilent hours of night ! we'll hear thee,
And mute attention ſhall await thy words.
    PHO This is not then the palace of *Damaſcus* !
If ye will hear, then I indeed have wrong'd you.
How can this be ?—When he for whom I've fought,
Fought againſt you, has yet refus'd to hear me !
You ſeem ſurpris'd.————It was ingratitude
That drove me out an exile fiom thoſe walls,
Which I ſo late defended.
    ABU. Can it be ?
Are theſe thy Chriſtian friends ?
    CAL. 'Tis well————we thank 'em.
They help us to ſubdue themſelves.——But who
Was that companion of thy flight ?——A woman,
So DARAN ſaid————
    PHO 'Tis there I am moſt wretched————
O I am torn from all my ſoul held dear,
And my life's blood flows out upon the wound !
That woman—'twas for her—how ſhall I ſpeak it ?—
EUDOCIA, O farewel !——I'll tell you then,
As faſt as theſe heart-rending ſighs well let me,
I lov'd the daughter of the proud EUMENES,

             D 3   And

And long in secret woo'd her; not unwelcome
To her my visits, but I fear'd her father,
Who oft I ad press'd her to detested nuptials,
And therefore durst not, till this night of joy,
Avow to him my courtship.   Now I thought her
Mine, by a double claim, of mutual vows,
And service yielded at his greatest need.
When as I mov'd my suit, with sour disdain
He mock'd my service and forbade my love;
Degraded me from the command I bore,
And with defiance bade me seek the foe.
How has his curse prevail'd!—The generous maid
Was won by my distress to leave the city;
And cruel fortune made me thus your prey.

ABU. [*Aside.*] My soul is mov'd.——Thou wert a
        man, O Prophet!
Forgive, if 'tis a crime, a human sorrow
For injur'd worth, tho' in an enemy!

PHO. Now—since you've heard my story, set me free,
That I may save her, yet dearer than life,
From a tyrannic father's threaten'd force,
Gold, gems and purple vests shall pay my ransom;
Nor shall my peaceful sword henceforth be drawn
In fight, nor break its truce with you for ever.

CAL. No;——there's one way, a better, and but one,
To save thyself, and make some reparation
For all the numbers thy bold hand has slain.

PHO. O name it quickly, and my soul will bless thee!

CAL. Embrace our faith, and share with us our for-
        tunes.

PHO. Then I am lost again!

CAL. What! when we offer
Not freedom only, but to raise thee high,
To greatness, conquest, glory, heav'nly bliss!

PHO. To sink me down to infamy, perdition,
Here and hereafter! make my name a curse
To present times, to ev'ry future age
A proverb and a scorn!——take back thy mercy,
And know I now disdain it.

CAL. As thou wilt.
The time's too precious to be wasted longer
In words with thee.   Thou know'st thy doom — Fare-   [wel.
                                                      ABU.

ABU. [*to* CALED, *afide.*] Hear me yet, CALED!
grant him fome fhort fpace;
Perhaps at length he will accept thy bounty.
Try him at leaft————

CAL. Well——be it fo then. DARAN,
Guard well thy charge.—Thou haft an hour to live;
If thou art wife, thou may'ft prolong that term,
If not——why——fare thee well, and think of death.
                    [*Exeunt* CALED *and* ABDUAH.
                    DARAN *waiting at a diftance*]

PHO. Farewel, and think of death! was it not fo?
Do murderers then preach morality?————
But how to think of what the living know not,
And the dead cannot, or elfe may not tell?————
What art thou, O thou great myfterious terror!
The way to thee we know; difeafes, famine,
Sword, fire, and all thy ever-open gates
That day and night ftand ready to receive us.
But what's beyond them?—Who will draw that veil?
Yet death's not there——no, 'tis a point of time,
The verge 'twixt mortal and immortal being.
It mocks our thought! on this fide all is life;
And when we've reach'd it, in that very inftant
'Tis paft the thinking of! O! if it be
The pangs, the throes, the agonizing ftruggle
When foul and body part, fure I have felt it,
And there's no more to fear.

DAR. [*Afide.*] Suppofe I now
Difpatch him?—right—what need to ftay for orders?
I wifh I durft?——Yet what I dare I'll do.
Your jewels, Chriftian—you'll not need thefe trifles——
                    [*Searching him.*

PHO. I pr'ythee, flave, ftand off—my foul's too bufy
To lofe a thought on thee.

        Enter ABUDAH,

ABU. What's this?————forbear!
Who gave thee leave to ufe this infolence?
        [*Takes the jewels from him, and lays 'em on a table.*

DAR. [*Afide*] Deny'd my booty?—Curfes on his head!
Was not the founder of our law a robber?
Why 'twas for that I left my country's gods,

                                        Menaph

Menaph and *Uzza.*   Better ftill be Pagan,
Than ftarve with a new faith.

ABU. What ?——doft thou mutter ?
DARAN, withdraw, and better learn thy duty.

[*Exit.* DARAN.

PHOCYAS, perhaps thou know'ft me not——

PHO. I know
Thy name ABUDAH, and thy office here
The fecond in command.   What more thou art
Indeed I cannot tell.

ABU. True, for thou yet
Know'ft not I am thy friend.

PHO Is't poffible ?
Thou fpeak'ft me fan.

ABU. What doft thou think of life ?

PHO. I think not of it ; death was in my thoughts.
On hard conditions, life were but a load,
And I wou'd lay it down.

ABU. Art thou refolv'd ?

PHO I am, unlefs thou bring'ft me better terms
Than thofe I have rejected.

ABU. Think again.
CALED, by me, once more renews that offer.   [try

PHO. Thou fay'ft thou art my friend ; why doft thou
To fhake the fettled temper of my breaft ?
My foul hath juft difcharg'd her cumbrous train
Of hopes and fears, prepar'd to take her voyage
To other feats, where fhe may reft in peace,
And now thou call'ft me back, to beat again
The painful roads of life.—Tempt me no more
To be a wretch, for I defpife the offer.

ABU. The general knows thee brave, and 'tis for that
He feeks alliance with thy noble virtues.

PHO. He knows me brave !——why does he then
          thus treat me ?
No ; he believes I am fo poor of foul,
That barely for the privilege to live,
I would be bought his flave.   But go and tell him,
The little fpace of life his fcorn bequeath'd me
Was lent in vain, and he may take the forfeit.

ABU Why wilt thou wed thyfelf to mifery,
When our faith courts thee to eternal bleffings ?

When

When truth itself is, like a seraph, come
To loose thy bonds?—The light divine, whose beams
Pierc'd thro' the gloom of *Hera's* sacred cave,
And there illumin'd the great MAHOMET,
Arabia's morning-stars, now shines on thee.
Arise, salute with joy the guest from Heav'n,
Follow her steps, and be no more a captive.

PHO. But whither must I follow?—answer that.
Is she a guest from Heav'n? What marks divine,
What signs, what wonders vouch her boasted mission?

ABU. What wonders?——turn thy eyes to *Mecca!*
mark
How from *Caaba* first, that hallow'd temple,
Her glory dawn'd?—then look how swift its course,
As when the sun beams shooting thro' a cloud
Drive o'er the meadow's face the flying shades!
Have not the nations bent before our swords,
Like ripen'd corn before the reaper's steel!
Why is all this? Why does success still wait
Upon our law, if not to shew that Heav'n
First sent it forth, and owns it still by conquest?

PHO. Dost thou ask why is this?—O why indeed?
Where is the man can read Heav'n's secret counsels?—
Why did I conquer in another cause,
Yet now am here?———

ABU. I'll tell thee—thy good angel
Has seiz'd thy hand unseen, and snatch'd thee out
From swift destruction; know, e're day shall dawn,
DAMASCUS will in blood lament its fall,
We've heard what army is design'd to march
Too late to save her. Now, e'en now, our force
Is just preparing to a fresh assault.
Now too thou might'st revenge thy wrongs— so CALED
Charg'd me to say; and more that he invites thee,
Thou know'st the terms——— to share with him the
conquest.

PHO. Conquest?—Revenge?—Hold, let me think—
O horror!
Revenge?—O what revenge? Bleed on my wounds;
For thus to be reveng'd, were it not worse
Than all that I can suffer?—But EUDOCIA———
Where will she then—Shield her, ye pitying pow'rs,
And

And let me die in peace!

ABU. Hear me once more,
'Tis all I have to offer; mark me now!
CALED has sworn EUDOCIA shall be safe.   [too?

PHO. Ha! safe?——but how? a wretched captive
ABU. He swears she shall be free, she shall be thine.

PHO. Then I am lost indeed————O cruel bounty!
How can I be at once both curs'd and happy?

ABU. The time draws near, and I must quickly leave
         thee;
But first reflect, that in this fatal night
Slaughter and rapine may be loos'd abroad,
And while they roam with undistinguish'd rage,
Should she thou lov'st—well may'st thou start—be made,
Perhaps unknown, some barbarous soldier's prey,
Should she then fall a sacrifice to lust,
Or brutal fury————

PHO. O—this pulls my heart-strings!   [Falls.
Earth open—save me, save me from that thought,
There's ruin in it, 'twill, it will undo me.

ABU. Nay do not plunge thyself in black despair;
Look up, poor wretch, thou art not shipwreck'd yet.
Behold an anchor, am not I thy friend?
Yet hear me, and be blest————

PHO. [*rising.*] Hah! who, what art thou? [*Raving.*
My friend? that's well; but hold—are all friends
         honest?
What's to be done?—Hush, hark! what voice is that!

ABU. There is no voice; 'tis yet the dead of night,
The guards, without, keep silent watch around us.

PHO. Again—it calls—'tis She—O lead me to her—
ABU. Thy passion mocks thee with imagin'd sounds.

PHO. Sure 'twas EUDOCIA's voice cry'd out—*Forbear.*
What shall I do?————O Heav'n!

ABU. Heav'n shews thee what.
Nay, now it is too late, see CALED comes
With anger on his brow; quickly withdraw
To the next tent, and there————

PHO. [*Raving.*] What do I see?
DAMASCUS? Conquest! ruin! rapes and murder!
Villains!————Is there no way—O save her, save her!
                    [*Exit with* ABUDAH.
                              Exit.

Enter CALED *and* DARAN.

DAR. Behold, on thy approach they shift their ground.

CAL. 'Tis as thou say'st, he trifles with my mercy.

DAR. Speak, shall I fetch his head?

CAL. No, stay thou here,
I cannot spare thee yet. RAPHAN, go thou [*To an officer.*
But hold—I've thought again,—he shall not die.
Go, tell him he shall live, till he has seen
DAMASCUS sink in flame, 'till he behold
That slave, the woman-idol he adores,
Or giv'n a prize to some brave *Mussulman*,
Or slain before his face; then if he sue
For death as for a boon—perhaps we'll grant it.
                                    [*Exit* RAPHAN.

DAR. The captains wait thy orders.

CAL. Are the troops
Ready to march?

DAR.   They are
          [*The captains pass by as they are nam'd.*
CAL. Where's *Abu-Taleb?*
Alcorash? ——O, your valiant tribes, I thank 'em,
Fled from their standard! Will they now redeem it?
Omar and *Serjabil?*—'tis well, I see 'em.
You know your duty. You, *Abdorraman*,
Must charge with *Raphan* Mourn, thou haughty city!
The bow is bent, nor can'st thou 'scape thy doom.
Who turns his back henceforth, our Prophet curse him!

DAR. But who commands the trusty bands of *Mecca?*
Thou know'st their leader fell in the last fight.

CAL. 'Tis true; thou, DARAN, well deserv'st that
          charge;
I've mark'd what a keen hatred, like my own,
Dwells in thy breast against these Christian dogs.

DAR. Thou dost me right.

CAL. And therefore I'll reward it.
Be that command now thine. And here—this sabre,
Bless'd in the field by MAHOMET himself
At *Chaibar's* prosp'rous fight, shall aid thy arm.

DAR. Thanks, my good chief, with this I'll better
          thank thee   [*Taking the scimitar.*

CAL. Myself will lead the troops of the Black-standard,
And at the Eastern gate begin the storm.

                                        DAR.

DAR But why do we not move ?. 'twill foon be day
Methinks I'm cold, and wou'd grow warm with action.

CAL. Then hafte and tell ABUDAH————O thou'it
welcome.

Enter A B U D A H.

Thy charge awaits thee. Where's the ftubborn captive?

ABU. Indeed he's brave. I left him for a moment
In the next tent. He's fcarcely yet himfelf.

CAL. But is he ours?

ABU. The threats of death are nothing ;
Tho' thy laft meffage fhook his foul, as winds
On the bleak hills bend down fome lofty pine ;
Yet ftill he held his root ; till I found means,
Abating fomewhat of thy firft demand,
If not to make him wholly ours, at leaft
To gain fufficient to our end.

CAL. Say how ?

ABU Oft he inclin'd, oft ftarted back ; at laft,
When juft confenting, for a while he paus'd,
Stood fix'd in thought, and lift his eyes to Heav'n;
Then, as with frefh recover'd force, cry'd out
Renounce my faith, Never————I anfwer'd, No,
That now he fhould not do it.

CAL. How ?

ABU. Yet hear.
For fince I faw him now fo loft in paffion,
That muft be left to his more temperate thoughts.
Mean time I urg'd, conjur'd, at laft conftrain'd him
By all he held moft dear ; nay, by the voice
Of Providence, that call'd him now to fave,
With her he lov'd, perhaps the lives of thoufands.
No longer to refift his better fate,
But join his arms in prefent action with us,
And fwear he would be faithful.

CAL. What, no more?
Then he's a Chriftian ftill?

ABU. Have patience yet ·
For if by him we can furprife the city————.

CAL. Say'ft thou?

ABU. Hear what's agreed ; but on the terms
That ev'ry unrefifting life be fpar'd.

I

I shall command some chosen faithful bands.
PHOCYAS will guide us to the gate, from whence
He late escap'd, nor do we doubt but there
With ease to gain admittance.

    CAL. This is something.
And yet I do not like this half-ally————————
Is he not still a Christian ?————but no matter————
Mean time I will attack the Eastern gate ;
Who first succeeds gives entrance to the rest.
Hear, all !————Prepare ye now for boldest deeds,
And know the Prophet will reward your valour.
Think that ye all to certain triumph move ;
Who falls in fight, yet meets the prize above.
There, in the gardens of eternal spring,
While birds of paradise around you sing,
Each, with his blooming beauty by his side,
Shall drink rich wines that in full rivers glide ;
Breathe fragrant gales o'er fields of spice that blow,
And gather fruits immortal as they grow
Ecstatic bliss shall your whole powers employ,
And ev'ry sense be lost in ev'ry joy.   [*Exeunt.*

ACT IV. SCENE I.

SCENE, *A great square in the city, before the
Governor's palace.*

Enter ABUDAH, *Saracen captains and soldiers ; with*
EUMENES, HERBIS, *and others of the Christians
unarm'd.*

EUMENES.

IT must be so————Farewel, devoted walls !————
  To be surpriz'd thus ?—Hell and all ye fiends,
How did ye watch this minute for destruction !

    HERB. We've been betray'd by riot and debauch ;
Curse on the traitor-guard !

    EUM. The guard above,
Did that sleep too ?

             E   ABU.

ABU. Chriſtians, complain no more.
What you have aſk'd is granted,   Are ye men,
And dare ye queſtion thus, with bold impatience,
Eternal Juſtice '—Know, the doom from Heav'n
Falls on your towers, reſiſtleſs as the bolt
That fires the cedars on your mountain tops.
Be meek, and learn with humble awe to bear
The mitigated ruin.   Worſe had follow'd,
Had ye oppos'd our numbers.   Now you're ſafe,
Quarter and liberty are giv'n to all ;
And little do ye think how much ye owe
To one brave enemy, whom yet ye know not.

Enter A R T A M O N *haſtily.*

ART. All's loſt '——Ha——Who are theſe'?
EUM. All's loſt indeed.
Yield up thy ſword, if thou wou'dſt ſhare our ſafety.
Thou com'ſt too late to bring us news.
ABU. O————no.
The news I bring is from the Eaſtern guard.
CALED has forc'd the gate, and——but he's here
    [*A cry without.*] Fly, fly, they follow——Quarter,
        mercy, quarter '
            [*Several perſons as purſu'd run over the ſtage*
    CALED. [*without.*] No quarter ! kill, I ſay, are they
        not Chriſtians ?
More blood ! our Prophet aſks it.————
            He enters with DARAN, *&c.*
What, ABUDAH ?
Well met '——but wherefore are theſe looks of peace ?
Why ſleeps thy ſword ?
ABU. CALED, our taſk is over.
Behold the chiefs, they have reſign'd the palace.
    CAL. And ſworn t' obey our law ?
    ABU. No.
    CAL. Then fall on.   [ſpar'd
    ABU. Hold yet, and hear me—Heav'n by me has
The ſword its cruel taſk   On eaſy terms
We've gain'd a bloodleſs conqueſt.
    CAL. I renounce it.
Curſe on thoſe terms, the city's mine by ſtorm.
Fall on, I ſay————

                                                    ABU

ABU. Nay then, I swear ye shall not
CAL. Ha!———Who am I?
ABU. The general, and I know
What reverence is your due.

      [CALED *signs to his men to fall on.*

————— —————Nay, he who stirs,
First makes his way thro' me. My honour's pledg'd;
Rob me of that who dares. [*They stop*] I know thee,
      CALED,
Chief in command, bold, valiant, wise and faithful:
But yet remember I'm a Mussulman;
Nay more, thou know'st, companion of the Prophet,
And what we vow is sacred.

    CAL. Thou'rt a Christian,
I swear thou art, and hast betray'd the faith.
Curse on thy new allies!

     ABU. No more———— this strife
But ill beseems the servants of the CALIPH,
And casts reproach—Christians, withdraw a while,
I pledge my life to answer the conditions———

      [*Exeunt* EUMENES, HERBIS, &c.

Why CALED, do we thus expose ourselves
A scorn to nations that despise our law?
Thou call'st me Christian————What? Is it because
I prize my plighted faith, that I'm a Christian?
Come, 'tis not well, and if————

     CAL. What terms are yielded?

     ABU. Leave to depart, to all that will; an oath
First giv'n, no more to aid the war against us,
An unmolested march. Each citizen
To take his goods, not more than a mule's burden;
The chiefs six mules, and ten the governor.
Besides some few slight arms for their defence
Against the mountain-robbers.

     CAL. Now, by MAHOMET,
Thou hast equipp'd an army.

     ABU. Canst thou doubt
The greater part by far will choose to stay,
Receive our law, or pay th' accustom'd tribute?
What fear we then from a few wretched bands
Of scatter'd fugitives?————besides, thou know'st
What towns of strength remain yet unsubdu'd.
Let us appear this once like generous victors,

So future conquests shall repay this bounty,
And willing provinces e'en court subjection.

CAL. Well——beit on thy head, if worse befall!
This once I yield——but see it then proclaim'd
Thro' all DAMASCUS, that who will depart
Must leave the place this instant—Pass, move on.

[*Exeunt.*

SCENE II. *The outside of a Nunnery.*

EUDOCIA.

Darkness is fled, and yet the morning light
Gives me more fears than did night's deadly gloom.
Within, without, all, all are foes——O PHOCYAS,
Thou art perhaps at rest, wou'd I were too!

[*After a pause.*

This place has holy charms, rapine and murder
Dire not approach it, but are aw'd to distance.
I've heard that e'en these infidels have spai'd
Walls sacred to devotion——World, farewel!
Here will I hide me, 'till the friendly grave
Open its arms and shelter me for ever.

[*Exit.*

Enter PHOCYAS.

PHO. Did I not hear the murmurs of a voice,
This way?—a woman's too?—and seem'd complaining!
Hark!—No—O torture! Whither shall I turn me?
I've search'd the palace rooms in vain; and now,
I know not why, some instinct brought me hither —
'Twas here last night we met; dear, dear EUDOCIA!
Might I once more—[*Going out he meets her entering.*

EUD. Who calls the lost EUDOCIA?
Sure 'tis a friendly voice.

PHO. 'Tis she——O rapture!

EUD. Is't possible——my PHOCYAS?——

PHO. My EUDOCIA!
Do I yet call thee mine?

EUD. Do I yet see thee?
Yet hear thee speak?——O how hast thou escap'd
From barbarous swords, and men that know not mercy

PHO. I've borne a thousand deaths since our last
    parting.

B

But wherefore do I talk of death?——for now,
Me thinks, I'm rais'd almost to life immortal,
And feel I'm blest beyond the pow'r of change.

E<small>UD</small>. O yet beware————lest some event unknown
Again shou'd part us.

P<small>HO</small> [*Aside.*] Heav'n avert the omen!
None can, my fair, none shall.

E<small>UD</small> Alas! thy transport
Makes thee forget; is not the city taken?

P<small>HO</small>. It is.

E<small>UD</small>. And are we not beset with foes?

P<small>HO</small>. There are no foes—or none to thee—no danger.

E<small>UD</small>. No foes?

P<small>HO</small>. I know not how to tell thee yet————
But think, E<small>UDOCIA</small>, that my matchless love
And wondrous causes pre-ordain'd, conspiring,
For thee have triumph'd o'er the fiercest foes,
And turn'd 'em into friends.

E<small>UD</small>. Amazement! Friends?————
O all ye guardian powers!—Say on—O lead me,
Lead me thro' this dark maze of Providence
Which thou hast trod, that I may trace thy steps
With silent awe, and worship as I pass.

P<small>HO</small>. Enquire no more—thou shalt know all here-
        after————
Let me conduct thee thence——

E<small>UD</small>. O whither next?
To what far distant home?————But 'tis enough,
That favour'd thus of Heav'n thou art my guide.
And as we journey on the painful way,
Say, wilt thou then beguile the passing hours,
And open all the wonders of thy story?

P<small>HO</small>. Indulge no more thy melancholly thoughts.
D<small>AMASCUS</small> is thy home.

E<small>UD</small>. And yet thou say'st
It is no longer Ours!——Where is my Father?

P<small>HO</small>. To shew thee too how fate seems every way
To guard thy safety, e'en thy father now,
Wert thou within his pow'r, wou'd stand defeated
Of his tyrannic vow. Thou know'st last night
What hope of aids flatter'd this foolish city;
At break of day th' A<small>RABIAN</small> scouts had seiz'd

E 3

A fecond courier, and from him 'tis learn'd
That on their march the army mutiny'd,
And EUTYCHES was flain.

EUD. And yet, that now ----
Is of the leaft importance to my peace.
But anfwer me; fay, where is now my father?

PHO. Or gone, or juft preparing to depart.

EUD. What! Is our doom revers'd? And is he then
The wretched fugitive?

PHO. Thou heav'nly maid!
To free thee then from every anxious thought,
Know, I've once more, wrong'd as I am, e'en fav'd
Thy father's threaten'd life, nay fav'd DAMASCUS
From blood and flaughter, and from total ruin.
Terms are obtain'd, and general freedom granted
To all that will, to leave in peace the city.

EUD. Is't poffible.—now truft me I cou'd chide thee:
'Tis much unkind to hold me thus in doubt;
I pr'y thee clear thefe wonders.

PHO. 'Twill furprife thee,
When thou fhalt know————

EUD. What?

PHO. To what deadly gulphs
Of horror and defpair, what cruel ftraits
Of agonizing thought I have been driv'n
This night 'ere my perplex'd bewilder'd foul
Cou'd find its way—thou faidft that thou wou'dft chide;
I fear thou wilt; indeed I have done that
I cou'd have wifh'd t' avoid————but for a caufe
So lovely, fo belov'd————

EUD. What doft thou mean?
I'll not indulge a thought that thou cou'dft do
One act unworthy of thyfelf, thy honour,
And that firm zeal againft thefe foes of heav'n,
Which won my heart at firft to fhare in all
Thy dangers and thy fame, and wifh thee mine.
Thou cou'dft not fave thy life by means inglorious.

PHO. Alas! thou know'ft me not—I'm man, frail
        man,
To error born; and who that's man is perfect?
To fave my life? O no, well was it rifk'd
For thee! had it been loft, 'twere not too much,

And

And thou but fafe ;——O what wou'dft thou have faid,
If I had rifk'd my foul to fave EUDOCIA ?

EUD. Ha ! Speak—O no, be dumb—it cannot be !
And yet thy looks are chang'd, thy lips grow pale.
Why doft thon fhake ?——alas ! I tremble too!
Thou cou'dft not, haft not fworn to *Mahomet* ?

PHO. No—I fhou'd firft have dy'd—nay giv'n up
  thee :

EUD. O PHOCYAS ! Was it well to try me thus ?——
And yet another deadly fear fucceeds.
How came thefe wretches hither ? Who reviv'd
Their fainting arms to unexpected triumph ?
For while thou fought'ft, and fought'ft the Chriftian
  caufe,
Thefe batter'd walls were rocks impregnable,
Their tow'rs of adamant. But O I fear
So ne act of thine————

PHO. No more————I'll tell thee all ;
But pr'ythee do not frown on me, EUDOCIA !——
I found the wakeful foe in midnight council
Refolv'd 'ere day to make a frefh attack,
Keen for revenge, and hungry after flaughter.
Cou'd my rack'd foul bear that, and think of thee !
Nay, think of thee expos'd a helplefs prey
To fome fierce ruffian's violating arms ?
O had the world been mine in that extreme
I fhould have giv'n whole provinces away,
Nay all————and thought it little for thy ranfom !

EUD. For this then,————oh————thou haft betray'd
  the city ?
Diftruftful in the righteous pow'rs above,
That ftill protect the chafte and innocent :
And to avert a feign'd uncertain danger,
Thou haft brought certain ruin on thy country !

PHO. No, thou forget'ft the friendly terms——the
  fword,
Which threaten'd to have fill'd thefe ftreets with blood,
Is fheath'd in peace ; thy father, thou, and all
The citizens are fafe, uncaptiv'd, free.

EUD. Safe ? free ? O no—Life, freedom, ev'ry good,
Turns to a curfe, if fought by wicked means.
Yet fure it cannot be! are thefe the terms

On which we meet?——No——we can never meet
On terms like these; the hand of death itself
Cou'd not have torn us from each others arms
Like this dire act, this more than fatal blow!
In death, the soul and body only part
To meet again, and be divorc'd no more,
But now——

   PHO. Ha! lightning blast me! Strike me,
Ye vengeful bolts! if this is my reward!
Are these my hop'd-for joys? Is this the welcome
The wretched PHOCYAS meets, from her he lov'd
More than life, fame—e'en to his foul's distraction?

   EUD. Hadst thou not help'd the slaves of *Mahomet*,
To spread their impious conquest o'er thy country,
What welcome was there in EUDOCIA's power
She had withheld from PHOCYAS? but alas!
'Tis thou hast blasted all our joys for ever,
And cut down hope like a poor short-liv'd flower,
Never to grow again!

   PHO. Cruel EUDOCIA!
If in my heart's deep anguish I've been forc'd
A while from what I was—dost thou reject me?
Think of the cause——

   EUD. The cause! There is no cause!
Not universal nature could afford
A cause for this; what were dominion, pomp,
The wealth of nations, nay of all the world,
The world itself, or what a thousand worlds,
If weigh'd with faith-unspotted, heav'nly truth,
Thoughts free from guilt, the empire of the mind,
And all the triumphs of a godlike breast
Firm and unmov'd in the great cause of virtue?

   PHO. How shall I answer thee?——my soul is aw'd,
And trembling owns th'eternal force of reason!
But oh! can nothing then atone, or plead
For pity from thee?

   EUD. Canst thou yet undo
The deed that's done, recal the time that past?
O call back yesterday, call back last night,
Tho with its fears, its dangers, its distress;
Bid the fair hours of innocence return,
When, in the lowest ebb of changeful fortune,

                      Thou

Thou wert more glorious in EUDOCIA's eyes
Than all the pride of monarchs !—but that deed—

PHO. No more—thou waken'st in my tortur'd heart
The cruel, confcious worm that ftings to madnefs.
O I'm undone !———I know it, and can bear
To be undone for thee, but not to lofe thee.

EUD. Poor wretch ! —— I pity thee !—but art thou
        PHOCYAS ?
The man I lov'd ?———I cou'd have dy'd with thee
'Ere thou didft this , then we had gone together,
A glorious pair, and foar'd above the ftars,
Bright as the ftars themfelves ; and as we pafs'd
The heav'nly roads and milky ways of light,
Had heard the bleft inhabitants with wonder
Applaud our fpotlefs love   But never, never
Will I be made the curft reward of treafon,
To feal thy doom, to bind a hellifh league,
And to infure thy everlafting woe.

PHO. What league ?—'tis ended—I renounce it—
        thus   [*Kneels.*
I bend to Heav'n and thee———O thou divine,
Thou matchlefs image of all perfect goodnefs !'
Do thou but pity yet the wretched PHOCYAS,
Heav'n will relent, and all may yet be well

EUD. No—we muft part. 'Twill afk whole years of
        forrow
To purge away this guilt.   Then do not think
Thy lofs in me is worth one dropping tear ,
But, if thou wou'dft be reconcil'd to Heav'n,
Firft facrifice to Heav'n that fatal paffion
Which caus'd thy fall—Farewel · forget the loft—
But how fhall I afk that ?———I wou'd have faid,
For thy foul's peace, forget the loft EUDOCIA
Canft thou forget her ?———O the killing torture
To think 'twas love, excefs of love, divorc'd us ?
Farewel for—ftill I cannot fpeak that word,
Thefe tears fpeak for me———O Farewel —   [*Exit*
    PHO [*Raving*] For ever !
Return, return and fpeak it, fay for ever '
She's gone———and now fhe joins the fugitives.
And yet fhe did not quite pronounce my doom———
O hear, all gracious Heav'n ! wilt thou at once

                                        Forgive,

Forgive, and O infpire me to fome act
This day, that may in part redeem what's paft !
Profper this day, or let it be my laft.   [*Exit.*

✛✛✛✛✛✛✛✛✛✛✛✛✛✛✛✛✛✛✛✛✛✛✛✛✛✛✛✛✛✛

A C T V.   S C E N E I.

S C E N E, *An open place in the city.*

Enter C A L E D *and* D A R A N *meeting.*

C A L E D.

SOLDIERS, what news ? thou look'ft as thou wert
          angry.
DAR. And durft I fay it, fo, my chief, I am,
I've fpoke—if it offends, my head is thine,
Take it, and I am filent.
CAL. No; fay on.
I know thee honeft, and perhaps I guefs
What knits thy brow in frowns————
DAR. Is this, my leader,
A conquer'd city !—View yon vale of palms :
Behold the vanquifh'd Chriftian triumphs ftill,
Rich in his flight, and mocks thy barren war.
CAL. The vale of palms !
DAR. Beyond thofe hills, the place
Where they agreed this day to meet and halt,
To gather all their forces; there, difguis'd,
Juft now I've view'd their camp—O I cou'd curfe
My eyes for what they've feen.
CAL. What haft thou feen ?
DAR. Why, all DAMASCUS ;—All its foul, its life,
Its heart's-blood, all its treafure, piles of plate,
Croffes enrich'd with gems, arras and filks,
And vefts of gold, unfolded to the fun,
That rival all his luftre.
CAL. How !
DAR. 'Tis true.
The bees are wifely bearing off their honey,
And foon the empty hive will be our own.
                                        CAL.

CAL. So forward too? Curſe on this fooliſh treaty.

DAR. Forward——it looks as they had been forewarn'd
By MAHOMET; the land wears not the face
Of war, but trade; and thou wou'dſt ſwear its mer-
-chants
Were ſending forth their loaded caravans
To all the neighbouring countries.

CAL. [*Aſide.*] Ha! this ſtarts
A lucky thought of MAHOMET's firſt exploit,
When he purſu'd the caravan of *Corafh*,
And from a thouſand mil-believing ſlaves
Wreſted their ill-heap'd goods, transferr'd to thrive
In holier hands, and propagate the faith.——————
{*To* DARAN.] 'Tis ſaid, the emperor had a wardrope here
Of coſtly ſilks.

DAR. That too they have remov'd.

CAL. Dogs! Infidels! 'tis more than was allow'd.

DAR And ſhall we not purſue 'em——robbers! thieves
That ſteal away themſelves and all they're worth,
And wrong the valiant ſoldier of his due.

CAL. [*Aſide*] The CALIPH ſhall know this——he ſhall,
    ABUDAH
is is thy coward bargain——I renounce it.
DARAN will ſtop their march, and make a ſearch.

DAR And ſtrip?

CAL. And kill.

DAR. That's well. And yet I fear
ABUDAH's Chriſtian friend——————

CAL. If poſſible,
He ſhou'd not know of this; no, nor ABUDAH.
By the ſeven heav'ns! his ſoul's a Chriſtian too,
And 'tis by kindred inſtinct he thus ſaves
Their curſed lives, and taints our cauſe with mercy.

DAR. I knew my general wou'd not ſuffer this,
Therefore I've troops prepar'd without the gate,
Juſt mounted for purſuit. Our *Arab* horſe
Will in few minutes reach the place; yet ſtill
I muſt repeat my doubts——that devil PHOCYAS
Will know it ſoon——I met him near the gate,
My nature ſickens at him, and forebodes
I know not what of ill.

CAL. No more, away

With

With thy cold fears————we'll march this very inſtant,
And quickly make this thriftleſs conqueſt good :
The ſword too has been wrong'd, and thirſts for blood.

SCENE II. *A valley full of tents, baggage and har-*
    neſs lying up and down amongſt them   The proſpect
    terminated with palm-trees and hills at a diſtance.

EUMENES, *with officers, attendants, and crouds of the*
    people of DAMASCUS.

EUM. [*Entring*] Sleep on—and angels be thy guard!
———— oft ſlumber
Has gently ſtole her from her griefs a while.
Let none approach the tent.——Are out-guards plac'd
On yonder hills?   [*To an officer.*
    1 OFF. They are.
    EUM. [*ſtriking his breaſt*] DAMASCUS! O————
Still art thou here?——Let me intreat you, friends,
To keep ſtrict order ; I have no command,
And can but now adviſe you.
    1 CIT. You are ſtill
Our head and leader.
    2 CIT   We reſolve t' obey you.
    3 CIT. We're all prepar'd to follow you.
    EUM. I thank you.
The ſun will ſoon go dówn upon our ſorrows,
And 'till to morrow's dawn this is our home :
Mean while, each, as he can, forget his loſs,
And bear the preſent lot ——
    OFF. Sir, I have mark'd
The camp's extent ; 'tis ſtretch'd quite thro' the valley,
I think that more than half the city's here.
    EUM. The proſpect gives me much relief. I'm pleas'd,
My honeſt countrymen, t' obſerve your numbers ;
And yet it fills my eyes with tears — 'tis ſaid
The mighty *Perſian* wept, when he ſurvey'd
His numerous army, but to think 'em mortal ;
Yet he then flouriſh'd in proſperity.
Alas! what's that ?————proſperity ? a harlot
That ſmiles but to betray ! O ſhining ruin !
Thou nurſe of paſſions, and thou bane of virtue !
O ſelf-deſtroying monſter ! that art blind ;

                                        Yet

Yet putt'ſt out reaſon's eyes, that ſtill ſhou'd guide thee;
Then plungeſt down ſome precipice unſeen,
And art no more '——Hear me, all gracious Heav'n!
Let me wear out my ſmall remains of life
Obſcure, content with humble poverty,
Or in afflictions hard but wholeſom ſchool,
If it muſt be——I'll learn to know myſelf,
And that's more worth than empire. But, O Heav'n,
Curſe me no more with proud proſperity!
It has undone me!—HERBIS; where, my friend,
Haſt thou been this long hour?

Enter H E R B I S.

'HER. On yonder ſummit,
To take a farewel proſpect of DAMASCUS.
EUM. And is it worth a look?
HERB. No————I've forgot it.
All our poſſeſſions are a graſp of air;
We're cheated whilſt we think we hold them faſt,
And when they're gone, we know that they were nothing.
But I've a deeper wound.
EUM. Poor good old man!
'Tis true;—thy ſon—there thou'rt indeed unhappy.

Enter A R T A M O N.

What, ARTAMON?—art thou here too?
ART Yes, Sir.
I never boaſted much of my religion,
Yet I've ſome honour and a ſoldier's pride;
I like not theſe new lords.
EUM. Thou'rt brave and honeſt.
Nay we'll not yet deſpair. A time may come
When from theſe brute barbarians we may wreſt
Once more our pleaſant ſeats——Alas! how ſoon
The flatterer Hope is ready with his ſong
To charm us to forgetfulneſs?——No more——
Let that be left to Heav'n,——ſee, HERBIS, ſee,
Methinks we've here a goodly city yet!
Was it not thus our great forefathers liv'd,
In better times?——in humble fields and tents,
With all their flocks and herds, their moving wealth?
See too! where our own *Pharphar* winds his ſtream

F   Thro'

Thro' the long vale, as if to follow us,
And kindly offers his cool wholesom draughts
To ease us in our march! why, this is plenty.

Enter EUDOCIA.

EUM My daughter? —— wherefore haft thou left thy
   tent?
What breaks so soon thy rest?

EUD. Rest is not there,
Or I have sought in vain, and cannot find it;
Oh no——we're wanderers, it is our doom;
There is no rest for us.

EUM. Thou art not well.

EUD. I wou'd, if possible, avoid myself.
I'm better now near you.

EUM. Near me?——alas!
The tender vine so wreaths its folded arms
Around some falling elm!—it wounds my heart
To think thou follow'st but to share my ruin.
I have lost all but thee.

EUD. O say not so.
You have lost nothing, no——you have preserv'd
immortal wealth, your faith inviolate
To Heav'n and to your country. Have you not
Refus'd to join with prosp'rous wicked men,
And hold from them a false inglorious greatness?
Ruin is yonder in DAMASCUS now
The seat abhorr'd of cursed infidels.
Infernal error, like a plague, has spread
Contagion thro' its guilty palaces,
And we are fled from death.

EUM. Heroic maid?
Thy words are balsam to my griefs. EUDOCIA,
I never knew thee till this day; I knew not
How many virtues I had wrong'd in thee.

EUD. If you talk thus you have not yet forgiv'n me

EUM. Forgiv'n thee?—why, for thee it is, thee only
I think Heav'n yet may look with pity on us;
Yes, we must all forgive each other now.
Poor HERBIS too ———we both have been to blame.
O PHOCYAS———but it cannot be recall'd.
Yet were he here, we'd ask him pardon too.

           My

My child !—I meet not to provoke thy tears.

Eud. [*Aside.*] O why is he not here ? why do I see
Thousands of happy wretches, that but seem
Undone, yet still are blest in innocence,
And why was he not one ?

Enter an OFFICER.

1 Off. Where is Eumenes ?

Eum. What means thy breathless haste ?

1 Off. I fear there's danger,
For as I kept my watch, I spy'd afar
Thick clouds of dust, and on a nearer view.
Perceiv'd a body of *Arabian* horse
Moving this way. I saw them wind the hill,
And then lost sight of 'em.

Herb. I saw 'em too,
Where the roads meet on t'other side these hills,
But took them for some band of Christian *Arabs*
Crossing the country.——This way did they move?

1 Off. With utmost speed.

Eum. If they are Christian *Arabs*,
They come as friends , if other, we're secure
By the late terms. Retire a while, Eudocia,
Till I return.   [*Exit* Eudocia.
I'll to the guard myself,
Soldier, lead on the way.

Enter another OFFICER.

2 Off. Arm, arm ! we're ruin'd !
The foe is in the camp.

Eum. So soon ?

2 Off. They've quitted
Their horses, and with sword in hand have forc'd
Our guards , they say they come for plunder.

Eum. Villains !
Sure Caled knows not of this treachery.
Come on——we can fight still. We'll make 'em know
What 'tis to urge the wretched to despair.   [*Exeunt.*
        [*A noise of fighting is heard for some time.*

Enter DARAN, *with a party of* Saracen *soldiers.*

Dar. Let the fools fight at distance.——Here's the
    harvest.

F 2   Reap,

Reap, reap, my countrymen! — Ay; there — first clear
Those further tents———

       [Exeunt soldiers bearing off baggage, &c.
[Looking between the tents.] What's here, a woman? — fair
She seems, and well attir'd! ———— It shall be so,
I'll strip her first, and then————

         [Exit, and returns with EUDOCIA.

EUD *[struggling]* Mercy! O spare me!
Help, save me! — What, no help! — Barbarian! monster!
Heav'n hear my cries.

    DAR. Woman, thy cries are vain,
No help is near.

Enter PHOCYAS.

PHO. Villain, thou ly'st! take that
To loose thy hold—   *[Pushing at him with his spear.*

    DAR. What, thou? my evil spirit!
Is't thou that haunt'st me still? — but thus I thank thee,

        [Offering to strike with his scimitar.
It will not be——lightning for ever blast
This coward arm that fails me! — O vile *Syrian*, *[Falls.*
I'm kill'd——O curse————   *[Dies.*

    PHO. Die then, thy curses cheak thee!————
EUDOCIA!

    EUD. PHOCYAS!————O astonishment!
Then is it thus that Heav'n has heard my pray'rs?
I tremble still——and scarce have power to ask thee
How thou art here? or whence this sudden outrage?

    PHO. *[Walking aside]* The blood ebbs back that fill'd
      my heart, and now
Again her parting farewel awes my soul,
As if 'twere fate, and not to be revok'd.
Will she not now upbraid me? see thy friends!
Are these, are these the villains thou hast trusted?

    EUD. What means this murmur'd sorrow to thyself?
Is it in vain that thou hast rescu'd me
From savage hands? —— Say, what's th' approaching
      danger?

    PHO. Sure ev'ry angel watches o'er thy safety!
Thou see'st 'tis death t' approach thee without awe,
And barbarism itself cannot profane thee.

    EUD. Thou dost not answer; whence are these alarms!
                         PHO.

PHO. Some stores remov'd, and not allow'd by treaty,
Have drawn the *Saracens* to make a search.
Perhaps 'twill quickly be agreed—but Oh!
Thou know'st, EUDOCIA, I'm a banish'd man,
And 'tis a crime I'm here once more before thee;
Else might I speak, 'twere better for the present
If thou would'st leave this place.

    EUD. No———I've a father,
(And shall I leave him?) whom we both have wrong'd,
Or he had not been thus driv'n out, expos'd
The humble tenant of this sheltring vale
For one poor night's repose.———And yet alas?
For this last act how wou'd I thank thee, PHOCYAS?——
I've nothing now but pray'rs and tears to give,
Cold fruitless thanks—but 'tis some comfort yet
That fate allows this short reprieve, that thus
We may behold each other, and once more
May mourn our woes, e'er yet we part———

    PHO. For ever!
'Tis then resolv'd———it was thy cruel sentence,
And I am here to execute that doom.

    EUD. What dost thou mean?

    PHO. [*Kneeling.*] Thus at thy feet———

    EUD. O rise!

    PHO. Never—no, here I'll lay my burden down;
I've try'd its weight, nor can support it longer.
Take thy last look, if yet thy eyes can bear
To look upon a wretch accurst, cast off
By Heav'n and thee———a little longer yet
And I am mingled with my kindred dust,
By thee forgotten and the world———

    EUD. Forbear!
O cruel man! why wilt thou rack me thus?
Didst thou not mark, thou didst, when last we parted,
The pangs, the strugglings of my suffering soul?
That nothing but the hand of Heav'n itself
Cou'd e'er divide me from thee?—Dost thou now
Reproach me thus? or can'st thou have a thought
That I can e'er forget thee?

    PHO. [*Rising.*] Have a care!
I'll not be tortur'd more with thy false pity.

No,

No, I renounce it. See, I am prepar'd.
                                        [*Shewing a dagger.*
Thy cruelty is mercy now——farewel.
And death is now but a releafe from torment.

    EUD. Hold——ftay thee yet——O madnefs of defpair!
And wou'dft thou die? think, e'er thou leap the gulph,
When thou haft trod that dark, that unknown way,
Canft thou return? what if the change prove worfe,
O think, if then————

    PHO. No——thought's my deadlieft foe;
'Tis lingring racks, and flow confuming fires,
And therefore to the grave I'd fly to fhun it.

    EUD. O fatal error——like a reftlefs ghoft,
It will purfue and haunt thee ftill, e'en there,
Perhaps in forms more frightful. Death's a name
By which poor guefling mortals are deceiv'd,
'Tis no where to be found. Thou fly'ft in vain
From life, to meet again with that thou fly'ft.
How wilt thou curfe thy rafhnefs then? how ftart,
And fhudder, and fhrink back? yet how avoid
To put on thy new being?

    PHO. So!——I thank thee!
For now I'm quite undone——I gave up all
For thee before, but this, this bofom friend,
My laft referve. — There—— [*Throws away the dagger.*
Tell me now, EUDOCIA,
Cut off from hope, deny'd the food of life,
And yet forbid to die, what am I now?
Or what will fate do with me?

    EUD. Oh!————   [*Turns away weeping.*
    PHO. Thou weep'ft!
Canft thou fhed tears, and yet not melt to mercy?
O fay, e'er yet returning madnefs feize me,
Is there in all futurity no profpect,
No diftant comfort? Not a glimmering light
To guide me thro' this maze? or muft I now
Sit down in darknefs and defpair for ever?
            [*Here they both continue filent for fome time.*
    PHO Still art thou filent?——Speak, difclofe my doom,
That's now fufpended in this awful moment!
O fpeak——for now my paffions wait thy voice;
My beating heart grows calm, my blood ftands ftill,
                                                Scarcely

Scarcely I live, or only live to hear thee.

EUD. If yet,—but can it be?—I fear—O PHOCYAS,
Let me be silent, still!

PHO. Hear then this last
This only pray'r!—Heav'n will consent to this.
Let me but follow thee, where-e'er thou goest,
But see thee, hear thy voice; be thou my angel,
To guide and govern my returning steps,
'Till long contrition and unweary'd duty
Shall expiate my guilt. Then say, EUDOCIA,
If like a soul anneal'd in purging fires,
After whole years thou feest me white again,
When thou, e'en thou shalt think——

EUD No more——This shakes
My firmest thoughts, and if——

[*Here a cry is heard of persons slaughter'd in the camp.*
——What shrieks of death!
I fear the treacherous foe——again! and louder!
Then they've begun a fatal harvest!——Haste,
Prevent——O wou'dst thou see me more with comfort,
Fly, save 'em, save the threaten'd lives of Christians,
My father and his friends!——I dare not stay——
Heav'n be my guide to shun this gathering ruin.
[*Exit* EUDOCIA.

Manet PHOCYAS *Enter* CALED.

CAL. [*Entering.*] So——Slaughter do thy work!
——These hands look well. [*Looking on his hands.*
The jovial hunter, e're he quits the field
First signs him in the stag's warm vital stream
With stains like these, to shew 'twas gallant sport.
PHOCYAS! Thou'rt met?—But whether thou art here
[*Comes forward.*
A friend or foe I know not; if a friend,
Which is EUMENES' tent?
PHO. Hold——pass no further.
CAL. Say'st thou, not pass?
PHO. No——on thy life no further.
CAL. What, dost thou frown too!—sure thou know'st
     me not! [now,
PHO. Not know thee?—Yes, too well I know thee
O murd'rous fiend! Why all this waste of blood?
Didst

Didſt thou not promiſe——

CAL. Promiſe? Inſolence!
'Tis well, 'tis well——For now I know thee too.
Perfidious mungrel ſlave! Thou double traitor!
Falſe to thy firſt and to thy latter vows!
Villain!——

PHO. That's well—Go on—I ſwear I thank thee.
Speak it again, and ſtrike it thro' my ear!
A villain! Yes, thou mad'ſt me ſo, thou devil!
And mind'ſt me now what to demand from thee.
Give, give me back my former ſelf, my honour,
My country's fair eſteem, my friends, my all——
Thou can'ſt not—O thou robber!—Give me then
Revenge, or death! The laſt I well deſerve,
That yeilded up my ſoul's beſt wealth to thee,
For which accurſt be thou, and curſt thy Prophet!

CAL. Hear'ſt thou this, MAHOMET?——Blaſpheming
      mouth!
For this thou ſoon ſhalt chew the bitter fruit
Of *Zacon's* tree, the food of fiends below.
Go————ſpeed thee thither——
      [*Puſhing at him with his lance, which* PHOCYAS
            puts by, and kills him.
PHO. Go thou firſt thyſelf.
CAL. [*Falling.*] O dog! Thou gnaw'ſt my heart!—
      falſe MAHOMET!
Is this, is this then my reward for——O——   [*Dies.*
                                    [*Exit* PHOCYAS.

*Several parties of Chriſtians and Saracens paſs over the
    farther part of the ſtage fighting. The former are
    beaten. At laſt* EUMENES *rallies them, and makes
    a ſtand. Then enter* ABUDAH *attended.*

ABU. Forbear, forbear, and ſheath thy bloody ſword!
EUM. ABUDAH! is this well!
ABU. No——I muſt own
You've cauſe——O Muſſulmans, look here, behold
Where like a broken ſpear your arm of war
Is thrown to earth!
EUM. Ha! CALED?
ABU. Dumb and breathleſs.
Then thus has Heav'n chaſtis'd us in thy fall,

                                            And

And thee for violated faith ; farewel,
Thou great, but cruel man !
 Eum. This thirst of blood
In his own blood is quench'd.
 Abu. Bear hence his clay
Back to Damascus. Cast a mantle first
O'er this sad sight : so shou'd we hide his faults,——
Now hear, ye servants of the Prophet, hear !
A greater death than this demands your tears,
For know, your Lord the Caliph is no more !
Good Abubeker has breath'd out his spirit
To him that gave it. Yet your Caliph lives,
Lives now in Omar. See, behold his signet,
Appointing me, such is his will, to lead
His faithful armies warring here in *Syria*.
Alas '——Foreknowledge sure of this event
Guided his choice !——obey me then your chief.
For you, O Christians ! know, with speed I came,
On the first notice of this foul design.
Or to prevent it, or repair your wrongs.
Your goods shall be untouch'd, your persons safe,
Nor shall our troops, henceforth, on pain of death,
Molest your march ——If more you ask, 'tis granted.
 Eum. Still just, and brave ! thy virtue wou'd adorns
A purer faith ! Thou better than thy sect,
That dar'st decline from that to acts of mercy !
Pardon, Abudah, if thy honest heart
Makes us e'en wish thee ours.
 Abu. [*Aside.*] O Power supreme,
That mad'st my heart, and know'st its inmost frame !
If yet I err, O lead me into truth,
Or pardon unknown error ! Now, Eumenes,
Friends as we may be, let us part in peace.
         [*Exeunt severally.*

   Enter EUDOCIA *and* ARTAMON.
 Eud. Alas ! but is my father safe ?
 Art. Heav'n knows.
I left him just preparing to engage ;
When doubtful of th' event he bade me haste
To warn his dearest daughter of the danger,
And aid your speedy flight.
            Eud.

EUD. My flight? but whether?
O no—if he is lost—
ART. I hope not so.
The noise is ceas'd.   Perhaps they're beaten off.
We soon shall know,—here's one that can inform us.

Enter first OFFICER.

Soldier, thy looks speaks well.   What says thy tongue?
1 OFF. The foe's withdrawn, ABUDAH has been
here
And has renew'd the terms.   CALED is kill'd——
ART. Hold—first, thank Heav'n for that!
EUD. Where is EUMENES?
1 OFF. I left him well, By his command I came
To search you out, and let you know this news.
I've more, but that——
ART. Is bad, perhaps; so says
This sudden pause.   Well, be it so; let's know it.
'Tis but life's checker'd lot.
1 OFF. EUMENES mourns
A friend's unhappy fall; HERBIS is slain;
A settled gloom seem'd to hang heavy on him,
Th' effect of grief, 'tis thought, for his lost son.
When, on the first attack, like one that sought
The welcome means of death, with desperate valour
He press'd the foe, and met the fate he wish'd.
ART. See, where EUMENES comes!—What's this?
He seems
To lead some wounded friend——Alas! 'tis——
[*They withdraw to one side of the stage.*

Enter EUMENES *leading in* PHOCYAS *with an arrow
in his breast*

EUM. Give me thy wound! O I could bear it for thee,
This goodness melts my heart.   What, in a moment,
Forgetting all thy wrongs, in kind embraces
T' exchange forgiveness thus!
PHO. Moments are few,
And must not now be wasted.   O EUMENES.
Lend me thy helping hand a little farther;
O where, where is she?
[*They advance.*
EUM. Look, look here EUDOCIA!

Behold

Behold a fight that calls for all our tears.

EUD. PHOCYAS, and wounded!—O what cruel hand—

PHO. No, 'twas a kind one—Spare thy tears, EU-
    DOCIA!

For mine are tears of joy.——

EUD. Is't possible?   [pray'r,

PHO. 'Tis done—the Pow'rs supreme have heard my
And prosper'd me with some fair deeds this day.
I've fought once more, and for my friends, my country.
By me the treacherous chiefs are flain; a while
I ftopp'd the foe, till, warn'd by me before
Of this their fudden march, ABUDAH came;
But firft this random fhaft had reach'd my breaft.
Life's mingled fcene is o'er——'tis thus that Heav'n
At once chaftifes, and I hope accepts me;
And now I wake as from the fleep of death.

EUD. What fhall I fay to thee, to give thee comfort?

PHO. Say only thou forgiv'ft me——O EUDOCIA!
No longer now my dazzled eyes behold thee
Thro' paffion's mifts; my foul now gazes on thee,
And fees thee lovelier in unfading charms,
Bright as the fhining angel hoft that ftood
Whilft I——but there, it fmarts——

EUD. Look down, look down,
Ye pitying Pow'rs! and heal his pious forrow!

EUM. 'Tis not too late, we hope, to give thee help.
See! yonder is my tent. We'll lead thee thither.
Come, enter there, and let thy wound be dref'd.
Perhaps it is not mortal.

PHO. No? not mortal?
No flattery now. By all my hopes hereafter,
For the world's empire I'd not lofe this death!
Alas! I but keep in my fleeting breath
A few fhort moments, till I have conjur'd you
That to the world you witnefs my remorfe
For my paft errors, and defend my fame.
For know——foon as this pointed fteel's drawn out
Life follows thro' the wound.

EUD. What doft thou fay?
O touch not yet the broken fprings of life?
A thoufand tender thoughts rife in my foul.
How fhall I give them words? O, till this hour

I

I fcarce have tafted woe !——this is indeed
To part——but oh——

PHO. No more——Death is now painful !
But fay, my friends, whilft I have breath to afk,
(For ftill methinks all your concerns are mine)
Whither have you defign'd to bend your journey ?

EUM. *Conftantinople* is my laft retreat,
If Heav'n indulge my wifh ; there I've refolv'd
To wear out the dark winter of my life,
An old man's ftock of days, I hope not many.

EUD. There will I dedicate myfelf to Heav'n.
O PHOCYAS, for thy fake, no rival elfe
Shall e'er poffefs my heart. My father too
Confents to this my vow. My vital flame
There, like a taper on the holy altai,
Shall wafte away ; till Heav'n relenting hear
Inceffant pray'rs for thee and for myfelf,
And wing my foul to meet with thine in blifs.
For in that thought I find a fudden hope,
As if infpir'd, fprings in my breaft, and tells me
That thy repenting fiaìty is forgiv'n,
And we fhall meet again, to part no more.

PHO. [*Plucking out the arrow*] Then all is done—
'twas the laft pang——at length
I've giv'n up thee, and the world now is—nothing.

EUM. Alas! he falls. Help, ARTAMON, fupport him.
Look, how he bleeds! Let's lay him gently down ;
Night gathers faft upon him——fo—look up,
Or fpeak, if thou haft life——Nay then—my daughter!
She faints——Help there, and bear her to her tent.

[EUDOCIA *is carry'd off.*

ART. [*Weeping afide.*] I thank ye, eyes ! this is but
decent tribute.
My heart was full before.

EUM. O PHOCYAS, PHOCYAS !
Alas ! he hears not now, nor fees my forrows !
Yet will I mourn for thee, thou gallant youth !
As for a fon——So let me call thee now !
A much-wrong'd friend ! and an unhappy Hero !
A fruitlefs zeal, yet all I now can fhew !
Tears vainly flow for errors learn'd too late,
When timely caution fhould prevent our fate.

[*Exeunt omnes*

E P I

EPILOGUE,

Spoken by Mr. WILKS.

WELL, Sirs; you've seen, his passion to approve,
A desperate lover give up all for love,
All but his faith ;—Methinks now I can spy,
Among you airy sparks, some who wou'd cry,
Phoo, pox !—for that—what need of such a pother ?
For one faith left, he wou'd have got another.——
True: 'twas your very case.   Just what you say,
Our rebel fools were ripe for, t'other day ;
Tho' disappointed now, they're wiser grown,
And, with much grief—are forc'd to keep their own.
These generous madmen *gratis* fought their ruin,
And set no price, not they ! on their undoing.
For gain, indeed, we've others wou'd not dally, ⎫
Or with stale principles stand shilli—shall I— ⎬
You'll find all their religion in CHANGE-ALLEY. ⎭
There all pursue, by better means or worse,
IAGO's rule, *Put money in thy purse.*
For tho' you differ still in speculation ;
For why——each head is wiser than the nation !
Tho' points of faith for ever will divide you,
And bravely you declare—none e'er shall ride you,
In practice all agree, and every man
Devoutly strives to get what wealth he can:

All

All parties at this golden altar bow,
GAIN, pow'rful GAIN's the new religion now.

But leave we this—Since in this circle smile
So many shining beauties of our Isle,
Who to more generous ends direct their aim,
And shew us virtue in its fairest frame;
To these with pride the Author bid me say,
'Twas for your sex he chiefly wrote this Play;
And if in one bright character you find
Superior honour, and a noble mind,
Know from the life EUDOCIA's charms he drew,
And hopes the piece shall live, that copies you;
Sure of success, he cannot miss his end,
If ev'ry BRITISH Heroine prove his fiend.

P R O·

PROLOGUE.

Spoken by Lord SANDWICH.

WHEN arts and arms, beneath ELIZA's fmile,
Spread wide their influence o'er this happy ifle ;
A golden reign, uncurs'd with party-rage,
That foe to tafte, and tyrant of our age ;
'E)e all our learning in a libel lay,
And all our talk, in politics, or play :
The Statefman oft would foothe his toils with wit ;
What SPENCER fung, and nature's SHAKESPEAR writ ;
Or to the laurel'd grove, at times, retire,
There, woo the Mufe, and wake the moving lyre.

As fair examples, like afcending morn,
The world at once enlighten and adorn ;
From them diffus'd, the gentle arts of peace
Shot bright'ning o'er the land, with fwift increafe ;
Rough nature foften'd into grace and eafe ;
Senfe grew polite, and fcience fought to pleafe.

RELIEV'D from yon rude *Scene* of party-din,
Where open bafenefs vyes with fecret fin,
And fafe embower'd in WOBURN's * airy groves,
Let us recall the times our tafte approves ;

* The *Siege of Damafcus* was acted at *Woburn*, by the
Duke of BEDFORD, the Earl of SANDWICH, and fome
other perfons of diftinction, in the month of *May* 1743.

Awaken

Awaken to our aid the mourning *Mufe* ;
Thro' every bofom tender thoughts infufe ;
Melt, angry faction into moral fenfe,
And to his guefts a BEDFORD's foul difpenfe.

AND now, while *Spring* extends her fmiling reign,
Green on the mountain, flowery in the plain ;
While genial *Nature* breathes, from hill and dale,
Health, fragrance, gladnefs, in the living gale ;
The various foftnefs, ftealing thro' the heart,
Impreffions, fweetly focial, will impart.
When fad EUDOCIA pours her hopelefs woe,
The tear of pity will unbidden flow !
When erring PHOCYAS, whom wild paffions blind,
Holds up himfelf a mirror for mankind ;
An equal eye on our own hearts we turn,
Where frailties lurk, where fond affections burn ;
And confcious, Nature is in all the fame,
We mourn the guilty, while the guilt we blame !

F I N I S.

THE

CHRISTIAN HERO:

A

TRAGEDY.

Written by Mr. LILLO.

EDINBURGH:

Printed for A. DONALDSON, at *Pope's* Head
oppofite the Exchange.

M,DCC,LIX.

PROLOGUE, spoken by Mr. *Cibber*.

SAcred to virtue, liberty, and truth,
The mufes bloom in everlafting youth.
Prefs'd, like the palm, they rife beneath their weight,
And foar above the reach of time, or fate.
When brafs, or marble, faithlefs to their truft,
No longer bear the name, nor guard the duft
Of kings, or heroes, to their charge confign'd,
But yield to age, and leave no track behind;
The poet's pen, with never dying lays,
Preferves their fame and celebrates their praife.

Let artful *Maro*, or bold *Lucan* tell,
How regal *Troy*, or *Rome*, more awful, fell;
Nations deftroy'd revive, loft empires fhine,
And freedom glows in each immortal line.
In vain would faction, war, or lawlefs power,
Which mar the patriot's fcheme, his fame devour;
When bards, by their fuperior force, can fave,
From dark oblivion and defeat the grave.
Say, *Britons*, muft this art forfake your ifle,
And leave, to vagrant apes, her native foil?
Muft fhe, the deareft friend that freedom knows,
Driv'n from her feat, feek refuge with her foes?
Forbid fo great a fhame, and fave the age
From fuch reproach, you patrons of the ftage.

Since well we know, there's not a theme fo dear,
As virtuous freedom, to a *Britifh* ear;
T' indulge fo juft a tafte, to night we fing
A pious Hero, and a patriot King;
By nature form'd, by providence defign'd
To fcourge ambition, and to right mankind;
Such *Cafiriot* was. O might it but appear,
That he retains the leaft refemblance here!
Should but the fmalleft portion of that fire,
Which fill'd his ample breaft our fcenes infpire,
The abject flave, to his reproach, fhall fee,
That fuch as dare deferve it, may be free:
And confcious tyranny confefs, with fhame,
That blind ambition wanders from her aim,
While virtue leads her votaries to fame.

DRAMATIS PERSONÆ.

TURKS.

AMURATH.	Mr. QUIN.
MAHOMET.	Mr. W. MILLS.
OSMYN.	Mr. BERRY.
KISLER AGA.	Mr. HEWIT.

CHRISTIANS.

SCANDERBEG.	Mr. MILWARD.
ARANTHES.	Mr. MILLS.
AMASIK.	Mr. CIBBER.
PAULINUS.	Mr. WINSTONE.

WOMEN.

HELLENA.	Mrs. THURMOND.
ALTHEA.	Mrs. BUTLER.
CLEORA.	Mrs. PRITCHARD.

Guards, Mutes, Eunuchs and Attendants.

Scene, the Plain and Mountains near Croia, *the Metropolis of* Epirus.

THE
CHRISTIAN HERO.

A
TRAGEDY.

ACT I. SCENE I.

A royal pavilion. HELLENA *on a Sofa in a melancholy posture.* CLEORA *attending near her. Eunuchs, mutes, singers and dancers.*

SONG.

The regent of night with her beams
Had chequer'd each valley and grove,
And swell'd with her influence the streams,
When Fatima, *pining for love,*
To the ocean, despair for her guide,
Repair'd for relief from her pain;
Where plunging, receive me, she cried,
I'm fair, young, and royal in vain.

HELLENA *rises and comes forward.*

HEILENA.

NO more, CLEORA! I accept thy love,
But thy officious kindness is in vain.
It is not music, nor the sprightly dance,
The harmony of motion, or of sound,
That can asswage my grief.
  CLE Let all retire.   [*Exeunt Eunuchs, &c.*
How long, my royal mistress! will you soothe

This

This secret, pining grief? How long, averse
To ev'ry dawn of joy, thus seek retirement;
And shun the gay delights, the pomp and power,
That ever wait the daughter of our Sultan,
And first of womankind?

HEL. How long shall love
And torturing despair, like ling'ring fevers,
Feed on the springs of life, and drink my blood?
How long shall AMURATH, my awful father,
Tho' press'd and overwhelm'd with disappointments,
Provoke the malice of his adverse stars,
And urge his own destruction; whilst in vain,
With unrelenting hatred, he pursues
Whom Heav'n protects, th'ever victorious Hero
Of *Epirus*.

CLE. Thus do you always talk,
Of love and death, despair and the *Epirot*.
Why will you ever strive to hide the cause,
The cruel cause of all this mighty anguish?
Believe me, Princess! 'tis better to intrust
A faithful slave, than keep the secret thus
To rack your breast, 'twill ease those pains——

HEL. That death
Alone can cure; but yet, my best CLEORA!
Such is thy truth, thy tenderness and love,
I can deny thee nought. Yes, thou shalt know
All thou desir'st, and share the very heart
Of sad HELLENA ——You must think I love.——
What else cou'd make thy Princess far more wretched
Than the meanest slave, and who but *Cashiot*
Cou'd merit so sublime a flame as mine?

CLE. 'Tis as I fear'd: she's lost beyond redemption.
[*Aside.*

HEL. A royal hostage to my father's court
When young he came, who lov'd him as a son,
I as a brother; so I fondly thought,
Nor found my error, 'till the fatal flame,
That now consumes me, cherish'd by my weakness,
Was grown too great, too fierce to be control'd
O matchless Prince! who can display thy worth?
Thou favourite of Heav'n, and first of men!
In courts more soft, more lovely, more attractive,

Than

Than thofe fair youths who with eternal bloom
Enjoy the fragrant manfions of the bleft;
In council wifer than a whole divan;
In anger awful; and in war as fierce
As thofe bright minifters, whom Heav'n fends forth
To punifh the prefuming fons of men;
In juftice th' image of that facred power,
Whom he ftill ferves with moft unfeign'd devotion;
Like him in mercy too, in bounty like him,
Excelling in magnificence the Princes
Of th' eaft, yet temperate and felf-denying
As a dervife ——Who know, and love thee not,
Avow their malice and contempt of virtue.

   CLE. Think, Princefs! think what 'tis you fay; of
        whom
It is you fpeak. Can he, that cruel Chriftian,
That enemy t'our Prophet and your father,
Deferve fuch praife from you;

   HEL. Unjuft CLEORA!
To call him cruel—But thou know'ft him not;
Or fure thy gentle nature wou'd abhor
To wrong him thus. And wherefore doft thou urge
His diff'rent faith to me? Love bufies not
Himfelf with reconciling creeds, nor heeds
The jarrings of contentious priefts: from courts
To fhades, from fhades to courts he flies
To conquer hearts, and overthrow diftinction,
Treating alike the monarch and the flave;
But fhuns the noify fchool, and leaves the race
Of proud, litigious men to their own folly,
Who, wife in words alone, confume their days
In fierce debate, nor know the end of life.

   CLE. Now I no longer wonder you contemn'd
AMASIE and his flame.

   HEL. O name him not,
The moft detefted traitor, who, tho' next
In blood, and late the deareft friend of his
Indulgent Prince, without a caufe renounc'd
His faith, his country, and his vow'd allegiance.

   CLE. Say not without a caufe, his love to you——

   HEL. Infolent flave! Ambitious, bloody traitor!
To claim my love for cruelty and fraud!

Muft

Muſt I have been a recompence for murder!
For regicide, the murder of his king!
But his defeat has freed me from that danger :
My father now retracts his former promiſe,
And treats him with averſion and contempt.

CLE. May treaſon ever meet the like reward ——
But ſee the man we ſpeak of comes this way.

HEL. I wou'd avoid him, do thou hear his meſſage,
His name is hateful, but whene'er I ſee him,
My blood runs back, my ſinews all relax,
And life itſelf ſeems ready to forſake me

[*Exit* HELLENA.

Enter AMASIE

CLE. What wou'd you Prince?

AMA I am inform'd the Sultan
Paſſed this way, and came in hopes t' have found him
With the princeſs

CLE Your hopes deceiv'd you, ſir.

AMA May I not ſee
The Princeſs?

CLE. No.

AMA I bring her happy news.

CLE. Nor happineſs, nor truth can come from thee;
For ev'ry word, and ev'ry thought of thine
Are full of deep deceit, and threaten miſchief.

(*Exit* CLEORA.

AMASIE *alone.*
Seen and avoided !——rated by her ſlave!——
Suſpected by the Sultan!——Scorn'd by all!——
Is this the gratitude of *Turkiſh* courts?
This my reward for Heav'n and honour loſt?——
Soul-poiſoning envy, eldeſt born of hell,
Thou ſin of devils, and their torment too,
To what contempt, what mis'ry haſt thou brought me?
Ill tim'd reflection!——I ſhall ſtill ſucceed——
Love and ambition, hatred and revenge——
There's not a wiſh my reſtleſs ſoul has form'd,
But ſhall be quickly crown'd——Then whence this
                anguiſh?

Sure

Sure 'tis much harder to attain Perfection
In ill, than to be truly good.——The Sultan——

Enter A M U R A T H *and* V I S I E R.

AM. Away; my fame is loft; my 'laurels won
With pain and toil, and water'd with my blood,
That well I hop'd would flourish o'er my grave;
When I that planted them shou'd be but duft,
Are wither'd all. O! wherefore did I tempt,
In the declining winter of my age,
The vigour of a youthful rebel's arms?
Whofe curft fuccefs, 'gainft fuch prodigious odds,
Makes credibility doubt what fhe fees,
And truth appear like falfehood.

AMA. Mighty Sultan!——

AM What wou'dft thou, flave!
Thou renegade, thou fpy!
Hence from my fight: avant, perfidious traitor.

VIS. My ever gracious lord, you wrong the prince,
None can be more devoted to your fervice.

AM. 'Tis falfe. Did he not lead my Spahi's forth
With hate profeft, and boafts of fure revenge
On SCANDERBEG; then leave my gallant troops
To fwell the triumph, and to glut the rage
Of that damn'd, damn'd deftroyer of the faithful.

VIS. O righteous Heav'n! when will thy judgments
ceafe?
For fix revolving moons have we in vain
Befieg'd yon city, proud, imperious *Croia*;
With famine, peftilence, and SCANDERBEG
More terrible than both, like threat'ning meteors,
Hov'ring o'er our heads. Our ftrength's confum'd:
By painful watchings and inceffant toils,
Do not our numbers ev'ry hour decreafe?
Are we not all devoted to deftruction?
Thofe that efcape the plague, of hunger die;
Or fav'd from famine, perifh by the fword.
Yet to behold you thus, burning with rage,
And tortur'd by defpair, afflicts us worfe
Than all our other griefs. Why will you ftill refufe
The only help your prefent ftate admits,
That fov'reign balm for minds like yours difeas'd,

B   And

And cure for ev'ry ill——All-healing patience?

AM. Name patience again, while th' *Epirot* lives,
And lives victorious, and thou art thyself
A base, insulting traitor. Hear me, *Allah*,
If thou art ought beside an empty name,
If thou dost still exist, as priests affirm,
Decree our fate, and govern all below ;
Behold, and aid a cause so much your own.
To slaves, to subjects, and to priests give patience,
But if it be within your power to grant
Ought that is worthy of a monarch's pray'r,
Give me revenge, or I'll renounce thy worship.
                                    (*Shouts.*
Ha ! whence those loud, those joyful acclamations.

AMA But that it pleas'd my lord to strike me dumb,
I had ere this inform'd him of the cause.
Just Heav'n, at length indulgent to your wishes,
Has blest you with the power to end our woes,
Or wreck your vengeance on the man you hate.

AM. Ha! what say'st thou ? take heed thou triflest
         not :
A second time thou'st rais'd my expectation ;
If thou deceiv'st it now, as at the first,
Death is the lightest ill thou hast to fear :
But if, beyond my hopes, thou tell'st me truth,
Thou shalt no longer droop beneath our frown,
(Your service slighted, and your love despis'd,)
Our former lavish grant shall be renew'd,
And my HELLENA be thy rich reward.

AMA (*Kneeling*) Bounty immense ! thus let——

AM. Rise, and proceed,
Make it appear that vengeance may be had ;
Let it be merely possible,——O *Allah* !
I ask no more,———and leave the rest to me.

AMA. Ever invincible, you are not to learn
That ARANTHES, Prince of *Durazzo*, who derives
His high descent from *Charlemain*, that most
Illustrious *Frank*, Santon and King, has long
Approv'd himself aspiring *Castriot*'s friend,
And firm ally. His wisdom, wealth and power
May well indear him to that haughty rebel ;
But yet a tie much stronger binds their friendship:

                                              The

The fair ALTHEA, daughter to ARANTHES,
Beholds the youthful conqueror her flave:
Nor are his ardent vows prefer'd in vain,
With confcious virtue, join'd with true affection,
With majefty and mildnefs fweetly temper'd,
The charming maid (for all who fee her muft
Confefs her charms,) returns his conftant flame.
This friend and miftrefs, the partner and the hop'd
Reward of all his toils, are in your power.

    AM. Prophet, thou'rt juft ; where are his conquefts
        now ?
Anguifh has left my foul to live in his
Perhaps ere this the news has reach'd his ears.
His promis'd joys are come to fwell my heart ;
I have 'em all, but doubled by his pain.
Hafte and inform us by what means, AMASIE,
Thefe precious pledges came into our hands.

    AMA. This morning from *Durazzo* they fet forth,
Slightly attended for the Chriftian camp,
Fearing no danger ; for they knew your army
Had been for months immur'd within thefe plains ;
The neighb'ring mountains being all poffeft
By their rebellious minion's conquering troops.
Of this inform'd, not daring to approach
Your facred prefence, I inform'd your fon,
Your empire's fecond hope, the brave Prince *Mahomet*.
Strait with two thoufand horfe, guided by me,
Who, as a native here, beft knew the route
The little troop muft take, he left the trenches:
The foe was quickly found ; tho' few in number
They yet refifted long, and dearly fold
Their liberty or lives : ARANTHES laft
Yielded himfelf and daughter to our power.   (*Shouts.*

Enter MAHOMET, ARANTHES, ALTHEA,
    Lords and Ladies in chains.

    MA. Long live great AMURATH, my royal father ;
O may his days for ages yet roll on,
And ev'ry day increafe his fame like this !
    AM. Rife to my arms : thou bring'ft me life and
        fame ;
And what my foul much more defir'd, revenge.

          When

When from the womb they brought thee to thefe arms,
The firft dear fruit of my *Maria*'s love,
And heir to all my kingdoms; ev'n then
I claps'd thee with lefs joy than at this moment.——
But let us view the captives thou has brought.
Now by our Prophet's head, a noble troop!
A fairer purchafe never grac'd my arms.
This muft be ARANTHES, and this his daughter.
They feem to fcorn their fortune: confcious majefty
Frowns on his brow, and beauty fmiles on hers.
Proud Chriftian, now where is your Prophet's power?

AR. Where it was ever, Sultan;—in himfelf.

AM If it be fuch as vainly you fuppofe,
Why art thou fallen thus beneath my power?
Whofe eyes ne'er pity'd, and whofe hand ne'er fpar'd
The followers of his fect.

AR. Prefumptuous man!
Shall finite knowledge tax eternal wifdom?
Or fhamelefs guilt dare, with invidious eyes,
To fearch for fpots in purity itfelf,
And call impartial Juftice to account?
Impious and vain! It is enough we know
Such is his will, who orders all things right,
To make e'en thefe thy chains, infulting king,
Eafy to us; and well content we bear 'em.

AM. Ill doth it fuit with your reputed wifdom
T'abet a rafh rebellious boy.

AR. Rebellious!
By the heroic virtue of the youth,
And more th'eternal juftice of our caufe,
I muft retort the charge. Since firft the angels
By their ambition fell; the greateft rebels,
The moft accurs'd, perfidious and ungrateful,
Are thofe, who have abus'd the fovereign power.
Why fhines the Sun, why do the feafons change,
The teeming earth lavifh her yearly ftore,
And all to blefs the fons of men in vain?
O! is it not that tyranny prevails,
And the true end of government is loft;
That thofe, who fhou'd defend each in his right,
Betray their truft, and feize upon the whole?
This, this is to rebel againft that power,

By

By which kings reign, and turn the arms of Heaven
Against itself. Then take the rebel back;
A virtuous prince, the patron of mankind,
With just contempt may hear a lawless tyrant
Arraign that conduct which condemns his own.

Aм 'Tis hard to say whether thy insolence,
Who, tho' in chains, dar'st brave me to my face,
Or the unprincely meanness of thy soul,
Who wou'd by law restrain the will of kings,
Amaze me most. Let SCANDERBEG and you,
Like fools contend, and shed your blood in vain,
While subjects reap the harvest of your toil ;
O'ercome, that you may live the slave of slaves ;
I fight to reign, and conquer for myself

Aʀ. A gen'rous slave wou'd scorn the abject thought,
What shou'd a king do then ?

Aм. Think like a king,
Whose glory is his power.

Aʀ Of doing good

Aм Of doing what he will, the other's none.

Aʀ. Has Heav'n no power because it doth no ill ?

Aм. Were these the thoughts of other Christian
princes,
Wou'd they stand neuter, and unmov'd behold
Th' *Epirot* and thyself sustain this war ;
Nor lend you their assistance ?

Aʀ Foul dishonour !
O everlasting shame ! wou'd they unite,
Afflicted *Europe* wou'd no longer groan
Beneath your yoke, and mourn her freedom lost :
Nor *Verna*'s nor *Basilia*'s fatal fields
Smoke with the blood of Christians unreveng'd :
But, to the scandal of our holy faith,
Some such there are, who owe their very lives,
Their peace and safety to the blood of others,
Yet think themselves born for themselves alone.

Aм. 'Tis time to quit a cause so ill supported ;
And your misfortunes may inform your friend,
What sure destruction waits the desp'rate wretch,
That tempts his wrath, who rules o'er half mankind,
And strikes the rest with terror at his name.

Aʀ.

AR. Ceafe thy vain boafts, and by example learn
The frail uncertain ftate of human greatnefs.
Where are now th' *Affyrians,* where the *Medes* ?
The *Perfians,* and their conquerors, the *Greeks* ;
Or the ftupendous power of ancient *Rome* ?
Has not the breath of time blafted their pride,
And laid their glory wafte ?

   AM. I'need not boaft
T'affert my power o'er thee. And yet perhaps
On SCANDERBEG's fubmiffion we may grant
Your freedom, and vouchfafe to give him peace.

   AR. If by fubmiffion vainly you defign
Difhonourable terms, a fhameful peace,
Give up fuch thoughts, thofe his great foul muft fcorn ;
Nor wou'd we be redeem'd at fuch a price :
Hope not to triumph over him in us.

   AM. Where is the majefty that us'd to awe
My trembling flaves ? art thou in love with death ?

    AR. No; nor with life, when purchas'd at th' ex-
      pence
Of others happinefs, or my own honour.

   AM. Behold this maid, this comfort of thy age.
I, as a father, know what 'tis to love
A child like this——I have been deem'd a man,
A brave one too——The fair, facred to peace,
Have never yet been number'd with my foes :
But if prefumptuoufly thou doft difpute
Thy own and daughter's ranfom on my terms ;
Or teach thy pupil to oppofe my will,
Renounce me, Heav'n, if like thy bloody priefts,
Thofe confecrated murderers of thy fect,
I caft not off all bowels of compaffion,
All pity, all remorfe——her tender fex,
Her youth, her blooming beauty fhall not fave her.
Away ; I'll hear no more. Prudence may yet
Inftruct you to avoid th' impending ruin.
AMASIE, we commit him to your charge.

   AL. O my father ! tho' torn from your embraces,
Your precepts, your example fhall be ever
Prefent with ALTHEA ; in doubts my guide,
In troubles my fupport.

   AR. This wounds indeed.

'Tis

'Tis hard to part and leave her thus expos'd;
But Heav'n muſt be obey'd (*Aſide.*). Farewel, my child!
Tho' reaſon and religion teach us patience,
Pain will be felt and nature have her courſe.　　[*Aſide.*
　　　　　　　　　　　　　　　　　[*Exit.* ARANTHES.

Am. Mourn not bright maid; you can have nought
　　　　to fear:
A father and a lover rule your fate.

Al. I ſee and ſcorn your arts, inſidious king.
And for your threats, purſue 'em when you dare;
Your pride to ſee your cruelty deſpis'd,
Shall give you greater pain than you inflict,
And turn your rage to ſhame. O prince belov'd!
O my affianc'd Lord! let not my danger
One moment ſtop the progreſs of your arms:
I have my wiſh, if dying I may ſhare
In your renown, and juſtify your choice.

Am. OSMYN, attend the lady to HELLENA.
　　　　　　　　　　　　　[*Exit* AMURATH, &c.

Vis. Fair princeſs, you ſhall know no more reſtraint
Than what is common to the ſex with us.

Al. Lead me to inſtant death, or let me groan
Whole years in chains————diſpoſe me as you pleaſe——
Tho' my lov'd Sire and Lord no more I ſee,
You hope in vain to conquer them in me.

ACT II.　SCENE I.

*A plain the whole length of the ſtage. One ſide lined
with Chriſtian, the other with Turkiſh ſoldiers.*

Enter VISIER *and* PAULINUS.

VISIER.

ALready has the trumpet's lofty ſound
From either camp twice eccho'd thro' the plain;
At the third ſummons both the kings appear.
May gracious Heav'n, in pity to mankind,

　　　　　　　　　　　　　　　　　Incline

Incline then breafts to fheath the fword, to ftop
The tide of blood, and give the world repofe.

PAUL. What may we not expect from fuch a treaty?
And yet the caution us'd on either fide
To guard againft furprife, betrays diftruft.

VIS A thoufand injuries, fuppos'd or real,
With keen refentment whet each jealous chief,
And feem to urge fufpicion.

PAUL. *Scipio*,
And the fierce *African* whom he fubdu'd,
With greater ardor never ftrove t'attain,
For *Rome* or *Carthage*, univerfal fway ;
Than your great Sultan to impofe the yoke
Of arbitrary power, and make men flaves ;
Or our brave prince to guard their liberties,
Or break their chains and purchafe freedom for 'em.

VIS Then their known zeal for their refpective faiths,
Muft yet much more alienate their minds.

PAUL. 'Tis hardly to be thought a youthful hero,
With victories replete, will ftoop to take
Abject conditions from a beaten foe.

VIS. Or that an artful prince will fail t'improve
Ev'ry advantage to increafe his power.

PAUL. Fortune ftands neuter, and impartial Heaven
Holds with an equal hand the trembling beam :
Superior wifdom, fortitude and courage
Muft turn the fcale. (*Trumpets*.) But fee their guards
          appear.
The great Intelligencies that inform
The planetary worlds, if fuch there be,
With all their vaft experience might attend
This interview, and pafs improv'd away.

Enter AMURATH, SCANDERBEG, MAHO-
     MET, ARANTHES, AMASIE, *&c.*

AM Doth it not fwell thy fond, ambitious heart ?
Doft thou not burft with pride, vain boy, to fee
The majefty of hoary AMURATH,
Whofe numerous years are fewer than his conquefts,
Reduc'd to terms, and ftoop to treat with thee?

SCAN. With gratitude and wonder I confefs
Myfelf th' unworthy inftrument of Heaven,

                                        To

To scourge thy falshood, cruelty and pride,
And free a virtuous people from thy chains.
With pity I behold your fierce impatience,
Your arrogance and scorn; ev'n while the hand
Of righteous Heaven is heavy on thy crimes,
And deals thee forth a portion of those woes,
Which thy relentless heart, with lawless lust
And never-sated avarice of power,
Has spread o'er half the habitable earth.

   Am. And must I answer to thy bold impeachment?
Thou infidel relasp'd! thou very Christian!
Without distinction and without a name
But what implies thy guilt. In vain thy flatt'rers
Proclaim thee king of *Macedon*, *Epirus*,
Illyria, *Albania* and *Dalmatia*;
Gain'd by surprize, by treachery and fraud;
What art thou but the more exalted traitor?

   Scan. Let abject minds, the slaves of mean ambition,
Affect vain titles and external pomp,
And take the shadow for substantial glory!
Superior birth, unmerited success,
The name of prince, of conqueror and king,
Are gifts of fortune and of little worth.
They may be, and too often are, possest
By sordid souls, who know no joy but wealth;
By ri'tous fools, or tyrants drench'd in blood;
A *Crœsus*, *Alexander*, or a *Nero*.
The best are sure the greatest of mankind.
Our actions form our characters. Let me
Approve myself a Christian and a soldier,
And flatt'ry cannot add, or envy take
Ought that I wish to have, or fear to lose.

   Am. Canst thou behold unmov'd, thou steady traitor,
Thy most munificent and loving patron,
Prest with the weight of more than fourscore years,
With feeble hands compell'd to reassume
The stubborn reins of power, and taste again,
When appetite is pall'd, the bitter sweets
Of sovereign command? shou'd I descend
To reason with thee, what cou'dst thou reply?
Have I not been a father to thy youth?
Did I not early form thy mind to greatness,

And

And teach thy infant hands the use of arms?
Tho' the unerring maxims of our state,
(The only rule of right and wrong in courts)
Had mark'd thee for destruction, still I spar'd thee:
Trusted, belov'd, advanc'd, thou hast betray'd me.
First seiz'd the provinces you call'd your own,
Then join'd my foes to rob me of my fame;
The perjur'd *Uladislaus*, fierce *Hunniades*,
And the *Venetians*, who have since forsook thee:
Tho' to remote *Magnesia* I retir'd,
Quitting the toils of empire to my son,
To seek for rest and find a peaceful grave;
Yet there the cries and clamours of my slaves,
Who fled the terrors of thy dreadful name,
Forbad their old o'erlabour'd king repose;
Forc'd me once more in hostile steel to cloth
These weary limbs, and rouse to their defence.
But that thy soul is lost to all remorse,
Thy black ingratitude must fright thyself?

SCAN. Can all your kingdoms bribe the voice of truth,
Which, while you speak, pleads for me in your breast?
Or rage efface the mem'ry of your guilt,
More than ten thousand witnesses against thee?
But slander, like the loathsome leper's breath,
Infects the healthful with its poisonous steams,
Unless repell'd, and bids me guard my fame.
My ancestors for ages fill'd this throne,
A brave, a virtuous, legal race of princes,
No arbitrary tyrants; the same laws
That made them kings, declar'd their people free.
My royal father, fam'd for his success
In war and love of peace, had govern'd long;
When with resistless force your conqu'ring troops
Pour'd like a deluge o'er the realms of *Greece*:
To save his people from impending ruin,
At your request, the pious, gen'rous prince
Gave up his sons as hostages of peace.
He died——the best of kings and men.   O *Castriot*!
I were unworthy of thy race and name
Cou'd I unmov'd remember thou'rt no more——
I wou'd have said, he died in firm reliance
On your promise given, your faith and honour;
                                                    But

But sure the memory of such a loss
May well o'er-bear, and drive me from my purpose.
'Twas then in scorn of ev'ry obligation,
Of truth and justice, gratitude and honour,
Of noblest trust and confidence repos'd ;
You like a lawless, most perfidious tyrant,
Amidst her griefs, seiz'd on his widow'd kingdom ;
And to secure your lawless acquisition ——
Oh ! how shall I proceed ! —— My bleeding heart!
Is pierc'd anew, new horrors wound my soul
At every pause, whenever I rehearse,
Whene'er I think upon thy monst'rous crimes ——
O *Reposio* ! *Stanissa* ! *Constantine* !
My slaughter'd brothers, whose dear blood still cries
Aloud to Heaven ,——your wrongs shall find redress.
Justice, defer'd, deals forth the heavier blow

   Am. Shall the great monarchs of our sublime race
Cut off their brothers, when they mount the throne,
Yet spare the lives of Christians they suspect :
Their death was wise, and I approve it yet,
But curse my folly that preserv'd thy life.

   Scan. What was then my life ? debarr'd of my right,
And kept t'augment the number of your slaves.
The only benefit you e'er conferr'd,
Was that you train'd me to the use of arms :
You had my service and was over-paid ;
Yet those whom I oppos'd were, like yourself,
Tyrants, who made a merchandize of men ;
And propagate religion by the sword.
Ever determin'd not to stain my hands
With Christian blood, when you commanded me
To turn my arms against th' *Hungarian* king,
I purpos'd from that hour, by Heaven's assistance,
At once t'avoid the guilt and free my country.

   Am. O traitor ! dost thou glory in thy shame ?
Think not I have forgot thy vile declension.
Yes on that fatal, that detested day,
When deep *Moravia*'s waves, dy'd with the blood
Of forty thousand of my faithful slaves,
Losing their azure, flow'd in purple Tides ;
Too well I know, thou didst forsake thy charge ;
And ere the news of thy revolt arriv'd,

Surpriz'd

Surpriz'd my Basha that commanded here;
Drove out my garrisons, and ravish'd from me
This fair and fertile kingdom.

    Scan. False aspersion !
The charge impos'd was ne'er accepted by me.
I arm'd my subjects for their common rights;
The love of liberty, that fired their souls,
That made them worthy, crown'd them with success.
I did my duty———'Twas but what I ow'd
To Heaven, an injur'd people and myself.

    Am. You will be justify'd in all that's past :
But I shall bend thy stubborn temper yet———
I know the worth of those dear pledges now
Within my power.   Thou know'st me too—Then think
And yield in time, while mercy may be had.

    Scan. I know your mercy by my brothers fate.

    Am. Then you may judge the future by the past.

    Scan. Tho' pity be a stranger to your breast,
Your present dang'rous state may teach you fear.

    Am Danger and I have been acquainted long ;
Full oft I've met her in the bloody field,
And drove her back with terror on my foes :
Your other phantom, Fear, I know her not;
Or in thy visage I behold her now.

    Scan. I fear not for myself.

    Am. Yet still thou fear'st.
Confess thyself subdu'd and sue for favour.   [conquest.

    Scan. When I submit to guilt, ——— I'll own your

    Am. Think on your friends.

    Scan. Afflictions are no crimes.

    Am. You wou'd redeem them !

    Scan. Yes; on any terms,
That honour may permit, and justice warrant.

    Am Hear the conditions then.

    Scan. Why sinks my heart ?
Why do I tremble thus ? When at the head
Of almost twice a hundred thousand souls,
I with a handful charg'd this fierce old chief,
Thou art my witness, Heav'n, I fear'd him not.
                          (*Aside.*

    Am. When I look back on what you were before
Your late revolt, charm'd with the pleasing view,

1

I wish to see those glorious days restor'd ;
When I with honour may indulge my bounty,
And make you great and happy as you're brave.

SCAN. Flattery!—Nay, then he's dangerous indeed!
(Aside.

AM. Renounce the errors of the Christian sect,
And be instructed in the law profest
By *Ishmael*'s holy race ; that light divine,
That darts from *Mecca*'s ever sacred fane,
T'illuminate the darken'd souls of men,
And fill 'em with its brightness.

SCAN. O ALTHEA! *(Aside.*

AM. Break your alliance with the Christian princes,
And let my foes be thine.

SCAN. That follows well ,
Th' abandon'd wretch, that breaks his faith with
Heav'n,
Will hardly stop at any future Crime. *(Aside.*

AM. Forego th' advantage that your arms have
won;
Give up this little part of spacious *Greece*,
Its cities and its people to my power :
And in return reign thou my substitute
O'er all my conquer'd provinces in *Europe*,
From *Adrianople* to the walls of *Buda*.

SCAN. Assist me, Heav'n! assist me to suppress
The rising indignation in my breast,
That struggles, heaves and rages for a vent————
ARANTHES ! ALTHEA ! How shall I preserve you ?
(Aside.

VIS. He's greatly mov'd, his visage flames with
wrath.

AMA. Just so he looks when rushing on the foe,
The eager blood starts from his trembling lips.

AM. I wait your resolution

SCAN. Three days the truce concluded is to last ,
That space I ask to answer your demands.

AM. 'Tis well , enjoy your wish————but yet remember
Honour and int'rest, gratitude and love
Bleed while you pause, and press you to comply.

C Farther

Farther, to favour you in all I may,
ARANTHES shall attend you to your camp:
Confult, refolve, your interefts are the fame;
ALTHEA juftly claims the care of both.

       [*Exit* AMURATH, &c.

 SCAN. O thou, who art my righteoufnefs and ftrength,
Diftrefs'd and tempted, ftill in thee I truft:
The pilot, when he fees the tempeft rife,
And the proud waves infult the low'ring fkies,
Fix'd to the helm, looks to that Power to lay
The raging ftorm, whom winds and feas obey.

       [*Exit* SCANDERBEG, &c.

A M A S I E *alone.*

Shou'd he comply? as fure he's hardly prefs'd;
Reftor'd to favour, where is my revenge?
He's but a man————lefs tempted I fell worfe;
But I'm not SCANDERBEG.————Say, he refufes,
It follows that the Sultan, in his rage,
Murders the captives, tho' we all fhou'd perifh,
Which fide foe'er I view, I like it not.
There is no peace for me, while *Caftriot* lives;
Plagu'd and diftrefs'd, he foars above me ftill;
Infults my hate, and awes me with his virtue.
His virtue! ha! How have I dream'd till now,
How 'fcap'd the thought? His virtue fhall betray him.
Hypocrify, that with an angel's likenefs
May well deceive the wifdom of an angel,
Shall re-inftate me in his gen'rous heart.
Which if I fail to pierce, may all the ill
I ever wifh'd to him fall on myfelf ————
The amorous Prince————I know his haughty foul
Ill brooks his fubtle father's peaceful fchemes.
He loves ALTHEA, and depends on me
T' affift his flame.

Enter M A H O M E T.

 MA. AMASIE, what fuccefs?
You faw the captive Princefs————
 AMA. Yes, my Lord.
 MA. Curfe on the jealous cuftoms of our court:

            Why

Why is that privilege deny'd to me?

AMA. You know why I'm indulg'd.

MA 'Tis true, but say,

What haft thou done that may advance my hopes!

AMA. I've thought, my Lord——

MA What tell'ft thou me of thoughts!

Haft thou not fpoke?—what fays the charming fair?

——Shall I be bleft?

AMA Spoke, what? alas! my Prince!

How little do you know that haughty Chriftian?

Bred in the rigid maxims of her fect,

Chafte as its precepts, moft feverely virtuous,

ALTHEA wou'd treat me with the laft contempt,

Shou'd I but name your gen'rous paffion to her,

And proudly term it fhameful and unjuft.

MA. Now as you wou'd avoid a Prince's hatred,

That muft one day command you; or expect

E'er to attain my fifter's love, the fcope

Of your ambition, aid me with your counfel.

My blood's on fire, and I will quench the flame,

Tho' univerfal ruin fhou'd enfue.

By Heaven I will; I'll plunge in feas of blifs,

And with repeated draughts of cordial love,

Expel the raging fever from my veins.

AMA. Glorious mifchief!——(*Afide*) If I judge right,

     her will

Is ne'er to be fubdu'd, you can't poffefs

Her mind, my Lord—and without that, you know—

MA Her mind! a fhadow? give me folid joys,

And let her Chriftian minion take the reft.

I love her for myfelf; my appetite

Muft be appeas'd, or live my conftant plague.

Let me but clafp her in my longing arms,

Prefs her foft bofom to my panting breaft,

And crown my wifhes; tho' attain'd by force,

Tho' amidft ftrugglings, fhrieks and gufhing tears;

Or while fhe faints beneath my ftrong embrace,

And I have all my raging paffions crave.

AM. Already I've conceiv'd the means to ferve you,

But time muft give th' imperfect embryo form,

And hail th' aufpicious birth.

MA. She's juftly mine,

         The

The purchase of my sword.   Our Prophet thus,
By manly force all prior right destroy'd ;
Power was his claim , he conquer'd and enjoy'd :
Beauty and fame alike his ardor mov'd ;
Fiercely he fought, and as he fought he lov'd.

ACT III. SCENE I.

The Christian camp.

Enter SCANDERBEG *and* ARANTHES.

ARANTHES.

ALTHEA mourns for this your fond delay,
  And thinks already she has liv'd too long ;
Since living she protracts the tyrant's fate,
And clouds the matchless lustre of your arms.
  SCAN. Justice herself would here suspend her sword ;
Nor with one undiscriminating blow,
Blind as she is, destroy both friends and foes.
  AR. It is appointed once for all to die :
Then what am I, or what a child of mine,
Weigh'd with the honour of the Christian name,
To bid the cause of liberty attend,
While gravely you debate those very trifles,
The time and circumstances of our death :
As justly nature might suspend her course
To wait the dissolution of an insect.
———No, let me bear defiance to the Sultan ;
Tell him, that you already are determin'd ;
And dare his worst.
  SCAN. Not for ten thousand worlds.
Wou'd I so tempt the fretful tyrant's rage ?
The pangs of death are light to those of absence ;
Then who can bear eternal separation ?
Transported as you are with pious zeal ;

Look inward, fearch your heart, and then confefs
The love of Heav'n excludes not facred friendfhip.
Think if my tafk were yours, how you wou'd act.
Wou'd you not paufe, conclude, retract, and paufe
     again,
To the laft moment of the time prefixt?
Wou'd you not count it virtue to contend,
Tho' againft hope, and ftruggle with defpair.
I know you wou'd; for tho' your tongue be mute,
Spite of yourfelf, your ftreaming eyes confefs it.
  Ar. My weaknefs is no precedent for you.
  Scan. If thus the friend, what muft the lover fuffer?
Think, good Aranthes, if you ever lov'd,
What I endure: think on Althea's charms,
And judge from thence the greatnefs of my pain.
  Ar. Why will you dwell upon the dang'ious theme?
The ftrength of *Sampfon* prov'd too weak for love,
David's integrity was no defence;
The King, the Hero, and the Prophet fell
Beneath the fame inevitable power:
The wifdom of his fon was folly here;
And he that comprehended all things elfe
Knew not himfelf, 'till dear experience taught
Him late repentance, anguifh, grief and fhame.
Then think no more, but give us up at once,
Give up Althea; Heav'n demands it of you;
For while fhe lives, your virtue is not fafe.
  Scan. Is this a father's voice?
  Ar. Wou'd I had died,
Ere I was honour'd with a father's name;
Or that my child had been lefs good and fair.
What was my greateft joy, is now my grief:
Ev'ry perfection wings my heart with pain.
For all her charms are now fo many fnares,
Which you muft break, or be undone for ever.
——Still unrefolv'd!——Forgive me, if I think,
You have the weaknefs now of other men.
  Scan. If to rejoice when virtue is rewarded;
Or mourn th' afflictions of the good and brave,
Who mourn not for themfelves; if love and friendfhip
Denote me weak, I wou'd be weaker ftill.
He who difclaims the foftnefs of humanity,

C 3

Afpiring

Aspiring to be more than man, is less.
Yet know, my father, rev'rend good ARANTHES!
Whatever tender sentiments I feel ;
Tho' as a man, a lover and a friend,
I fear the Sultan's cruelty and malice ;
Yet as a Christian, I despise 'em both.
'Tis not for man to glory in his strength;
The best have fallen, and the wisest err'd.
Yet when the time shall come, when Heaven shall by
Its Providence declare, this is my will,
And this the sacrifice that I demand,
Why, who can tell, but full of that same energy,
Which swells your breast, I may reply, ev'n so
Thy will be done.

    AR How have my fears deceiv'd me ?

    SCAN. The careful gard'ner turns the limpid stream,
This way, or that ; as suits his purpose best.
The wrath of man shall praise his Maker's name,
The residue, restrain'd, rest on himself.
Let us not rashly antedate our woes.
Tho' I defer the sentence of your death,
Tho' I cou'd die ten thousand times to save you,
I do not, nay I dare not, bid you live.

    AR Excellent man! why did I ever doubt thee?
Your zeal's no less, your wisdom more than mine.
My time's expir'd, illustrious Prince,——farewel !

    SCAN My father! my ALTHEA !——

    AR. O my son !
Our part is little in this noble conflict,
The worst is death , your's harder, but more glorious,
To live and suffer.   Heaven inspire thy soul
With more than *Roman* fortitude and courage
They poorly fled to death, t'avoid misfortunes ,
May Christian patience teach thee to o'ercome 'em,
                     [*Exit* ARANTHES.

SCANDERBEG *alone.*
In this extremity shall I invoke
Thy awful genius, O majestic *Rome*;
Or *Junius Brutus*, thine; who sacrific'd,
To public liberty, paternal love·
The younger *Brutus* , or the *Greek* Timoleon ;

                                Of

Of self denial, great examples all :
But all far short of what's requir'd of me.
These patriots offer'd to an injur'd world
But guilty wretches, who deserv'd their fates.
Wou'd they have given up the best of men,
And the most perfect of the gentler sex
To death, to worse than death, a tyrant's rage?
No, nature unassisted cannot do it.
To thee, I bow me then, fountain of life,
Of wisdom and of power,
Who know'st our frame, and mad'st us what we are ;
I ask not length of days, nor fame, nor empire :
Give me to know and to discharge my duty,
And leave th' event to thee——AMASIE here ——

Enter AMASIE, *who kneels and lays his sword at* SCAN-
DERBEG's *feet.*

AMA Well may you turn away, justly disdain
To cast one look upon the lost AMASIE.
Constant as truth, inflexible as justice,
Above ambition, and the joys of sense,
You must abhor the wretch, whose fatal weakness
Betray'd him to such crimes, as make him hateful
To Heaven, to all good men, and to himself.
    SCAN. What com'st thou for, what canst thou hope
            from me ?
    AMA I come for justice.
    SCAN Justice must condemn thee.
    AMA I have condemn'd myself ; but dare not die,
Till you, the proper judge, confirm the sentence. [loss
    SCAN. When first you fell, I deeply mourn'd your
But from that moment gave you up for ever :
    AMA. Still you're my prince ! my native, rightful
            prince.
    SCAN. Then what art thou ?
    AMA. The blackest, worst of traitors.
    SCAN Be that thy punishment.
    AMA. Dreadful decree !
'Tis more than I can bear —— leave me not thus.
Is not the blood that runs in either's veins,
Deriv'd from the same source ? was I not once,
Howe'er unworthy, honour'd with your friendship,
                                    named

Named your fucceffor? fo lov'd, fo trufted,
That all the envious pin'd, and all the good,
Look'd up with wonder at the glorious height,
To which your partial fondnefs had advanc'd me.

SCAN. Ill-judging man, thou aggravat'ft thy crimes.

AMA. That cannot be; I but excite your juftice.
Behold my guilty breaft; ftrike and maintain
The honour of our houfe, wipe out this ftain
Of its illuftrious race and blot of friendfhip.

SCAN. If your ambition be to fall by me,
You fhou'd have met me in the front of battle
With manly oppofition, and receiv'd
The death thou feek'ft for in the rage of war.
My fword defcends not on a proftrate foe:
Tho' you've deferv'd to die, I've not deferv'd
To be your executioner.

AMA. Juft Heavens!
Are you a Chriftian prince, and will you fpare
A black apoftate?

SCAN. Heaven can right itfelf
With my aid, nor do I know on earth
So great, fo juft an object of compaffion.
Live and repent.

AMA. I have and do repent,
But cannot live.   The court of AMURATH
Abhors a Chriftian; ev'ry Chriftian court
Detefts a traitor.

SCAN. Miferable man!   [*Afide.*

AMA. We're taught that Heav'n is merciful and kind,

SCAN. What wretch dares doubt of that?

AMA. Then why am I
Deny'd to fue for peace and pardon there,
Since I muft never hope for them on earth?

SCAN. Have I the feeds of frailty in my nature?
Am I a man, like him, and can I fee,
Unpitying and unmov'd, the bitter anguifh,
The deep contrition of his wounded foul?
It will not be———O nature take your courfe,
I'll not refift your tendereft impreffions.   [*Afide.*
Supprefs the tumult of your troubled mind,
You have o'ercome; I feel and fhare your forrows.

AMA. O be lefs good, or I fhall die with fhame.
                                          SCAN.

SCAN. I've been too flow to pardon.   [*Embracing.*
AMA. O my Prince!
My injur'd Prince!
SCAN. Thy friend, thy friend, AMASIE.
AMA. How have you rais'd me from the laft defpair?
And dare you truft this rebel, this apoftate?
SCAN. 'Tis Heav'n's prerogative alone to fearch
The hearts of men, and read their inmoft thoughts:
I wou'd be circumfpect, not over wife;
Nor, for one error, lofe a friend for ever:
No, let me be deceiv'd e're want humanity.
AMA. The wifdom and beneficence of Heav'n
Flow in your words, and blefs all thofe who hear 'em.
                    [*Trumpets found a parley.*
SCAN. What means this fummons to a fecond parley?
AMA. The Sultan's hafte anticipates my purpofe.
                              [*Afide.*
Something that much concerns your love and honour,
I have to fay, but muft defer it now,
And once more join his council; if I'm feen,
I lofe the only means that's left to ferve you.
SCAN. You will return——————
AMA. As certain as the night,
About the midft of which you may expect me.
SCAN. You'll find me in my tent; the word's,
    ALTHEA.

Enter OFFICER.

OFF. The Vifier with the princefs of *Durazzo,*
Demands an audience.
SCAN. Fly; and introduce 'em.
Can this be true?
AMA. Moft true. The Sultan hopes
That your ALTHEA's eyes will conquer for him:
Heav'n guard your heart. Farewel — at night expect me.
He's well deceiv'd; hypocrify, I thank thee.
Dark and profound as hell, what line can fathom,
Or eye explore the fecret thoughts of men?
Yet once I fear'd I fhou'd betray myfelf,
And be indeed the penitent I feign'd;
So much his virtue mov'd me. Curfe his virtue!
He ever will excell me — Let him die,

                              Tho'

Tho' all my peace die with him—wretched man !
When shall I rest from envy and remorse ?   (*Aside.*
                                        Ext AMASEM.

SCAN. I shall once more behold ALTHEA then.
So wretches are indulg'd the sight of Heav'n
To sharpen pain, and aggravate their loss.
The blended beauties of the teeming spring,
Whate'er excells in nature's works besides,
Are vile to her, the glory of the whole.
Flowers fade and lose their odours, gems their brightness,
And gold its estimation in her presence.
But see, she comes——Sure such a form betray'd
The first of men to quit his paradise,
And all the joys of innocence and peace,
For those he found in her : yet had the lovely,
Alas too lovely parent of mankind,
Possess'd a mind, as much superior to
Her outward form, as my ALTHEA doth ;
Mankind had never fall'n.

Enter VISIER, ALTHEA, *&c.* SCANDERBEG
        kneels and kisses her hand.

SCAN. O my princess !
AL   My ever honour'd Lord !
SCAN. To be your slave,
A captive to your charms, is more than to
Be lord of humankind.
        AL. The Visier, prince —— (SCANDERBEG *rises*
        VIS. Far be it noble SCANDERBEG from me
To intercept my royal master's bounty,
Who wills you to enjoy freedom of speech,
Uninterrupted with the Christian princess
I'll with the guards retire and wait your leisure
                        Exit Visier, *&c.*

SCAN. O my ALTHEA !
    AL. Speak, I'm all attention.
    SCAN. O who can raise his thoughts to the occasion ?
Or, doing that, reduce such thoughts to words ?
    AL. I will assist you—we must part for ever.
    SCAN. Is that, is that so easy ? Righteous Heaven !
It doth amaze me, and confound my reason
To hear thee, thus calm and serene, pronounce

                                        The

The dreadful sentence.

AL. Is it not determin'd?

SCAN. To give thee back to slavery and chains!
To bear the malice of a bloody tyrant,
Inrag'd by my refusal!————O ALTHEA!
Tho' Heav'n must be obey'd, something is due
To virtuous love. We may, we must confess
A sense of such unutterable woe.
When in return of my inceffant vows,
You deign'd to crown my love; when expectation
Of the long sigh'd for bliss had raised my joys
To that exalted pitch, that I look'd down
With pity on mankind, and only griev'd
To think they stood expofed to disappointment,
Misery and pain, while I alone was happy
Then, then to lose thee————

AL. O complain no more.
You move a weaknefs here, unworthy her,
Who wou'd afpire but to deferve your love.
I wou'd have died like the mute facrifice,
Who goes as chearful, and as unconcern'd,
To bleed upon the altar, as to sleep
Within its nightly fold.

SCAN. Coud'st thou do this!

AL. Had I not feen you thus, I think I shou'd;
But at your grief my refolution fails me:
I'm fubdued the woman, the weak, fond woman,
Swells in my heart, and gufhes from my eyes.

SCAN. What have I done? the greatnefs of thy foul,
Not to be comprehended but by minds
Exalted as thy own, ftagger'd my reafon;
And what was prudence and fuperior virtue,
I thought a wrong to love. Rafh, thoughtlefs man!
To force a tendernefs thou can'ft not bear,
That ftabs the very foul of refolution,
And leaves thee without ftrength to ftem a torrent,
That afks an angel's force to meet its rage.

AL. To combat inclination, to fubdue
Our own defires, and conquer by fubmiffion;
Are virtues, prince, no angel ever knew.
While thefe are your's, fhall I indulge my grief?
————The ftorm is over, and I'm calm again.

SCAN.

SCAN. O thou eternal fource of admiration!
What new wonder haft thou prepar'd to charm
My ravifh'd foul ? where didft thou learn the art
To ftop the tide of grief in its full flow,
And triumph o'er defpair ?

　AL. In you I triumph.
Tho' rack'd and torn with more than mortal grief,
Amidft the pangs of difappointed love
And fuff'ring friendfhip, do I not behold thee,
Still conftant as the Sun, that keeps its courfe,
Tho' ftorms and tempefts vex the nether fky,
And low'ring clouds a while obfcure his brightnefs.

　SCAN Excellent, heavenly maid ; thou rob'ft thyfelf,
And attribut'ft to me thy own perfections.

　AL. Have you once queftion'd whether you fhould part
With two the deareft things to man on earth,
A friend and miftrefs ; or renounce your faith,
The int'reft of mankind and caufe of virtue ?

　SCAN That were to purchafe ev'n thee too dear :
That were a mifery beyond thy lofs :
That were, my princefs ! to deferve to lofe thee.

　AL.　That gracious power that wrought you for this
　　　　purpofe,
That made you great to ftruggle with adverfity,
And teach luxurious princes, by example,
What kings fhou'd be, and fhame 'em into virtue ;
Beholds, with pleafure, you difcharge the truft,
And act up to the dignity you're form'd for.

　SCAN.　O whether wou'd thy dazzling virtue foar ?
Is't not enough we yield to our misfortunes,
And bear afflictions, tho' with bleeding hearts.
Wou'dft thou attempt to raife pleafure from pain,
And teach the voice of mourning, fongs of joy ?

　AL. Small is my part, and fuited to my ftrength.
What is dying ? A wanton CLEOPATRA
Cou'd fmile in death, and infans die in fleep.
What tho' my days are few and fill'd with forrow !
Cou'd vain profperity to hoary age
Afford a happinefs to be compar'd
To dying now in fuch a glorious caufe ;
Lamented and belov'd by thee, the beft
And greateft of mankind——Then let us hafte

And clofe the fcene ——You, good PADLINUS, let
The Vifier know, I'm ready to return.
Why are you pale, and why do gufhing tears
Blot the majeftic beauty of your face?
Why is the Hero in the Lover loft?

 SCAN. Let angels, who attend in crouds to hear
   thee;
Let all the fons of liberty and fame;
Thofe, who ftill wait, and thofe who have obtain'd
The end of all then labours, heaven and earth,
Angels and men; the living and the dead,
Behold and judge if ever man before
Purchas'd the patriot's name, or fav'd his country,
His faith and honour, at a price fo dear.

Enter VISIER.

 VIS. Well Prince, may we not hope that thofe bright
   eyes
Have charm'd your foul to peace? Who wou'd refift,
When honour's gain'd by being overcome?
To yield to beauty, crowns the warrior's fame.

 SCAN I'm not to learn how to efteem the Princefs;
But know the Sultan over-rates his power,
When he prefumes to barter for her love.
Her mind is free and royal as his own;
Nor is fhe to be gain'd by doing what
Wou'd forfeit her efteem. And I muft think
This hafte to know my mind, is fraud or fear.
What needs there more? The truce is unexpu'd:
If your proud mafter wifhes for a peace,
We yet may treat on honourable terms.
In the mean time receive the Princefs back.

 VIS Think what you do, great fir.
 SCAN. I know my duty.
 AL. Farewel, my Lord!
 SCAN Farewel!——protect her, Heaven!
 AL Now let the fretful tyrant ftorm and rage,
The only danger we cou'd fear is paft.
      [*Exit* ALTHEA *and* VISIER.
 SCAN. T'encounter hofts of foes is eafier far,
Than to fuftain this innate, bofom war,

D   This

This one unbloody conqueſt coſts me more,
Than all the battles I e'er won before.

><><><><><><><><><><><><><><><><><><><><><

A C T IV. S C E N E I.

The outward apartment in the womens tent.
A guard of Eunuchs.

Enter K I S L E R A G A.

AGA 'TIS as I thought: our maſter is betray'd.
      Whoever knew a renegade ſincere?
This dog's a Chriſtian ſtill !

Enter A M A S I E.

AMA The victim's prepar'd.
If luſt holds on her courſe, and revels yet
In the hot veins of raſh, luxurious youth,
This Chriſtian Heroine, this ſecond *Lucrece,*
In MAHOMET ſhall find another TARQUIN,
As cruel and remorſeleſs as the firſt.
If I ſhou'd fail in my attempt to night,
And SCANDERBEG ſurvive——ALTHEA raviſh'd——
He'll wiſh himſelf, I had ſucceeded better.   [*Aſide.*
Diſmiſs your uſeleſs train of prying ſlaves;
I've buſineſs that requires your ear alone.
                                    [*Exeunt Eunuchs.*
A *Grecian* chief, who owns our maſter's cauſe,
Muſt be admitted to the captive Princeſs.
'Tis of importance to the Sultan's ſervice,
That he ſhou'd enter and depart unknown:
I'll introduce him, while you watch without
That none approach to give him interruption.
  AGA. This I conceive, but why he mov'd the lady
To the remoteſt part of the pavilion
I cannot comprehend.   [*Aſide.*
                                    AMA.

AMA. You know your duty ; ·
Your life fhall anfwer for the leaft neglect. ·
AGA. I fhall take care——(*Exit* AMASIE.) to ruin
thee, thou traitor.

SCENE II.

*Another apartment; Stage darken'd; Table and
Lamp.*

ALTHEA *difcovered.*

AL. Is this a time and place for virtuous love ?
This is the wanton's hour: now fhe forfakes
Her home, and, hid in darknefs, watches for her prey:
The foul, whom Heav'n abhors, falls in her fnares ;
And pierc'd with guilt, as with an arrow, dies.
Thou fickly lamp, that glimmers thro' my tears,
Faintly contending with prevailing darknefs,
Spreads o'er the place a melancholy gloom,
That fooths the joylefs temper of my mind.
So a pale meteor's dull and beamlefs flame
To the bewilder'd traveller appears,
And adds new horrors to the cheerlefs night.
——Is error then the lot of all mankind ?
It is, it is.—for SCANDERBEG is fall'n ——
O ! what could move him to the rafh attempt ?
If he fhou'd perifh, as the danger's great,
How will th' infulting infidels rejoice ?
How will the foe, with fcornful triumph, fing,
As a fool dies, fo dy'd this mighty chief ;
His hands unbound, no fetters on his feet,
But as an ideot by his folly falls,
So fell the champion of the Chriftian caufe.

Enter MAHOMET *dreft like* SCANDERBEG, *faft-
'ning the door on the infide*

He's come, and all my forrows are compleat.
Are you purfued ?—O my prophetic fears !—
If undifcover'd you have enter'd here,
This caution's needlefs, if betray'd, in vain.

MA.

MA. Of such a prize who can be too secure?

AL. 'Tis not his voice—defend me, O defend me,
All gracious Heaven!

MA. Dost thou not know me, Princess?

AL. Alas! too well! (*Aside.*) Sure you've mistook
　　your way,
Or came perchance to seek some other here;
Howe'er that be, permit me to retire.

MA. Mistaken fair; or is this ign'rance feign'd?
'Tis you alone I seek   Impetuous love,
That will not be resisted, brought me here
To lay my life and fortune at your feet.

AL. Then I'm betray'd, basely betray'd; just Hea-
　　ven!
Expos'd, perhaps devoted, to a ruin,
From which the grave itself is no retreat,
And time can ne'er repair—Be gracious, sir,-
To an unhappy maid!—Or I'm deceiv'd,
Or you, my Lord, were pleas'd to mention love;
Of that, alas! I am forbid to hear;
Compassion better suits my humble state,
That I intreat; have pity on me, Prince,
Dispel my fears, and send me from your presence.

MA. Grant what you ask, I need compassion too:
Your beauty's necessary to my peace:
Then yield, in pity to yourself and me,
What else I'll take by force: consent to make me
Happy, and in return, when time shall give
The scepter to my hand, I'll make thee queen
Of half the conquer'd globe.

AL. Know, impious Prince!
If one loose thought wou'd buy the whole, I'd scorn
It at that price.

MA. Then rifl'd and abandon'd,
Live thou the scorn both of the world and me.
You have your choice, I came not here to talk

AL. O! what were all my former woes to this?
Under the pain of absence, hard captivity
And my late fears, patience and fortitude
Were my support; patience and fortitude
Are useless now. Shame and dishonour are
Not to be born. Father! ARANTHES! haste,

And

And like *Virginius* preſerve your daughter.
Come *Caſtriot*, come! ALTHEA calls thee now
To certain death, to ſave her from pollution

MA Call louder yet, your idols do not hear.

AL. Tho' none ſhou'd hear, yet ſorrow muſt complain.

MA. Your moving ſoftneſs fans my am'rous flame——
No help can reach thee——All thy friends are abſent;
Wiſely comply, and make a friend of me.

AL All are not abſent, he whoſe preſence fills
Both Heaven and earth; he, he is with me ſtill;
Sees my diſtreſs, numbers my flowing tears,
And underſtands the voice of my complainings,
Tho' ſorrow drowns my ſpeech.

MA I'll wait no longer;
Nor aſk again for that I've power to take.
Now you may ſtrive, as I have begg'd, in vain.

AL. O thou, whoſe hand ſuſtains the whole creation,
Who cloth'ſt the woods, the vallies and the fields,
Who hear'ſt the hungry lion when he roars;
And feed'ſt the eagle on the mountain's top,
Shut not thine ear——turn not away thy face,
Be not as one far off, when danger's near,
Or like an abſent friend to the diſtreſs'd——
Aſſiſt me, ſave me——only thou canſt ſave——
O let me not invoke thy aid in vain

AM. [*Without*] Force, force an entrance.

MA. Ha! who dares do this? [*The door burſts open.*

Enter AMURATH, VISIER, *Kiſler* AGA *and Guards*

MA. Sham'd and prevented! O my curſed fortune!

AL My pray'rs are heard, let virtue ne'er deſpair.

VIS. Guard well the paſſage.

K AGA. Who ſecures his ſword?

VIS. SCANDERBEG yield! thou canſt not hope
t'eſcape.

AM. To fall ſo meanly after all thy wars——
Well may'ſt thou hide thy face.

VIS Blinded by love,
My Lord, he miſs'd his way.

AM. True, OSMIN, true:
That poor excuſe for madneſs, vice and folly,

D 3   Is

Is all this mighty hero has to plead.
—A fair account of life and honour loft !
I hop'd not triumph—Prophet, 'tis too much——
I afk'd but vengeance——Bring him to my tent.
When mirth declining calls for fomething new,
We'll think upon the manner of his death.

MA. Away, you dogs ! confusion, death and hell !
[*Exit*.

AI. They ftand agaft.   Deliverance waits the juft,
But fh)rt's the triumph of deceitful men.
Turn'd on themfelves, their own devices cover
Them with fhame.   (*Afide*)   [*Exit*.

VIS   I'm loft in admiration !
It is the Prince MAHOMET.

AM. Wonder, rage
And difappointment drive me to diftraction.
KISLER AGA, expect to anfwer this.

K. AGA. Let not my Lord condemn his flave unheard,
AMASIE, whom I ever thought a villain,
Going this evening to the captive Princefs ;
I follow'd unperceiv'd, and fo difpos'd me
As to o'erhear him ; who with many oaths,
Affur'd ALTHEA, SCANDERBEG was come ;
Conceal'd by night, and in his faith fecure,
Once more to fee her, and repeat his vows.
Of this I thought myfelf in duty bound
T'inform my royal mafter.

AM. You are clear.

K. AGA. The caution us'd to introduce the Prince,
Seem'd to confirm the truth of what I heard.

AM. Leave us—enough ; your conduct merits praife.
[*Exit* K AGA.

VIS   Th'affrighted fair is fled to her apartment.

AM. Degenerate boy ? thou art my witnefs, ALLAH,
Not fo I fpent my youth, and won his mother ;
Tho' much I lov'd, and long I figh'd in vain.
'Tis vile and bafe to do a private wrong :
When kings, as kings, do ill, the office then
Muft juftify the man.

VIS   A believing monarch,
Obedient to the meffenger of Heaven,
Can never err.

AM.

AM. Our Prophet, by the fword,
Firft taught the ftubborn Arabs to believe,
And writ his laws in blood.

VIS. He knew mankind;
Nay, yet the priefts of all religions teach,
Whate'er is done to propagate the faith,
Muft from its end be good.

AM. Thus do I ftand
Acquitted to myfelf; and SCANDERBEG,
Tho' by affaffination, juftly falls.
To-morrow's fun fhall fhine for me alone.
Yet, O! my faithful OSMIN, all's not well:
I know not how, my fpirits kindle not
As they were wont, when glory was in view.
True, I rejoice, and yet, methinks, my joy
Is like the mirth wrung from a man in pain,

VIS. Guard, righteous Heaven, thy great Vicegerent's
AM. The body fympathizes with the mind, - [health.
As that with what we love. My languor may
Be the effect of my HELLENA's grief,
I live in her. My pleafures are improv'd,
My pains forgot, when I behold her face;
The tend'reft, fondeft, moft belov'd of children.

VIS. O! what has happen'd, Sir?
AM. This evening, OSMIN,
When I commanded her to love AMASIE;
And look upon him as her future lord,
An afhy palenefs fpread o'er all her face,
And gufhing tears befpoke her ftrong averfion:
But when, t'enhance his merit, I difclofed
The purpos'd murder of his native Prince;
Had I pronounc'd the fentence of her death,
Sure lefs had been her terror and furprize.
Kneeling, fhe call'd on Heaven and earth to witnefs
Her utter deteftation of the fact,
And everlafting hatred of AMASIE,
His perfon and defign.

VIS. Unhappy Princefs!
To be compell'd to marry where fhe hates.

AM. O! fhe abhors him, loaths his very name;
Yet ftill her filial piety prevail'd,
She hung upon my neck, pray'd for my life,

My

My honour, my fuccefs; and took her leave
In fuch endearing ftrains, as if fhe never
Had been to fee me more.   Her moving foftnefs
Melted my old tough heart—I kifs'd her—figh'd,
And wept as faft as fhe.   Our mingled tears
Together flow'd down my fhrunk wither'd cheeks,
And trickled from my beard——O! fhou'd my thirft
Of vengeace kill my child, fhou'd fhe, t' avoid
AMASIE, fly to death—what cou'd fupport me?

[*Exeunt.*

SCENE III.

A Wood, thro' which is feen the Chriftian *Camp.*

Enter HELLENA *and* CLEORA *in mens apparel*

CLE. Where are we, Princefs! whither will you wan-
        der?   [tain.
HEL   We've gain'd the utmoft fummit of the moun-
I hear the neigh of horfes—See'ft thou not
Thofe lights that glimmer thro' the trees, CLEORA!
The Chriftian camp's before us.
    CLE. Righteous ALLAH! the Chriftian camp!——
    HEL. 'Tis thither I am bound.
    CLE. Diftraction!
    HEL. I am determin'd.
    CLE. Hear me, Princefs?
Once take the counfel of your faithful flave,
And yet return before our flight be known.
    HEL. O! no, CLEORA! I muft ne'er return.
    CLE. Then in your father's empire let us feek
Some far remote and unfrequented village;
Where, thus difguis'd, you may remain unknown
To all but me; 'till death fhall end your forrows.
Why are you come to find new dangers here?
Alas! I thought you only fled AMASIE.
    HEL. Why fhould I fly from him? in his defpite
I cou'd have dy'd, even in my father's arms.
Death, ever at my call, had been a fure
Defence from his more loath'd embraces. Gentle maid,
Think it not hard, that I've conceal'd from thee

My

My real intention, till 'twas paſt thy power,
Hid'ſt thou the inclination to prevent it.

CLE. Break, break, my heart, for I've liv'd too long,
Since I'm ſuſpected by my royal miſtreſs.

HEL. I fear'd thy fond affection would have weigh'd
Each danger with too ſcrupulous a hand
I know 'twill ſtrike thee with the laſt amazement
To hear I've left the boſom of a father,
Howe'er ſevere to others, kind to me,.
To ſeek his mortal foe.

CLE. Your reaſon's loſt.

HEL. No ; I remember well the terrors paſt,
And count on thoſe to come ; both worſe than death.
Conſcious of my weak ſex, with all its fears,
To paſs by night thro' camps of hoſtile men,
And urge the preſence of that awful prince,
My ſoul in ſecret has ſo long ador'd————
When I ſhall ſee him, ſhou'd his piercing eye
Trace me thro' my diſguiſe !————O my CLEORA !
Will not my fault'ring tongue, my crimſon cheeks,
My panting heart and trembling limbs betray me ?
What think'ſt thou ? Say, ſhall I not die with ſhame
When I wou'd ſpeak, and leave my tale untold.

CLE. Theſe and a thouſand difficulties more
Oppoſe your purpoſe; then in time retire.

HEL. No more , away ; my reſolution's fixt.
The glory and the danger's both before me,
And both are mine——you were neceſſary
To my eſcape—That's paſt—'Tis true, indeed,.
Your ſervice has by far excell'd my bounty :
Here take theſe jewels, and go ſeek thy ſafety :
I can purſue my purpoſe by myſelf.

Enter PAULINUS, *with a guard , who come from the
farther part of the ſtage to the front, and ſtand liſte-
ning for ſome time.*

CLE. O how have I deſerv'd this cruel uſage !
If I've diſcover'd any ſigns of fear,
'Twas never for myſelf——Go where you pleaſe,
I'll follow you to death.

HEL.

HEL. Kind, faithful maid——

Wherefore fhou'd I involve thee in my ruin?

CLE. 'Tis ruin to forfake you.

HEL. Mine is certain;

Thou may'ft have many happy years to come.

PAU. Stand, there.——Who are you?——Anfwer to the

HEL. Fatal furprize! what muft we anfwer?   [guard.

CLE. Friends.

PAU. Make it appear—this inftant—Give the word.

——Silent——Some fpies fent from the Sultan's camp.

Left, favour'd by the darknefs of the night,

The traitors fhou'd efcape, guard ev'ry paffage.

HEL. SCANDERBEG muft die.   } [Guards fur-

OFF. Not by thy hand,   } round them.

If mine can aim aright, thou bloody villain!

[Wounds HELLENA. She falls.

HEL. Untimely fate!

CLE. Where are you?

HEL. Here, on the earth.

CLE. You're wounded then?

HEL. Alas! to death, CLEORA.

CLE. Prophet, I do not charge you with injuftice;

But I muft grieve, and wonder things are thus.

HEL. Too hafty death! cou'dft thou not ftay a little,

Little longer? the bufinefs of my life

Had foon been done, and I had come to thee.

PAU. Moving founds! I fear you've been too rafh.

Ill fated youths, who are you, and from whence?

What dire misfortune brought you to this place?

HEL. It matters not, who, or from whence we are;

But as you prize your royal mafter's life,

Conduct me to him ftrait: mine ebbs apace,

Yet on its fhort duration his depends.

PAU. Your adjuration is of fuch a force,

His own commands wou'd fcarce oblige me more.

Sir, I'll attend you

HEL. All you fleeting powers,

Sight, fpeech and motion, O! forfake me not

So near my journey's end, affift me to

Perform this only tafk, and take your flight for ever.

SCENE

SCENE IV.

SCANDERBEG'S *Tent.*

SCAN. Degenerate *Rome*! by godlike *Brutus* freed
From *Cæsar* and his temporary chain,
Your own ingratitude renew'd those bonds,
Beneath whose galling weight you justly perish'd.
If freedom be Heaven's universal gift,
Th' unalienable right of human kind,
Were all men virtuous, there would be no slaves.
Despotic power, that root of bitterness,
That tree of death, that spreads its baleful arms
Almost from pole to pole; beneath whose cursed shade,
No good thing thrives, and ev'ry ill finds shelter.;
Had found no time for its detested growth,
But for the follies and the crimes of men.
In ev'ry climate, and in ev'ry age,
Where arts, and arms, and public virtue flourish'd,
Ambition, dangerous only to itself,
Crush'd in its infancy, still found a grave
Where it attempted to erect a throne.

Enter HELLENA, *supported by* PAULINUS, *and*
CLEORA, *guards following*

HEL. My blood flows faster, and my throbbing heart
Beats with redoubl'd force, now I behold him,
O take me to thy arms—I die, CLEORA! (*Swoons.*)
PAU. He faints, support him, while we search his
            wound.
CLE. Away; and touch him not—O gracious Prince!
If ever pity mov'd your royal breast,
Let all depart except yourself and us.
SCAN Let all withdraw   (*Exit* PAULINUS, &c.
Now, gentle youth, inform me,
Why you oppose th' assistance of your friend?
CLE She's gone, she's gone: O Heavens! she's past
            assistance.
SCAN. Think what you say, and recollect your reason.
CLE O mighty Prince! we are not what we seem,
But hapless women.
                                    SCAN·

Scan. Ha!

Cle. Women; and fure
The moft diftrefs'd, and wretched of our fex.
T'increafe your admiration, view this face.

Scan. Sure I have known thefe lovely features well,
But when, or where, my recollection fails me.

Cle. And well it may. O! who cou'd know thee now?
Never enough deplor'd, unhappy Princefs.

Scan. Fearful fuggeftion! fure my eyes deceive me!
Forbid it Heaven, that this fhou'd be Hellena.

Hel. Who was it call'd upon the loft Hellena?

Scan. Ha! fhe revives; fly inftantly for aid.

Hel. It was his voice —— falfe maid, thou haft be-
     tray'd me.
Stay—whether wou'dft thou go! I'm paft all aid:
The friendly hand of death will quickly clofe
Thefe ever ftreaming eyes, and end my fhame.
O Prince! the moft diftinguifh'd and belov'd
By righteous *Allah*, of his works below;
You fee the daughter of relentlefs Amurath,
Sunk with her father's crimes, o'erwhelm'd with fhame,
Expiring at your feet. My weaknefs ftands
Confefs'd, but be it fo, I will no more
Lament my painful, hopelefs, fatal flame,
Since Heaven ordain'd it for your prefervation.

Scan. When will my wonder and my anguifh ceafe?

Hel. I'm come to fave you, Prince, from falling by
A vile affaffin's aim; the falfe Amasie
Has deeply fworn your death; ev'n now he comes
To plunge his bloody poniard in your breaft.

Scan. Fatal miftake! what bafe detractor has
Traduc'd my friend; and wrought thee, gen'rous Princefs,
To thy ruin?

Hel. Doth not the traitor come
Here by appointment?

Scan. Ha!

Hel. Whence learnt I that?
Be not deceiv'd, but guard your precious life;
Or I fhall die in vain For me this bloody
Enterprize was form'd; my feeble charms,
That wound but where I hate, the motive to
This crime.

SCAN Juft Heav'n! that I cou'd longer doubt it!

CLE. Alas! fhe's going, raife her, gently raife her.

HEL. My head grows dizzy.

SCAN. Lean it on my breaft.

HEL This is indeed no time to ftand on forms.

SCAN. The pains, the agonies of death are on her;
And yet fhe fuffers lefs, much lefs, than I.
What generous heart can bear it?

HEL. Do not grieve:
And yet methinks your pity fooths my pain.   (mine?

SCAN Why wou'dft thou give thy life to ranfom
Wou'd I had dy'd, or yet cou'd die, to fave thee

HEL I'd not exchange my death, lamented thus,
And in your arms, for any other's life————
Unlefs ALTHEA's.

SCAN Were ALTHEA here
She wou'd forget her own fevere diftrefs,
And only weep for yours.

HEL. May fhe be happy!
Yet had you never feen her, who can tell?
You fometimes might, perhaps, have thought on me.

SCAN He in my place, who cou'd refrain from tears?
Unenvied let him boaft of his brutality:
I'm not afham'd to own myfelf a man.

HEL. Farewel, CLEORA!————weep not, gentle maid;
I recommend her, Sir, to your protection.
And, O victorious Prince, if e'er hereafter
Conqueft fhou'd give my father to your fword————
————Then think on me —— fufpend your lifted arm,
And fpare————O fpare his life————forget your wrongs;
Or think them punifhed in his daughter's lofs   (*Dies.*

SCAN. Her gentle foul is fled, fhe refts in peace;
While we, methinks, like gratitude and grief,
Form'd by the fculpture's art to grace her urn;
Moving, tho' lifelefs, eloquent, tho', dumb,
Excite incurious mortals to explore,
Virtues fo rare, and trace the fhining ftore,
That cou'd a life fo fhort fo well fupply;
Yet mourn with us fuch excellence fhou'd die.

E   A C T

ACT V.   Scene I.

Christian Camp.

Enter SCANDERBEG AMASIE *in chains,* PAU-
LINUS *&c.*

SCANDERBEG.

COU'D love, that fills each honeſt gen'rous breaſt
   With double ardour to excell in virtue,
Conclude, thou wretch! what malice firſt begun,
And finiſh thee a villain? thou wou'dſt die——
We'll diſappoint thee — Live, tortur'd with guilt,
A terror to thyſelf: or let the Sultan,
The vile abettor of thy crimes, reward thee;
We know no puniſhment to ſuit thy guilt.
This is a Chriſtian land.   Our laws were made
For men, not monſters.——Take him from my ſight.
'Tis needleſs to repeat that by hoſtility,   (*Exit* AMASIE.
Of the worſt kind, our faithleſs enemies
Have broke the truce.   We're now again prepar'd
Once more to prove the fortune of our arms;
And try by honeſt force, ſeeing all treaties
With ſuch perfidious men are vain, to free
Our captive friends, and drive theſe fierce deſtroyers
From *Epirus* PAULINUS, with your ſquadrons
Attack the trenches weſtward of the city,
T'amuſe the foe, and draw their force that way;
Then I'll, with the remaining troops, aſſault
The eaſt; where doubly intrench'd the royal tents,
The priſon of ALTHEA and her father,
Raiſe their aſpiring heads.   I need not ſay,
Acquit yourſelves like men; I know you well;
Nor ſpur you on with hopes of promis'd wealth.
I have no uſeleſs ſtores of hoarded gold:
My revenues, you know, have been the ſpoils
Of vanquiſh'd foes, theſe I have ſhar'd amongſt you.
Wou'd you have more? our enemies have enoug :
Subdue your foes, and ſatiſfy yourſelves.
Let each commit himſelf to that juſt Power,

Who

Who ſtill has been our guide and ſure defence.
Be valiant, not preſumptuous. Seek his aid,
Who by our weakneſs magnifies his ſtrength.
Now follow me, my fellow ſoldiers, and remember
You ſight the cauſe of liberty and truth,
Your native land, ARANTHES and ALTHEA.

Drawing his ſword.

ALL. Huzza! liberty! juſtice! ARANTHES and
ALTHEA! [*Exeunt.*

S C E N E II.

The Sultan's tent.

AMURATH, KAGA, *and an Officer.*

AM. AMASIE's not return'd ——ſhou'd he betray me
And join with SCANDERBEG to free the captives! ——
That officer's his creature —— MUSTAPHA!
Reſign ARANTHES to the KISLER AGA——
Conduct him to ALTHEA. Let AMASIE,
That unauſpicious ſlave, be true or falſe,
Succeed or periſh, they ſhall ſurely die:
So tell the father—Hence, you ſlaves, be gone.
Now let me think—there muſt have been a change,
A revolution in the ſcource of things.
The former chain of beings is diſſolv'd:
Effects roll backward, and direct their cauſes,
And nature is no more. Thou hoary wretch,
Tear thy white locks, abandon ev'ry hope,
Renounce humanity and all its ties.
Duty and virtue, gratitude and love,
Forſook the world, when my HELLENA fled.
May order ne'er return to bleſs mankind;
Let diſcord rage, ne'er let affections meet;
But parents curſe, and children diſobey;
Or either's kindneſs be repaid with hate.
'Till ev'ry child, and ev'ry ſire on earth,
Be in each other curs'd, as me and mine.

Enter VISIER.

VIS. Not yet at reſt?

E 2

AM.

Am. A parent and at reft!———— (the weft

Vis. The Chriftians have ftorm'd the trenches toward
Unle's our prefence animate the troops
All will be loft

Am. HELLENA's loft already!

Vis. Sine AMASIE has fail'd, and SCANDERBEG
Is come upon us to revenge th' attempt

Am. 'Tis well Wak'd from my lethargy of grief,
I yet may reach his heart.

Vis. Regard your health,
And leave the bufinefs of this night to us;
A burning fever rages in your blood. (*Alarm.*

Am. Fame calls me forth. Again I hear her voice;
Earth fhakes, and Heaven reverberates the found.
Affrighted night fits trembling on her throne,
Tumult has driven filence from her confines,
And half her empire's loft. When glory calls,
Shall age or ficknefs keep me from the field?
No, in fpite of both I'll die like AMURATH yet,
Like what I've liv'd, a foldier and a king

Vis. He's defperate and will not be oppos'd.

S C E N E III.

Turkifh *Camp.*

Alarm, foldiers flying.

[*Soldiers within*] Fly, fly, SCANDERBEG, SCAN-
DERBEG; fly, fly.

Enter A M U R A T H *and* V I S I E R *meeting the rout*

Am. Turn back you flaves.

[*Soldiers within*] Fly, fly; SCANDERBEG, fly

Am. Ah! cowards, villains! doth his name affright
you?
Are there fuch terrors in an empty found?
And is my rage contemn'd? but you fhall find
Death is as certain from my arm as his.

Vis. O fpare your faithful flaves! What can men do
Againft a power, invincible, like Heav'n's?

Am. And muft it be, like Heav'n's, eternal too?

Vis.

Vis Retire, my Lord, into the inner camp,
And there securely wait a better hour :
For this is the *Epirot*'s.

Am. Slave, thou lieft !
This hour is mine · I'll triumph o'er him yet.
This hour his friend and miftrefs both fhall die.
The royal brute, tho' in the hunters toils,
Pierc'd with a thoufand wounds is ftill a lion ;
Dreadful in death, and dang'rous to the laft.   [*Exeunt.*

S C E N E IV.

A L T H E A'S *Apartment.*

Al. Was ever night like this? what terrors have
I paft? and, O! what terrors yet furround me?
A loud and deaf'ning found, that feem'd the voice
Of a chac'd multitude, or many waters
Vex'd to a Storm, firft fpread thro' all the camp;
Then fhrieks, and cries, and yellings of delpair,
Mix'd with the fhouts of victory and joy.
Sure fleep has left all eyes, as well as mine.
Fate is at work, I fink beneath my fears.
Since I have known a danger worfe than death,
My courage has forfook me.

Enter A R A N T H E S.

Ha! who comes
At this late hour? Protect me righteous Heaven!

Ar Why, my ALTHEA! doft thou fly thy father?

Al. Sure 'tis his voice! O gracious Heaven! it is,
It is my father ——Moft unlook'd for joy!

Ar Do I once more behold thee, my ALTHEA!

Al. To whofe blefs'd bounty do we owe this meeting?

Ar Thou deareft earthly blifs, this moment's ours,
No matter how attain'd ; I have thee now
In my fond arms, and wou'd indulge my joy,
Nor think how foon 'twill end. Why fhou'd poor
mortals,
To trouble born, anticipate their pains?

Al. I can't conceal my fears · if you again

                                                       Muft

Muft leave me here, the fun in all its courfe,
Sees not a wretch fo loft as poor ALTHEA.

AR. Alas! why will you urge me to difclofe
What wou'd, tho' I were filent, foon be known?
The wrathful Sultan has pronounc'd our death.
Yes, I am come to die with thee, my child!

AL. Then we fhall part no more.
My foul's at peace——Forgive, O righteous Heaven!
My weak diftruft of thy Almighty Power,
Thy kindnefs and protection. O my father!
I wifh'd t'have dy'd alone, yet at your death,
I muft not, dare not murmur or complain;
Since Heaven with you permits me to defcend,
Pure and unfpotted to the peaceful grave.

AR. Heroic maid! O moft exalted virtue.
                              [*Afide, weeping.*

AL. Why do you hide your face, why turn you from
B'not furpriz'd, nor charge me with unkindnefs. [me?
There is, my deareft father! one calamity,
Tho' fure but one, by far more dreadful
Ev'n than thy death——O fpeak, fpeak to me, fir!

AR. Good Heav'n! my joy's too great,—I cannot
        fpeak.
Tears muft relieve me, or my heart will burft
I thank thee, Heaven! I have not liv'd in vain.
This happy hour o'erpays an age of forrow.
My child! my life! my foul! my dear ALTHEA!
Thy bright example fires my emulation,
Thou haft the ftart, but muft not bear away
The victor's palm alone, and fhame thy father.
No, my ALTHEA! to that bounteous hand
Which made thee what thou art, and made thee mine,
Without the leaft reluctance, I'll refign thee.——
And fee the trial comes.

          Enter KAGA *and Mutes*
AGA. Forgive, fair Princefs, a devoted flave,
                              [*Kneeling.*
Who knows no will, but his Imperial Lord's;
No merit, but obedience Cou'd my tears
Have mov'd the Sultan, I had been excufed
This fatal vifit.

                                        AL.

AL. KISLER AGA, rise,
Spite of thy office, thou haft a human foul.
What are thy mafter's orders? Art thou come
A fecond time to my deliv'rance?

AGA. If
Death, fudden, violent and immature,
Be a deliverance, you will foon be free. [rors,

AL. To minds prepar'd, death ftrip'd of all its ter-
In any form, at any hour is welcome.

AGA. Whether the Sultan, raging for the lofs
Of his lov'd daughter, thinks that other's pain,
In the fame kind, wou'd mitigate his own,
Or from fome other caufe, I cannot fay,
But he has order'd that the lady firft
Shou'd fuffer death, her father being prefent —
I fee you're mov'd.

AR I am.—But 'tis with fcorn
Of your proud mafter's impotence and malice,
Alas! I'm not to learn my child is mortal.

AGA. Thefe eager blood-hounds growl at my delay,
And will, perhaps, accufe me to the Sultan.

AL. Obey the tyrant, let them do their office.

AGA. I muft, but Heaven can tell with what reluc-
The only favour in my power to grant, [tance.
Is the fad choice of dying by the bowftring,
The fatal poinard, or this pois'nous draught.

AL. Give me the bowl. Death, this way feems lefs
frightful,
Than from the hands of rude and barbarous men,

AR Farewel, my child!

AL. Affift me with your prayers.

AR. My prayers have been inceffant as thy own,
And both are heard—Fear not—thy crown's prepar'd;
And Heav'n, with all its glories, lies before thee:
Millions of angels wait to guard the paffage;
Thou can'ft not mifs thy way.

AL. Shou'd Heav'n preferve you?—
Shou'd you live to fee him?—commend me to
My Lord—Tell him, that I die his—That Heaven,
Which calls me now, is only lov'd beyond him —
That I'm not loft—That we fhall meet again.—
Bid him not grieve.—
[*Alarm.*
Enter

Enter SCANDERBEG, &c,

He flies to ALTHEA.

SCAN. Away you facrilegious flaves——She lives——
I have her warm and panting in my arms——
Lift up thy eyes, dearer to mine than light——
O let me hear the mufic of thy voice,
Left I fhou'd doubt I come too late to fave 'thee,
And difcord feize my foul.

AL. Surprize is dumb.
So fudden a tranfition who can bear ?
My thoughts were all juft reconcil'd to death,
But thou haft call'd them back.   The love of life,
That feem'd extinguifh'd in me, now returns.
O ! if there is a happinefs on earth,
Here I muft find it, here and only here.   [joy !

SCAN. ARANTHES too !——He lives !——Confummate

AR. And lives by thee, thou glorious happy youth !
O let me prefs thee in my longing arms——
My child too !——My ALTHEA !——

AL. O my father !

AR. Compleat felicity !

AL. O dangerous blifs ! (*weeps.*)

SCAN. Why weeps my life ?

AL Some have their portion here :
Flatt'ring profperity has ruin'd thoufands,
Whom death with all its terrors cou'd not fhake. [ger.

SCAN. Thy pious tears fh·ll guard us from that dan-

AL. Is not the glory of both worlds too much
For frail, imperfect mortals to expect ?

SCAN. Our happinefs, tho' great, is far from perfect,
Since fhe, the fair unfortunate HELLENA,
To whom next Heav'n we owe it, is no more,
I cannot blame your tears ; this is no time
To tell the mournful tale, that muft, when e'er
Remember'd, make me fad, tho' crown'd with victory,
And in thy arms, CROIA reliev'd, expects us :
My grateful fubjects will for thy deliv'rance
Exprefs more joy, than that their foes are fled.

Enter PAULINUS, *and the Sultan Prifoner*

PAU. Hail glorious King ! Your conqueft is compleat·

Behold ambitious AMURATH your captive.

SCAN. Take off his chains.

AM. What pageantry is this?

SCAN. Sound a retreat, since none refift, let war,
And flaughter ceafe. It grieves my foul to think
The crimes of one fhou'd coft mankind fo dear.

PAU. Sir, how will you difpofe the cruel tyrant?

SCAN Give him his liberty, and leave him here
Till he fhall think it proper to retire.
Such of his fubjects as attend him now,
Or fhall repair hither to do him fervice,
Shall all be fafe. His lovely, virtuous daughter,
Worthy a better race and happier fate,
Preferv'd my life,

AM. Dogs! flaves! will none difpatch me?
Muft I hear this, yet be compell'd to live?

SCAN. Unhappy man! how will he bear the reft?
When juftice ftrikes let guilty mortals tremble,
And all revere her power, but none infult
The miferable. Her impartial fword
Scorns to affift man's felfifh low revenge:
T'avoid her anger let us fhun the thought.
Be witnefs, Heaven! I pity and forgive him.
    [*Exeunt* SCANDERBEG, ARANTHES *and* ALTHEA,

AM. Can this be true! am I caft down from that
Majeftic height, where, like an earthly God,
For more than half an age, I fate enthron'd,
To the abhor'd condition of a flave?
A pardon'd flave! What! live to be forgiv'n!
And all this brought upon me by HELLENA!
Shou'd our Prophet return to earth and fwear it,
I'd tell him to his face that he was perjur'd.
Hell wants the power, and Heaven wou'd never curfe,
To that degree, a doating, fond, old man —
What make my child! my loving, gentle child!
The inftrument and author of my ruin!

Enter V I S I E R, *Officers and* A M A S I E.

VIS. Beg them to halt; blaft not a parent's eye
With fuch a fight.

AM. What fight? but 'tis no matter;
There's nothing left for me to hope or fear.

                                    VIS.

VIS. A mourning troop of Chriſtians from their camp
In ſolemn pomp's arriv'd; who bath'd in tears,
(What en'my cou'd refrain?) attend a chariot,
That bears HELLENA bleeding, pale and dead.

AM. Falſe MAHOMET! [*Swoons.*

OFF. Our Royal Maſter's dead!

VIS. No! he revives, alas! he's not ſo happy!

AM. I ſaw AMASIE.

VIS. Here the traitor ſtands,
By SCANDERBEC committed to your mercy.

AMA. HELLENA did prevent me.——

AM. Damn'd apoſtate!
I've heard enough and have no time to loſe.——
See him impal'd alive; we'll let him know
As much of hell as can be known on earth,

[*Exit* AMASIE.

And go from pain to pain.
Where is my ſon?

VIS. Fled towards *Andrianople.*

AM. He doth well:
Death has o'ertook me here. Lord of ſo many
Fair, ſpacious kingdoms, in a hoſtile land,
Oppreſs'd with age, misfortunes, grief and ſhame,
AMURATH breathes his laſt, and leaves his bones
To beg from foes an ignominious grave.
Falſe or ungrateful Prophet! have I ſpread
Fell devaſtation over half the globe,
To raiſe thy creſcent's pale, uncertain light,
Above the Chriſtian's glowing, crimſon croſs:
In hoary age to be rewarded thus!——
When the *Hungarian* King had broke his faith;
Diſtreſs'd, to his own Prophet I appeal'd,
A ſtranger, and an enemy; he did me right;
Reſtor'd loſt vict'ry to my flying troops,
And gave the perjur'd monarch to my ſword.
But I have done——Cou'dſt thou repent, there's nothing
In thy power worth my acceptance now.
Glory, to thee I've liv'd, but pining grief
Robs thee of half the honour of my death.
OSMIN, and you my other faithful chiefs,
The poor remains of all the mighty hoſt
[nown,
I brought to this curs'd ſiege, this grave of my re-
If

If you return, and live to fee my fon,
Bid him remember how his father fell;
Bid him ne'er fheath the fword,
Till my diminfh'd fame fhine forth, and blaze a-new
In his revenge—Revenge me—Oh! Revenge. [*Dies.*

VIS. Eclips'd and in a ftorm our fun is fet:
And now, methinks, as when our Prophet fled,
Terror fhou'd feize on each believing heart:
Let fome inform the King—This was his fate;
'Tis ours thus to be left without a guide,
Difperfe, wander, away, our fhepherd's loft.

Exeunt.

S C E N E V.

Enter S C A N D E R B E G, A R A N T H E S, A L T H E A,
P A U L I N U S, *and Guards*

SCAN. That you are free and happy I rejoice;
If I have faithfully difcharged my truft
I'm well rewarded here,

PAUL. O Royal Sir!
Your happinefs is ours, this virtuous Princefs
An equal blefling to yourfelf and people.

2d *Off.* To fay each fubject loves you as himfelf,
Is lefs than truth: we love you as we ought,
As a free people fhou'd a patriot King,

SCAN. This is to reign, this is to be a king,
Who can controul his power, who rules the will
Of thofe o'er whom he reigns? or count his wealth,
Who has the hearts of fubjects that abound?
Was ever Prince fo abfolute as I?

PAU. Or ever fubjects fo intirely free?
Whofe duty's intereft, and obedience choice.

SCAN. For this alone was government ordain'd;
And kings are Gods on earth but while, like Gods,
They do no ill, but reign to blefs mankind.
May proud, relentlefs AMURATH's misfortunes
Teach future monarchs to avoid his crimes
Th' impious prince, who does all laws difown,
Yet claims from Heaven a right to hold his throne,
Blafphemes that power which righteous kings obey;
For Juftice and Mercy bound e'en th' Almighty's fway.

End of the fifth Act.

EPILOGUE,

Spoken by Mrs. CLIVE.

THE ferious bus'nefs of the night being over,
Pray, ladies, your opinion of our lover?
Will you allow the man deferves the name,
Who quits his miftrefs to preferve — his fame?
And what was fame in that romantic age?——
But fure fuch whims ne'er were but on the ftage.
A ftatefman rack his brains, a foldier fight——
Merely to do an injur'd people right'——
What! ferve his country, and get nothing by't!
Why, ay, fays *Bays*, *George Caftriot* was the man;
'Tis a known truth—— believe him thofe who can.
Not but we've patriots too, tho' I am told
There's a vaft diff'rence 'twixt the new and old
Say, theirs cou'd fight, I'm fure that ours can—fcold.
But to the glory of the prefent race,
No ftubborn principles their worth debafe,
Patriots when out, are courtiers when in place
So, *vice verfa*, turn a courtier out,
No weather-cock more fwiftly veers about
His country now, good man! claims all his care. ——
Who'd fee it plunder'd? — that's deny'd his fhare.

SINCE courtiers and anti-courtiers both have fhown
That by the public good they mean their own,
What if each BRITON, in his private ftation,
Should try to bilk thofe, who imbroil the nation,
Quit either faction, and, like men, unite
To do their king and injur'd country right
Both have been wrong'd prevent their guilty joy,
Who wou'd your mutual amity deftroy
Wou'd you preferve your freedom? guard his throne,
Who makes your peace and happinefs his own
Wou'd you be grateful? let your Monarch know,
Which way you wou'd be beft, and make him fo

But foft! methinks, I hear fome fops complain,
Who came prepar'd to give the ladies pain,   [vain
That they have drefs'd and fpent — Gad's curfe — three hours in
No hints obfcene, improved by their broad ftare,
Have given confufion to the tortur'd fair
We own the charge Let Monfieur *Harlequin*,
And his trim troop, your loofe applaufes win
Too much already has each modeft ear
Been there infulted, we'll protect them here.

FINIS

DON SEBASTIAN,

KING of *Portugal*.

A

T R A G E D Y.

Written by Mr. D R Y D E N.

————*Nec tarda Senectus*
Debilitat vires animi, mutatque vigorem. VIRG.

E D I N B U R G H.

Printed for A DONALDSON, at *Pope's* Head
oppofite the Exchange.

M,DCC,LIX.

PROLOGUE.

Spoken by a Lady.

THE judge remov'd, tho' he's no more my Lord,
   May plead at bar, or at the council-board :
So may caſt poets write ; there's no pretenſion.
To argue loſs of wit from loſs of penſion.
Your looks are chearful ; and in all this place,
I ſee not one that wears a *damning face*.
The BRITISH nation is too brave to ſhew
Ignoble vengeance on a vanquiſh'd foe.
At leaſt be civil to the wretch imploring,
And lay your paws upon him, without roaring :
Suppoſe our poet was your foe before ,
Yet now, the bus'neſs of the field is o'er ;
'Tis time to let your civil wars alone,
When troops are into winter-quarters gone.
JOVE was alike to LATIAN and to PHRYGIAN ;
And you well know, a play's of no religion.
Take good advice, and pleaſe yourſelves this day ,
No matter from what hands you have the play.
Among good fellows ev'ry health will paſs,
That ſerves to carry round another glaſs :
When with full bowls of Burgundy you dine,
Tho' at the mighty monarch you repine,
You grant him ſtill Moſt Chriſtian in his wine.
   Thus far the poet ; but his brains grow addle ,
And all the reſt is purely from his noddle.
You've ſeen young ladies at the ſenate-door,
Prefer petitions, and your grace imploie ;
However grave the legiſlators were,
Their cauſe went ne'er the worſe for being fair.
Reaſons as weak as theirs, perhaps I bring ;
But I cou'd bribe you with as good a thing.
I heard him make advances of good nature,
That he, for once, would ſheath his cutting ſatire -
Sign but his peace, he vows he'll ne'er again
The ſacred names of fops and beaus profane.
Strike up the bargain quickly ; for I ſwear,
As times go now, he offers very fair.

PROLOGUE.

Spoken by a Lady.

THE judge remov'd, tho' he's no more my Lord,
   May plead at bar, or at the council-board :
So may caſt poets write ; there's no pretenſion.
To argue loſs of wit from loſs of penſion.
Your looks are chearful ; and in all this place,
I ſee not one that wears a *damning face.*
The BRITISH nation is too brave to ſhew
Ignoble vengeance on a vanquiſh'd foe.
At leaſt be civil to the wretch imploring,
And lay your paws upon him, without roaring :
Suppoſe our poet was your foe before ;
Yet now, the bus'neſs of the field is o'er ;
'Tis time to let your civil wars alone,
When troops are into winter-quarters gone.
JOVE was alike to LATIAN and to PHRYGIAN ;
And you well know, a play's of no religion
Take good advice, and pleaſe yourſelves this day ,
No matter from what hands you have the play.
Among good fellows ev'ry health will paſs,
That ſerves to carry round another glaſs :
When with full bowls of Burgundy you dine,
Tho' at the mighty monarch you repine,
You grant him ſtill Moſt Chriſtian in his wine.

   Thus far the poet ; but his brains grow addle,
And all the reſt is purely from his noddle.
You've ſeen young ladies at the ſenate door,
Prefer petitions, and your grace implore ,
However grave the legiſlators were,
Their cauſe went ne'er the worſe for being fair.
Reaſons as weak as theirs, perhaps I bring ;
But I cou'd bribe you with as good a thing.
I heard him make advances of good nature,
That he, for once, would ſheath his cutting ſatire :
Sign but his peace, he vows he'll ne'er again
The ſacred names of fops and beaus profane.
Strike up the bargain quickly , for I ſwear,
As times go now, he offers very fair.

Be

Be not too hard on him with statutes neither;
Be kind, and do not set your teeth together,
To stretch the laws, as coblers do their leather.
Horses by Papists are not to be ridden;
But sure the Muses horse was ne'er forbidden:
For in no rate-book, it was ever found
That PEGASUS was valued at five pound:
Fine him to daily drudging and inditing;
And let him pay his taxes out in writing.

DRAMATIS PERSONÆ.

M E N.

DON SEBASTIAN, King of *Portugal*,
MULEY-MOLUCH, Emperor of *Barbary*.
DORAX, a noble *Portuguese*, now a Renegade, former-
  ly DON ALONZO DE SELVERA, Alcaide, or Govern-
  or of *Alcazar*.
BENDUCAR, chief Minister, and Favourite to the Em-
  peror.
ABDALLA, the Mufti.
MULEY ZEYDAN, Brother to the Emperor.
DON ANTONIO, a young, noble, amorous *Portuguese*,
  now a Slave.
DON ALVAREZ, an old Counsellor to DON SEBASTIAN,
  now a Slave also.
MUSTAPHA, Captain of the Rabble.

W O M E N.

ALMEYDA, a Captive Queen of *Barbary*.
MORAYMA, Daughter to the Mufti.
JOHAYMA, chief Wife to the Mufti.
Two Merchants.
Rabble.
A Servant to BENDUCAR.
A Servant to the Mufti.

SCENE, the Castle of *Alcazar*.

DON

Don SEBASTIAN,

King of *Portugal.*

A

TRAGEDY.

ACT I.   SCENE I.

*The Scene at Alcazar, reprefenting a market-place
under the caftle.*

MULEY-ZEYDAN, BENDUCAR.

MULEY-ZEYDAN.

NOW *Africa's* long wars are at an end ;   [blood,
   And our parch'd earth is drench'd in Chriftian
My conquering brother will have flaves enow,
To pay his cruel vows for victory.
What hear you of SEBASTIAN, King of *Portugal?*
   BEND. He fell among a heap of flaughter'd Moors ;
Though yet his mangled carcafe is not found.
The rival of our threaten'd empire, MAHOMET,
Was clofe purfu'd ; and, in the general rout,
Miftook a fwelling current for a ford ;
And in *Mucazar's* flood was feen to rife.
Thrice was he feen , at length his courfer plung'd,
And threw him off ; the waves whelm'd over him,
And helplefs in his heavy arms he drown'd.
   MUL-ZEYD. Thus then a doubtful title is extinguifh'd :
Thus, MOLUCH, ftill the favourite of fate,

Swims

Swims in a fanguine torrent to the throne,
As if our Prophet only work'd for him:
As MULEY-ZEYDAN were not worth his care,
And younger brothers but the draff of nature.

BEND. Be ftill, and learn the foothing arts of court;
Adore his fortune, mix with flattering crouds,
And when they praife him moft, be you the loudeft :
Your brother is luxurious, clofe and cruel,
Generous by fits, but permanent in mifchief:
The fhadow of a difcontent wou'd ruin us ;
We muft be fafe before we can be great :
Thefe things-obferv'd, leave me to fhape the reft.

MUL.-ZEYD. You have the key , he opens inward to
            you.

BEND. So often try'd, and ever found fo true,
Has given me truft, and truft has given me means
Once to be falfe for all. I truft not him :
For now his ends are ferv'd, and he grown abfolute,
How am I fure to ftand who ferv'd thofe ends ?
I know your nature, open, mild, and grateful ;
In fuch a prince the people may be bleft,
And I be fafe.

MUL.-ZEYD. My father !   [*Embracing him*

BEND. My future King ! aufpicious MULEY-ZEYDAN.
Shall I adore you ? no, the place is public ;
I worfhip you within, the outward act
Shall be referv'd till nations follow you,
And Heav'n fhall envy you the kneeling world.
You know th' Alcaide of *Alcazar*, DORAX ?

MUL.-ZEYD. The gallant renegade, you mean ?

BEND. The fame :
That gloomy outfide, like a rufty cheft,
Contains the fhining treafure of a foul,
Refolv'd and brave . he has the foldiers hearts.
And time fhall make him ours.

MUL.-ZEYD. He's juft upon us.

BEND. I know him from afar,
By the long ftride, and by the fullen port:
Retire, my Lord.
Wait on your brother's triumph, yours is next;
His growth is but a wild and fruitlefs plant,

I'll

I ll cut his barren branches to the ftock,
And graft you on to bear.

MUL-ZEYD. My oracle!   [*Exit* MULEY-ZEYD.

BEND. Yes, to delude your hopes,
This eafy fool muft be my ftale, fet up
To catch the people's eyes , he's tame and merciful ;
Him I can manage, till I make him odious
By fome unpopular act, and then dethrone him.

Enter DORAX.

Now DORAX!

BEND, Bare BENDUCAR!

DORAX. Well, BENDUCAR!

DOR. Thou wou'dft have titles, take 'em then, chief
Minifter, firft hangman of the ftate.

BEND. Some call me favourite.

DOR. What's that, his minion?
Thou art too old to be a catamite!
Now prithee tell me, and abate thy pride,
Is not BENDUCAR bare, a better name
In a friend's mouth, than all thofe gawdy titles,
Which I difdain to give the man I love?

BEND. But always out of humour,——

DOR. I have caufe :
Tho' all mankind is caufe enough for fatire.

BEND. Why then thou haft reveng'd thee on mankind;
They fay, in fight thou hadft a thirfty fword,
And well 'twas glutted there.   But let me know,
Brave renegade! cou'dft thou not meet SEBASTIAN?
Thy mafter had been worthy of thy fword.

DOR. My mafter! by what title?
Becaufe I happen'd to be born where he
Happen'd to be a king? and yet I ferv'd him ,
Nay, I was fool enough to love him too.
You know my ftory, how I was rewarded
For fifteen hard campaigns, ftill hoop'd in iron,
And why I turn'd Mahometan : I'm grateful ,
But whofoever dares to injure me,
Let that man know, I dare to be reveng'd.

BEND. Still you run off from biafs ; fay what moves
Your prefent fpleen?

DOR. Yow mark'd not what I told you :

I

I kill'd not one that was his maker's image;
I met with none but vulgar two-legg'd brutes.
SEBASTIAN was my aim; he was a man:
Nay, though he hated me, and I hate him,
Yet I muſt do him right, he was a man,
Above man's height, e'en tow'ring to *Divinity*.
Brave, pious, generous, great, and liberal;
Juſt as the ſcales of Heav'n that weigh the ſeaſons;
He lov'd his people, him they idoliz'd,
And thence proceeds my mortal hatred to him;
That thus, unblameable to all beſides,
He err'd to me alone:
His goodneſs was diffus'd to human kind,
And all his cruelty confin'd to me.
 BEND. You cou'd not meet him then?
 DOR. No, though I fought
Where ranks fell thickeſt; 'twas indeed the place
To ſeek SEBASTIAN: through a track of death
I followed him, by groans of dying foes;
But ſtill I came too late; for he was flown
Like lightning, ſwift before me to new ſlaughters;
I mow'd acroſs, and made irregular harveſt,
Defac'd the pomp of battle, but in vain;
For he was ſtill ſupplying death elſe-where:
This mads me, that perhaps ignoble hands
Have overlaid him, for they cou'd not conquer:
Murder'd by multitudes, whom I alone
Had right to ſlay; I too wou'd have been ſlain,
That catching hold upon his flitting ghoſt
I might have robb'd him of his opening Heav'n;
And dragg'd him down with me, ſpight of predeſtina-
  tion.
 BEND. 'Tis of as much import as *Afric's* worth
To know what came of him, and of ALMEYDA,
The ſiſter of the vanquiſh'd MAHOMET,
Whoſe fatal beauty to her brother drew
The land's third part, as *Lucifer* did Heav'n's.
 DOR. I hope ſhe periſh'd in the general rout.
As for SEBASTIAN we muſt ſearch the field,
And, where we ſee a mountain of the ſlain,
Send one to climb, and looking down below,
There he ſhall find him at his manly length

With

With his face lift up to Heav'n, in the red monument,
Which his true sword has digg'd.

BEND. Yet we may poffibly hear farther news;
For while our *Africans* purfu'd the chace,
The captain of the rabble iffued out,
With a black fhirtlefs train to fpoil the dead,
And feize the living.

DOR. Each of 'em an hoft,
A million ftrong of vermin ev'ry villain :
No part of government, but lords of anarchy,
Chaos of power, and privileg'd deftruction.

BEND. Yet I muft tell you, friend, the great muft ufe 'em,
Sometimes as neceffary tools of tumult.

DOR. I wou'd ufe 'em
Like dogs in times of plague, out-laws of nature,
Fit to be fhot and brain'd, without a procefs,
To ftop infection; that's their proper death.

BEND. No more,
Behold the Emperor coming to furvey
The flaves, in order to perform his vow.

Enter M U L E Y - M O L U C H *the Emperor, with attendants*
The M U F T I, *and* M U L E Y - Z E Y D A N.

M. MOL. Our armour now may ruft, our idle fcimitars
Hang by our fides, for ornament not ufe :
Children fhall beat our atabals and drums,
And all the noify trades of war, no more
Shall wake the peaceful morn · the *Xeriff*'s blood
No longer in divided channels runs,
The younger houfe took end in MAHOMET.
Nor fhall SEBASTIAN's formidable name
Be longer us'd to lull the crying babe !

MUFTI. For this victorious day our mighty Prophet
Expects your gratitude, the facrifice
Of Chriftian flaves, devoted, if you won.

M. MOL. The purple prefent fhall be richly paid:
That vow perform'd, fafting fhall be abolifh'd :
Preach abftinence no more ; I tell thee, MUFTI,
Good feafting is devout : and thou, our head,
Haft a religious, ruddy countenance ;
We well have learned luxury : our lean faith
Gives fcandal to the Chriftians : they feed high:

B.   Then

Then look for shoals of converts, when thou hast
Reform'd us into fasting.

MUF. Fasting is but the letter of the law:
Yet it shows well to preach it to the vulgar.
Wine is against our law; that's literal too,
But not deny'd to kings and to their guides:
Wine is a holy liquor, for the great.   [*English*

DOR [*aside*] This MUFTI, in my conscience, is some
Renegade, he talks so favourably of toping.

M. MOL. Bring forth th' unhappy relicks of the war.

Enter MUSTAPHA, *Captain of the rabble, with his followers
of the black guard, &c. and other Moors: with them a
company of* Portuguese *slaves without any of the chief
persons.*

M MOL. These are not fit to pay an Emperor's vow;
Our bulls and rams had been more noble victims;
These are but garbage, not a sacrifice.   [*off'rings:*

MUF The Prophet must not pick and choose his
Now he has giv'n the day, 'tis past recalling:
And he must be content with such as these.   [*masters.*

M MOL. But are these all? Speak you who are their

MUST. All, upon my honour. If you will take 'em as
their fathers got 'em, so. If not, you must stay till they
get a better generation.

M MOL. Pain of your lives let none conceal a slave.

MUST. Let every man look to his own conscience, I
am sure mine shall never hang me.

BEND. Thou speak'st as thou wert privy to conceal-
ments. Then thou art an accomplice.

MUST. Nay, if accomplices must suffer, it may go
hard with me; but here's the devil on't, there's a great
man, and a holy man too, concern'd with me. Now if I
confess, he'll be sure to 'scape between his greatness and
his holiness, and I shall be murder'd because of my poverty and rascality.

MUF. [*winking at him.*] Then if thy silence save the
          great and holy,
'Tis sure thou shalt go straight to paradise.

MUST. 'Tis a fine place they say, but, Doctor, I am
not worthy on't: I am contented with this homely
                                        world,

woild , 'tis good enough for fuch a poor rafcally Muffulman as I am : befides I have learnt fo much good manners, Doctor, as to let my betters be ferv'd before me.

M Mol. Thou talk'ft as if the MUFTI were concern'd.

MUST. Your Majefty may lay your foul on't : but for
my part, though I am a plain fellow, yet I fcorn to be
trick'd into paradife , I wou'd he fhou'd know it. The
truth on't is an't like you, His reverence bought of me the
flower of all the market, thefe—thefe are but dogs meat
to 'em, and a round price he paid me too, I'll fay that
for him , but not enough for me to venture my neck for.
If I get paradife when my time comes, I can't help myfelf , but I'll venture nothing before-hand, upon a blind
bargain.

M. Mol. Where are thofe flaves ? produce 'em.

Muf. They are not what he fays.

M. Mol. No more excufes. [*One goes out to fetch them*.
Know thou may'ft better dally
With a dead Prophet, than a living King.

Muf, But I referv'd 'em to prefent thy greatnefs
An off'ring worthy thee.

MUST. By the fame token there was a dainty virgin,
(Virgin faid I! but I wont be too pofitive of that neither)
with a roguifh leering eye ! he paid me down for her
upon the nail a thoufand golden *Sultanis* ; or he had
never had her, I can tell him that : Now is it very likely
he would pay fo dear for fuch a delicious morfel, and
give it away out of his own mouth , when it had fuch a
farewel with it too ?

Enter SEBASTIAN *conducted in mean habit, with* ALVAREZ,
ANTONIO, *and* ALMEYDA *her face veil'd with a* Barnus,

M Mol. Ay , Thefe look like the workmanfhip of
This is the porcelain clay of human-kind,   [Heav'n.
And therefore caft into thefe noble moulds.

DORAX *afide, while the* EMPEROR *whifpers* BENDUCAR:

By all my wrongs 'tis he ; he's poifon to me ;
My injur'd honour, and my ravifh'd love,
Bleed at their murderer's fight.

BENDUCAR *to* DORAX *afide*.

The Emperor wou'd learn thefe pris'ners names ;
You know 'em.

DOR,

Dor, Tell him, No;
And trouble me no more.——I will not know 'em.
Aside.] Revenge muſt be my own; I ſcorn a proxy.
　M. Mol. 'Tis decreed,
Theſe of a better aſpect, with the reſt,
Shall ſhare one common doom, and lots decide it.
For ev'ry number'd captive put a ball
Into an urn; three only black be there,
The reſt, all white, are ſafe.
　Muf. Hold, ſir, the woman muſt not draw.
　M. Mol. O Mufti,
We know your reaſon, let her ſhare the danger.
　Muf. Our law ſays plainly women have no ſouls:
　M. Mol. 'Tis true, their ſouls are mortal, ſet her by:
Yet were Almeyda here, though fame reports her
The faireſt of her ſex, ſo much unſeen,
I hate the ſiſter of our rival houſe,
Ten thouſand ſuch dry notions of our *Alcoran*
Shou'd not protect her life, if not immortal:.
Die as ſhe cou'd, all of a piece, the better,
That none of her remain.

Here an urn is brought in; the pris'ners approach with
great concern; and among the reſt Sebastian, Al-
varez and Antonio; *who come more chearfully.*

　Dor. Poor abject creatures how they fear to die!
　　　　　　　　　　　　　　　　　　[*Aſide.*
Theſe never knew one happy hour in life,
Yet ſhake to lay it down: is load ſo pleaſant?
Or has Heav'n hid the happineſs of death
That men may bear to live?——Now for our heroes.

　　　　　The three approach.

O, theſe come up with ſpirits more reſolv'd!
Old venerable Alvarez, well I know him,
The fav'rite once of this Sebastian's father:
Now miniſter, (too honeſt for his trade),
Religion bears him out, a thing taught young,
In age ill practis'd, yet his prop in death.
O, he has drawn a black; and ſmiles upon't,
As who ſhould ſay, my faith and ſoul are white

　　　　　　　　　　　　　　　　Tho'

Tho' my lot's fwarthy : Now if there be hereafter,
He's bleft ; if not, well cheated, and dies pleas'd.

ANTON. *holding his lot in his clench'd hand.*]
Here I have thee,
Be what thou wilt, I will not look too foon.
Thou haft a colour, if thou prov'ft not right,
I have a minute good 'ere I behold thee.
Blind men fay white feels fmooth, and black feels rough:
Thou haft a rugged fkin ; I do not like thee.   ⎰ *Draws*
     SEBASTIAN *comes up to draw.*   ⎱ *a black.*

M. MOL. *to* BEN. Mark him who now approaches to
     the lott'ry ;
He looks fecure of death, fuperior greatnefs,
Like Jove, when he made fate, and faid thou art
The flave of my creation ; I admire him.

BEND. He looks as man was made with face erect,
That fcorns his brittle corps, and feems afham'd
He's not all-fpirit, his eyes with a dumb pride,
Accufing fortune that he fell not warm :
Yet now difdains to live.   [SEBAST. *draws a black.*

M. MOL. He has his wifh,
And I have fail'd of mine.]

DOR. Robb'd of my vengeance by a trivial chance !
Shall I difcover him ? no, 'twere low and bafe !
Ev'n abject, and below thofe vulgar fouls,
That fhar'd his danger, yet not one difclos'd him :
But ftruck with rev'rence, kept an awful filence.
I'll fee no more of this : dog of a Prophet !   [*Ex* DOR.

M. MOL. One of thefe three is a whole hecatomb,
And therefore only one of 'em fhall die.
The reft are but mute cattle ; and when death
Comes, like a rufhing lion, couch like fpaniels,
With lolling tongues, and tremble at the paw ;
Let lots again decide it.

[*The three draw again, and the lot falls on* SEBASTIAN.

SEBAST. Then there's no more to manage ! if I fall,
It fhall be like myfelf, a fetting fun
Shou'd leave a track of glory in the fkies.
Behold SEBASTIAN King of *Portugal.*

M. MOL. SEBASTIAN ! ha ! it muft be he ; no other
Cou'd reprefent fuch fuff'ring Majefty :

I saw him, as he terms himself, a sun
Struggling in dark eclipse, and shooting day
On either side of the black-orb that veil'd him.

SEBAST. Not less ev'n in this despicable now,
Than when my name fill'd *Afric* with affrights,
And froze your hearts beneath your torrid zone.

BEND. *to* M. MOL. Extravagantly brave! ev'n to an
Impudence of greatness.

SEBAST. Here satiate all your fury;
Let fortune empty her whole quiver on me,
I have a soul, that like an ample shield
Can take in all, and verge enough for more.
I would have conquer'd you; and ventur'd only
A narrow neck of land for a third world;
To give my loosen'd subjects room to play.
Fate was not mine,
Nor am I fate's, now I have pleas'd my longing,
And trod the ground which I beheld from far.
I beg no pity for this mould'ring clay:
For if you give it burial there, it takes
Possession of your earth ·
If burnt and scatter'd in the air, the winds,
That strow my dust, diffuse my royalty,
And spread me o'er your clime: for where one atom
Of mine shall light, know there SEBASTIAN reigns.

M MOL. What shall I do to conquer thee?
SEB. Impossible!
Souls know no conquerors.
M. MOL. I'll show thee for a monster thro' my *Afric.*
SEB. No, thou canst only show me for a man:
Afric is stor'd with monsters; man's a prodigy
Thy subjects have not seen.
M. MOL. Thou talk'st as if
Still at the head of battle.
SEB. Thou mistak'st,
For then I would not talk.
M. MOL. Thou'rt brave too late:
Thou shou'dst have dy'd in battle, like a soldier.
SEB. I fought and fell like one, but death deceiv'd me,
I wanted weight of feeble Moors upon me,
To crush my soul out.

M. MOL

M. Mol. Still untameable!
In what a ruin has thy head-ftrong pride,
And boundlefs thirft of empire, plung'd thy people.

Sebast. What fay'ft thou, ha! No more of that.

M. Mol. Behold,
What carcafes of thine thy crime has ftrew'd,
And left our *Afric* vultures to devour.

Bend. Thofe fouls were thofe thy God intrufted with
        thee,
To cherifh not deftroy.

Sebast. Witnefs, O Heav'n, how much
This fight cencerns me! wou'd I had a life
For each of thefe; how gladly wou'd I pay
The ranfom down: But fince I have but one,
'Tis a king's life; and freely 'tis beftow'd.
Not your falfe Prophet, but eternal Juftice
His deftin'd me the lot, to die for thefe:
'Tis fit a Sovereign fo fhou'd pay fuch fubjects;
For fubjects fuch as they are feldom feen,
Who not forfook me at my greateft need;
Nor for bafe lucre fold their loyalty,
But fhar'd my dangers to the laft event,
And fenc'd 'em with their own: Thefe thanks I pay
        you,   [*Wipes his eyes.*
And know that when Sebastian weeps, his tears
Come harder than his blood.

M. Mol. They plead too ftrongly
To be withftood: my clouds are gath'ring too,
In kindly mixture with his royal fhow'r:
Be fafe, and owe thy life, not to my gift,
But to the greatnefs of thy mind, Sebastian:
Thy fubjects too fhall live; a due reward
For their untainted faith, in thy concealment.

Mufti. Remember, fir, your vow.

M. Mol. Do thou remember
Thy function, mercy, and provoke not blood.

Sebast. A mercy unexpected, undefir'd,
Surprizes more: You've learnt the art to vanquifh;
You cou'd not (give me leave to tell you, fir)
Have giv'n me life but in my fubjects fafety,
Kings, who are fathers, live but in their people.

M. Mol. Still great, and grateful, that's thy cha-
        racter.   Unveil

Unveil the woman, I wou'd view the face
That warm'd our MUFTI's zeal:
Thofe pious parrots peck the faireft fruit;
Such taftets are for kings

           [*Officers go to unveil* ALMEYDA.

   ALM. Stand off ye flaves, I will not be unveil'd.

   M. MOL. Slave is thy title: force her.

   SEB. Or your lives,
Approach her not.

   M. MOL. How's this!

   SEB. Sir, pardon me,
And hear me fpeak ——

   ALM. Hear me, I will be heard:
I am no flave; the nobleft blood of *Afric*
Runs in my veins; a purer ftream than thine,
For though deriv'd from the fame fource, thy current
Is puddled and defil'd with tyranny.

   M. MOL. What female fury have we here!

   ALM. I fhou'd be one,
Becaufe of kin to thee: wou'dft thou be touch'd
By the prefuming hands of faucy grooms?
The fame refpect, nay more, is due to me:
More for my fex; the fame for my defcent.
Thefe hands are only fit to draw the curtain,
Now, if thou dar'ft behold ALMEYDA's face.

           [*Unveils herfelf*

She whom thy *Mufti* tax'd to have no foul,
Let *Afric* now be judge;
Perhaps thou think'ft I meanly hope to 'fcape,
As did SEBASTIAN when he own'd his greatnefs.
But to remove that fcruple, know, bafe man,
My murder'd father, and my brother's ghoft
Still haunt this breaft, and prompt it to revenge.
Think not I could forgive, nor dare thou pardon.

   M. MOL. Would'ft thou revenge thee, traitrefs, hadft
      thou pow'r?

   ALM. Traitor, I wou'd, the name's more juftly thine:
Thy father was not more than mine, the heir
Of this large empire; but with arms united
They fought their way, and feiz'd the crown by force:
And equal as their danger was their fhare:
For where was elderfhip, where none had right

                      But

But that which conqueſt gave ? 'twas thy ambition
Pull'd from my peaceful father what his ſword
Help'd thine to gain : ſurpriz'd him and his kingdom,
No provocation given, no war declar'd.

M. Mol. I'll hear no more.

Alm. This is the living coal that burning in me
Wou'd flame to vengeance, cou'd it find a vent.
My brother too, that lies yet ſcarcely cold
In his deep wat'ry bed : my wand'ring mother,
Who in exile died.
O that I had the fruitful heads of Hydra,
That one might bourgeon where another fell ;
Still wou'd I give thee work ; ſtill, ſtill, thou tyrant
And hiſs thee with the laſt.   [ine :

M. Mol. Something, I know not what, comes over
Whether the toils of battle, unrepair'd
With due repoſe, or other ſudden qualm.
Benducar do the reſt.   [Goes off, the court follows him.

Bend. Strange ; in full health this pang is of the ſoul,
The body's unconcern'd : I'll think hereafter.
Conduct theſe royal captives to the caſtle ;
Bid Dorax uſe 'em well, till farther order,
                                        [Going off, ſtops.
Th' inferior captives their firſt owners take,
To ſell, or to diſpoſe.——You Mustapha,
Set ope the market for the ſlaves.   [Exit Benducar.

The maſters and ſlaves come forward, and buyers of ſe-
veral qualities come in and chaffer.

Must. My chattels are come into my hands again,
and my conſcience will ſerve me to ſell 'em twice over,
any price now, before the Mufti comes to claim 'em.

Firſt Merchant *to* MUSTAPHA.
What doſt hold that bold fellow at ?
                                [*Pointing to* Alvarez.
He's tough and has no ſervice in his limbs.

Must. I confeſs he's ſomewhat tough ; but I ſuppoſe
you wou'd not boil him. I aſk for him a thouſand crowns.

1. Mer. Thou mean'ſt a thouſand marvedi's.

Must. Prithee friend, give me leave to know my
own meaning.

                                        1. Mer.

1 MER. What virtues has he to deserve that price ?

MUST. Marry come up sir! virtues quotha! I took him in the king's company ; he's of a great family, and rich, what other virtues wou'dst thou have in a Nobleman ?

1 MER. I buy him with another man's purse, that's my comfort.

My lord DORAX, the governor, will have him at any rate :———

There's handsel.

Come old fellow to the castle.

ALVAR. To what is miserable age reserv'd !   [Aside.
But Oh the King! and Oh the fatal secret !
Which I have kept thus long, to time it better,
And now I wou'd disclose 'tis past my pow'r
                              [Exit with his master.

MUST. Something of a secret, and of the king I heard him mutter: a pimp I warrant him ; for I am sure he is an old courtier.

Now to put off t'other remnant of my merchandize.——

Enter a Second MERCHANT.

2 MER. You, friend, what do you ask for this bauble?

MUST. Bauble do you call him ; he's a substantial true-bred beast ; bravely fore-handed ; mark but the cleanness of his shapes too ; his dam may be a *Spanish* gennet, but a true Barb by the sire, or I have no skill in horse-flesh.——

Marry, I ask six hundred *Xeriffs* for him.

Enter MUFTI

MUFTI. What's that you are asking, sirrah ?

MUST. Marry, I ask your reverence six hundred pardons ; I was doing you a small piece of service here, putting off your chattels for you.

MUFTI. And putting the money into your own pocket.

MUST. Upon vulgar reputation, no my Lord, it was for your profit and emolument. What, wrong the head of my religion ? I was sensible you wou'd have damn'd me, or any man that shou'd have injur'd you in a single farthing ; for I knew that was sacrifice.

MUFTI, Sacrilege you mean, sirrah, —and damning
                                                    shall

ſhall be the leaſt part of your puniſhment; I have taken you in the fact, and have the law upon you.

MUST. Good my Lord, take pity upon a poor man in this world, and damn him in the next.

MUFTI. No ſirrah, ſo you may repent and 'ſcape puniſhment: did not you ſell this very ſlave amongſt the reſt to me, and take money for him.

MUST. Right, my Lord.

MUFTI, And ſelling him again? take money twice for the ſame commodity? Oh, villain!
But did you not know him to be my ſlave, ſirrah?

MUST. Why ſhou'd I lye to your honour, I did know him, and thereupon, ſeeing him wander about, I took him up for a ſtray, and impounded him, with intention to reſtore him to the right owner.

MUFTI. And yet at the ſame time was ſelling him to another · how rarely the ſtory hangs together.

MUST. Patience, my Lord.
I took him up, as your heriot, with intention to have made the beſt of him, and then have brought the whole product of him in a purſe to you; for I know you wou'd have ſpent half of it upon your pious pleaſures, have hoarded up the other half, and given the remainder in charities to the poor.

MUFTI. And what's become of my other ſlave? thou haſt ſold him too, I have a villainous ſuſpicion.

MUST I know you have, my Lord, but while I was managing this young robuſtous fellow, that old ſpark, who was nothing but ſkin and bone, and by conſequence, very nimble, ſlipt through my fingers like an eel; for there was no hold faſt of him, and ran away to buy himſelf a new maſter.

MUFTI *to* ANTONIO.
Follow me home, ſirrah: [*to* MUST] I ſhall remember you ſome other time. [*Exit* MUFTI *with* ANTONIO.

MUST I never doubted your Lordſhip's memory, for an ill turn and I ſhall remember him too in the next riſing of the mobile, for this act of reſumption, and more eſpecially for the ghoſtly counſel he gave me before the Emperor, to have hang'd myſelf in ſilence, to have ſav'd his reverence The beſt on't is, I am beforehand with him, for ſelling one of his ſlaves twice over. ——

And

And if he had not come juft in the nick, I might have pocketted up t'other : for what fhould a poor man do, that gets his living by hard labonr, but pray for bad times when he may get it eafily. O, for fome incomparable tumult⁴ then fhou'd I naturally wifh, that the beaten party might prevail, becaufe we have plundered t'other fide already, and there's nothing more to get of 'em.

> Both rich and poor for their own intereft pray,
> 'Tis our's to make our fortunes while we may ;
> For kingdoms are not conquer'd every day.
> [*Exit.* MUSTAPHA.

✚✚✚✚✚✚✚✚✚✚✚✚✚✚✚✚✚✚✚✚✚✚✚✚✚✚✚✚✚✚

ACT II. SCENE I.

Suppofed to be a terrace-walk, on the fide of the caftle of Alcazar.

EMPEROR, BENDUCAR,

EMPEROR.

AND think'ft thou not it was difcovered ?
 BEND No :
The thoughts of kings are like religious groves,
The walks of muffled Gods , Sacred retreat,
Where none but whom they pleafe t' admit, approach.

EMP. Did not my confcious eyes flafh out a flame
To lighten thofe brown horrors, and difclofe
The fecret path I trode ?

BEND. I cou'd not find it, 'till you lent a clue
To that clofe labyrinth ; how then fhou'd they ?

EMP. I wou'd be loth they fhou'd : It breeds contempt
For herds to liften, or prefume to pry,
When the hurt lion groans within his den :
But is't not ftrange ?

BEND. To love ? not more than 'tis to live ; a tax
Impos'd on all by nature, paid in kind,
Familiar as our being.

EMP. ftill 'tis ftrange

To

To me: I know my soul as wild as winds,
That sweep the desarts of our moving plains:
Love might as well be sow'd upon our sands,
As in a breast so barren:
To love an enemy, the only one
Remaining too, whom yester sun beheld,
Must'ring her charms, and rolling, as she past
By every squadron, her alluring eyes;
To edge her champion swords, and urge my ruin!
The shouts of soldiers, and the burst of cannon,
Maintain e'en still a deaf and murm'ring noise;
Nor am I yet recover'd of the sound
Her battle rous'd: yet spite of me I love.

BEND. What then controuls you,
Her person and her p r y in your power?

EMP. A thousand things controul this conqueror,
My native pride to own th' unworthy passion,
Hazard of int'rest, and my people's love:
To what a storm of fate am I expos'd!
What if I had her murd'red? 'tis but what
My subjects all expect, and she deserves.
Wou'd not th' impossibility
Of ever, ever seeing, or possessing,
Calm all this rage, this hurrican of soul?

BEND. That ever, ever!
I mark'd the double shows extreme reluctance
To part with her for ever.

EMP Right, thou hast me,
I wou'd but cannot kill: I must enjoy her:
I must, and what I must I surely will.
What's royalty but pow'r to please myself?
And if I dare not, then am I a slave,
And my own slaves the sov'reigns.———'Tis resolv'd
Weak princes flatter when they want the pow'r
To crub their people, tender plants must bend,
But when a government is grown to strength,
Like some old oak, rough with its armed bark,
It yeilds not to the tug, but only nods,
And turns to sullen state

BEND. Then you resolve
T' implore her pity, and to beg relief?

EMP Death, must I beg the pity of a slave?

C

Muft a king beg ? Yes love's a greater King ;
A tyrant, nay, a devil that poffeffes me,
And drives me on by force———
Say I fhou'd wed her, wou'd not my wife fubjects.
Take check, and think it ftrange ? perhaps revolt ?

    BEND. I hope they wou'd not.

    EMP. Then thou doubt'ft they wou'd ?

    BEND. To whom ?

    EMP. To her

Perhaps, to my brother, or to thee.

    BEND. [*in diforder*.

To me ! me did you mention ? how I tremble !
The name of treafon fhakes my honeft foul.
If I am doubted, Sir,
Secure yourfelf this moment, take my life.

    EMP. No more : If I fufpected thee——I wou'd.

    BEND. I thank your kindnefs : guilt had almoft loft
        me !   [*Afide.*

    EMP. But clear my doubts : think'ft thou they may
        rebel.

    [BEND. *Afide.*

This goes as I wou'd wifh :———(*to the* EMP.) 'Tis
    poffible.

A fecret party ftill remains, that lurks
Like embers rak'd in afhes——wanting but
A breath to blow afide th' involving duft,
And then they blaze abroad.

    EMP. They muft be trampled out.

    BEND. But firft be known.

    EMP. Torture fhall force it from 'em.

    BEND. You wou'd not put a nation to the rack ?

    EMP. Yes, the whole world ; fo I be fafe, I care not.

    BEND. Our limbs and lives

Are yours, but mixing friends with foes is hard.

    EMP. All may be foes ; or how to be diftinguifh'd,
If fome be friends ?

    BEND. They may with eafe be winnow'd ;
Suppofe fome one, who has deferv'd your truft,
Some one, who knows mankind, fhou'd be employ'd
To mix among 'em, feem a malecontent,
And dive into their breafts, to try how far
They dare oppofe your love ?

                                    EMP.

EMP. I like this well: 'tis wholesome wickedness.

BEND. Whomever he suspects, he fastens there,
And leaves no cranny of his soul unsearch'd:
Then like a bee bagg'd with his honey'd venom,
He brings it to your hive. If such a man,
So able, and so honest, may be found;
If not, my project dies———

EMP. By all my hopes thou hast describ'd thyself:——
Thou, thou alone are fit to play that engine,
Thou only cou'd'st contrive.

BEND. Sure, I cou'd serve you:
I think I cou'd:———but here's the difficulty,
I'm so entirely yours,
That I shou'd scurvily dissemble hate;
The cheat wou'd be too gross.

EMP. Art thou a statesman,
And canst not be a hypocrite?———Impossible!
Do not distrust thy virtues.

BEND. If I must personate, this seeming villain,
Remember 'tis to serve you.

EMP No more words:
Love goads me to ALMEYDA. All affairs
Are troublesome but that; and yet that most.
                                             [Going.

Bid DORAX treat SEBASTIAN like a king;
I had forgot him,——— but this love marrs all,
And takes up my whole breast.   [Exit EMPEROR.

BEND (to the EMP). Be sure I'll tell him———
With all the aggravating circumstances   [Alone.
I can, to make him swell at that command,
The tyrant first suspected me:
Then, with a sudden gust, he whirl'd about,
And trusted me too far: madness of pow'r!
Now, by his own consent, I ruin him.
For, shou'd some feeble soul, for fear or gain,
Bolt out t' accuse me, ev'n the king is cozen'd,
And thinks he's in the secret.
How sweet is treason when the traytor's safe!
(Sees the MUFTI and DORAX entering, and seeming to
                    confer.)
    The MUFTI, and with him my sullen DORAX,
That first is mine already.

'Twas eafy work to gain a cov'tous mind,
Whom rage to lofe his pris'ners had prepar'd:
Now, caught himfelf,
He wou'd feduce another; I muft help him:
For church men, though they itch to govern all,
Are filly, woeful, awkward politicians;
They make lame mifchief, though they mean it well.

  MUF. He'll tell you more.

  DOR. I've heard enough already
To make me loath thy morals.

  BEND *to* DOR. You feem warm:
The good man's zeal, perhaps, is gone too far.

  DOR. Not very far; not farther than zeal goes
Of courfe, a fmall day's journey fhort of treafon.

  MUF. By all that's holy, treafon was not nam'd:
I fpar'd the Emperor's broken vows to fave
The flave from death, though it was cheating Heav'n,
But I forgave him that

  DOR. And flighted o'er   [*fcorrfully.*
The wrongs himfelf fuftain'd in property:
When his bought flaves were feiz'd by force, no lofs
Of his confider'd, and no coft repaid.

  MUF. Not wholly flighted o'er, not abfolutely:
Some modeft hints of private wrongs I urg'd.

  DOR. Two thirds of all he faid: there he began;
To fhew the fulnefs of his heart, there ended,
Some fhort excurfions of a broken vow
He made indeed, but flat infipid ftuff:
But when he made his lofs the theme, he flourifh'd,
Reliev'd his fainting rhetoric with new figures,
And thunder'd at oppreffing tyranny.

  MUF. Why not, when facrilegious pow'r wou'd feize
My property; 'tis an affront to Heav'n,
Whofe perfon, though unworthy, I fuftain.

  DOR. You've made fuch ftrong alliances above,
That 'twere profanenefs in us laity
To offer earthly aid.
I tell thee, MUFTI, if the world were wife,
They wou'd not wag one finger in your quarrels;
Your Heav'n you promife, but our earth you covet:
The *Phaethons* of mankind, who fire that world,
Which you were fent, by preaching, but to warn

  BEND. This goes beyond the mark.   MUF

MUF. No, let him rail;
His Prophet works within him;
He's a rare convert.

DOR. Now his zeal yearns,
To fee me burnt; he damns me from his church,
Becaufe I wou'd reftrain him to his duty;
Is not the care of fouls a load fufficient?
Are not your holy ftipends paid for this?
Were you not bred apart from worldly noife,
To ftudy fouls, their cures and their difeafes?
If this be fo, we afk you but our own:
Give us your whole employment, all your care:
The province of the foul is large enough
To fill up every cranny of your time,
And leave you much to anfwer, if one wretch
Be damn'd by your neglect.

BEND. *to the* MUFTI. He fpeaks but reafon.

DOR. Why then thefe foreign thoughts of ftate-
employments,
Abhorrent to your function and your breeding?
Poor dioning truants of unpractis'd cells,
Bred in the fellowfhip of bearded boys,
What wonder is it if you know not men?
Yet there you live demure, with down-caft eyes,
And humble as your difcipline requires,
But, when let loofe from thence to live at large,
Your little tincture of devotion dies:
Then luxury fucceeds, and, fet agog
With a new fcene of yet untafted joys,
You fall with greedy hunger to the feaft.
Of all your college virtues, nothing now
But your original ignorance remains:
Bloated with pride, ambition, avarice,
You fwell to counfel kings and govern kingdoms.

MUF. He prates as if kings had not confciences,
And none requir'd directors but the croud,

DOR. As private men they want you, not as kings;
Nor wou'd you care t' infpect their public confcience,
But that it draws dependencies of pow'r,
And earthly intereft which you long to fway.
Content you with monopolizing Heav'n,
And let this little hanging ball alone,

For

For give you but a foot of confcience there,
And you, like *Archimedes*, tofs the globe.
We know your thoughts of us, that laymen are
Lag fouls, and rubbifh of remaining clay,
Which Heav'n, grown weary of more perfect work,
Set upright with a little puff of breath,
And bid us pafs for men.

    MUF I will not anfwer,
Bale foul mouth'd renegade, but I'll pray for thee,
To fhew my charity.   [*Exit* MUFTI.

    DOR Do; but forget not him who needs it moft:
Allow thyfelf fome fhare: He's gone too foon;
I had to tell him of his holy jugglings;
Things that would ftartle faith, and make us deem
Not this or that, but all religions falfe.

    BEND Our holy orator has loft the caufe;   [*Afide*.
But I fhall yet redeem it——[*to* DORAX] let him go;
For I have fecret orders from the Emperor,
Which none but you muft hear: I muft confefs,
I cou'd have wifh'd fome other hand had brought 'em.
When did you fee your pris'ner great SEBASTIAN?

    DOR. You might as well have afk'd me when I faw
A crefted dragon, or a bafilifk;
Both are lefs poifon to my eyes and nature.
He knows not I am I; nor fhall he fee me
Till time has perfected a lab'ring thought
That rolls within my breaft.

    BEND 'Twas my miftake;
I guefs'd indeed that time and his misfortunes,
And your returning duty had effac'd
The memory of paft wrongs; they wou'd in me;
And I judg'd you as tame and as forgiving.

    DOR Forgive him! no, I left my foolifh faith,
Becaufe it wou'd oblige me to forgivenefs.

    BEND. I can but grieve to find you obftinate;
For you muft fee him; 'tis our Emperor's will,
And ftrict command.

    DOR I laugh at that command.   [him.

    BEND. You muft do more than fee; ferve and refpect

    DOR. See, ferve him, and refpect; and after all
My yet uncancell'd wrongs, I muft do this!
But I forget myfelf.

    BEND. Indeed you do.   [DOR

DOR The Emperor is a stranger to my wrongs;
I need but tell my story to revoke
This hard commiffion.

BEND. Can you call me friend,
And think I cou'd neglect to fpeak, at full,
Th' affronts you had from your ungrateful mafter.

DOR. And yet enjoin'd my fervice, and attendance?

BEND. And yet enjoin'd 'em both. Wou'd that were [all;
He fcrew'd his face into a harden'd fmile,
And faid, SEBASTIAN knew to govern flaves.

DOR. Slaves are the growth of *Afric*, not of *Europe :*
By Heav'n I will not lay down my commiffion;
Not at his foot, I will not ftoop fo low,
But if there be a part in all his face
More facred than the reft, I'll throw it there.

BEND. You may; but then you lofe all future means
Of vengeance on SEBASTIAN, when no more
Alcaide of this fort.

DOR That thought efcap'd me. [both:

BEND. Keep your command; and be reveng'd on
Nor foothe yourfelf, you have no power t' affront him:
The Emp'ror's love protects him from your power,
And he, who fpoke that proud ill-natur'd word,
Following the bent of his impetuous temper,
May force your reconcilement to SEBASTIAN;
Nay, bid you kneel, and kifs th' offending foot
That kick'd you from his prefence.
But think not to divide their punifhment;
You cannot touch a hair of loath'd SEBASTIAN
While MULEY-MOLUCH lives.

DOR. What means this riddle?

BEND. 'Tis out; there needs no *Oedipus* to folve it.
Our Emp'ror is a tyrant, fear'd and hated;
I fcarce remember, in his reign, one day
Pafs guiltlefs o'er his execrable head.
He thinks the fun is loft that fees not blood;
When none is fhed we count it holiday.
We, who are moft in favour, cannot call
This hour our own!—you know the younger brother
Mild MULEY ZEIDAN.

DOR. Hold, and let me think.

BEND. The foldiers idolize you;

He

He trufts you with the caftle,
The key of all his kingdom.

 DOR. Well, and he trufts you too.

 BEND. Elfe I were mad,
To hazard fuch a daring enterprize.   [him?

 DOR He trufts us both; mark that: fhall we betray
A mafter who repofes life and empire
In our fidelity: I grant he is a tyrant,
That hated name my nature moft abhors;
More, as you fay, has loaded me with fcorn:
Ev'n with the laft contempt, to ferve SEBASTIAN.
Yet more, I know he vacates my revenge;
Which, but by this revolt, I cannot compafs:
But while he trufts me, 'twere fo bafe a part
To fawn and yet betray, I fhould be hifs'd
And whoop'd in hell for that ingratitude.

 BEND. Confider well what I have done for you.

 DOR. Confider thou what thou wou'dft have me do.

 BEND. You've too much honour for a renegade.

 DOR. And thou too little faith to be a fav'rite.
Is not the bread thou eat'ft, the robe thou wear'ft,
Thy wealth, and honours, all the pure indulgence
of him thou wou'dft deftroy ?
And wou'd his creature, nay his friend betray him ?
Why then no bond is left on human kind :
Diftrufts, debates, immortal ftrifes enfue :
Children may murder parents, wives their hufbands;
All muft be rapine, wars, and defolation,
When truft and gratitude no longer bind.

 BEND Well have you argued in your own defence :
You, who have burft afunder all thofe bonds,
And turn'd a rebel to your native Prince.

 DOR. True, I rebell'd, but when did I betray ?
Indignities, which man cou'd not fupport,
Provok'd my vengeance to this noble crime.
But he had ftripp'd me firft of my command,
Difmifs'd my fervice, and abfolv'd my faith;
And, with difdainful language, dar'd my worft.
I but accepted war, which he denounc'd;
Elfe had you feen, not DORAX, but ALONZO,
With his couch'd lance againft your foremoft *Moors:*
Perhaps too turn'd the fortune of the day,

        Made

Made *Afric* mourn, and *Portugal* triumph.

BEND. Let me embrace thee.

DOR. Stand off, fycophant,
And keep infection diftant.

BEND. Brave and honeft.

DOR. In fpite of thy temptations.

BEND. Call 'em trials ;
They were no more : thy faith was held in balance,
And nicely weigh'd, by jealoufy of pow'r ;
Vaft was the truft of fuch a royal charge ;
And our wife Emperor might juftly fear
SEBASTIAN might be freed and reconcil'd,
By new obligements to thy former love.

DOR. I doubt thee ftill ; thy reafons were too ftrong,
And driv'n too near the head to be but artifice.
And after all, I know thou art a ftatefman,
Where truth is rarely found.

BEND. Behold the Emperor.:
              [*Enter* EMP. SEB. *and* ALMEYDA.
Afk him, I beg thee to be juftify'd,
If he employ'd me not to ford thy foul,
And try the footing, whether falfe or firm.

DOR. Death to my eyes, I fee SEBASTIAN with him!
Muft he be ferv'd ! avoid him ; if we meet,
It muft be like the crufh of heav'n and earth,
T" involve us both in ruin.   [*Exit* DORAX.

BEND. 'Twas a bare faving game I made with DORAX ;
But better fo than loft ; he cannot hurt me,
That I precaution'd · I muft ruin him.
But now this love, Ay, there's the gathering ftorm !
The Tyrant muft not wed ALMEYDA ; no,
That ruins all the fabric I am raifing.
Yet feeming to approve it gave me time,
And gaining time gains all.

[BENDUCAR *goes and waits behind the* EMPEROR. *The*
    EMPEROR, SEBASTIAN *and* ALMEYDA *advance*
    to the front of the ftage] *Guards and Attendants.*

EMP. *to* SEB. I bade 'em ferve you, and if they obey not,
I keep my lions keen within their dens,
To ftop their maws with difobedient flaves.

                   SEB.

SEB. If I had conquer'd,
They wou'd not have with more observance waited:
Their eyes, hands, feet,
Are all so quick, they seem t' have but one motion,
To catch my flying words. Only the *Alcaide*
Shuns me, and, with a grim civility,
Bows, and declines my walks.

EMP. A renegade: —
I know not more of him; but that he's brave,
And hates your Christian sect. If you can frame
A farther wish, give wing to your desires,
And name the thing you want.

SEB. My liberty;
For were ev'n paradise itself my prison,
Still I should long to leap the crystal walls.

EMP. Sure our two souls have somewhere been ac-
        quainted
In former beings; or, struck out together,
One spark to *Afric* flew, and one to *Portugal*.
Expect a quick deliverance: [*turning to* ALM.] here's a
        third,
Of kindred soul to both: pity our stars
Have made us foes! I shou'd not wish her death.

ALM. I ask no pity——If I thought my soul
Of kin to thine, soon wou'd I rend my heart-strings,
And tear out that alliance: but thou viper
Hast cancell'd kindred, made a rent in nature,
And thro' her holy bowels gnaw'd thy way
Through thy own blood to empire.

EMP. This again,
And yet she lives, and only lives t' upbraid me.

SEB. What honour is there in a woman's death!
Wrong'd as she says, but helpless to revenge;
Strong in her passion, impotent of reason,
Too weak to hurt, too fair to be destroy'd.
Mark her majestic fabrick; she's a temple
Sacred by birth, and built by hands divine.
Her soul's the deity that lodges there;
Nor is the pile unworthy of the god.

EMP. She's all that thou canst say, or I can think:
But the perverseness of her clam'rous tongue
Strikes pity deaf.

                                                    SEB.

SEB. Then only hear her eyes;
Though they are mute, they plead; nay more, command,
For beauteous eyes have arbitrary power.
All females have prerogative of fex,
The she's ev'n of the favage herd are safe;
And, when they snarl or bite, have no return
But courtship from the male.

EMP. Were she not she, and I not MULEY-MOLUCH,
She's mistress of inevitable charms,
For all but me; not am I so exempt,
But that——I know not what I was to say——
But I am too obnoxious to my friends;
And sway'd by your advice.

SEB. Sir, I advis'd not.
By Heav'n I never counsell'd love, but pity.

EMP. By Heav'n thou didst: deny it not, thou didst;
For what was all that prodigality
Of praise, but to inflame me?——

SEB. Sir,——

EMR. No more:
Thou hast convinc'd me, that she's worth my love.

SEB. Was ever man so ruin'd by himself! [*Aside.*

ALM. Thy love; that odious mouth was never fram'd
To speak a word so soft:
Name death again, for that thou canst pronounce
With horrid grace, becoming of a tyrant.
Love is for human hearts, and not for thine,
Where the brute beast extinguishes the man.

EMP. Such if I were, yet rugged lions love,
And grapple, and compel their savage dams——
Mark, my SEBASTIAN, how that sullen frown, ⎫ *She*
Like flashing lightning, opens angry Heav'n, ⎬ *frowns.*
And while it kills, delights. But yet, insult not ⎭
Too soon, proud beauty, I confess no love.

SEB. No sir, I said so, and I witness for you,
Not love, but noble pity mov'd your mind:
Int'rest might urge you too to save her life,
For those, who with her party lost, might murmur
At shedding royal blood.

EMP. Right, thou instruct'st me;
Int'rest of state requires not death, but marriage,
T' unite the jarring titles of our line.

SEB.

SEB. Let me be dumb for ever, all I plead, [*Aside.*
Like wild-fire thrown against the wind, returns
With double force to burn me.

EMP Cou'd I but bend to make my beauteous foe
The partner of my throne, and of my bed ————

ALM. Still thou disemblest; but I read thy heart,
And know the power of my own charms; thou lov'st,
And I am pleas'd for my revenge thou dost.

EMP And thou hást cause.

ALM. I hate; for I have pow'r to make thee wretched.
Be sure I will, and yet despair of freedom.

EMP. Well then, I love————
And 'tis below my greatness to disown it:
Love thee implacably, yet hate thee too,
Wou'd hunt thee bare-foot, in the mid-day sun,
Through the parch'd desarts, and the scorching sands,
T' enjoy thy love, and once enjoy'd to kill thee

ALM. 'Tis a false courage, when thou threaten'st me,
Thou canst not stir a hand to touch my life:
Do not I see thee tremble while thou speak'st;
Lay by the lions hide, vain conqueror,
And take the distaff; for thy soul's my slave.

EMP. Confusion! how thou view'st my very heart!
I cou'd, as soon,
Stop a spring-tide blown in, with my bare hand,
As this impetuous love ————Yes, I will wed thee;
In spite of thee and of myself, I will.

ALM. For what? to people *Afric* with new monsters,
Which that unnatural mixture must produce?
No, were we join'd, e'en tho it were in death,
Our bodies burning in one funeral pile,
The prodigy of THEBES wou'd be renew'd,
And my divided flames shou'd break from thine.

EMP. Serpent, I will engender poison with thee;
Join hate with hate, and venom to the birth:
Our offspring, like the seed of dragons teeth,
Shall issue arm'd, and fight themselves to death.

ALM. I'm calm again, thou canst not marry me.

EMP. As gleams of sun-shine soften storms to show'rs,
So, if you smile, the loudness of my rage
In gentle whispers shall return, but this,————
That nothing can divert my love but death.

ALM.

ALM. See how thou art deceiv'd, I am a Christian;
'Tis true, unpractis'd in my new belief,
Wrongs I resent, nor pardon yet with ease:
Those fruits come late, and are of flow increase
In haughty hearts like mine: now, tell thyself
If this one word deftroy not thy defigns:
Thy law permits thee not to marry me.

EMP. 'Tis but a fpecious tale to blaft my hopes,
And baffle my pretenfions.   Speak, SEBASTIAN,
And, as a king, fpeak true.

SEBAST. Then, thus adjur'd,
On a king's word 'tis truth, but truth ill-tim'd:
For her dear life is now expos'd a-new:
Unlefs you wholly can put on divinity,
And gracioufly forgive.

ALM   Now learn by this,
The little value I have left for life,
And trouble me no more.

EMP. I thank thee, woman;
Thou haft reftor'd me to my native rage;
And I will feize my happinefs by force.

SEBAST. Know, MULY-MOLUCH, when thou dar'ft
Attempt————

EMP. Beware, I wou'd not be provok'd to ufe
A conqu'ror's right, and therefore charge thy filence.
If thou wou'dft merit to be thought my friend,
I leave thee to perfuade her to compliance.
If not, there's a new guft in ravifhment,
Which I have never try'd.

BEND. They muft be watch'd;
For fomething I obferv'd creates a doubt.   [*Afide.*
                    Exeunt EMPEROR *and* BENDUCAR.

SEB I've been too tame, have bafely born my wrongs,
And not exerted all the king within me,
I heard him, O fweet Heav'ns, he threaten'd rape,
Nay infolently urg'd me to perfuade thee,
Ev'n thee, thou idol of my foul and eyes;
For whom I fuffer life, and drag this being.

ALM. You turn my prifon into paradife;
But I have turn'd your empire to a prifon:
In all your wars good fortune flew before you;
Sublime you fat in triumph on her wheel;

D   Till

Till in my fatal cause your sword was drawn ;
The weight of my misfortunes dragg'd you down.

 SEB. And is't not strange, that Heav'n shou'd bless
   my arms
In common causes and desert the best ?
Now in your greatest last extremity,
When I wou'd aid you most, and most desire it,
I bring but sighs, the succours of a slave.

 ALM. Leave then the luggage of your fate behind,
To make your flight more easy, leave ALMEYDA.
Nor think me left a base-ignoble prey,
Expos'd to this inhuman Tyrant's lust ;
My virtue is a guard beyond my strength,
And death, my last defence, within my call.

 SEB. Death may be call'd in vain, and cannot come ;
Tyrants can tye him up from your relief :
Nor has a Christian privilege to die.

 ALM. If shunning ill be good, then death is good
To those who cannot shun it but by death :
Divines but peep on undiscover'd worlds,
And draw the distant landscape as they please :
But who has e'er return'd from these bright regions,
To tell their manners, and relate their laws ?
I'll venture landing on that happy shore
With an unsully'd body and white mind ;
If I have err'd, some kind inhabitant
Will pity a stray'd soul, and take me home.

 SEB. Beware of death, thou canst not die unperjur'd,
And leave an unaccomplish'd love behind :
Thy vows are mine ; nor will I quit my claim :
The ties of minds are but imperfect bonds,
Unless the bodies join to seal the contract.

 ALM. What joys can you possess, or can I give,
Where groans of death succeed the sighs of love ?
Our *Hymen* has not on his saffron robe ;
But muffled up in mourning, downward holds
His drooping torch, extinguish'd with his tears.

 SEB. The god of love stands ready to revive it
With is ætherial breath.

 ALM. 'Tis late to join, when we must part so soon.

 SEB. Nay, rather let us haste it, e're we part :
Our souls, for want of that acquaintance here,

          May

May wander in the starry walks above,
And, forc'd on worse companions, miss ourselves:

ALM. The Tyrant will not long be absent hence;
And soon I shall be ravish'd from your arms.

SEB. Wilt thou thyself become the greater tyrant,
And give not love, while thou haft love to give?
In dang'rous days, when riches are a crime,
The wise betimes make over their estates:
Make o'er thy honour, by a deed of trust,
And give me seisure of the mighty wealth.

ALM What shall I do! O teach me to refuse——
I wou'd; and yet I tremble at the grant.
For dire presages fright my soul by day,
And boding visions haunt my nightly dreams:
Sometimes, methinks, I hear the groans of ghosts;
Thin, hollow sounds, and lamentable screams,
Then, like a dying echo, from afar,
My mother's voice, that cries, Wed not ALMEYDA!
Forewarn'd ALMEYDA, marriage is thy crime.

SEB. Come laugh at fond presages; I had some;
Fam'd *Nostrudamus*, when he took my horoscope,
Foretold my father I shou'd wed with incest:
'Ere this unhappy war my mother dy'd;
And sisters I had none; vain augury!
A long religious life, a holy age,
My stars assign'd me too, impossible.
For how can incest suit with holiness,
Or priestly orders with a princely state?

ALM. Old venerable ALVAREZ!——— [*sighing.*

SEB. But why that sigh in naming that good man?

ALM. Your father's counsellor and confident———

SEB. He was; and, if he lives, my second father:

ALM. Mark'd our farewel, when going to the fight,
You gave ALMEYDA for the word of battle,
'Twas in that fatal moment, he discover'd
The love that long we labour'd to conceal.
I know it; though my eyes stood full of tears,
Yet through the mist, I saw him stedfast gaze
Then knock'd his aged breast, and inward groan'd;
Like some sad prophet, that foresaw the doom
Of those whom best he lov'd, and cou'd not save.

D 2   SEB.

SEB It ſtartles me! and brings to my remembrance,
That, when the ſhock of battle was begun,
He wou'd have much complain'd, but had not time,
Of our hid paſſion ; then, with lifted hands,
He begg'd me by my father's ſacred ſoul,
Not to eſpouſe you, if he dy'd in fight :
For if he liv'd, and we were conquerors,
He had ſuch things to urge againſt our marriage,
As, now declar'd, wou'd blunt my ſword in battle,
And daſtardize my courage.

ALM. My blood curdles ;
And cakes about my heart.

SEB. I'll breathe a ſigh ſo warm into thy boſom,
Shall make it flow again. My love, he knows not
Thou art a Chriſtian , that produc'd his fear ;
Leſt thou ſhould'ſt ſooth my ſoul with charms ſo ſtrong,
That Heav'n might prove too weak.

ALM. There muſt be more -
This cou'd not blunt your ſword.

SEB. Yes, if I drew it with a curſt intent,
To take a miſbeliever to my bed ;
It muſt be ſo.

ALM. Yet————

SEB. No, thou ſhalt not plead
With that fair mouth againſt the cauſe of love.
Within this caſtle is a captive prieſt,
My holy confeſſor, whoſe free acceſs
Not ev'n the barb'rous victors have refus'd ;
This happy hour his hands ſhall make us one.

AM. I go, with love and fortune, two blind guides,
To lead my way ;' half loth, and half conſenting.
If, as my ſoul forebodes, ſome dire event
Purſue this union, or ſome crime unknown,
Forgive me, Heav'n , and, all ye bleſt above,
Excuſe the frailty of unbounded love.

SCENE

S c e n e II.

A Garden; with Lodging-rooms behind it; or on the fides.

Enter M U F T I, A N T O N I O *as a flave, and* J O H A Y M A *the* M U F T I's *wife.*

MUFTI. And how do you like him, look upon him well, he's a perfonable fellow of a Chriftian dog. Now I think you are fitted, for a gardner · ha! what fay'ft thou JOHAYMA ?

JOH. He may make a fhift to fow lettice, raife melons, and water a garden plat.

MUFTI Why, honey-bird, I bought him a purpofe for thee; didft not thou fay thou long'ft for a Chriftian flave ?

JOH. Ay, but the fight of that loathfome creature has almoft cur'd me.

And befides, I have always long'd for an eunuch, for they fay that's a civil creature, and almoft as harmlefs as yourfelf, hufband. fpeak, fellow, are not you fuch a kind of peaceable thing ?

ANT I was never taken for one in my own country; and not very peaceable neither, when I am well provok'd.

MUFTI. To your occupation, dog, bind up the jeffamines in yond' arbour, and handle your pruning knife with dexterity, tightly I fay, go tightly to your bufinefs; you have coft me much, and muft earn it in your work, here's plentiful provifion for you, rafcal, fallating in the garden, and water in the tank, and on holydays the licking of a platter of rice, when you deferve it.

JOH. What have you been bred up to, firrah, and what can you perform to recommend you to my fervice ? [ANTONIO *making legs.*

Why madam, I can perform as much as any man in a fair lady's fervice

I can play upon the flute, and fing; I can carry your umbrella, and fan your ladyfhip, and cool you when you are too hot; in fine, no fervice either by day or by night fhall come amifs to me, and befides I am of fo quick

D 3   an

an apprehenfion that you need but wink upon me at any time to make me underftand my duty. [*She winks at him.*

ANT. Very fine, fhe has tip'd the wink already.——

[*Afide.*

JOH. The whelp may come to fomething in time.

MUFTI. A very malapert cur, I can tell him that I do not like his fawning; you muft be taught your diftance, firrah. [*Strikes him.*

JOH. Hold, hold ——

He has deferv'd it I confefs; but for once let his igno-rance plead his pardon, we muft not difcourage a begin-ner. Your Reverence has taught us charity ev'n to birds and beafts: here you filthy brute you: —— take this little alms to buy you plaifters.

[*Gives him a piece of money.*

ANT. Money and a love-pinch into the bargain.

[*Afide.*

Enter a SERVANT

Sir, my Lord BENDUCAR is coming to wait on you, and is already at the palace-gate.

MUFTI. Come in JOHAYMA, regulate the reft of my wives and concubines, and leave the fellow to his work.

JOH. Look how ftupidly he ftares about him, like a calf new come into the world. I fhall teach you firrah, to know your bufinefs a little better. —— this way, you aukward rafcal, here lies the arbour, muft I be fhow-ing you eternally? [*turning him about.*

MUFTI. Come away, minion, you fhall fhow him nothing

JOH. I'll but bring him into the arbour, where a rofe-tree and a myrtle are juft falling for want of a prop, if they were bound together they would help to keep up one another. —— he's a raw gardener, and 'tis but charity to teach him.

MUFTI. No more deeds of charity to day; come in, or I fhall think you a little better difpos'd than I could wifh you.

JOH. Well, go before, I will follow my paftor.

MUFTI. So you may caft a fheep's eye behind you in before me. And you, faucinefs, mind your pruning knife, or I may chance to ufe it for you.

[*Exeunt* MUFTI *and* JOHAYMA.

ANT.

ANT *alone.* Thank you for that, but I am in no such haste to be made a Muſſulman. For his wedlock, with all her haughtineſs, I find her coming. How far a Chriſtian ſhou'd reſiſt, I partly know, but how far a young Chriſtian can reſiſt is another queſtion She's tolerable, and I am a poor ſtranger, far from better friends, and in a bodily neceſſity · now have I a ſtrange temptation to try what other females are belonging to this family : I am not far from the womens apartment I am ſure ; and if theſe birds are within diſtance, heie's that will chuckle 'em together.

[*Pulls out his flute and plays.*

A grate opens, and MORAYMA *the* MUFTI's *daughter appears at it.*

ANT. Ay there's an apparition ! that is a morſel worthy of a Mufti; ha ! ſee, ſhe beckons too ——

[*She beckons to him.*

MOR. Come a little nearer and ſpeak ſoftly.

ANT I come, I come I warrant thee, the leaſt twinkle had brought me to thee, ſuch another kind ſyllable or two wou'd turn me to a meteor and diaw me up to thee.

MOR. I dare not ſpeak, for fear of being over-heard ; but if you think my perſon worth your hazard, and can deſerve my love——the reſt this note ſhall tell you—— (*throws down a handkerchief*). No more, my heart goes with you. [*Exit from the grate*

ANT. O thou pretty little heart, art thou flown hither ? I'll keep it warm I warrant it, and brood upon it in the new neſt but now for my treaſure trove, that's wrapt up in the handkerchief : no peeping here, though I long to be ſpelling her *Arabic* ſcrawls and pot-hooks. But I muſt carry off my prize, as robbers do, and not think of ſharing the booty, before I am free from danger, and out of eye-ſhot from the other windows. If her wit be as poignant as her eyes, I am a double ſlave. Our northern beauties are meer dough to theſe, inſipid white earth, meer tobacco-pipe-clay, with no more ſoul and motion in 'em, than a fly in winter,

Here the warm planet ripens, and ſublimes
The well bak'd beauties of the ſouthern climes;

Our

Our Cupid's but a bungler in his trade,
His keeneſt arrows are in *Afric* made.

[*Exit.* ANTONIO.

✤✤✤✤✤✤✤✤✤✤✤✤✤✤✤✤✤✤✤✤✤✤✤✤✤✤✤✤✤✤✤

ACT III. Scene I.

*A terrace-walk; or ſome other public place near the
Caſtle of* ALCAZAR.

EMPEROR, MULEY-MOLUCH, BENDUCAR.

EMPEROR.

MArry'd ! I'll not believe it ; 'tis impoſture,
Improbable they ſhould preſume t' attempt,
Impoſſible they ſhould effect their wiſh.

BEND Have patience till I clear it.

EMP I have none :
Go bid our moving plains of ſand lie ſtill,
And ſtir not when the ſtormy ſouth blows high :
From top to bottom thou haſt toſs'd my ſoul,
And, now 'tis in the madneſs of the whirl,
Requir'ſt a ſudden ſtop ? unſay, they lye,
That may in time do ſomewhat.

BEND. I have done :
For, ſince it pleaſes you it ſhould be forg'd,
'Tis fit it ſhould : far be it from your ſlave,
To raiſe diſturbance in your ſacred breaſt.

EMP. SEBASTIAN is my ſlave as well as thou ;
Nor durſt offend my love by that preſumption.

BEND. Moſt ſure he ought not.

EMP. Then all means are wanting ;
No prieſt, no ceremonies of their ſect,
Or, grant we theſe defects cou'd be ſupply'd,
How cou'd our Prophet do an act ſo baſe,
So to reſume his gifts, and curſe my conqueſts
By making me unhappy ! No, the ſlave,
That told thee ſo abſur'd a ſtory, ly'd.

BEND. Yet till this moment I have found him faithful:

He

He said he saw it too.

EMP. Difpatch; what faw he?

BEND. Truth is, confidering with what earneftnefs,
SEBASTIAN pleaded for ALMEDYA's life,
Inhanc'd her beauty, dwelt upon her praife,——

EMP. O ftupid and unthinking as I was!
I might have maik'd it too: 'twas grofs and palpable!

BEND. Methought I trac'd a lover ill-difguis'd;
And fent my fpy, a fharp obferving flave,
T' inform me better, if I guefs'd aright.
He told me that he faw SEBASTIAN's page
Run crofs the marble fquare; who foon return'd,
And after him there lag'd a puffing Fryar;
Clofe wrap't he bore fome facred inftrument
Of Chriftian fuperftition in his hand:
My fervant follow'd faft, and, through a chink,
Perceiv'd the royal captives hand in hand:
And heard the hooded father mumbling charms,
That make thofe mifbelievers man and wife.
Which done, the fpoufes kifs'd with fuch a fervour,
And give fuch furious earneft of their flames,
That their eyes fparkled, and there mantling blood
Flew flufhing o'er their faces.

EMP. Hell, confound 'em!

BEND. The reverend father, with a holy leer,
Saw he might well be fpar'd, and foon withdrew:
This forc'd my fervant to a quick retreat,
For fear to be difcover'd; guefs the reft.

EMP. I do. My fancy is too exquifite,
And tortures me with their imagin'd blifs.
Some earthquake fhou'd have ris'n, and rent the ground,
Have fwallow'd him, and left the longing bride,
In agony of unaccomplifh'd love.   (*Walks diforderly.*)

Enter the MUFTI.

BEND. In an unluckly hour   [*Afide.*
That fools intrudes, raw in this great affair,
And uninftructed how to ftem the tide.

Coming up to the MUFTI, *afide.*

The Emp'ror muft not marry, nor enjoy;
Keep to that point, ftand firm, for all's at ftake.

EMPEROR

EMPEROR *seeing him.* You druggerman of Heav'n,
Muft I attend
Your droning prayers? Why came you not before?
Do'ft thou not know the captive king has dar'd·
To wed ALMEYDA? Cancel me that marriage,
And make her mine; about the bufinefs, quick!
Expound thy *Mahomet;* make him fpeak my fenfe,
Or he's no Prophet here, and thou no MUFTI,
Unlefs thou know'ft the trick of thy vocation,
To wreft and rend the law to pleafe thy prince.

MUF. Why verily the law is monftrous plain:
There's not one doubtful text in all the Alcoran,
Which can be wrench'd in favour to your project.

EMP Forge one, and foift it into fome by-place,
Of fome old rotten roll, do't, I command thee,
Muft I teach thee thy trade?

MUF. It cannot be;
For matrimony being the deareft point
Of Law, the people have it all by heart ·
Befides th' offence is fo exorbitant, [*In a higher tone.*
To mingle with a mifbelieving race,
That fpeedy vengeance wou'd purfue your crime.

*Emperor, taking him by the throat with one hand, fnatch-
es out his fword with the other, and points it to his
breaft.*

EMP. Slave, have I rais'd thee to this pomp and pow'r,
To preach againft my will? know I am law,
And thou not *Mahomet*'s meffenger, but mine:
Make it, I charge thee, make my pleafure lawful:
Or firft I ftrip thee of thy ghoftly greatnefs,
Then fend thee poft to tell thy tale above,
And bring thy vain memorials to thy Prophet
Of juftice done below for difobedience,

MUF. For heav'n's fake hold, the refpite of a moment,———
To think for you.

EMP. And for thyfelf———
MUF. For both,
BEND. Difgrace, and death, and avarice have loft
him! [*Afide.*
MUF.

MUF. 'Tis true, our law forbids to wed a Christian;
But it forbids you not to ravish her.
You have a conqueror's right upon your slave;
And then, the more despight you do a Christian,
You serve the Prophet more who loaths that sect.

EMP. Oh now it mends; and you talk reason,
  MUFTI.
But stay! I promis'd freedom to SEBASTIAN:
Now shou'd I grant it, his revengeful soul
Wou'd ne'er forgive his violated bed.

MUF. Kill him, for then you give him liberty:
His soul is from his earthly prison freed.

EMP. How happy is the Prince who has a churchman
So learn'd and pliant to expound his laws.

BEND. Two things I humbly offer to your prudence.

EMP. Be brief; but let not either thwart my love.

BEND. First, since our holy man has made rape
  lawful,
Fright her with that: proceed not yet to force:
Why shou'd you pluck the green distasteful fruit
From the unwilling bough,
When it may ripen of itself and fall?

EMP. Grant her a day; tho' that's too much to give
Out of a life which I devote to love.

BEND. Then next, to bar
All future hopes of her desir'd SEBASTIAN,
Let DORAX be enjoin'd to bring his head.

  EMPEROR *to the* MUFTI.

Go, MUFTI, call him to receive his orders.
      [*Exit* MUFTI.
I take thy counsel, her desires new rouz'd,
And yet unslak'd, will kindle in her fancy,
And make her eager to renew the feast.

BEND. [*Aside,*] DORAX, I know before, will disobey:
There's a foe's head well cropt ——
But this hot love precipitates my plot;
And brings it to projection 'ere its time.

         Enter

Enter SEBASTIAN *and* ALMEYDA *hand in hand,
upon sight of the* EMPEROR, *they separate and seem
disturb'd*

ALM. He breaks, at unawares, upon our walks,
And like a mid-night wolf invades the fold:
Make speedy preparation of your soul,
And bid it arm apace.   He comes for answer,
And brutal mischief sits upon his brow.
　　　　EMPEROR *coming up to them.*
EMP. Have you perform'd
Your embassy, and treated with success?
　SEBAST. I had not time.
　EMP. No, not for my affairs,
But for your own too much.
　SEBAST. You talk in clouds, explain your meaning,
　　Sir,
　EMP Explain yours first : What meant you hand in
　　hand,
And when you saw me, with a guilty start,
You loos'd your hold, affrighted at my presence?
　SEBAST Affrighted?
　EMP. Yes, astonish'd, and confounded.
　SEB. What mak'st thou of thyself, and what of me?
Art thou some ghost, some demon, or some God?
That I shou'd stand astonish'd at thy sight?
If thou cou'dst deem so meanly of my courage,
Why didst thou not engage me man for man,
And try the virtue of that *Gorgon* face,
To stare me into statue?
　EMP Oh, thou art now recover'd, but by Heav'n,
Thou wer't amaz'd at first, as it surpris'd
At unexpected baseness brought to light.
　SEB. Base and ungrateful never was I thought ;
Nor, till this turn of fate, durst thou have call'd me ;
Say, in what cranny of SEBASTIAN's soul,
Unknown to me, so loath'd a crime is lodg'd ?
　EMP. Thou hast not broke my trust repos'd in thee?
　SEB Impos'd, but not receiv'd : take back that false-
　　hood.
　EMP. Thou art not marry'd to ALMEYDA ?
　SEB. Yes,
　　　　　　　　　　　　　　　EMP.

EMP And own'ft the ufurpation of my love?

SEB. I own it in the face of Heav'n and thee,
No ufurpation, but a lawful claim,
Of which I ftand poffefs'd.

EMP. Sh' has chofen well,
Betwixt a captive and a conqueror.

ALM. Betwixt a monfter and the beft of men.
He was the envy of his neighb'ring kings,
To fhare his noble chains is more to me,
Than all the favage greatnefs of thy throne.

SEB. Were I to chufe again, and knew my fate,
For fuch a night I would be what I am.
The joys I have poffefs'd are ever mine,
Out of the reach, behind eternity,
Hid in the facred trealure of the paft;
But blefs'd remembrance brings 'em hourly back.

EMP. Hourly indeed, who haft but hours to live:
O mighty purchafe of a boafted blifs!
To dream of what thou had'ft one fugitive night,
And never fhall have more!

ALM. Thou wilt not dare to break what Heav'n has
        join'd?

EMP. Not break the chain, but change a rotten link,
And rivet one to laft.
Think'ft thou I come to argue right and wrong?
Why lingers DORAX thus? Where are my guards,

    [BENDUCAR *goes out for the Guards, and returns.*
To drag that flave to death?

                    [*Pointing to* SEBASTIAN.

Now ftorm and rage,
Call vainly on thy Prophet, then defy him
For wanting power to fave thee.

SEB That were to gratify thy pride: I'll fhew thee
How a man fhou'd, and how a king dare die

    ALMEYDA, *to the* EMPEROR

Expect revenge from Heav'n, inhuman wretch!
Nor hope t' afcend SEBASTIAN's holy bed.

            Enter two of the Guards

EMP. Go, bear the captive to a fpeedy death,
And let my foul at eafe.

ALM. I charge you, hold, ye minifters of death
                E   Speak,

Speak, my SEBASTIAN;
Plead for thy life: Oh afk it of the Tyrant;
'Tis no difhonour, truft me, Love, 'tis none:
I wou'd die for thee, but I cannot plead;
My haughty heart difdains it, e'en for thee.
Still filent! Will the King of PORTUGAL
Go to his death, like a dumb facrifice?
Beg him to fave my life in faving thine.

 SEB. Farewel, my life's not worth another word.

 EMP [*To the Guards.*] Perform your orders.

 ALM. Stay, take my farewel too:
Farewel the greatnefs of ALMEYDA's foul!
Look, Tyrant, what excefs of love can do,
It pulls me down thus low, as to thy feet,
        [*Kneels to him.*
Nay, to embrace thy knees with loathing hands,
Which blifter when they touch thee; yet e'en thus,
Thus far I can to fave SEBASTIAN's life.

 EMP. A facred pleafure trickles thro' my veins:
It works about the inlets of my foul,
To feel thy touch, and pity tempts the pafs;
But the tough metal of my heart refifts,
'Tis warm'd with the foft fire, not melted down.

 ALM. A flood of fcalding tears will make it run;
Spare him, oh fpare; can you pretend to love,
And have no pity? Love and that are twins.
Here will I grow;
Thus compafs you with thefe fupplanting cords,
And pull fo long till the proud fabric falls.

 EMP. Still kneel, and still embrace, 'tis double
   pleafure
So to be hugg'd, and fee SEBASTIAN die.

 ALM. Look, Tyrant, when thou nam'ft SEBASTIAN's
  death,
Thy very executioners turn pale.
Rough as they are, and harden'd in the trade
Of death, they ftart at an anointed head,
And tremble to approach —He hears me not,
Nor minds th' impreffion of a God on kings;
Becaufe no ftamp of Heav'n was on his foul;
But the refifting mafs drove back the feal.
Say, tho' thy heart be rock of adamant,
Yet rocks are not impregnable to bribes:

          Inftruct

Inftruct me how to bribe thee: name thy price;
Lo, I refign my title to the crown;
Send me to exile with the man I love,
And banifhment is empire.

  Emp. Here's my claim;

                    [*Clapping his hand to his Sword.*

And this extinguifh'd thine, thou giv'ft me nothing.

  Alm. My father's, mother's, brother's death I par-
          don:
That's fomewhat, fure; a mighty fum of murder,
Of innocent and kindred blood ftruck off
My prayers and penance fhall difcount for thefe,
And beg of Heav'n to charge the bill on me.
Behold what price I offer, and how dear,
To buy Sebastian's life.

  Emp. Let after reck'nings trouble fearful fools,
I'll ftand the trial of thofe trivial crimes
But, fince thou begg'ft me to prefcribe my terms,
The only I can offer are thy love,
And this one day of refpite to refolve.
Grant or deny; for thy next word is fate,
And fate is deaf to pray'r.

  Alm. May Heav'n be fo   [*Rifing up.*
At thy laft breath to thine: I curfe thee not,
For who can better curfe the plague or devil,
Than to be what they are? that curfe be thine.
Now, do not fpeak, Sebastian, for you need not,
But die, for I refign your life   look, Heav'n,
Almeyda dooms her dear Sebastian's death!

                Enter D O R A X *attended by three Soldiers.*

  Emp. Thou mov'ft a tortoife pace to my relief.
Take hence that, once a king, that fullen pride
That fwells to dumbnefs, lay him in the dungeon,
And fink him deep with irons, that, when he wou'd,
He fhall not groan to hearing, when I fend,
The next commands are death.

  Alm. Then prayers are vain as curfes.

  Emp. Much at one
In a flave's mouth, againft a monarch's pow'r.
This day thou haft to think;
At night, if thou wilt curfe, thou fhalt curfe kindly;

                          E 2   Make

Make hafte; feize, force her, bear her hence.

ALM. Farewel, my loft SEBASTIAN!
I do not beg, I challenge juftice now;
O Pow'rs, if kings be your peculiar care,
Why plays this wretch with your prerogative?
Now flafh him dead, now crumble him to afhes;
Or henceforth live confin'd in your own palace,
And look not idly out upon a world
That is no longer yours.

She is carried off ftruggling, the EMPEROR *and* BEN-
DUCAR *follow;*

SEBASTIAN *ftruggles in his Guards arms, and fhakes off
on of them, but two others come in, and hold him;
he fpeaks not all the while.*

DOR. I find I'm but a half ftrain'd villain yet;
[*Afide.*

But mungril mifchievous! for my blood boil'd,
To view this brutal act, and my ftern foul
Tugg'd at my arm to draw in her defence.
Down, thou rebelling Chriftian, in my heart;
Redeem thy fame on this SEBASTIAN firft;
Then think on others wrongs, when thine are righted.
[*Walks a turn.*

But how to right 'em? on a flave difarm'd,
Defenceless, and fubmitted to my rage?
A bafe revenge is vengeance on myfelt?
[*Walks again.*

I have it, and I thank thee honeft head,
Thus prefent to me at my great neceffity.
[*Comes up to* SEBASTIAN.

You know me not?
SEB. I hear men call thee DORAX
DOR. 'Tis well, you know enough for once: you
fpeak too;
You were ftruck mute before.
SEB. Silence became me then.
DOR. Yet we may talk hereafter.
SEB. Hereafter is not mine. ———
Difpatch thy work, good executioner.

DOR.

DOR. None of my blood were hangmen, add that
falshood
To a long bill that yet remains unreckon'd.

SEB. A king and thou can never have a reck'ning.

DOR. A greater sum perhaps than you can pay.
Mean time I shall make bold t' increase your debt;
          [*gives him his sword.*
Take this, and use it at your greatest need.

SEB. This hand and this have been acquainted well;
[*Looks on it.*]
It shou'd have come before into my grasp,
To kill the ravisher.   [life.

DOR. Thou heard'st the Tyrant's orders, guard thy
When 'tis attack'd, and guard it like a man.

SEB. I'm still without thy meaning, but I thank thee.

DOR. Thank me when I ask thanks, thank me with

SEB. Such surly kindness did I never see!   [that.

   DORAX, *to the Captain of his Guards.*

MUZA, draw out a file, pick man by man,
Such who dare die, and dear will sell their death.
Guard him to th' utmost, now conduct him hence,
And treat him as my person.

SEB. Something like
That voice, methinks I shou'd have somewhere heard:
But floods of woes have hurry'd it far off,
Beyond my ken of soul.
    [*Exit* SEBASTIAN *with the soldiers.*

DOR. But I shall bring him back, ungrateful man;
          [*solus.*

I shall, and set him full before thy sight,
When I shall front thee, like some staring ghost,
With all my wrongs about me.——What so soon
Return'd? This haste is boding.

Enter to him EMPEROR, BENDUCAR, MUFTI.

EMP. She's still inexorable, still imperious:
And loud, as if like *Bacchus* born in thunder
Be quick, ye false physicians of my mind,
Bring speedy death or cure.   [lives:

BEND. What can be counsell'd, while SEBASTIAN
The vine will cling, while the tall poplar stands;
       E 3   But

But, that cut down, creeps to the next fupport,
And twines as clofely there   [ceed.

    EMP. That's done with eafe, I fpeak him dead, pro-

    MUF. Proclaim your marriage with ALMEYDA next,
That civil wars may ceafe ; this gains the crowd;
Then you may fafely force her to your will :
For people fide with violence and injuftice,
When done for public good.

    EMP. Preach thou that doctrine.

    BEND. Th' unreafonable fool has broach'd a truth
                                    [*Afide*.
That blafts my hopes ; but fince 'tis gone fo far,
He fhall divulge ALMEYDA is a Chriftian :
If that produce no tumult, I defpair.

    EMP. Why fpeaks not DORAX ?

    DOR. Becaufe my foul abhors to mix with him.
Sir, let me bluntly fay, you went too far
To truft the preaching pow'r on ftate affairs,
To him or any heavenly demagogue.
'Tis a limb lopt from your prerogative,
And fo much of Heav'ns image blotted from you.

    MUF. Sure, thou haft never heard of holy men,
(So Chriftians call 'em) fam'd in ftate affairs ?
Such as in *Spain Ximenes, Albornoz*,
In *England Wolfey*, match me thefe with laymen.

    DOR. How you triumph in one or two of thefe,
Born to be ftatefmen, happ'ning to be churchmen !
Thou call'ft 'em holy, fo their function was,
But tell me, MUFTI, which of them were faints,
Next, Sir, to you, the fum of all is this,
Since he claims pow'r from Heav'n, and not from kings,
When 'tis his int'reft he can int'reft Heav'n
To preach you down, and ages oft depend
On hours, uninterrupted, in the chair.

    EMP. I'll truft his preaching, while I rule his pay :
And I dare truft my *Africans* to hear
Whatever he dare preach.

    DOR. You know 'em not,
The genius of your Moors is mutiny ;
They fcarcely want a guide to move their madnefs :
Prompt to rebel on every weak pretence,
Bluftring when courted, crouching when opprefs'd

                                       Wife

Wife to themfelves, and fools to all the world.
Reftlefs in change, and perjur'd to a proverb.
They love religion fweeten'd to the fenfe;
A good luxurious, palatable faith.
Thus vice and godlinefs, prepoft'rous pair!
Ride cheek by joul, but churchmen hold the reins:
And, whene'er kings wou'd lower clergy greatnefs,
They learn too late what pow'r the preachers have,
And whofe the fubjects are, the MUFTI knows it,
Nor dares deny what pafs'd betwixt us two.

    EMP. No more, whate'er he faid was by command
    DOR. Why then no more, fince you will hear no more;
Some kings are refolute to their own ruin.
    EMP Without your meddling where you are not afk'd,
Obey your orders, and difpatch SEBASTIAN.
    DOR. Truft my revenge, be fure I wifh him dead.
    EMP. What mean'ft thou! what's thy wifhing to my
        will?
Difpatch him, rid me of the man I loath.
    DOR. I hear you, Sir, I'll take my time and do't——
    EMP. Thy time? what's all thy time, what's thy
        whole life
To my one hour of eafe; no more replies,
But fee thou doft it; or——
    DOR. Choak in that threat: I can fay OR as loud.
    EMP. 'Tis well, I fee my words have no effect,
But I may fend a meffage to difpofe you.
                         [*Is going off.*
    DOR. Expect an anfwer worthy of that meffage.
    MUF. The Prophet ow'd him this?   [*Afide.*
And thank'd be Heav'n, he has it.
    BEND. By holy *Alba*, I conjure you ftay,
And judge not rafhly of fo brave man.
    [*Draws the* EMPEROR *afide and whifpers him.*
I'll give you reafons why he cannot execute
Your orders now, and why he will hereafter.
    MUF BENDUCAR is a fool to bring him off, *Afide.*
I'll work my own revenge, and fpeedily.
    BEND. The fort is his, the foldiers hearts are his;
A thoufand Chriftian flaves are in the caftle,
Which he can free to reinforce his pow'r,

                                Your

Your troops far off, beleaguering *Larache*,
Yet in the Christians' hands.

EMP. I grant all this;
But grant me he must die.

BEND. He shall, by poison ·
'Tis here, the deadly drug prepar'd in powder,
Hot as hell-fire———then, to prevent his soldiers
From rising to revenge their general's death,
While he is struggling with his mortal pangs,
The rabble on the sudden may be rais'd
To seize the castle.

EMP. Do't; 'tis left to thee.

BEND. Yet more, but clear your brow, for he observes.
                    [*They whisper again.*

DOR. What, will the fav'rite prop my falling fortunes?
O prodigy of court!

EMPEROR *and* BENDUCAR *return to* DORAX.

EMP. Your friend has fully clear'd your innocence:
I was too hasty to condemn unheard,
And you perhaps too prompt in your replies.
As far as fits the majesty of kings,
I ask excuse.

DOR. I'm sure I meant it well.

EMP. I know you did.—this to our love renew'd—
                    [EMPEROR *drinks.*

BENDUCAR, fill to DORAX.
          [BENDUCAR *turns and mixes a powder in it.*

DOR. Let it go round, for all of us have need
To quench our heats : 'tis the king's health, BENDUCAR,
                    [*He drinks.*
And I wou'd pledge it though I knew 'twere poison.

BEND. Another bowl, for what the King has touch'd,
                    [*Drinks out of another bowl.*
And you have pledg'd, is sacred to your loves ———

MUF. Since charity becomes my calling, thus
Let me provoke your friendship : and Heav'n bless it,
As I intend it, well———

*Drinks, and turning aside pours some drops out of a
    little phial into the bowl, then presents it to* DORAX.

DOR. Heav'n make thee, honest,
On that condition we shall soon be friends——— [*Drinks.*
                                            MUF.

Muf.)Yes, at our meeting in another world ; [*Aside.*
For thou haft drunk thy pafsport out of this.
Not the *Nonacrean* fount, nor *Lethe*'s lake,
Cou'd fooner numb thy nimble faculties,
Than this to fleep eternal,

Emp. Now farewel, Dorax; this was our firft quarrel,
And I dare prophefy will prove our laft.

Exit Emperor *with* Benducar *and the* Mufti.

Dor. It may be fo : I'm ftrangely difcompos'd ,
Quick fhooting through my limbs, and pricking pains,
Qualms at my heart, convulfions in my nerves,
Shiv'rings of cold, and burnings of my entrails
Within my little world make medley war;
Lofe and regain, beat and are beaten back,
As momentary victors quit their ground.
Can it be poifon ! poifon's of one tenour,
Or hot or cold ; this neither, and yet both.
Some deadly draught, fome enemy of life
Boils in my bowels, and works out my foul.
Ingratitude's the growth of ev'ry clime ;
Afric, the fcene remov'd, is *Portugal.*
Of all court fervice learn the common lot ;
To-day 'tis done, to-morrow 'tis forgot.
Oh, were that all ! my honeft corpfe muft lie
Expos'd to fcorn, and public infamy :
My fhameful death will be divulg'd alone ,
The worth and honour of my foul unknown.   [*Exit.*

S c e n e II.

A night fcene in the Mufti's *Garden, where an
arbour is difcover'd.*

Enter ANTONIO

Ant. She names herfelf Morayma ; the Mufti's
only daughter, and a virgin ! This is the time and place
that fhe appointed in her letter, yet fhe comes not.
Why, thou fweet delicious creature, why, to torture me
with thy delay ! dar'ft thou be falfe to thy affignation ?
What, in the cool and filence of the night, and to a new
lover ? Pox on the hypocrite thy father, for inftructing
thee

thee so little in the sweetest point of his religion. Hark, I hear the rustling of her silk mantle. Now she comes, now she comes; no, hang't, that was but the whistling of the wind through the *Orange* trees. Now again, I hear the pit-a-pat of a pretty foot through the dark alley: No, 'tis the son of a mare that's broken loose and munching upon the melons ——Oh the misery of an expecting lover! Well, I'll e'en despair; go into my arbour, and try to sleep; in a dream I shall enjoy her in despight of her. [*Goes into the arbour and lies down.*

Enter JOHAYMA *wrapt up in a Moorish mantle.*

JOH. Thus far my love has carried me, almost without my knowledge whither I was going: shall I go on, shall I discover myself?——What an injury am I doing to my old husband?——Yet what injury——?
[*She comes a little nearer the arbour.*

ANTONIO *raising himself a little and looking.*

At last 'tis she: this is no illusion I am sure, 'tis a true she devil of flesh and blood; and she cou'd never have taken a fitter time to tempt me——

JOH. He's young and handsome——

ANT. Yes, well enough, I thank nature. [*Aside.*

JOH. And I am yet neither old nor ugly: sure he will not refuse me.

ANT. No, thou may'st pawn thy maiden head upon't he wo'not.

He rushes out and embraces her.

I can hold no longer from embracing thee, my dear MORAYMA the old unconscionable whore-'on thy father cou'd he expect cold chastity from a child of his begetting?

JOH. What nonsense do you talk? do you take me for the MUFTI's daughter?

ANT. Why, are you not, Madam?
[*Throwing off her* Barnus.

JOH. I find you had an appointment with MORAYMA.

ANT. By all that's good the nauseous wife! [*Aside.*

JOH. What are you confounded and stand mute?

ANT. Somewhat nonplus'd I confess, to hear you deny your name so positively: why, are you not MORYAMA the MUFTI's daughter? did I not see you with him? did not he present me to you? were you not so charitable as
to

to give me money ? if I may be fo bold to remember you of paft favours.

Joh. And you fee I am come to make 'em good ; but I am neither MORAYMA, nor the MUFTI's daughter.

ANT. Nay, I know not that . but I am fure he is old enough to be your father ; and either father, or reverend father, I heard you call him.

Joh. Once again, how came you to name MORAYMA?

ANT. Another damn'd miftake of mine : for, afking one of my fellow flaves, who were the chief ladies about the houfe, he anfwered me MORAYMA and JOHAYMA ; but fhe it feems is his daughter, with a pox to her, and you are his beloved wife.

Joh Say your beloved miftrefs, if you pleafe , for that's the title I defire. This moon-fhine grows offen-five to my eyes ; come, fhall we walk into the arbour ? there we may rectify all miftakes.

ANT. That's clofe and dark.

Joh And are thofe faults to lovers ?

ANT. But there I cannot pleafe myfelf with the fight of your beauty, nor is there a breath of air ftirring.

Joh. The breath of lovers is the fweeteft air , but you are fearful

ANT. I am confidering, indeed, that if I am taken with you ——— a ——— pray where lodges your hufband ?

Joh. Juft againft the face of this open walk.

ANT. Then he has feen us already, for ought I know.

Joh. You make fo many difficulties, I fear I am dif-pleafing to you.

ANT. *Afide.* If MORAYMA comes and takes me in the arbour with her, I have made a fine exchange of that diamond for this pebble.

Joh. You are much fall'n off, let me tell you from the fury of your firft embrace.

ANT I confefs, I was fomewhat too furious at firft ; but you will forgive the tranfport of my paffion ; now I have confider'd it better, I have a qualm of confcience.

Joh. Of confcience ! why, what has confcience to do with two young lovers that have opportunity ?

ANT Why, truly, confcience is fomething to blame for interpofing in our matters : but how can I help it, if I have a fcruple to betray my mafter ?

Joh.

JOH. There muſt be ſomething more in it; for your conſcience was very quiet, when you took me for MO-RAYMA.

ANT I grant you, madam, when I took you for his daughter : for then I might have made you an honourable amends by marriage I muſt be plain with you, you are married, and to a holy man, the head of your religion : go back to your chamber, and conſider of it ; who knows, but, at our next meeting, the ſweet devil may have more power over me ? I am true fleſh and blood, I can tell you that for your comfort.

JOH. Fleſh without blood I think thou art ; or if any, it is as cold as that of fiſhes. But I'll teach thee, to thy coſt, what vengeance is in ſtore for refuſing a lady, who has offer'd thee her love · —— Help, help, there , will no body come to my aſſiſtance ?

ANT. What do you mean, madam , for Heav'n's ſake, peace ' your huſband will hear you ; think of your own danger, if you will not think of mine.

JOH Ungrateful wretch, thou deſerv'ſt no pity · Help, help, huſband, or I ſhall be raviſh'd : the villain will be too ſtrong for me ! Help, help, for pity of a poor diſtreſſed creature !

ANT. Then I have nothing but impudence to aſſiſt me ; I muſt drown her clamour whate'er comes on't
*He takes out his flute, and plays as loud as he poſſibly can,
and ſhe continues crying out.*

Enter the MUFTI *in his night-gown, and two ſervants.*

MUF. O thou villain, what horrible impiety art thou committing ' what ! raviſhing the wife of my boſom ' take him away, gauch him, impale him, rid the world of ſuch a monſter.   [*Servants ſeize him.*

ANT. Mercy, dear maſter, mercy. Hear me firſt, and after, if I have deſerv'd hanging, ſpare me not . what have you ſeen to provoke you to this cruelty '

MUF. I have heard the out-cries of my wife ; the bleatings of the poor innocent lamb : ſeen nothing, ſay'ſt thou '

ANT Pray think in reaſon, Sir, is a man to be put to death for a ſimilitude ? no violence has been committed,
none

none intended : the lamb's alive ; and, if I durſt tell you ſo, no more a lamb than I am a butcher.

Jo h. How's that, villain, dar'ſt thou accuſe me?

A n t. Be patient, madam, and ſpeak but truth, and I'll do any thing to ſerve you : I ſay again, and ſwear it too, I'll do any thing to ſerve you.

Jo h [*Aſide.*] I underſtand him, but I fear, 'tis now too late to ſave him :——Pray hear me ſpeak, huſband; perhaps he may ſay ſomething for himſelf, I know not.

Mu f. Speak thou, has he not violated my bed and thy honour?

Jo h. I forgive him freely · for he has done nothing : what he will do hereafter, to make me ſatisfaction, him-ſelf beſt knows.

A n t. Any thing, any thing, ſweet Madam : I ſhall refuſe no drudgery.

Mu f. But did he mean no miſchief? was he endea-vouring nothing?

Jo h. In my conſcience, I begin to doubt he did not.

Mu f. 'Tis impoſſible : then what meant all theſe out-cries?

Jo h. I heard muſic in the garden, and at an unſea-ſonable time of night; and I ſtole ſoftly out of my bed, as imagining it might be he.

Mu f. How's that Jo h a y m a? imagining it was he, and yet you went?

Jo h. Why not, my Lord? am not I the miſtreſs of the family? and is it not my place to ſee good order kept in it? I thought he might have allured ſome of the ſhee ſlaves to him; and was reſolved to prevent what might have been betwixt him and them, when on the ſudden he ruſh'd out upon me, caught me in his arms with ſuch a fury ——

Mu f. I have heard enough, away with him ——

Jo h. Miſtaking me, no doubt, for one of his fellow-ſlaves · with that, affrighted as I was, I diſcovered my-ſelf, and cried aloud : but as ſoon as ever he knew me, the villain let me go ; and I muſt needs ſay, he ſtarted back, as if I were ſome ſerpent, and was more 'affraid of me than I of him.

Mu f. O thou corrupter of my family, that's cauſe enough of death, once again. away with him.

F Jo h.

JOH. What, for an intended trespass? No harm has been done, whatever may be. He cost you five hundred crowns, I take it.——

MUF. Thou say'st true, a very considerable sum: he shall not die, though he had committed folly with a slave; 'tis too much to lose by him.

ANT. My only fault for ever has been to love playing in the dark, and the more she cry'd, the more I play'd; that it might be seen I intended nothing to her.

MUF. To your kennel, sirrah; mortify your flesh, and consider in whose family you are.

JOH. And one thing more, remember from henceforth to obey better.

MUF. [*Aside*] For all her smoothness, I am not quite cur'd of my jealousy; but I have thought of a way that will clear my doubts.

[*Exit* MUFTI *with* JOHAYMA *and servants.*]

ANT. I am mortify'd sufficiently already, without the help of his ghostly counsel. Fear of death has gone farther with me in two minutes, than my conscience wou'd have gone in two months: and if MORAYMA shou'd now appear, I say no more, but alas for her and me,

[MORAYMA *comes out of the arbour, she steals behind him, and claps him on the back*]

MOR. And if MORAYMA shou'd appear, as she does appear, alas you say for her and you!

ANT. Art thou there, my sweet temptation! my eyes, my life, my soul, my all!

MOR. A mighty compliment, when all these, by your own confession, are just nothing.

ANT. Nothing, till thou cam'st; thou dost not know the power of thy own charms: let me embrace thee.

MOR. No, now I think on't, you are already enter'd into articles with my enemy JOHAYMA: any thing to serve you, madam; I shall refuse no drudgery: whose words were those, gentleman? was that like a cavalier of honour?

ANT. Not very heroic, but self-preservation is a point above honour and religion too——ANTONIO was a rogue, I must confess; but you must give me leave to love him.

MOR.

Mor. To beg your life fo bafely, and to prefent your fword to your enemy ; Oh recreant!

Ant. If I had died honourably, my fame indeed wou'd have founded loud, but I fhou'd never have heard the blaft · Come, don't make yourfelf worfe natur'd than you are · to fave my life, you wou'd be content I fhou'd promife any thing. Can you fufpect I wou'd leave you for Johayma?

Mor. No; but I can expect you wou'd have both of us; love is covetous, heart for heart is an equal truck. In fhort I am younger ; I think handfomer ; and am fure I love you better; fhe has been my ftep-mother for fifteen years · you think that's her face you fee, but 'tis only a daub'd vizard : fhe wears an armour of proof upon't, an inch thick of paint, befides the wafh : her face is fo fortify'd that you can make no approaches to it without a fhovel.

Ant. By this hand——(*taking it.*)

Mor. Which you fhall never touch ; but upon better affurances than you imagine. (*Pulling her hand away*)

Ant. I'll marry thee, and make a Chriftian of thee, thou pretty infidel!

Mor. I mean you fhall · but no earneft; till the bargain be made before witnefs : there's love enough to be had, and as much as you can turn you to, never doubt it, but all upon honourable terms.

Ant. I vow and fwear by love , and he's a deity in all religions; that I'll adore thee to revenge myfelf upon thy father, for being the head of a falfe religion.

Mor. And fo you fhall , I offer you his daughter for your fecond : but fince you are fo preffing, meet me under my window, to morrow-night, body for body, about this hour; I'll flip down out of my lodging, and bring my father in my hand.

Ant. How, thy father !

Mor. I mean all that's good of him , his pearls, and his jewels, his whole contents, his heart, and foul ; as much as ever I can carry. I'll leave him his Alcoran ; that's revenue enough for him : every page of it is gold and diamonds. He has the turn of an eye, a demure fmile, and a godly cant, that are worth millions to him. I forgot to tell you that I will have a flave prepared at the

poftern

postern-gate, with two horses ready sadled : no more, for I fear I may be miss'd ; and think I hear 'em calling for me——if you have constancy and courage——

ANT. Never doubt it : and love in abundance, to wander with thee all the world over.

MOR The value of twelve hundred thousand crowns in a casket !

ANT A heavy burden, Heav'n knows ! but we must pray for patience to support it.

MOR. Besides a willing tit that will venture her corpse with you ·——Come I know you long to have a parting blow with me ; and therefore to shew you I am in charity—— [*He kisses her.*

ANT. Once more, for pity ; that I may keep the flavour upon my lips till we meet again.

MOR. No , frequent charities make bold beggars : and besides I have learnt of a falconer, never to feed up a hawk when I wou'd have him fly : that's enough—— but if you will be nibbling, here's a hand to stay your stomach. [*Kissing her hand.*

ANT. Thus conquer'd infidels, that wars may cease, Are forc'd to give their hands, and sign the peace.

MOR. Thus Christians are outwitted by the foe , You had her in your pow'r, and let her go. If you release my hand, the fault's not mine ; You shou'd have made me seal, as well as sign.

She runs off, he follows her to the door , then comes back again, and goes out at the other.

+++

ACT IV. SCENE I.

BENDUCAR'*s Palace in the Castle of* ALCAZAR.

BENDUCAR *solus.*

MY future fate, the colour of my life, My all depends on this important hour : ALMEYDA and the crown have push'd me forward;

'Tis

'Tis fix'd, the Tyrant muſt not raviſh her ·
He and SEBASTIAN ſtand betwixt my hopes;
He moſt; and therefore fiſt to be diſpatch'd.
Theſe and a thouſand things are to be done
In the ſhoit compaſs of this rolling night,
And nothing yet perform'd,
None of my emiſſaries yet return'd.

Enter H A L Y,——*Firſt Servant*

Oh HALY! thou haſt held me long in pain.
What haſt thou learnt of DORAX, is he dead?

HAL. Two hours I warily have watch'd his palace;
All doors are ſhut, no ſervant peeps abroad,
Some officers with ſtriding haſte paſs'd in,
While others outward went on quick diſpatch;
Sometimes huſh'd ſilence ſeem'd to reign within,
Then cries confus'd, and a joint clamour follow'd:
Then lghts went gliding by, from room to room,
And ſhot like thwaiting meteors croſs the houſe:
Not daring farther to enquire; I came
With ſpeed, to bring you this imperfect news.

BEND. Hence I conclude him either dead or dying:
His mournful friends, ſummon'd to take their leaves,
Are throng'd about his couch, and ſit in council,
What thoſe caballing captains may deſign,
I muſt prevent,
By being fiſt in action.
To MULEY-ZEYDAN fly with ſpeed, deſire him
To take my laſt inſtructions, tell th' impoitance,
And haſte his preſence here.   [*Exit* HALY.

How has this poiſon loſt its wonted way?
It ſhou'd have burnt its paſſage, not have linger'd
In the blind labyrinths and crooked turnings
Of human compoſition, now it moves
Like a ſlow fire that works againſt the wind,
As if his ſtronger ſtars had interpos'd.

Enter H A M E T,

Well, HAMET, are our friends the rabble rais'd?
From MUSTAPHA, what meſſage?

HAM. What you wiſh:
The ſtreets are thicker in this noon of night,

F 3   Than

Than at the mid-day fun : a drowzy horror
Sits on their eyes like fear not well awake :
All croud in heaps, as at a night alarm,
The bees drive out upon each other's backs
T' imbofs their hives in clufters; all afk news :
Their bufy captain runs the weary round
To whifper orders, and commanding filence
Makes not noife ceafe, but deafens it to murmurs.

  BEND. Night waftes apace ; when, when will he
  HAM. He only waits your fummons. [appear ?
  BEND. Hafte their coming.
Let feerecy and filence be enjoin'd
In their clofe march : what news from the lieutenant ?
  HAM. I left him at the gate, firm to your int'reft,
T' admit the townfmen at their firft appearance.
  BEND. Thus far 'tis well: go, haften MUSTAPHA.
          Exit HAMET.

    Enter ORCHAN, *the Third Servant*.
O, ORCHAN, did I think thy diligence
Wou'd lag behind the reft ? what from the MUFTI ?
  ORCH. I fought him round his palace ; made enquiry
Of all the flaves : in fhort, I us'd your name
And urg'd th' importance home; but had for anfwer
That fince the fhut of evening none had feen him.
  BEND. O the curft fate of all confpiracies !
They move on many fprings, if one but fail
The reftive Machine ftops —In an ill hour he's abfent;
'Tis the firft time, and fure will be the laft,
That e'er a churchman was not in the way,
When tumult and rebellion fhou'd be broach'd:
Stay by me, thou art refolute and faithful ;
I have employment worthy of thy arm. [*Walks.*

    Enter MULEY-ZEYDAN
  MUL-ZEYD. You fee me come impatient of my hopes,
And eager as the courfer for the race :
Is all in readinefs ?
  BEND All but the MUFTI.
  MUL-ZEYD. We muft go on without him,
  BEND. True we muft ;
For 'tis ill ftopping in the full career,
            How

How e'er the leap be dangerous and wide.   [afar;

ORCH. [*looking out*] I see the blaze of torches from
And hear the trampling of thick-beating feet ;
This way they move.

BEND. No doubt the Emperor.
We muſt not be ſurpriz'd in conference.
Truſt to my management the Tyrant's death ;
And haſte yourſelf to join with MUSTAPHA.
The Officer who guards the gate is yours ;
When you have gain'd that paſs, divide your force :
Yourſelf in perſon head one choſen half,
And march t' oppreſs the faction in conſult
With dying DORAX : Fate has driv'n 'em all
Into the net · you muſt be bold and ſudden :
Sp re none, and if you find him ſtruggling yet
With pangs of death, truſt not his rolling eyes
And heaving galps ; for poiſon may be falſe,
The home thruſt of a friendly ſword is ſure.

MUL.-ZEYD. Doubt not my conduct : they ſhall be
            ſurpriz'd ;
Mercy may wait without the gate one night,
At morn I'll take her in————

BEND. Here lies your way,
You meet your brother there.

MUL.-ZEYD. May we ne'er meet :
For, like the twins of *Leda,* when I mount
He gallops down the ſkies.————
                        [*Exit* MULEY-ZEYDAN.

BEND. He comes : now, heart,
Be ribb'd with iron for this one attempt :
Set ope thy ſluices, ſend the vigorous blood
Through every active limb for my relief :
Then, take thy reſt within thy quiet cell,
For thou ſhalt drum no more.

Enter MULEY-MOLUCH, *and Guards attending him.*

MUL.-MOL, What news of our affairs, and what of
            DORAX ?
Is he no more ? ſay that, and make me happy.

BEND. May all your enemies be like that dog,
Whoſe parting ſoul is lab'ring at the lips.

MUL.-MOL. The people, are they rais'd ?
                                        BEND.

BEND. And marfhall'd too :
Juft ready for the march

MUL.-MOL. Then I'm at eafe.

BEND. The night is yours, the glitt'ring hoft of Heav'n
Shines but for you, but moft the ftar of love,
That twinkles you to fair ALMEYDA's bed.
Oh there's a joy to melt in her embrace,
Diffolve in pleafures ;
But hafte, and make 'em yours.

MUL.-MOL I will, and yet
A kind of weight hangs heavy at my heart ;
My fenfes too are dull and ftupify'd,
Their edge rebated ; fure fome ill approaches,
And fome kind fpirit knocks foftly at my foul,
To tell me fate's at hand.

BEND Mere fancies all—no danger can be near,
But of a furfeit at too full a feaft.

MUL.-MOL. It may be fo · it looks fo like the dream
That overtook me at my waking hour
This morn, and dreams they fay are then divine,
When all the balmy vapours are exhal'd,
And fome o'er pouring God continues fleep.
'Twas then methought ALMEYDA, fmiling, came
Attended with a train of all her race.
Whom in the rage of empire I had murder'd.
But now, no longer foes, they gave me joy
Of my new conqueft, and with helping hands
Heav'd me into our holy Prophet's arms,
Who bore me in a purple cloud to Heav'n.

BEND Good omen, Sir, I wifh you in that Heav'n
Your dream portends you.
Which prefages death———   [*Afide*.

MUL.-MOL. Thou too wert there ;
And thou methought didft pufh me from below,
With thy full force to Paradife.

BEND. Yet better.

MUL.-MOL. Ha ! what's that grizly fellow that attends thee ?

BEND. Why afk you, Sir !

MUL. MOL. For he was in my dream ;
And help'd to heave me up.

                              BEND.

BEND. With pray'rs and wifhes;
For I dare fwear him honeft,

MUL.-MOL. That may be;
But yet he looks damnation.

BEND. You forget,
The face would pleafe you better: do you love,
And can you thus forbear?

MUL.-MOL. I'll head my people;
Then think of dalliance, when the danger's o'er.
My warlike fpirits now work another way;
And my foul's tun'd to trumpets,

BEND. You debafe yourfelf,
To think of mixing with th'ignoble herd.
Let fuch perform the fervile work of war,
Such who have no ALMEYDA to enjoy.
What! fhall the people know their godlike prince
Skulk'd in a nightly fkirmifh? ftole a conqueft,
Headed a rabble, and profan'd his perfon,
Shoulder'd with filth, born in a tide of ordure,
And ftifled with their rank offenfive fweat?

MUL.-MOL. I am off again: I will not proftitute
The regal dignity fo far, to head 'em.

BEND. There fpoke a king.
Difmifs your guards to be employ'd elfewhere
In ruder combats, you will want no feconds
In thofe alarms you feek.

MUL.-MOL. Go join the croud; [*to the Guards.*
BENDUCAR, thou fhalt lead 'em in my place.
[*Exeunt Guards.*
The God of love once more has fhot his fires
Into my foul, and my whole heart receives him.
ALMEYDA now returns with all her charms;
I feel her as fhe glides along my veins,
And dances in my blood: fo when our Prophet
Had long been hamm'ring in his lonely cell,
Some dull, infipid, tedious paradife,
A brifk *Arabian* girl came tripping by;
Paffing fhe caft at him a fide long glance,
And look'd behind in hopes to be purfu'd:
He took the hint, embrac'd the flying fair;
And having found his Heav'n, he plac'd it there.
[*Exit* MUL.-MOL.
BEND.

BEND. That paradife thou never fhalt poffefs.
His death is eafy now, his guards are gone,
And I can fin but once to feize 'the throne.
All after-acts are fanctify'd by pow'r.
ORCH. Command my fword and life.
BEND. I thank thee, ORCHAN,
And fhall reward thy faith : this mafter-key
Frees every lock, and leads us to his perfon ;
And fhou'd we mifs our blow, as Heav'n forbid,
Secures retreat : leave open all behind us ;
And firft fet wide the MUFTI's garden gate,
Which is his private paffage to the palace :
For there our mutineers appoint to meet,
And thence we may have aid. Now fleep, ye ftars,
That filently o'er watch the fate of kings ;
Be all propitious influences barr'd,
And none but murd'rous planets mount the guard.
[*Exit with* ORCHAN.

A Night Scene of the MUFTI's *Garden.*

Enter the MUFTI *alone, in a Slave's Habit like that of* ANTONIO.

MUF. This 'tis to have a found head-piece ; by this I
have got to be chief of my religion ; that is, honeftly
fpeaking, to teach others what I neither know nor believe myfelf For what's MAHOMET to me, but that
I get by him ? Now for my policy of this night · I have
mew'd up my fufpected fpoufe in her chamber.   No
more embaffies to that lufty young ftallion of a gard'ner.
Next my habit of a flave ; I have made myfelf as like
him as I can, all but his youth and vigour, which when
I had, I pafs'd my time as well as any of my holy pre-
deceffors.   Now walking under the windows of my fera-
glio, if JOHAYMA look out fhe will certainly take me
for ANTONIO, and call to me ; and by that I fhall
know what concupifcence is working in her, fhe cannot
come down to commit iniquity, there's my fafety ; but
if fhe peep, if fhe put her nofe abroad, that's demonftra-
tion of her pious will : And I'll not make the firft precedent for a churchman to forgive injuries.

Enter

Enter MORAYMA, *running to him with a casket in her hand, and embracing him.*

MOR. Now I can embrace you with a good confcience; here are the pearls and jewels, here's my father.

MUF. I am indeed thy father, but how the devil didft thou know me in this difguife; and what pearls and jewels doft thou mean?

MOR. [*going back*]——What have I done, and what will become of me!

MUF. Art thou mad, MORAYMA?

MOR. I think you'll make me fo.

MUF. Why, what have I done to thee? recollect thy felf and fpeak fenfe to me.

MOR. Then give me leave to tell you, you are the worft of fathers.

MUF. Did I think I had begotten fuch a monfter? Proceed, my dutiful child, proceed, proceed.

MOR. You have been raking together a mafs of wealth, by indirect and wicked means; the fpoils of orphans are in thefe jewels, and the tears of widows in thefe pearls.

MUF. Thou amazeft me!

MOR I wou'd do fo. This cafket is loaded with your fins, 'tis the cargo of rapines, fimony, and extortions, the iniquity of thirty years Muftifhip, converted into diamonds.

MUF. Wou'd fome rich railing rogue wou'd fay fo much to me, that I might fqueeze his purfe for fcandal.

MOR. No, fir, you get more by pious fools than railers, when you infinuate into their families, manage their fortunes while they live, and beggar their heirs by getting legacies when they die. And do you think I'll be the receiver of your theft? I difcharge my confcience of it · Here take again your filthy mammon, and reftore it you had beft to the true owners.

MUF. I am finely documented by my own daughter.

MOR. And a great credit for me to be fo · do but think how decent a habit you have on, and how becoming your function to be difguis'd like a flave, and eves-dropping under the womens windows If I had not known you cafually by your fhambling gate, and a certain reverend awkwardnefs that is natural to all of your function, here you had been expos'd to the laughter of your own

fervants,

servants, who have been in search of you through your whole Seraglio, peeping under every petticoat to find you.

MUF. Prithee child reproach me no more of human failings, they are but a little of the pitch and spots of the world that are still sticking on me, but I hope to scour 'em out in time I am better at bottom than thou think'st; I am not the man thou tak'st me for.

MOR No, to my sorrow, Sir, you are not.

MUF It was a very odd beginning, tho' methought, to see thee come running in upon me with such a warm embrace, prithee what was the meaning of that violent hot hug ?

MOR. I am sure I meant nothing by it, but the zeal and affection which I bear to the man of the world who n I may love lawfully.

MUF. But thou wilt not teach me at this age the nature of a close embrace ?

MOR. If you mistook my innocent embrace for sin, I wish heartily it had been given where it wou'd have been more acceptable.

MUF. Why, this is as it shou'd be now: take the treasure again, it can never be put into better hands.

MOR Yes, to my knowledge, but it might. I have confess'd my soul to you, if you can understand me rightly ; I never disobey'd you till this night ; and now since, through the violence of my passion, I have been so unfortunate, I humbly beg your pardon, your blessing, and your leave, that upon the first opportunity I may go for ever from your sight for Heaven knows, I never desire to see you more

MUF. [*Wiping his eyes*] Thou mak'st me weep at thy unkindness, indeed, dear daughter, we will not part.

MOR. Indeed, but we will.

MUF Why, if I have been a little pilfering, or so, I take it bitterly of thee to tell me of it, since it was to make thee rich, and I hope a man may make bold with his own soul, without offence to his own child. here, take the jewels again, take 'em I charge thee upon thy obedience.

MOR. Well then, in virtue of obedience I will take 'em, but on my soul, I had rather they were in a better hand.

Muf. Meaning mine, I know it.

Mor. Meaning his, whom I love better than my life.

Muf. That's me again.

Mor. I wou'd have you think so.

Muf. How thy good nature works upon me! well I can do no less than venture damning for thee, and I may put fair for it, if the rabble be order'd to rise to night.

Enter ANTONIO *in an African rich habit.*

Ant What do you mean, my dear, to stand talking in this suspicious place, just underneath JOHAYMA's window? *(to the* MUFTI*).* You are well met, comerade, I know you are the friend of our flight. Are the horses ready at the postern gate?

Muf. ANTONIO, and in disguise! now I begin to smell a rat.

Ant. And I another, that out-stinks it: false MORAYMA, hast thou thus betray'd me to thy father!

Mor. Alas, I was betray'd myself he came disguis'd like you, and I poor innocent ran into his hands.

Muf. In good time you did so; you wou'd fain break loose now, though you left a limb behind you, but I am yet in my own territories, and in call of company, that's my comfort. [ANTONIO, *taking him by the throat.*

Ant. No, I have a trick left to put thee past thy squeaking. I have given thee the quinsey; that ungracious tongue shall preach no more false doctrine.

Mor. What do you mean? you will not throttle him? consider, he's my father.

Ant Prithee let us provide first for our own safety; if I do not consider him, he will consider us with a vengeance afterwards.

Mor. You may threaten him for crying out, but for my sake give him back a little cranny of his wind-pipe and some part of speech.

Ant Not so much as one single interjection: come away father in law, this is no place for dialogues, when you are in the mosque you talk by hours, and there no man must interrupt you, this is but like for like, good father in law; now I am in the pulpit, 'tis your turn to hold your tongue [*He struggles.*

G

Nay

Nay if you be hanging back, I shall take care you shall hang forward.

[Pulls him along the stage; with a sword at his reins.

MOR. T' other way, to the arbour with him; and make haste before we are discovered.

ANT. If I only bind and gag him there, he may commend me hereafter for civil usage, he deserves not so much favour by any action of his life.

MOR. Yes, pray bate him one, for begetting your mistress.

ANT. I wou'd, if he had not thought more of thy mother than of thee; once more come along in silence, my Pythagorean father in law.

JOH [*At the balcony.*] —— A bird in a cage may peep at least, though she must not fly, what bustle's there beneath my window? ANTONIO, by all my hopes! I know him by his habit: but what makes that woman with him, and a friend, a sword drawn, and hasting hence? this is no time for silence Who's within call there? where are the servants? why Omar, Abedin, Hassan, and the rest, make haste and run into the garden; there are thieves and villains; arm all the family, and stop 'em. [ANTONIO *turning back.*

ANT. O that screech-owl at the window! we shall be pursu'd immediately; which way shall we take?

[MORAYMA *giving him the casket.*

MOR. 'Tis impossible to escape them, for the way to our horses lies back again by the house, and then we shall meet 'em full in the teeth; here take these jewels, thou may'st leap these walls, and get away.

ANT. And what will become of thee then, poor kind soul.

MOR. I must take my fortune; when you are got safe into your own country, I hope you will bestow a sigh on the memory of her who lov'd you!

ANT. It makes me mad, to think how many a good night will be lost betwixt us! take back thy jewels; 'tis an empty casket without thee: besides I shou'd never leap well with the weight of all thy father's sins about me; thou and they had been a bargain.

MOR. Prithee take 'em, 'twill help me to be reveng'd on him.

ANT.

A̓NT. No; they'll ferve to make thy peace with him.

MOR. I hear 'em coming; fhift for yourfelf at leaft; remember I am yours for 'ever.

[*Servants crying*, this way, this way, *behind the fcenes*.

ANT. And I but the empty fhadow of myfelf without thee! farewel, father-in-law, that fhould have been—— Now which way fortune ——

[*Runs amazedly backwards and forwards*.
Servants within Follow, follow, yonder are the villains.

ANT. O here's a gate open; but it leads into the caftle; yet I muft venture it.   [*Going out*.
[*A fhout behind the fcenes, where* ANTONIO *is going out*.

ANT. There's the rabble in a mutiny, what, is the devil up at midnight! ———— however 'tis good herding in a croud.   [*Runs out*.

[MUFTI *runs to* MORAYMA *and lays hold on her, then fnatches away the casket*.]

MUF. Now, to do things in order, firft I feize upon the bag, and then upon the baggage: for thou art but my flefh and blood, but thefe are my life and foul.

MOR. Then let me follow my flefh and blood, and keep to yourfelf your life and foul.

MUF. Both or none; come away to durance.

MOR. Well, if it muft be fo; agreed, for I have another trick to play you, and thank yourfelf for what fhall follow.

                    Enter S E R V A N T S.

JOH   [*From above*] One of them took through the private way into the caftle, follow him be fure, for thefe are yours already.

MOR. Help here, quickly, *Omar*, *Abedin*; I have hold on the villain that ftole my jewels, but 'tis a lufty rogue, and he will be too ftrong for me, what, help I fay, do you not know your mafter's daughter.

MUF. Now if I cry out they will know my voice; and then I am difgraced for ever: O thou art a venomous cockatrice!

MOR. Of your own begetting.

                    [*The fervants feize him*.

Firft fervant. What a glorious deliverance have you had, madam, from this bloody-minded chriftian!

          G 2   MOR.

MOR. Give me back my jewels, and carry this notorious malefactor to be punish'd by my father.

I'll hunt the other dry-foot. [*Takes the jewels, and runs out after* ANTONIO *at the same passage*.

First servant. I long to be handselling his hide, before we bring him to my master.

Second servant. Hang him for an old covetous hypocrite . he deserves a worse punishment himself for keeping us so hardly.

First servant. Ay, wou'd he were, in this villain's place ; thus wou'd I lay on him, and thus,
(*Beats him*.

Second servant. And thus wou'd I revenge myself of my last beating. (*He beats him too, and then the rest*.

MUF. Oh, oh, oh !

First servant. Now supposing you were the MUFTI. Sir, ——— (*Beats him again*.

MUF. The devil's in that supposing rascal ; I can bear no more ; and I am the MUFTI : now, suppose yourselves my servants, and hold your hands, an anointed halter take you all.

First servant My master ! you will pardon the excess of our zeal for you, Sir , indeed we all took you for a villain, and so we us'd you

MUF. Ay, so I feel you did , my back and sides are abundant testimonies of your zeal. Run rogues, ar d bring me back my jewels, and my fugitive daughter : run, I say.

(*They run to the gate, and the first servant runs back again*.

Second servant Sir, the castle is in a most terrible combustion ! you may hear 'em hither.

MUF. 'Tis a laudable commotion : the voice of the mobile is the voice of Heav'n. I must retire a little, to strip me of the slave, and to assume the MUFTI, and then I will return : for the piety of the people must be encouraged ; that they may help me to recover my jewels, and my daughter. [*Exit* MUFTI *and servants*.

Scene changes to the castle-yard, and discovers ANTONIO, MUSTAPHA, *and the rabble shouting, they come forward*.

ANT. And so at length, as I inform'd you, I escap'd out of his covetous clutches ; and now fly to your illustrious feet for my protection.

MUST.

Must. Thou fhall have it, and now defy the Mufti. 'Tis the fiift petition that has been made to me fince my exaltation to tumult, in this fecond, night of the month, *Abib*, and in the year of the *Hegyra*; the lor' knows what year; but 'tis no matter, for when I am fettled, the learned are bound to find it out for me. For I am refolved to date my authority over the rabble, like other monarchs.

Ant. I have always had a longing to be yours again; though I cou'd not compafs it before, and had defign'd you a cafket of my mafter's jewels too, for I knew the cuftom, and wou'd not have appear'd before a great perfon, as you are, without a prefent. But he has defrauded my good intentions, and bafely robb'd you of 'em, 'tis a prize worth a million of crowns, and you carry your letters of Mark about with you.

Must. I fhall make bold with his treafure, for the fupport of my new government.
[The people gather about him.
What do thefe vile raggamuffins fo near our perfon? Your favour is offenfive to us; bear back there, and make room for honeft men to approach us; thefe fools and knaves are always impudently crouding next to princes, and keeping off the more deferving, bear back, I fay.
[They make a wider circle.
That's dutifully done, now fhout to fhew your loyalty (*A great fhout*) Hear'ft thou that, flave Antonio? Thefe obftreperous villains fhout, and know not for what they make a noife. You fhall fee me manage 'em, that you may judge what ignorant beafts they are. For whom do you fhout now? who's to live and reign? tell me that, the wifeft of you.

Firft Rabble. Even who you pleafe, captain.

Must. La you there; I told you fo.

Second Rabble. We are not bound to know who is to live and reign, our bufinefs is only to rife upon command, and plunder.

Third Rabble. Ay, the riches of both parties; for they are our enemies.

Must. This laft fellow is a little more fenfible than the reft; he has enter'd fomewhat upon the merits of the cause,

First Rabble. If a poor man may speak his mind, I think, captain, that yourself are the fittest to live and reign; I mean not over, but next and immediately under the people: and thereupon I say, a MUSTAPHA! a MUSTAPHA!

(*All cry*) a MUSTAPHA! a MUSTAPHA!

MUST. I must confess the sound is pleasing, and tickles the ears of my ambition, but alas! good people, it must not be: I am contented to be a poor simple viceroy; but Prince MULEY-ZEYDAN is to be the man: I shall take care to instruct him in the arts of government; and in his duty to us all: And therefore mark me cry, a MULEY ZEYDAN! a MULEY-ZEYDAN!

(*All cry*) A MULEY-ZEYDAN! a MULEY-ZEYDAN!

MUST. You see, slave ANTONIO, what I might have been.

ANT. I observe your modesty.

MUST. But for a foolish promise I made once to my lord BENDUCAR, to set up any one he pleas'd.

Re-enter the MUFTI *with his servants.*

ANT. Here's the old hypocrite again; now stand your ground, and bate him not an inch. Remember the jewels, the rich and glorious jewels; they are destin'd to be yours, by virtue of prerogative.

MUST. Let me alone to pick a quarrel, I have an old grudge to him upon thy account.

MUFTI, *making up to the mobile.*

Good people, here you are met together.

First Rabble Ay, we know that without your telling; but why are we met together, doctor? for that's it which no body here can tell.

Second Rabble. Why to see one another in the dark; and to make holy-day at midnight.

MUF. You are met, as becomes good Mussulmen; to settle the nation, for I must tell you, that though your tyrant is a lawful Emperor, yet your lawful Emperor is but a tyrant

ANT. What stuff he talks!

MUST. 'Tis excellent fine matter indeed, slave ANTONIO; he has a rare tongue; oh, he wou'd move a rock of elephant!

ANT,

ANT. [*Aside*] What a block have I to work upon, [*To him*] But still remember the jewels, sir, the jewels.

MUST. Nay that's true on t'other side: The jewels muft be 'mine', but he has a pure fine way of talking: my conscience goes along with him, but the jewels have set my heart against him.

MUF. That your Emperor is a tyrant is moft manifeft; for you were born to be *Turks*: but he has play'd the *Turk* with you, and is taking your religion away.

Second Rabble We find that in our decay of trade; I have feen, for thefe hundred years, that religion and trade always go together.

MUF. He is now upon the point of marrying himfelf, without our fovereign confent; and what are the effects of marriage?

Third Rabble. A fcolding domineering wife, if fhe prove honeft, and, if a whore, a fine gaudy minx, that robs our counters every night, and then goes out, and fpends it upon our cuckold-makers.

MUF. No, the natural effects of marriage are children: Now on whom wou'd he beget thefe children? even upon a Curiftian! O horrible; how can you believe me, though I am ready to fwear it upon the ALCORAN! Yes, true believers, you may believe me, that he is going to beget a race of mifbelievers.

MUST. That's fine in earneft; I cannot forbear harkening to his enchanting tongue.

ANT. But yet remember——

MUST. Ay, ay, the jewels! Now again I hate him; but yet my confcience makes me liften to him.

MUF. Therefore to conclude all, believers, pluck up your hearts, and pluck down the tyrant. Remember the courage of your anceftors; remember the majefty of the people, remember yourfelves, your wives and children; and laftly, above all, remember your religion, and our holy MAHOMET; all thefe require your timeous affiftance; fhall I fay they beg it? No, they claim it of you, by all the neareft and deareft ties of thefe three P's, Self-Prefervation, our Property, and our Prophet. Now anfwer me with an unanimous chearful cry, and follow me, who am your leader, to a glorious deliverance.

(*All*

(All cry, a MUFTI*! a* MUFTI*! and are following
him off the Stage.)*

ANT. Now you see what becomes of our foolish qualms
of conscience: The jewels are lost, and they are all
leaving you.

MUST. What, am I forsaken of my subjects? Wou'd
the rogue purloin my liege-people from me! I charge you
in my own name, come back, ye deserters; and hear me
speak.

First Rabble. What, will he come with his balderdash,
after the MUFTI's eloquent oration?

Second Rabble. He's our captain lawfully pick'd up,
and elected upon a stall, we will hear him.

Omnes. Speak, captain, for we will hear you.

MUST. Do you remember the glorious rapines and
robberies you have committed? Your breaking open and
gutting of houses, your rummaging of cellars, your de-
molishing of Christian temples, and bearing off in triumph
the superstitious plate and pictures, the ornaments of
their wicked altars? when all rich moveables were sen-
tenc'd for idolatrous, and all that was idolatrous, was
seiz'd? Answer first for your remembrance, of all these
sweetnesses of mutiny, for upon those grounds I shall
proceed.

Omnes. Yes, we do remember, we do remember.

MUST. Then make much of your retentive faculties,
And who led you to those honey-combs? Your MUFTI?
No, believers, he only preach'd you up to it; but durst
not lead you; he was but your counsellor, but I was
your captain, he only loo'd you, but 'twas I that led
you.

Omnes. That's true, that's true.

- ANT. There, you were with him for his figures.

MUST. I think I was, slave ANTONIO. Alas! I was
ignorant of my own talent.——Say then, believers,
will you have a captain for your MUFTI? or a MUFTI
for your captain? and further to instruct you how to
cry, will you have a MUFTI, or no MUFTI?

Omnes. No MUFTI, no MUFTI.

MUST. That I laid in for 'em, slave ANTONIO.——
Do I then spit upon your faces? Do I discourage rebellion,

on, mutiny, rapine and plundering? You may think I
do, believers; but Heaven forbid: no, I encourage you
to all these laudable undertakings; you shall plunder,
you shall pull down the government; but you shall do
this upon my authority, and not by his wicked instiga-
tion.

Third Rabble. Nay, when his turn is serv'd, he may
preach up loyalty again, and restitution, that he might
have another snack among us.

First Rabble. He may, indeed; for 'tis but his saying
'tis sin, and then, we must restore; and therefore I would
have a new religion, where half the commandments shou'd
be taken away, the rest mollifi'd, and there shou'd be little or no sin remaining.

Omnes. Another religion, a new religion, another religion!

MUST. And that may easily be done, with the help
of a little inspiration: for I must tell you, I have a pige-
on at home, of *Mahomet's* own breed; and when I have
learn'd her to pick pease out of my ear, rest satisfy'd till
then, and you shall have another. But now I think
on't, I am inspir'd already, that 'tis no sin to depose the
MUFTI.

ANT. And good reason; for when kings and queens
are to be discarded, what shou'd knaves do any longer in
the pack?

Omnes. He is depos'd, he is depos'd, he is depos'd.

MUST. Nay, if he and his Clergy will needs be preaching up rebellion, and giving us their blessing, 'tis but justice they should have the first fruits of it. Slave ANTO-
NIO, take him into custody, and dost thou hear, boy,
be sure to secure the little transitory box of jewels · if he
be obstinate, put a civil question to him upon the rack,
and he squeaks I warrant him.

ANT. *Seizing the* MUFTI. Come, my *quondam* master, you and I must change qualities.

MUF. I hope you will not be so barbarous to torture
me, we may preach suffering to others, but alas! holy
flesh is too well pamper'd to endure martyrdom.

MUST Now, late MUFTI, not forgetting my first
quarrel to you, we will enter ourselves with the plunder

of

of your palace: 'tis good to fanctify a work, and begin a God's name.

Firft Rabble. Our Prophet, let the devil alone with the laft *Mob.*

Mob. But he takes care of this himfelf.

As they are going out, enter BENDUCAR *leading* AL-MEYDA: *he with a fword in one hand,* BENDUCAR'S *flave follows with* MULY-MOLUCH'S *head upon a fpear.*

MUST. Not fo much hafte, mafters; come back again: you are fo bent upon mifchief, that you take a man upon the firft word of plunder. Here's a fight for you: the Emperor is come upon his head to vifit you. [*Bowing.*] Moft noble Emperor' now, I hope you will not hit us in the teeth, that we have pull'd you down, for we can tell you to your face, that we have exalted you. [*They all fhout.*

[BENDUCAR *to* ALMEYDA, *apart.*]
Think what I am, and what yourfelf may be,
In being mine: refufe not proffer'd love
That brings a crown.

[ALMEYDA *to him.*]
I have refolv'd,
And thefe fhall know my thoughts.

[BENDUCAR *to her.*]
On that I build.———
(*He comes up to the rabble.*
Joy to the people for the tyrant's death!
Oppreffion, rapine, banifhment and blood
Are now no more; but fpeechlefs as that tongue
That lies for ever ftill.
How is my grief divided with my joy,
When I muft own I kill'd him' bid me fpeak,
For not to bid me is to difallow
What for your fakes is done.

MUST. In the name of the people we command you fpeak; but that pretty lady fhall fpeak firft, for we have taken fomething of a liking to her perfon. Be not afraid, lady, to fpeak to thefe rude raggamuffins; there's nothing fhall offend you.

[*Making a leg.*
ALM.

ALM. Why ſhould I fear to ſpeak, who am your queen?
My peaceful father ſway'd the ſceptre long;
And you enjoyed the bleſſings of his reign,
While you deſerv'd the name of *Africans.*
Then not commanded, but commanding you,
Fearleſs I ſpeak . know me for what I am.   [*aſide.*

BEND. How ſhe aſſumes! I like not this beginning.

ALM. I was not born ſo baſe to flatter crouds,
And move your pity by a whining tale:
Your Tyrant would have forc'd me to his bed;
But in th'attempt of that foul brutal act,
Theſe loyal ſlaves ſecur'd me by his death.
                    [*Pointing to* BENDUCAR.

BEND. Makes ſhe no more of me than of a ſlave; [*aſide.*
Madam, I thought I had inſtructed you   [*To* ALM.
To frame a ſpeech more ſuiting to the times:
The circumſtances of that dire deſign,
Your own deſpair, my unexpected aid,
My life endanger'd by his bold defence,
And, after all, his death and your deliv'rance,
Were themes that ought not to be ſlighted o'er.

MUST. She might have paſs'd over all your petty
buſineſſes, and no great matter: but the raiſing of my
rabble is an exploit of conſequence, and not to be mum-
bled up in ſilence, for all her pertneſs.

ALM. When force invades the gift of nature, life,
The eldeſt law of nature bids defend:
And if, in that defence, a Tyrant fall,
His death's his crime, not ours:
Suffice it that he's dead; all wrongs die with him.
When he can wrong no more I pardon him:
Thus I abſolve myſelf, and him excuſe,
Who ſav'd my life and honour; but praiſe reither.

BEND. 'Tis cheap to pardon whom you would not pay·
But what ſpeak I of payment and reward?
Ungrateful woman, you are yet no queen;
No more than a proud haughty Chriſtian ſlave;
As ſuch I ſeize my right.   [*Going to lay hold on her.*

ALMEYDA [*drawing a dagger.*]
    Dare not t'approach me;
Now *Africans,*
He ſhews himſelf to you; to me he ſtood

                                        Confeſs'd

Confefs'd before, and own'd his infolence
T' efpoufe my perfon, and affume the crown;
Claim'd in my right: for this he flew your Tyrant:
Oh no, he only chang'd him for a worfe,
Imbas'd your flavery by his own vilenefs,
And loaded you with more ignoble bonds:
Then think me not ungrateful, not to fhare
Th' imperial crown with a prefuming traitor.
He fays I am a Chriftian, true I am,
But yet no flave: if Chriftians can be thought
Unfit to govern thofe of other faith,
'Tis lett for you to judge.

BEND. I have not patience; fhe confumes the time
In idle talk, and owns her falfe belief:
Seize her by force, and bear her hence unheard.

ALMEYDA *to the people.*

No, let me rather die your facrifice
Than live his triumph;
I throw myfelf into my people's arms;
As you are men, compaffionate my wrongs,
And as good men protect me.

ANTONIO *afide to* MUSTAPHA.

Something muft be done to fave her.
This is all addrefs'd to you, fir: fhe fingled you out with
her eye, as commander in chief of the mobility.

MUST. Think'ft thou fo, flave ANTONIO?

ANT. Moft certainly, fir; and you cannot in honour
but protect her. Now look to your hits, and make your
fortune.

MUST. Methought indeed fhe caft a kind leer towards
me: our Prophet was but juft fuch another fcoundrel as
I am, till he rais'd himfelf to power, and confequently
to holinefs, by marrying his mafter's widow I am refolv'd I'll put forward for myfelf, for why fhould I be
my Lord BENDUCAR's fool and flave, when I may be
my own fool and his mafter

BEND. Take her into poffeffion, MUSTAPHA.

MUST. That's better counfel than you meant it:
yes, I do take her into poffeffion, and into protection too
what fay you, mafters, will you ftand by me?

Omnes. One and all, one and all.

BEND. Haft thou now betray'd me, Traitor?
MUFTI fpeak, and mind 'em of religion.

MUFTI *fhakes his head.*

MUST. Alas! the poor gentleman has gotten a cold,
with a fermon of two hours long, and a prayer of four:
And befides, if he durft fpeak, mankind is grown wifer at
this time of day, than to cut one another's throats about
religion. Our MUFTI's is a green coat, and the Chriftian's is a black coat; and we muft wifely go together by
the ears, whether green or black fhall fweep our fpoils.

[*Drums within and fhouts.*

BEND. Now we fhall fee whofe numbers will prevail:
The conquering troops of MULEY-ZEYDAN come
To crufh rebellion, and efpoufe my caufe

MUST. We will have a fair trial of fkill for't, I can
tell him that. When we have difpatch'd with MULEY-
ZEYDAN, your lordfhip fhall march in equal proportions
of your body, to the four gates of the city, and every
tower fhall have a quarter of you

[ANTONIO *draws them up, and takes* ALMEYDA *by the
Hand*]   [*Shouts again and drums.*

Enter DORAX *and* SEBASTIAN, *attended by* African
foldiers and Portuguefe.

ALMEYDA *and* SEBASTIAN *run into each other's arms,
and fpeak together.*

ALM. *and* SEB. My SEBASTIAN! my ALMEYDA!

ALM. Do you then live?

SEB And live to love thee ever.

BEND. How! DORAX and SEBASTIAN ftill alive.
The Moors and Chriftians join'd! I thank thee, Prophet.

DOR The citadel is ours; and MULEY-ZEYDAN
Safe under guard, but as becomes a prince.
Lay down your arms: fuch bafe Plebeian blood
Would only ftain the brightnefs of my fword,
And blunt it for fome noble work behind.

MUST I fuppofe you may put it up, without offence
to any man here prefent? For my part I have been loyal
to my fovereign lady· Though that villain BENDUCAR,
and that hypocrite the MUFTI, would have corrupted
me, but if thofe two 'fcape publick juftice, then I, and
all my late honeft fubjects here, deferve hanging.

H   BEND.

[BEND. I am fure I did my part to poifon thee,
to DORAX.] What faint foe'er has folder'd thee again.
A dofe lefs hot had burft through ribs of iron.

MUF. Not knowing that, I poifon'd him once more,
And drench'd him with a draught fo deadly cold,
That, had'ft not thou prevented, had congeal'd
The channel of his blood, and froze him dead.

BEND. Thou interpofing fool, to mingle mifchief,
And think to mend the perfect work of hell!

DOR. Thus, when Heav'n pleafes, double poifons cure.
I will not tax thee of ingratitude
To me thy friend, who haft betray'd thy prince;
Death he deferv'd indeed, but not from thee:
But fate it feems referv'd the worft of men
To end the worft of tyrants.
Go, bear him to his fate,
And fend him to attend his mafter's ghoft:
Let fome fecure my other pois'ning friend,
Whofe double diligence preferv'd my life.

ANT. You are fall'n into good hands, father-in-law;
Your fparkling jewels, and MORAYMA's eyes
May prove a better bail than you deferve.

MUF. The beft that can come of me in this condition,
is, to have my life begg'd firft, and then to be begg'd for
a fool afterwards.

Exit ANTONIO *with the* MUFTI, *and at the fame time*
BENDUCAR *is carry'd off.*

DORAX *to* MUSTAPHA. You and your hungry herd de-
part untouch'd;
For juftice cannot ftoop fo low to reach
The groveling fin of crouds; But curft be they
Who truft revenge with fuch mad inftruments,
Whofe blindfold bufinefs is but to deftroy:
And like the fire, commiffion'd by the winds,
Begins on fheds, but, rowling in a round,
On palaces returns. Away, ye fcum,
That ftill rife upmoft when the nation boils!
Ye mungril work of Heav'n, with human fhapes,
Not to be damn'd, or fav'd, but breathe, and perifh;
That have but juft enough of fenfe to know
The mafter's voice, when rated, to depart!

(*Exeunt* MUSTAPHA *and* Rabble

ALM

ALMEYDA, *kneeling to him.*
With gratitude as low as knees can pay
To those blest holy fires, our guardian angels;
Receive these thanks till altars can be rais'd.

DORAX, *raising her up.*
Arise, fair excellence, and pay no thanks,
Till time discover what I have deserv'd.

SEB. More than reward can answer,
If *Portugal* and *Spain* were join'd to *Afric,*
And the main ocean crusted into land;
If universal monarchy were mine,
Here shou'd the gift be plac'd

DOR. And from some hands I shou'd refuse that gift:
Be not too prodigal of promises;
But stint your bounty to one only grant,
Which I can ask with honour.

SEB. What I am
Is but thy gift; make what thou can'st of me,
Secure of no repulse.

DOR. *to* SEBASTIAN. Dismiss your train.
To ALMEYDA. You, madam, please one moment to
retire.

[SEBASTIAN *signs to the* Portuguese *to go off.* AL-
MEYDA *bowing to him, goes off also: The* Africans
follow her]

DORAX, *to the Captain of his Guard.*
With you one word in private
(*Goes out with the Captain.*

SEB. *solus.* Reserv'd behaviour, open nobleness,
A long mysterious track of a stern bounty!
But now the hand of fate is on the curtain,
And draws the scene to sight.

[*Re-enter* DORAX, *having taken off his turban and put
on a peruke, hat and cravat.*]

DOR. Now, do you know me?
SEB. Thou shou'd'st be ALONZO.
DOL. So you should be SEBASTIAN:
But when SEBASTIAN ceas'd to be himself,
I ceas'd to be ALONZO.

SEB. As in a dream
I see thee here, and scarce believe mine eyes.

DOR. Is it so strange to find me, where my wrongs,

H 2
And

And your inhuman tyranny have sent me ?
Think not you dream · Or, if you did, my injuries
Shall call so loud, that lethargy should wake;
And death shou'd give you back to answer me.
A thousand nights have brush'd their balmy wings
Over these eyes, but, ever when they clos'd,
Your tyrant image forc'd 'em ope again,
And dry'd the dews they brought.
The long expected hour is come at length,
By manly vengeance to redeem my fame,
And that once clear'd, eternal sleep is welcome.

SEB. I have not yet forgot I am a king,
Whose royal office is redress of wrongs:
If I have wrong'd thee, charge me face to face;
I have not yet forgot I am a soldier.

DOR. 'Tis the first justice thou hast ever done me:
Then, though I loath this woman's war of tongues,
Yet shall my cause of vengeance first be clear:
And, honour, be thou judge.

SEB. Honour befriend us both.
Beware, I warn thee yet, to tell thy griefs
In terms becoming majesty to hear ·
I warn thee thus, because I know thy temper
Is insolent and haughty to superiors:
How often hast thou brav'd my peaceful court,
Fill'd it with noisy brawls, and windy boasts,
And with past services, nauseously repeated,
Reproach'd ev'n me thy prince ?

DOR. Well I might, when you forgot reward,
The part of heav'n in kings, for punishment
Is hangman's work, and drudgery for devils.
I must and will reproach thee with my service,
Tyrant (it irks me so to call my prince) ·
But just resentment and hard usage coin'd
Th'unwilling word, and, grating as it is,
Take it, for 'tis thy due.

SEB How, tyrant!
DOR. Tyrant.
SEB. Traitor! that name thou canst not echo back:
That robe of infamy, that circumcision
Ill hid beneath that robe, proclaim thee traitor:
And, if a name

More

More foul than traitor be, 'tis renegade.

DOR. If I'm a traitor, think and blush, thou Tyrant,
Whose injuries betray'd me into treason;
Effac'd my loyalty, unhing'd my faith,
And hurry'd me from hopes of heav'n to hell.
All these, and all my yet unfinish'd crimes,
When I shall rise to plead before the saints,
I'll charge on thee, to make thy damning sure.

SEB. Thy old presumptuous arrogance again,
That bred my first dislike, and then my loathing?
Once mo e, be warn'd, and know me for thy king.

DOR. Too well I know thee, but for king no more:
This is not *Lisbon*, nor the circle this,
Where, like a statue, thou hast stood besieg'd
By sycophants and fools, the growth of courts:
Where thy gull'd eyes, in all the gaudy round,
Met nothing but a lie in every face;
And the gross flattery of a gaping croud,
Envious who first should catch and first applaud
The stuff of royal nonsense: when I spoke,
My honest homely words were carp'd and censur'd
For want of courtly stile: related actions,
Though modestly reported, pass'd for boasts:
Secure of merit, if I ask'd reward,
Thy hungry minions thought their rights invaded,
And the bread snatch'd from pimps and parasites.
Henriquez answer'd, with a ready lie,
To save his king's, the boon was begg'd before.

SEB. What say'st thou of *Henriquez?* now by Heav'n
Thou mov'st me more by barely naming him,
Than all thy foul unmanner'd scurril taunts.   [him:

DOR. And therefore 'twas to gall thee that I nam'd
That thing, that nothing, but a cringe and smile;
That woman, but more daub'd; or, if a man,
Corrupted to a woman: thy man mistress.

SEB. All false as hell, or thou.

DOR. Yes, full as false
As that I serv'd thee fifteen hard campaigns,
And pitch'd thy standard in these foreign fields:
By me thy greatness grew; thy years grew with it;
But thy ingratitude outgrew 'em both.

SEB. I fee to what thou tend'ft; but tell me firft,
If thofe gieat acts were done alone for me
If love pioduc'd not fome, and pride the reft.

DOR Why love does all that's noble heie below;
But all'th' advantage of that love was thine :
Foi, coming fraughted back, in either hand,
With palm and olive, victory and peace,
I was indeed prepar'd to afk my own :
Foi *Violante*'s vows were mine before :
Thy malice had prevention, e're I fpoke,
And afk'd me *Violante* foi *Henriquez*.

SEB. I meant thee a reward of greater worth :

DOR. Where juftice wanted, could reward be hop'd ?
Could the robb'd paffenger expect a bounty,
Fiom thofe iapacious hands who ftript him fiift ?

SEB. He had my promife 'ere I knew thy love.

DOR. My fervices deferv'd thou fhould'ft revoke it.

SEB. Thy infolence had cancell'd all thy feivice :
To violate my laws, even in my court,
Sacred to peace, and fafe from all affronts;
Ev'n to my face, as done in my defpight,
Under the wing of awful majefty
To ftrike the man I lov'd !

DOR. Ev'n in the face of Heav'n, a place more facred,
Would I have ftiuck the man, who, prop'd by power,
Would feize my right, and rob me of my love :
But for a blow provok'd by thy injuftice,
The hifty product of a juft defpaii,
When he refus'd to meet me in the field,
That thou fhould'ft make a coward's caufe thy own !

SEB. He durft; nay more, defir'd and begg'd with
         tears,
To meet thy challenge fairly : 'twas thy fault
To make it public; but my duty, then,
To interpofe, on pain of my difpleafure,
Betwixt your fwords.

DOR On pain of infamy
He fhou'd have difobey'd.

SEB. In' indignity thou didft, was meant to me;
Thy gloomy eyes were caft on me, with fcoin,
As who fhould fay the blow was there intended ;
But that thou didft not daie to lift thy hands

Againft

Againſt anointed power : ſo was I forc'd
To do a ſovereign juſtice to myſelf,
And ſpurn thee from my preſence.

    DOR. Thou haſt dar'd
To tell me, what I durſt not tell myſelf:
I durſt not think that I was ſpurn'd, and live;
And live to hear it boaſted to my face.
All my long avarice of honour loſt,
Heap'd up in youth, and hoarded up for age !
Has honour's fountain then ſuck'd back the ſtream ?
He has , and hooting boys may dry-ſhod paſs,
And gather pebbles from the naked ford.
Give me my love, my honour, give 'em back: . . . .
Give me revenge ; while I have breath to aſk it . . . .

    SEB. Now, by this honour'd order which I wear,
More gladly would I give, than thou dar'ſt aſk it:
Nor ſhall the ſacred character of King
Be urg'd, to ſhield me from thy bold appeal.
If I have injur'd thee, that makes us equal :
The wrong, if done, debas'd me down to thee ;
But thou haſt charg'd me with ingratitude .
Haſt thou not charg'd me ; ſpeak ?

    DOR. Thou know'ſt I have :
If thou diſown'ſt that imputation, draw,
And prove my charge a lie.

    SEB. No; to diſprove that lie, I muſt not draw:
Be conſcious to thy worth, and tell thy ſoul
What thou haſt done this day in my defence :
To fight thee, after this, what were it elſe,
Than owning that ingratitude thou urgeſt ?
That *Iſthmus* ſtands betwixt two ruſhing ſeas,
Which, mounting, view each other from afar,
And ſtrive in vain to meet.

    DOR. I'll cut that *Iſthmus.*
Thou know'ſt I meant not to preſerve thy life,
But to reprieve it, for my own revenge.
I ſav'd thee out of honourable malice :
Now draw, I ſhould be loth to think thou dar'ſt not:
Beware of ſuch another vile excuſe.

    SEB. O patience, Heaven !

    DOR. Beware of patience too ;
That's a ſuſpicious word : it had been proper

Before

Before thy foot had fpurn'd me; now 'tis bafe :
Yet, to difarm thee of thy laft defence,
I have thy oath for my fecurity :
The only boon I begg'd was this fair combat ;
Fight or be perjur'd now ; that's all my choice.
    [SEB. *drawing*] Now I can thank thee, as thou
       would'ft be thank'd :
Never was vow of honour better paid,
If my true fword but bold, than this fhall be.
The fprightly bridegroom, on his wedding night,
More gladly enters not the lifts of love.
Why, 'tis enjoyment to be fummon'd thus.
Go : bear my meffage to *Henriquez'* ghoft ;
And fay his mafter and his friend reveng'd him.
    DOR. His ghoft ! then is my hated rival dead ?
    SEB. The queftion is befide our prefent purpofe,
Thou feeft me ready, we delay too long
    DOR. A minute is not much in either's life,
When there's but one betwixt us ; throw it in,
And give it him of us who is to fall.
    SEB. He's dead · make hafte, and thou may'ft yet
       o'ertake him.
    DOR. When I was hafty, thou delay'd'ft me longer.
I prithee let me hedge one moment more
Into thy promife, for thy life preferv'd ;
Be kind : and tell me how that rival dy'd,
Whofe death next thine I wifh'd.
    SEB. If it would pleafe thee, thou fhould'ft never
       know :
But thou, like jealoufy, enquir'ft a truth,
Which, found, will torture thee : he dy'd in fight :
Fought next my perfon ; as in concert fought :
Kept pace for pace, gave blow for every blow ;
Save when he heav'd his fhield in my defence;
And on his naked fide receiv'd my wound.
Then, when he could no more, he fell at once :
But roll'd his falling body crofs their way,
And made a bulwark of it for his Prince.
    DOR. I never can forgive him fuch a death !
    SEB I prophefy'd thy proud foul could not bear it.
Now, judge thyfelf, who beft deferv'd my love.
I knew you both ; (and durft I fay), as Heaven
           Foreknew,

Foreknew, among the shining angel hoft,
Who would ftand firm, who fall.

DOR. Had he been tempted fo, fo had he fall'n;
And fo had I been favour'd, had I ftood.

SEB. What had been, is unknown, what is, appears:
Confefs he juftly was preferr'd to thee.

DOR. Had I been born with his indulgent ftars,
My fortune had been his, and his been mine.
O, worfe than hell! what glory have I loft,
And what has he acquir'd, by fuch a death!
I fhould have fallen by SEBASTIAN's fide:
My corpfe had been the bulwark of my King.
His glorious end was a patch'd work of fate,
Ill forted with a foft effeminate life:
It fuited better with my life than his
So to have dy'd: mine had been of a piece,
Spent in your fervice, dying at your feet.

SEB. The more effeminate and foft his life,
The more his fame, to ftruggle to the field
And meet his glorious fate: confefs, proud fpirit,
(For I will have it from thy very mouth),
That better he deferv'd my love than thou.

DOR. O, whether would you drive me! I muft grant,
Yes I muft grant, but with a fwelling foul,
Henriquez had your love with more defert:
For you he fought, and dy'd, I fought againft you;
Through all the mazes of the bloody field,
Hunted your facred life, which that I mifs'd,
Was the propitious error of my fate,
Not of my foul, my foul's a regicide.

SEB. Thou might'ft have given it a more gentle name:
[*more calmly*]. Thou meant'ft to kill a tyrant, not a
         King ·
Speak, didft thou not, ALONZO?

DOR. Can I fpeak!
Alas, I cannot anfwer to ALONZO:
No, DORAX cannot anfwer to ALONZO:
ALONZO was too kind a name for me
Then, when I fought and conquer'd with your arms,
In that bleft age I was the man you nam'd:
Till rage and pride debas'd me into DORAX,
And loft, like *Lucifer*, my name above.

                                              SEB.

SEB. Yet twice this day, I ow'd my life to DORAX.

DOR. I fav'd you, but to kill you; there's my grief.

SEB. Nay if thou canft be griev'd, thou canft repent.
Thou could'ft not be a villain, tho' thou would'ft:
Thou own'ft too much, in owning thou haft err'd;
And I too little, who provok'd thy crime.

DOR. O ftop this headlong torrent of your goodnefs:
It comes too faft upon a feeble foul,
Half drown'd in tears before; fpare my confufion:
For pity fpare, and fay not, firft, you err'd.
For yet I have not dar'd, thro' guilt and fhame,
To throw myfelf beneath your Royal feet.

(Falls at his feet)

Now fpurn this rebel, this proud renegade:
'Tis juft you fhould, nor will I more complain

SEB. Indeed thou fhould'ft not afk forgivenefs firft,
(taking him up) But thou prevent'ft me ftill, in all that's
noble
Yet I will raife thee up with better news:
Thy *Violante's* heart was ever thine,
Compell'd to wed, becaufe fhe was my ward,
Her foul was abfent when fhe gave her hand:
Nor could my threats, or his purfuing courtfhip,
Effect the confummation of his love:
So, ftill induiging tears, fhe pines for thee,
A widow and a maid.

DOR. Have I been curfing Heav'n, while Heav'n blefs'd
me!
I fhall run mad with extafy of joy:
What, in one moment, to be reconcil'd
To Heaven, and to my king, and to my love!
But pity is my friend, and ftops me fhort,
For my unhappy rival: poor *Henriquez*!

SEB. Art thou fo generous too, to pity him?
Nay, then I was unjuft to love him better.
Here let me ever hold thee in my arms:

[*Embracing him.*

And all our quarrels be but fuch as thefe,
Who fhall love beft, and clofeft fhall embrace:
Be what *Henriquez* was; be my ALONZO.

DOR. What, my ALONZO, faid you? my ALONZO!
Let my tears thank you, for I cannot fpeak:

And

And, if I cou'd,
Words were not made to vent such thoughts as mine.

SEB. Thou can'ft not fpeak, and I can ne'er be filent.
Some ftrange reverfe of fate muft, fure, attend
This vaft profufion, this extravagance
Of Heaven, to blifs me thus. 'Tis gold fo pure,
I cannot bear the ftamp, without allay :
Be kind, ye powers, and take but half away.
With eafe the gifts of fortune I refign ;
But, let my love, and fiiend, be ever mine.

Exeunt.

ACT V.

The SCENE *is a Room of State.*

Enter ANTONIO *and* DORAX.

ANTONIO I had forgot
T'enquire before, but long to be inform'd,
How, poifon'd and betray'd, and round befet,
You could unwind yourfelf from all thefe dangers ;
And move fo fpeedily to our relief !

DOR. The double poifons, after a fhort combat,
Expell'd each other in their civil war,
By nature's benefit , and rous'd my thoughts
To guard that life which now I found attack'd.
I fummon'd all my officers in hafte,
On whofe experienc'd faith I might rely:
All came ; refolv'd to die in my defence,
Save that one villain who betray'd the gate.
Our diligence prevented the furprize
We juftly fear'd : fo, MULEY-ZEYDAN found us
Drawn up in battle, to receive the charge.

ANT. But how the *Moors* and *Chriftian* flaves were
        join'd,
You have not yet unfolded.

DOR. That remains.
We knew their int'reft was the fame with ours :

And

And tho' I hated, more than death, SEBASTIAN,
I could not fee him die by vulgar hands :
But prompted by my angel, or by his,
Freed all the flaves, and plac'd him next myfelf,
Becaule I would not have his perfon known.
I need not tell the reft, th' event declares it.

    ANT Your conqueft came of courfe , their men were
       raw,
And yours were difciplin'd : one doubt remains,
Why you induftrioufly conceal'd the King,
Who, known, had added courage to his men ?

    DOR. I would not hazard civil broils, betwixt
His friends and mine, which might prevent our combat:
Yet, had he fall'n, I had difmifs'd his troops ;
Or, if victorious, order'd his efcape.
But I forget a new increafe of joy,
To feaft him with furprize ; I muft about it :
Expect my fwift return.

                       [*Exit* DORAX.

Enter a Servant to ANTONIO

    Serv Here's a lady at the door that bids me tell you,
fhe is come to make an end of the game, that was broken
off betwixt you.

    ANT. What manner of woman is fhe ? does fhe not
want two of the four elements? has fhe any thing about
her but air and fire ?

    Serv. Truly, fhe flies about the room, as if fhe had
wings inftead of legs, I believe fhe's juft turning into
a bird: a houfe-bird I warrant her : and fo hafty to
fly to you, that, rather than fail of entrance, fhe
would come tumbling down the chimney, like a fwallow.

Enter MORAYMA.

[ANTONIO *running to her and embracing her.*
    Look if fhe be not here already : what, no denial it
feems will ferve your turn ? Why thou little dun, is thy
debt fo preffing ?

    MOR Little devil, if you pleafe !

    ANT Where the devil haft thou been ? and how the
devil didft thou find me here ?

                      MOR.

MOR I follow'd you into the castle-yard; but there was nothing but tumult, and confusion: and I was bodily afraid of being pick'd up by some of the rabble · considering I had a double charge about me,——my jewels and my maiden head.

ANT. Both of 'em intended for my worship's sole use and property.

MOR. And what was poor little I among 'em all?

ANT. Not a mouthful a-piece: 'twas too much odds in conscience.

MOR. So, seeking for shelter, I naturally ran to the old place of assignation, the garden-house; where, for want of instinct, you did not follow me.

ANT. Well, for thy comfort, I have secur'd thy father; and I hope thou hast secur'd his effects for us.

MOR. Yes truly, I had the prudent foresight to consider that when we grow old, and weary of solacing one another, we might have, at least, wherewithal to make merry with the world, and take up with a worse pleasure of eating and drinking, when we were disabled for a better.

ANT. Thy fortune will be e'en too good for thee: for thou art going into the country of serenades, and gallantries; where thy street will be haunted every night, with thy foolish lovers, and my rivals; who will be sighing, and singing, under thy inexorable windows, lamentable ditties, and call thee cruel, and goddess, and moon, and stars, and all the poetical names of wicked rhime.

Re-enter DORAX *with* SEBASTIAN *and* ALMEYDA. SEBASTIAN *enters speaking to* DORAX, *while* ANTONIO *presents* MORAYMA *to* ALMEYDA.

SEB. How fares our royal pris'ner, MULEY ZEYDAN?
DOR. Dispos'd to grant whatever I desire,
To gain a crown, and freedom: well I know him,
Of easy temper, naturally good,
And faithful to his word.

SEB. Yet one thing wants,
To fill the measure of my happiness;
I'm still in pain for poor ALVAREZ' life.

I

DOR.

DOR. Releafe that fear , the good old man is fafe:
I paid his ranfom ,
And have already order'd his attendance.

SEB. O bid him enter, for I long to fee him.

Enter ALVAREZ *with a fervant, who departs when* AL-
VAREZ *is enter'd.*

[ALVAREZ *falling down and embracing the King's knees.*]
  Now, by my foul, and by thefe hoary hairs,
I'm fo o'er-whelm'd with pleafure, that I feel
A latter fpring within my with'ring limbs,
That fhoots me out again.

[SEBASTIAN *raifing him*] Thou good old man!
Thou haft deceiv'd me into more, more joys;
Who ftood brim-full before.

ALV O my dear child !
I love thee fo, I cannot call thee King,
Whom I fo oft have dandled in thefe arms !
What, when I gave thee loft to find thee living !
'Tis like a father, who himfelf had 'fcap'd
A falling houfe, and, after anxious fearch,
Hears, from afar, his only fon within ;
And digs thro' rubbifh, till he drags him out
To fee the friendly light.
Such is my hafte, fo trembling is my joy,
To draw thee forth from underneath thy fate!

SEB. The tempeft is o'er-blown ; the fkies are clear,
And the fea charm'd into a calm fo ftill
That not a wrinkle ruffles her fmooth face.

ALV. Juft fuch fhe fhows before a rifing ftorm :
And therefore am I come, with timely fpeed,
To warn you into port.

ALM. My foul forebodes   (*Afide.*
Some dire event involv'd in thofe dark words ;
And juft difclofing in a birth of fate.

ALV Is there not yet an heir of this vaft empire,
Who ftill furvives, of MULEY-MOLUCH's branch ?

DOR Yes, fuch an one there is, a captive here,
And brother to the dead

ALV The pow'rs above
Be prais'd for that : my prayers for my good mafter
I hope are heard.

                        SEB.

SEB Thou haft a right in Heav'n;
But why thefe prayers for me?

ALV. A door is open yet for your deliv'rance,
Now, you my countrymen, and you ALMEYDA,
Now all of us; and you (my all in one),
May yet be happy in that captive's life

SEB. We have him here an honourable hoftage
For terms of peace: what more he can contribute
To make me bleft; I know not.

ALV, Vaftly more:
ALMEYDA may be fettled in the throne,
And you review your native clime with fame:
A firm alliance, and eternal peace,
(The glorious crown of honourable war),
Are all included in that prince's life:
Let this fair queen be giv'n to MULEY-ZEYDAN;
And make her love the fanction of your league.

SEB. No more of that · his life's in my difpofe;
And prifoners are not to infift on terms.
Or if they were, yet he demands not thefe.

ALV. You fhou'd exact 'em.

ALM. Better may be made;
Thefe cannot: I abhor the tyrant's race;
My parents murderers; my throne's ufurpers:
But, at one blow to cut off all difpute,
Know this; thou bufy, old, officious man,
I am a Chriftian; now be wife no more;
Or if thou would'ft be ftill thought wife, be filent.

ALV O! I perceive you think your int'reft touch'd:
'Tis what before the battle I obferv'd:
But I muft fpeak and will.

SEB. I prithee peace;
Perhaps fhe thinks they are too near of blood.

ALV I wifh fhe may not wed to blood more near.

SEB. What if I make her mine?

ALV. Now Heav'n forbid! Have you forgot——

SEB Thou mean'ft my father's will,
In bar of marriage to ALMEYDA's bed:
Thou feeft my faculties are ftill entire,
Though thine are much impair'd, I weigh'd that will,
And found 'twas grounded on our diff'rent faiths,
But had he liv'd to fee her happy change,

I 2   He

He wou'd have cancell'd that harsh interdict,
And join'd our hands himself.

    ALV. Still had he liv'd, and seen this change,
He still had been the same.

    SEB. I have a dark remembrance of my father;
His reas'nings and his actions both were just;
And, granting that, he must have chang'd his measures.

    ALV. Yes, he was just, and therefore cou'd not change.

    SEB. 'Tis a base wrong thou offer'st to the dead.

    ALV. Now Heav'n forbid,
That I shou'd blast his pious memory :
No, I am tender of his holy fame;
For, dying, he bequeath'd it to my charge.
Believe I am , and seek to know no more,
But pay a blind obedience to his will.
For to preserve his fame I wou'd be silent.

    SEB. Craz'd fool! who woud'st be thought an oracle;
Come down from off thy tripos, and speak plain.
My father shall be justify'd, he shall :
'Tis a son's part to rise in his defence,
And to confound thy malice, or thy dotage.

    ALV. It does not grieve me that you hold me craz'd;
But, to be clear'd at my dead master's cost ;
O there's the wound! but let me first adjure you,
By all you owe that dear departed soul,
No more to think of marriage with ALMEYDA.

    SEB. Not Heav'n and earth, combin'd, can hinder it.

    ALV. Then, witness Heav'n and earth, how loth I am
To say, you must not, nay, you cannot wed;
And since not only a dead father's fame,
But more, a lady's honour must be touch'd,
Which nice as ermins will not bear a soil,
Let all retire, that you alone may hear
What ev'n in whispers I wou'd tell your ear.

                         [All are going out.

    ALM. Not one of you depart; I charge you, stay.
And were my voice a trumpet loud as fame,
To reach the round of Heav'n, and earth, and sea,
All nations shou'd be summon'd to this place,
So little do I fear the fellow's charge :
So shou'd my honour, like a rising swan,
Brush, with her wings, the falling drops away,

                                 And

And proudly plow the waves.

SEB. This noble pride becomes thy innocence;
And I dare trust my father's memory,
To stand the charge of that foul forging tongue.

ALV. It will be soon discover'd if I forge.
Have you not heard your father in his youth,
When newly marry'd, travell'd into *Spain,*
And made a long abode in PHILIP's court?

SEB Why so remote a question? which thyself
Can answer to thyself, for thou wert with him,
His fav'rite, as I oft have heard thee boast,
And nearest to his soul.

ALV Too near indeed; forgive me, gracious Heav'n!
That ever I should boast I was so near,
The confident of all his young amours—
(*To* ALMEYDA) And have not you, unhappy beauty,
            heard,
Have you not often heard your exil'd parents
Were refug'd in that court, and at that time?

ALM. 'Tis true: and often since, my mother own'd
How kind that Prince was, to espouse her cause;
She counsell'd, nay, enjoin'd me on her blessing
To seek the sanctuary of your court;
Which gave me first encouragement to come,
And, with my brother, beg SEBASTIAN's aid.

[SEB *to* ALM] Thou help'st me well to justify my war:
My dying father swore me, then a boy;
And made me kiss the cross upon his sword,
Never to sheath it, till that exil'd queen
Were by my arms restor'd.

ALV And you can find
No mystery, couch'd in this excess of kindness?
Were kings e'er known, in this degenerate age,
So passionately fond of noble acts,
Where int'rest shar'd not more than half with honour?

SEB. Base grov'ling soul, who know'st not honour's
            worth,
But weigh'st it out in mercenary scales:
The secret pleasure of a generous act,
Is the great mind's great bribe.

ALV. Show me that king, and I'll believe the phœnix.
But knock at your own breast, and ask your soul,

I 3   If

If thofe fair fatal eyes edg'd not your fword
More than your father's charge, and all your vows?
If fo; and fo your filence grants it is,
Know, King, your father had, like you, a foul;
And love is your inheritance from him.
ALMEYDA's mother too had eyes, like her,
And not lefs charming; and were charm'd no lefs
Than yours are now with her, and hers with you.

　ALM. Thou ly'ft, impoftor, perjur'd fiiend, thou ly'ft.

　SEB　Was't not enough to brand my father's fame,
But thou muft load a lady's memory!
O infamous, bafe e'en beyond repair!
And, to what end this ill-concerted lie,
Which palpable and grofs, yet granted true,
It bars not my inviolable vows.

　ALV. Take heed and double not your father's crimes;
To his adult'ry do not add your inceft.
Know, fhe's the product of unlawful love:
And 'tis your carnal fifter you wou'd wed.

　ALM. Out, bafe impofture! 'tis as falfe as hell!

　DOR. It looks not like impofture: but a truth,
On utmoft need reveal'd.

　SEB. Did I expect from DORAX this return?
Is this the love renew'd?

　DOR. Sir, I am filent;
Pray Heav'n my fears prove falfe.

　SEB. Away, you all combine to make me wretched.

　ALV. But hear the ftory of that fatal love;
Where every circumftance fhall prove another;
And truth fo fhine, by her own native light,
That if a lie were mix'd, it muft be feen.

　SEB. No, all may ftill be forg'd, and of a piece.
No; I can credit nothing thou can'ft fay:

　ALV　One proof remains, and that's your father's
　　　hand
Firm'd with his fignet; both fo fully known,
That plainer evidence can hardly be,
Unlefs his foul wou'd want her Heav'n a while,
And come on earth to fwear.

　SEB. Produce that writing.

　ALV. *to* DORAX.] ALONZO has it in his cuftody.
The fame, which when his noblenefs redeem'd me,

　　　　　　　　　　　　　　　　　　And

And in a friendly vifit own'd himfelf
For what he is, I then depofited :
And had his faith to give it to the King. -

           DORAX *giving a feal'd paper to the King.*

Untouch'd, and feal'd as when intrufted with me ;
Such I reftore it, with a trembling hand,
Left ought within difturb your peace of foul.

           SEBASTIAN *tearing open the feals.*

Draw near, ALMEYDA ; thou art moft concern'd :
For I am moft in thee
ALONZO, mark the characters :
Thou know'ft my father's hand, obferve it well :
And if th' impofture's pen have made one flip,
That fhows it counterfeit, mark that and fave me.

    DOR It looks, indeed, too like my mafter's hand :
So does the fignet ; more I cannot fay ;
But wifh 'twere not fo like.

    SEB. Methinks it owns
The black adult'ry, and ALMEYDA's birth ;
But fuch a mift of grief comes o'er my eyes,
I cannot, or I would not read it plain.

    ALM. Heav'n cannot be more true, than this is falfe.

    SEB. O could'ft thou prove it, with the fame affurance !
Speak, haft thou ever feen my father's hand ?

    ALM. No, but my mother's honour has been read
By me, and by the world, in all her acts,
In characters more plain and legible,
Than this dumb evidence, this blotted lie.
Oh that I were a man, as my foul's one,
To prove thee, traitor, an affaffinate
Of her fair fame : thus would I tear thee, thus: *(Tearing*
And fcatter o'er the field thy coward limbs,   *the paper*)
Like this foul offspring of thy forging brain

                   (Scattering the paper.

    ALV Juft fo, fhalt thou be torn from all thy hopes.
For know, proud woman, know, in thy defpight,
The moft authentic proof is ftill behind.
Thou wear'ft it on thy finger · 'tis that ring,
Which, match'd with that on his, fhall clear the doubt.
'Tis no dumb forgery : for that fhall fpeak,
And found a rattling peal to either's confcience

    SEB. This ring, indeed, my father, with a cold

                            And

And fhaking hand, juft in the pangs of death, ,
Put on my finger,. with a parting figh ;
And wou'd have fpoke, but falter'd in his fpeech,
With undiftinguifh'd founds.

  ALV. I know it well,
For I was prefent : now ALMEYDA, fpeak ;
And truly tell us, how came you by yours?

  ALM. My mother, when I parted from her fight, .
To go to Portugal, bequeath'd it to me, ,
Prefaging fhe fhould never fee me more :
She pull'd it from her finger, fhed fome tears,
Kifs'd it ,. and told me 'twas a pledge of love.;
And had a myftery of great importance
Relating to my fortunes.

  ALV. Mark me now,
While I difclofe that fatal myftery.
Thofe rings, when you were born, and thought another's,
Your parents, glowing yet in finful love,
Bid me befpeak : a curious artift wrought 'em,
With joints fo clofe as not to be perceiv'd ;
Yet are they both each other's counterpart.
Her part had JUAN infcrib'd, and his had ZAYDA.
(You know thofe names are theirs). And in the midft,.
A heart divided in two halves was plac'd
Now if the rivets of thofe rings inclos'd,
Fit not each other, I have forg'd this lie :
But if they join, you muft for ever part,
  [*They pull off their rings and give them to* ALVAREZ,
   who unfcrews 'em and fits 'em to each other]
  SEB. Now, life or death !
  ALM. And either thine or our——I'm loft for ever !
   [*She fwoons and is taken off.*
  SEBASTIAN *ftands fixt and motionlefs for fome time.*]
  SEB. Look to the queen my wife, for I am paft
All power of aid to her, or to myfelf.

  ALV. His wife ! faid he, his wife ? Oh fatal found !
For, had I known it, this unwelcome news
Had never reach'd their ears.
So they had ftill been bleft in ignorance,
And I alone unhappy.
   [SEBASTIAN *ftarting out of his amazment.*
         SEB.

SEB. I will not live, no not a moment more;
I will not add one moment more to inceſt,

                     [*Draws, they hold him.*

   ALV. For Heav'n's ſake hold, and recollect your mind.
   SEB. Stand off, and let me take my fill of death:
For I can hold my breath in your deſpight,
And ſwell my heaving ſoul out when I pleaſe.
   ALV. Heav'n comfort you!
   SEB. What, art thou giving comfort!
Wou'd'ſt thou give comfort who haſt given deſpair?
No palliation e'er can heal my wound;
For, ſhou'd you argue all you can, 'tis inceſt:
No, 'tis reſolv'd, I charge you plead no more;
I cannot live without ALMEYDA's ſight,
Nor can I ſee ALMEYDA but I ſin.
Heav'n has inſpir'd me with a ſacred thought,
To live alone to Heav'n, and die to her.
   DOR. Mean you to turn an *Anchoret* ?
   SEB. What elſe?
The world was once too narrow for my mind,
But one poor little nook will ſerve me now;
To hide me from the reſt of human-kind.
   ALV. You may repent, and wiſh your crown too late.
   SEB. Never, my dear ALVAREZ. He who leaves
ALMEYDA, may renounce the reſt with eaſe.
   DOR. Oh truly great!
A ſoul fix'd high, and capable of Heav'n.
Old as he is, your uncle Cardinal
Is not ſo far enamour'd of a cloyſter,
But he will thank you for the crown you leave him.
   SEB. To pleaſe him more, let him believe me dead:
That he may never dream I may return.
ALONZO, I am now no more thy king,
But ſtill thy friend, and, by that hol'y name,
Adjure thee to perform my laſt requeſt:
Make our conditions with you captive king,
Secure me but my ſolitary cell;
'Tis all I aſk him for a crown reſtor'd.
   DOR. I will do more:
But fear not MULEY-ZEYDAN, his ſoft metal
Melts down with eaſy warmth, runs in the mould,
And needs no farther forge.   [*Exit* DORAX.
                            Re-

Re-enter ALMEYDA, *led by* MORAYMA, *and followed by her attendants.*

SEB. See where she comes again.
By Heav'n, when I behold these beauteous eyes,
Repentance lags, and sin comes hurrying on:

ALM. This is too cruel!

SEB. Speak'st thou of love, of fortune, or of death?
Or double death? for we must part, ALMEYDA.

ALM. Yes we must part, SEBASTIAN;
That's all the name that I have left to call thee.
I must not call thee by the name I wou'd;
But when I say SEBASTIAN, dear SEBASTIAN,
I kiss the name I speak.———
Here comes the sad denouncer of my fate,
To toll the mournful knell of separation:
While I, as on my death-bed, hear the sound
That warns me hence for ever
          [SEBASTIAN *to* DORAX] Now be brief,
          And I will try to listen,
And share the minute that remains, betwixt
The care I owe my subjects and my love.

DOR. Your fate has gratify'd you all she can;
Gives easy misery, and makes exile pleasing.
I trusted MULEY-ZEYDAN as a friend,
But swore him first to secrecy: He wept
Your fortune, and with tears, not squeez'd by art,
But shed by nature, like a kindly shower:
In short, he proffer'd more than I demanded;
A safe retreat, a gentle solitude,
Unvex'd with noise, and undisturb'd with fears:
I chose you one.———

ALM. O do not tell me where:
For if I knew the place of his abode,
I shou'd be tempted to pursue his steps,
And then we both were lost.

SEB. Ev'n past redemption.
For, if I knew thou wert on that design,
As I must know, because our souls are one,
I shou'd not wander, but by sure instinct
Shou'd meet thee just half-way, in pilgrimage,
And close for ever:—For I know my love
More strong than thine, and I more frail than thou.

                                        ALM.

ALM. Tell me not that : for I muſt boaſt my crime,
And cannot bear that thou ſhou'dſt better love.

DOR. I may inform you both : for you muſt go,
Where ſeas, and winds, and deſarts will divide you.
Under the ledge of *Atlas* lies a cave,
Cut in the living rock, by nature's hands ;
The venerable ſeat of holy hermits :
Who there, ſecure in ſeparated cells,
Sacred ev'n to the *Moors*, enjoy devotion ;
And from the purling ſtreams and ſavage fruits,
Have wholeſome bev'rage, and unbloody feaſts.

SEB. 'Tis penance too voluptuous for my crime.

DOR. Your ſubjects, conſcious of your life, are few :
But all deſirous to partake your exile :
And to do office to your ſacred perſon.
The reſt, who think you dead, ſhall be diſmiſs'd,
Under ſafe convoy till they reach your fleet.

ALM. But how am wretched I to be diſpos'd ?
A vain enquiry, ſince I leave my lord :
For all the world beſide is baniſhment !

DOR. I have a ſiſter, abbeſs in *Tercera's*,
Who loſt her lover on her bridal day.———

ALM. There fate provided me a fellow-turtle ;
To mingle ſighs with ſighs, and tears with tears.

DOR. Laſt, for my ſelf, if I have well fulfil'd
My ſad commiſſion, let me beg the boon,
To ſhare the ſorrows of your laſt receſs :
And mourn the common loſſes of our loves.

ALV. And what becomes of me ? muſt I be left,
As age and time had worn me out of uſe ?
Theſe ſinews are not yet ſo much unſtrung,
To fail me when my maſter ſhou'd be ſerv'd :
And when they are, then will I ſteal to death,
Silent, and unobſerv'd, to ſave his tears.

SEB. I've heard you both: ALVAREZ, have thy wiſh:
But thine, ALONZO, thine, is too unjuſt.
I charge thee with my laſt commands, return,
And bleſs thy *Violante* with thy vows.
ANTONIO, be thou happy too, in thine.
Laſt, let me ſwear you all to ſecrecy ;
And to conceal my ſhame, conceal my life.

DOR. ANT. MOR. We ſwear to keep it ſecret.

ALM.

ALM. Now I wou'd speak the last farewel, I cannot:
It wou'd be still farewel, a thousand times,
And, multiply'd in echo's, still farewel.
I will not speak; but think a thousand, thousand,
And be thou silent too, my lost SEBASTIAN;
So let us part in the dumb pomp of grief.
My heart's too great; or I wou'd die this moment:
But death I thank him, in an hour, has made
A mighty journey, and I haste to meet him.

[*She staggers, and her women hold her up*]

SEB Help to support this feeble drooping flower:
This tender sweet, lo shaken by the storm.
For these fond arms must thus be stretch'd in vain,
And never, never must embrace her more.
'Tis past—my soul goes in that word,—farewel:

*ALVAREZ goes with SEBASTIAN to one end of the
Stage. Women with ALMEYDA to the other.*

*DORAX coming up to ANTONIO and MORAYMA,
who stand on the middle of the stage.*

DOR. Haste to attend ALMEYDA: For your sake
Your father is forgiven: But for ANTONIO,
He forfeits half his wealth: Be happy both:
And let SEBASTIAN and ALMEYDA's fate
This dreadful sentence to the world relate,
That unrepented crimes of parents dead
Are justly punish'd on their children's head.

F I N I S.

CPSIA.information can be obtained at www.ICGtesting.com

234060LV00006B/72/P